Flexibility in Teaching

Flexibility in Teaching

An Excursion into the Nature of Teaching and Training

Edited by

Bruce R. Joyce
Clark C. Brown
Lucy Peck

With these colleagues:

Lenora F. Butler
Christopher Clark
Janet Crist-Witzel
Peter Dirr
JoAnn Greenwood
Richard E. Hodges
David E. Hunt
Elizabeth Joyce

Thomas Kluwin
Michael McKibbin
Ronald Marx
Joyce E. Noy
Katherine O'Donnell
Penelope Peterson
Roma Reid
Mary Rosser

Marvin Seperson
Irene S. Shigaki
Beverly Showers
Stewart Tinsman
Rhoada Wald
Marsha Weil

LONGMAN

New York and London

FLEXIBILITY IN TEACHING
An Excursion into the Nature of Teaching and Training

Longman Inc., New York
Associated companies, branches, and
representatives throughout the world.

Developmental Editor: Nicole Benevento
Editorial and Design Supervisor: Joan Matthews
Cover Design: Dan Serrano
Manufacturing and Production Supervisor: Robin Besofsky
Composition: Kingsport Press
Printing and binding: BookCrafters Inc.

Library of Congress Cataloging in Publication Data
Main entry under title:

Flexibility in teaching.

   Bibliography: p.
   Includes index.
   1. Teaching—Addresses, essays, lectures. I. Joyce,
Bruce R. II. Brown, Clark C. III. Peck, Lucy.
LB1025.2.F547   371.1'02   80–16927
ISBN 0–582–28125–3

Manufactured in the United States of America

9 8 7 6 5 4 3 2 1

Acknowledgments

The editors wish to thank the following authors for their kind permission to reprint:

"The Roots of Humanity: Views of Humankind and the Education of Teachers," by Bruce R. Joyce. First appeared as "Conceptions of Man and Their Implications for Teacher Education" in *Teacher Education:* The Seventy Fourth Yearbook of the National Society for the Study of Education, Part II. Edited by Kevin Ryan. Chicago: The University of Chicago Press, 1975.

"The Models of Teaching Community: Overview of a Struggle to Understand Teaching and Teacher Education," by Bruce R. Joyce. From the *Texas Tech Journal of Education,* 1975.

"Flexibility as Repertoire," by Bruce R. Joyce and Richard E. Hodges. First appeared as "A Rationale for Teacher Education" in the *Elementary School Journal,* February 1975.

"Teachers' Adaptation: 'Reading' and 'Flexing' to Students", by David E. Hunt. First appeared as "Teacher Adaptation to Students: From Implicit to Explicit Matching." Prepared for the Program in Teaching Effectiveness to the Stanford Center for Research and Development in Testing.

"Strength and Sensitivity: The Battleground of Explicit Matching Behavior," by Lucy Peck. First appeared as "Situational Assessment of Strength and Sensitivity in Teaching," in the *Journal of Teacher Education,* Spring 1972.

"Sensitivity Training: An Experiment for Teachers," by Bruce R. Joyce, Peter Dirr, and David E. Hunt. From *Journal of Teacher Education,* Spring 1969.

"Teacher Training Personality and Initial Teaching Style," by David E. Hunt and Bruce R. Joyce. From the *American Educational Research Journal,* May 1967.

"The Relationship between Teaching Styles, Personality, and Setting," by Clark C. Brown. First appeared as "The Initial Teaching Style of Student Teachers," in *Educational Leadership,* May 1974.

"The Relationship between the Teaching Styles of Student Teachers and Those of the Cooperating Teachers," by Marvin Seperson and Bruce R. Joyce. First appeared as "The Teaching Styles of Students Teachers as Related to the Teaching Styles of Their Cooperating Teachers," in *Education Leadership,* November 1973.

"The Effects of Instructional Flexibility Training on Teaching Styles in Controlled Repertoire," by Stewart Tinsman. An original paper.

"A Structure for Pluralism in Teacher Education," by Bruce R. Joyce, Marsha Weil, and Rhoada Wald. First appeared as "The Training of Educators: A Structure of Pluralism" in *Teacher College Research,* Winter 1971.

"Can Teachers Learn Repertoires of Models of Teaching?" by Bruce R. Joyce, Rhoada Wald, and Marsha Weil. First appeared as "The Teacher Innovator: Models of Teaching as the Core of Teacher Education," in *Interchange,* Fall 1973.

"The Relationship of Teacher Characteristics to the Utilization of Models of Teaching," by Irene S. Shigaki and Clark C. Brown. An original paper.

"Improving Inservice Training," by Bruce R. Joyce and Beverly Showers. From *Educational Leadership,* February 1980.

"Student Conceptual Level and Models of Teaching: Theoretical and Empirical Coordination of Two Models," by David E. Hunt. An original paper.

"Studies in Role Playing: MOTAC III," by David E. Hunt, Lenora F. Butler, Joyce Noy, and Mary Rosser. An original paper.

"Teacher Decision Making and Teacher Effectiveness," by Christopher Clark and Bruce R. Joyce. Originally presented to the 1975 Annual Meeting of the American Educational Research Association.

"The Nature of Teacher Decision Making," by Ronald Marx and Penelope Peterson. Originally presented to the 1975 Annual Meeting of the American Educational Research Association.

"Teachers' Utilization of Feedback from Students," by Janet Crist-Witzel. Originally presented to the 1976 Annual Meeting of the American Educational Research Association.

"Toward a Theory of Information Processing in Teaching: The South Bay Study," by Bruce R. Joyce. From the *Educational Research Quarterly,* Winter 1978-9.

"Vehicles for Controlling Content in the Study of Teaching," by Bruce R. Joyce. Originally presented to the 1975 Annual Meeting of the American Educational Research Association.

"The Relative Effects of Content Vehicles in Educational Research," by Thomas Kluwin, Ronald Marx, and Elizabeth Joyce. An original paper.

"The Short-Term Effects of Self-Administrated Teacher Training Products," by Thomas Kluwin, Michael McKibbin, and Elizabeth Joyce. An original paper.

Contents

Tables

Figures

Preface

This book presents part of the work of fifteen years by about fifty people. The authors and editors share an appreciation of the "art of teaching," and a commitment to translating that art into scientific terms and relationships, thereby trying to give teaching a new language, new models, and new directions.

Special thanks go to David Hunt and his colleagues for their major contribution to the ideas and prose of this book. Also, to Pamela David and Susan Kuhner for providing essential editorial assistance; and to Elinore Brown and Shirley Stone for typing and retyping an incredible amount of text, tables, and references.

Teaching is presented here as a combined product of personality, the nature of schools, and training events. It is viewed in terms of its potential as a life-giving symbiotic relationship between motivated teachers and learners, both of whom live much of their daily lives in the exhilarating, frustrating, rewarding, punishing environment of the public school.

The studies and speculative papers presented here view teaching as the gentle, persistent adaptation of people to other people. Teacher education, we believe, should increase the flexibility and focus of this interaction. In Hunt's terms, it is the coordination of objectives (purposes), the environment (instrument and context), and learner (who and what s/he is).

While empirical and reasoned for the most part, the essays and research reports presented here represent a view of humankind that envisions people-in-teaching and people-in-learning as the creators of themselves through their interaction. Flexibility, from that stance, becomes an essential characteristic of the teacher as s/he creates her/himself, offers possibilities to his/her students, and creates the schools of the future.

Flexibility in
Teaching

PART I

The Social and Technical Context

In the first of these papers the history of teacher education is described as the product of a series of reform movements in education.

In the second an overview is given of the fifteen-year struggle to understand teaching and teacher education—a struggle that is the substance of this book.

All the concepts presented in this part stem from the conviction that the essence of teaching is flexibility. We see students as voracious, energy-expending, experience-consuming creatures. We see the teacher's task as interacting with these omnivores of emotions and ideas, contrasting and blending with them, creating with and for them the environments that will most productively feed their appetites.

However, to think about the teachers, to study them, to educate and help them educate themselves, we need concepts that cover their behaviors. We have to somehow describe the act of teaching in terms that have fidelity to the teacher's act and that also enable us to orient teacher education programs. We need, in short, to define the whole and parts of teaching so that we can construct environments from which the novice and the experienced teacher can grow in competence and empathy for the learner.

1

The Roots of Humanity: Views of Humankind and the Education of Teachers

Bruce R. Joyce

THE ROOT IN THE CULTURE

Schools, as social institutions, are dominated by the mainstream cultural values that perpetuate *traditional* practices for educating the young. Any very great deviation immediately stimulates a negative reaction, frequently a severe one. Thus most schools are minor variations on the basic cultural theme.

The purpose of teacher education is to provide personnel for schools. Tied thus to the schooling process, teacher education is not much freer to experiment with alternatives than are the schools themselves. It is, therefore, remarkable that we have seen as many variations as we have, both in schooling and in the preparation of teachers. Because ideas that are not brought to fruition are less threatening than are those that are acted upon, we find a much greater diversity of ideas than we do of practices.

The normative schooling process within the culture probably represents the dominant view of humankind; that is, the one most comfortably held by most members of society. Equally, the dominant mode of the education of teachers represents the mainstream conception of the nature of people and the place of education in their lives. Both schooling and the process of educating the teacher have been well coordinated with respect to the culture.

As a consequence, the mainstream ideas are so dominant in practice that they form the ground against which we see competing alternatives in the processes of schooling and of teacher education. Thus, we begin our analysis by attempting to characterize the presently ascendant practices of schooling and teacher education and to infer the view of humanity which these practices appear to imply. We will then turn to other conceptions and project them as figures against the ground of the normative practice. The conceptions represent one effect of pluralism in Western culture—this essay would be pointless in a society that was not somewhat pluralistic. As it is, the alternatives are really variations on the central themes of the culture—they represent a small part of what the liberated mind might create.

The Ground: The School of the Industrial Society

Thesis: Schools and teacher-education programs are most commonly based on an economic conception of humanity. This conception forms the ground against which competing alternatives vie for attention.

The "common school" was established largely during the nineteenth century.[22] Its curricular content, the processes used to teach that content, and the social structure of the school reflected the educational needs of the society in the early days of the Industrial Revolution, as well as the need to establish a common heritage for people who came to the United States from Europe.

Before the establishment of the common school, most members of society were functionally illiterate. Participation in a mass society, its governmental processes, and its emerging economic system required literacy and occupationally relevant skills. Content related to literacy and computation, therefore, became the staple fare of the primary curriculum, and it has remained so until the present time. The view of children which was dominant in that day was derived largely from the Puritan heritage. The child was seen as an inferior being who needed discipline in order to (literally!) save his/her soul.[27] Thus the common methods of schooling—regimentation through lessons, and severe discipline—were sanctioned by moral authority translated into pedagogical principles. The Lockian psychology that prevailed in those times (and that still does to a surprising degree among many lay people and practitioners) lacked any coherent conception of individual differences. Failure to learn was largely attributed to lack of motivation or laziness, and the carrot and the stick were recommended as the remedies for that condition. Recitation lessons, the workbook, and the copy book became the tools of the trade. The stern, regimented environment fit with the view of the child as an inferior who had to be disciplined for his/her moral and intellectual benefit. Alvin Toffler [99] views form, structure, and substance of that kind of school as perfectly suited for the requirements of the early industrial society.

> Mass education was the ingenious machine constructed by industrialism to produce the kind of adults it needed. The problem was inordinately complex. How to preadapt children for a new world—a world of repetitive indoor toil, smoke, noise, machines, crowded living conditions, collective discipline, a world in which time was to be regulated not by the cycle of sun and moon, but by the factory whistle and the clock.

The solution was an educational system that, in its very structure, simulated this new world. This system did not emerge instantly. Even today it retains throwback elements from pre-industrial society. Yet the whole idea of assembling masses of students (raw material) to be processed by teachers (workers) in a centrally located school (factory) was a stroke of industrial genius. The whole administrative hierarchy of education, as it grew up, followed the model of industrial bureaucracy. The very organization of knowledge into permanent disciplines was grounded on industrial assumptions. Children marched from place to place and sat in assigned stations. Bells rang to announce changes of time.

The inner life of the school thus became an anticipatory mirror, a perfect introduction to industrial society. The most criticized features of education today—the regimentation, lack of individualization, the rigid systems of seating, grouping, grading and marking, the authoritarian role of the teacher—are precisely those that made mass public education so effective an instrument of adaptation for its place and time.

Young people passing through this educational machine emerged into an adult society whose structure of jobs, roles, and institutions resembled that of the school itself. The schoolchild did not simply learn facts that he could use later on; he lived, as well as learned, a way of life modeled after the one he would lead in the future." [99]

As secondary schools and colleges were established, the school system became even more closely tied to the status system of the society. Education became an indispensable means of status maintenance and acquisition for most persons. To acquire status or to maintain it (unless one's family was unassailably wealthy), one had to acquire education. It is not surprising that a schooling so tied to the economic system would reflect economic values. The school's system of rewards and punishments (currently given for work done) was based on the establishment of lower levels of education as prerequisites for higher ones. This permitted the student to be kept in line by means of the threat that if s/he did not behave, s/he would fall—not only from the academic, but from the economic ladder as well. Suspension and expulsion from school became powerful disciplinary weapons. Expulsion particularly represented a fine that a person would pay throughout his/her lifetime in terms of earnings not received. The structure of the school was designed to facilitate this conception of education and to permit the easy maintenance of order and regimentation. Departmentalized systems with students moving from class to class, where they would be under the supervision of a particular teacher, emphasized the role of the teacher as taskmaster and disciplinarian. The segmented day provided conditions for the teacher under which most student-centered modes of education were extremely difficult to carry out. The structure of secondary education, with students passing from station to station, mimicked the assembly line in the factory. Individuals were seen as producers and as consumers. The purpose of education was to make them better at both.

Most liberal movements in American education have focused on the extension of educational opportunity and its concomitant economic benefits for more and more members of the society. These movements have not challenged the economic view of humanity, but have tried to be egalitarian in focus. (Only a few of the reform movements have been based on different ideologies, that is, on conceptions that are not primarily economic in focus.) Under the influence of politically liberal but still economic views of humanity, the universities and high schools have been expanded. More kinds of higher-education institutions have been developed to provide for more and more people. In recent years national programs such as Head Start, Follow Through, and Upward Bound have been designed to make it possible for more children to fit into the economic order by first fitting into the educational system.

Conceptions of education derived from an economic point of view have dominated American society since the 1830s. The community closely guards the economic conception. Parents put enormous pressure on schools to teach their children to read early because they are fearful of the disadvantages that will accrue later if the children are poor readers. The substance and methods attendant to innovative practices are scrutinized carefully to determine whether they threaten either the economic view of the child or the industrial view of the school. Child-centered methods of education—that is, methods that suggest education should be paced by the child's needs and interests—seriously threaten the economic view of humankind. Consequently, child-centered methods are difficult to implement without considerable political strife. Although the society has gradually become more sympathetic to a personalistic view of the child, when it comes to serious decision making, efficiency is usually preferred to the risks taken when the child is permitted to set his/her own pace or learn in his/her own way. Private schools, very few of which are innovative in educational method or substance, are highly prized for their economic value. Families that are enraged at rising rates of taxation tax themselves heavily to purchase a private education, not least because of the utility of its credentials. Credentialing processes receive especially careful protection because they open doors to many jobs more effectively than competence can. The bachelor's degree is a clear example. It has been several generations since there was a clear correlation between the substance of a liberal education in a college and performance in business. Yet the economic value of the liberal arts credential has long been recognized, and it is desired by many for this reason much more than for its intrinsic worth.

Teacher Education in the Industrial Society

The education of the teacher was beautifully crafted to fit the industrial conception of humanity. In the first place, nearly all teachers were raising their status, and, as a consequence, were very much locked into the whole system—people who are successfully raising their social positions are rarely radical. In addition, teachers' colleges and education departments occupied relatively low status positions in the academic firmament. The normal schools and the education departments in the state universities were only a little way from the bottom of the academic pecking order, but they looked very good to people who were on the way up.

The substance and methods of teacher education curriculums were carefully structured to represent and reflect the normative schooling practices. The core component of the traditional teacher-education program was student teaching, an apprenticeship system designed to socialize the young teachers into the practices of the older ones. *(No more effective method has ever been devised for preventing change in a social institution than to apprentice the novice to his/her elder.)* The methods courses dealt largely with the traditional curriculum areas of the school and were designed to introduce the teacher candidates to the trends of the time in those subject areas. The methods courses, of course, were carefully separated from the apprenticeship experience to ensure that any new idea or any idea too deviant from present practice would be removed from the clinical situation in time and space. That is, the methods courses were placed before student teaching so they could not influence it as directly as if they had occurred, say, in the schools themselves and during student teaching. In addition, educational theory came to be separated from methods courses. The social, psychological, and philosophical foundations, designed to provide the teacher with the perspectives s/he would need to make curricular and instructional decisions, and the substantive courses, designed to provide her/him with the content s/he would need to teach, were clearly differentiated from the pragmatism of the methods.

There has always been a certain amount of tension in this normative teacher-training system. Some instructors of substance, foundations, and methods have always been more radical than was anticipated. The separation of theory from practice, however, made it fairly easy to deal with these people. They might be permitted to present their radical ideas in the psychology class, but these could be dismissed as "just theory" when the apprenticeship situation began.

In summary, teacher education was built around the socialization of the novice teacher to the prevailing industrial conception of humankind and its schooling. Upwardly mobile people were gathered together in relatively low-status institutions in order to be socialized into the existing practices of the schools. Higher-education institutions controlled the subject matter, materials, methods, and success of teachers in training, chiefly through the cooperating teacher.

Although there was tension between theoretical and practical components of programs, it was by no means total. Most of the theories that were taught to the young teacher reflected the industrial values. The very language of curriculum, "select objectives, organize learning experiences, evaluate outcomes" was efficiency-oriented. Industrial models of individualization were recommended. (The extent to which this is still true can be seen in the kinds of theories which are presently being taught to novice teachers. The contingency version of behavior modification is sweeping teacher education. The incorporation of Piaget's ideas into curricula directed at accelerating cognitive development is basically *industrial conversion of development theory*.)

The way research is presented to educators is equally reflective of this stance. For example, when one looks at presentations of research on reading instruction as these are prepared for the profession, one finds that they compare methods by criteria of efficiency in achievement of specific goals. The bulk of scientific literature on education is as economic in mode as is the dominant theory and practice of the field. Thus the young teacher is socialized to stances toward curriculum and research that are compatible with the mainstream.

As the culture changes, the adequacy of this mode of education, developed in the early industrial age and reflecting its values and practices, is coming under increasing fire. The tension produced by social change is developing rapidly but, thus far, is represented more in social criticism than in the generation of new forms. The issue of obsolescence is a powerfully important one, however, and we will return to it later.

Before doing so, however, it is important to identify the competing ideologies that have risen during the present century, for they not only represent alternative views of humankind but express some of the tension of cultural change.

The Ideological Spread

Thus, against the backdrop of a teacher education that uses apprenticeship—the classic mode of industrial education—as its core, we can identify four major reform movements in teacher education which have had some impact during this century. These are: the *progressive reform* movement, the *academic reform* movement, the *personalistic reform* movement, and the *competency orientation*. Each of these movements has embodied a view of humankind which contrasts interestingly with the industrial orientation, so that we can compare their stances with that of the mainstream practices in teacher education.

The Progressive Movement: The Social Orientation

Thesis: The *progressive movement* saw people as creators of their culture, and they saw knowledge as emergent. Thus the teacher was to lead children to identify and solve problems and learn how to create knowledge.

The attempts to reform teacher education during the twentieth century have varied considerably in the extent to which they have challenged the traditional practices that so clearly reflect the early industrial era. The most extensive of the reform movements is in some ways the most paradoxical. We shall call it the *progressive reform movement* because it emmanated from the mainstream of the progressive movement.[23] It is illustrated most power-fully in the writings of John Dewey and Dewey's interpreters in the progressive movement itself.[26] It is paradoxical in its mixture of the radical and the conservative. It stood for social change and for changes in educational method and substance, and rooted these in a conception of humanity that was nontra-ditional. However, it utilized many traditional educational procedures and structures. Especially, it embraced the common components of teacher educa-tion. *Thus it was not as different as it might have become had it been more radical in its invention of instructional forms.*

Although the progressive movement was in many ways quite diffuse, it represented a blending of the child-study movement that began in the latter part of the nineteenth century with the translation of the work of the pragmatic philosophers into educational terms. To the child-study movement it owed its focus on the student as an individual and its recognition that education had to begin on terms understandable to her/him. Thus the student was conceived of as an emotional and intellectual being in his/her own right. S/he was not simply an economic entity, raw material to be processed into the system of the Industrial Revolution. Within progressive circles the student came to be seen as a self, struggling to become. William James stated the position clearly in *Talks to Teachers,* [48] when he emphasized that the student had to be understood in terms of his/her personal cognitive development and that his/her emotions were legitimate emphases in the educational pro-cess.

Dewey's pragmatism contained the expression of the two major ideas from which the progressive movement drew its strength. One was the *constructionist view of knowledge,* which saw knowledge as a product of think-ing—an ever-changing set of conceptions which had to be held tentatively because it would be modified as new experience was acquired and processed differently. Knowledge was seen as a function of purpose, since the individual's purposes would affect the questions s/he would ask and the way s/he would process information. The constructionist view of knowledge conflicted enor-mously with the way the acquisition of knowledge was controlled in the schools. Both the recitation method and the kinds of content that were taught proceeded from a static conception of knowledge and deemphasized the role of the individual mind in processing information. Where Dewey saw people seeking information in terms of their purposes, developing and constantly changing their conceptions, having to become aware of their own frames of reference in order to understand their knowledge and communicate it to others, the industrial conception emphasized the stability of the external world and diminished the role of the individual.

Dewey was also concerned with the revitalization of democracy and with the reconstruction of society on terms that would enable its continued improve-ment. This view of society and of the role of the citizen in improving it was consistent with his stance toward knowledge. He saw the society at any given time as a product of the limitations of thought and the possibilities of social action that were prevalent during that period.[26] To reconstruct the society, citizens needed to work together to try to comprehend their lives and develop more effective social arrangements. In keeping with this, the teacher's task was to organize her/his class as a democratic problem-solving group, a miniature democracy. His/her students would work together to create a social system in which they could begin the process of social problem solving. The instructor would teach them to use scientific methods to solve the kinds of problems that were within their grasp.

Dewey's perception of knowledge as ever-changing and the ideal society as an organization of people who would recognize this and work together to define and attack their most important problems represented a massive challenge to traditional conceptions of knowledge and social process. The view of education as an emergent group process was equally confrontational. It implied a type of teacher education which was bound to be controversial. The teacher could not be presented with the knowledge and methods that s/he would need throughout his/her career. Because s/he had to take each group of students on its own terms, s/he had to be prepared to organize it into a problem-solving group. The teacher would have to make decisions which would fit the characteristics of the individuals s/he was working with and the kinds of problems that they were able to define and attack. Thus the teacher her/himself had to be seen as a problem solver, one who would continually invent methodology, reselecting substance and methods as the life of each classroom group created and recreated itself. These conceptions of the teacher's role had a considerable impact on the theory of teacher education and a lesser but perceptible impact on practice as well. The influence persists today, especially in contemporary supervisory theory which is rooted more firmly in the conceptions of the progressive movement than in any formulations that have been developed since.[6]

Although its views of knowledge and social process were considerably different from those of the industrial conceptions, the progressive movement worked within the traditional schools and programs of teacher education, thereby achieving only limited modifications. Progressives were instrumental in increasing the amount of child study that was included in the teacher-preparation curriculum, particularly with respect to elementary teaching. The emphasis on apprenticeship continued, but stress was placed on creating relationships between schools and colleges that would coordinate changes in the schools with changes in the education of the teacher. Methods courses were retained but were reshaped. Often democratic practices were instituted within them with the college instructor playing a facilitative role to a group of problem-solving students. Occasional programs were run entirely in a problem-solving mode.[97]

The methods courses were changed the most. Previously they had emphasized what to teach and how to teach it. Under the progressive influence, the courses became less systematic, more oriented toward emergent methodologies of teaching, and less oriented toward the substance of the disciplines. Science courses began to emphasize problem solving with materials gathered by the teacher and children.[11] "Resource" units, rather than structured curriculums, were presented to the young teacher, who was taught how to create units which would meet the particular needs of the students and their communities.

Social studies as a curriculum area is a good example, for it was created to help students study contemporary problems of their choosing, and then help them learn to *identify* problems. The methodologies recommended for Problems of Democracy courses and for elementary social studies emphasized democratic problem solving and the creation by the teacher of unique substances and resources needed by his/her students. Many methods courses themselves used emergent, group-dynamics-oriented methods to prepare the novice teacher to employ them. Methods courses also began to emphasize field trips and the function of the community in the education of the child. A course known as Community Forces and Resources * was created to train the young teacher to study the community and to tailor education to the unique needs of that community. Courses such as Human Development emphasized child study, helping the novice teacher to relate education to the needs of the specific children s/he would teach. Educational philosophy became especially attuned to the progressive movement, partly because its origins had been in the work of philosophers. The categories that dominated educational philosophy for years, "essentialism," "perrenialism," and "pragmatism" stressed the differences between the pragmatic approach and the essentialistic and perrenialistic views that had dominated education. Books by Kilpatrick [60] and other interpreters of Dewey became the standard texts in educational philosophy. The educational philosophers separated themselves from the philosophy departments in universities and colleges in order to attempt to make their work more relevant to the needs of the schools and to escape the more abstract constraints of their parent discipline.

These trends in teacher education warred with the apprenticeship experience. There was increasing conflict between the "theory" of education, as taught in the methods courses and the social, philosophical, and psychological foundations courses, and the kinds of experiences the young teacher had in the schools. The great teacher educators during the period stretching from the early 1930s until the present devoted most of their energies to organizational and procedural matters designed to reduce this gulf.[66] They concentrated especially on improving relationships among cooperating teachers, student teachers, and college supervisors. They developed a great number of procedural devices by which the theories of the colleges could be brought into closer alignment with the practices of the schools, so that the apprentice-

---

* The course derived from Dewey's stance toward school-community relations. Kilpatrick, W. H. *Philosophy of Education.* New York: Macmillan, 1951.

ship experience would reinforce what was being taught in the methods courses and, reciprocally, the "real world" would affect the colleges. The view of the individual as a socially committed problem solver combined with the constructionist view of knowledge to create a view of the teacher as one whose competence in democratic leadership overshadowed his/her other attributes.

As the progressive movement in schooling began to decline, its influence on teacher education also declined, although more slowly. It continues today to have considerable influence both on what is taught in teacher education and how it is taught. The conflict between theory and practice that was made virtually inevitable by the failure to reconstruct teacher education more radically continues wherever progressive courses conflict with the apprenticeship experience. (However, probably no reform movement in teacher education can avoid this type of conflict unless it accompanies or follows rather than precedes radical school reform.)

The progressives, in stressing the emergence of the democratic process, were present- and future-oriented. They stressed that continuing change was a part of social life and that all institutions, including education, would need continual revision and, even, replacement. They stressed student-centered, problem-oriented, hypothesis-generating modes of education and saw teachers as part of the process for adapting the society to changing conditions.

The Academic Orientation

Thesis: The *academic reform movement* viewed the individual as a scholar. Its approach to teacher education was direct—to train the teacher to think like a scholar and to "practice the disciplines" with children.

It is debatable how far the academic community resides within the mainstream of American society. The existence of such a vast number of higher-education institutions and the predominance of academic content within the schooling process might be taken as evidence that the work of the scholar obtains high recognition within the culture. The roles of scholars as advisors to government attest to a certain degree of acceptance. Yet it is possible to have a post secondary education without a high degree of intellectuality, and the scholar certainly is not embraced by all segments of the culture. Intellectuals frequently express alienation from the center of the society. Hofstadter and his students have taken great pains to point out and document the extent to which antiintellectualism characterizes mainstream America.[43] Much of the literature of this century is a reaction by intellectuals to the barbarism of humans as economic beings. Sinclair Lewis's *Babbitt* has great symbolic value in this respect, as does Savage in Aldous Huxley's *Brave New World.* The expatriate writers of the twenties and thirties found it literally impossible to maintain and nurture ideas in a normal American environment. Hutchins's view of higher education generated considerable controversy, partly because of suspicions of his intellectuality, especially fears about the kinds of social thoughts that intellectuals generate. (His orientation toward the scholarship of the past also infuriated the future-oriented progressives.) In the 1950s and 60s, the academic community rose up and unified itself, although scarcely in a mood of radical social reform.* It obtained larger appropriations from the National Science Foundation and the academic wings of the U.S. Office of Education. It capitalized on the Russian achievements with Sputnik and the subsequent widespread criticism of education to generate a large-scale reform movement. The academic reform movement [16,40] dominated the headlines of innovation in American education from about 1955 to 1965. Scholar-led projects in sciences, mathematics, social studies, English and foreign languages created materials for children built around the ideas and methods of the academic disciplines. Large-scale programs were launched to train teachers to implement those curriculums. In these programs great prominence was given to the information-processing power of the academic disciplines. The effort was focused on conceptual capacities of people and the potential contribution of scholarly concepts to improvement of their lives. The movement clearly intended to make academic thought more intelligible to the citizen and to prepare more students for a life of scholarship. The teacher was to be the surrogate of this process (although in many cases s/he was prepared to use "teacher-proof" materials rather than to lead the children directly).

A meeting (the Woods Hole Conference) that focused the beginning of the movement resulted in the popularization of the term, "the structure of the discipline." The four advantages cited by Bruner in *The Process of Education* for organizing instruction around the central concepts of the academic disciplines supply a good basis for our inference of the view of humankind that is embodied in the academic reform movement.

1. Organizing teaching around the structure of the disciplines would increase memory by providing the student with an ideational scaffolding on which to organize and retain information.

2. It would give the student greater comprehension and greater intellectual power by providing unifying ideas to help him/her comprehend his/her world.

3. The major concepts would increase the transfer of education to problem-solving situations by providing an intellectual structure for thinking about problems.

4. The education of the child would be brought closer to the forefront of knowledge. S/he would be learning the same types of concept that advanced scholars use, rather than distillations and assertions far removed from the ideas that inspire advanced technique.

The view deemphasized emotion. Nowhere in *The Process of Education* were the emotions of the student discussed except in the assumption that

---

* The academic community is only one segment of the intellectual community, of course. The reform movement does not represent writers, artists, journalists, and others outside the academic community. Nor do their views necessarily coincide with the academic stance.

knowledge is itself intrinsically motivating. The act of knowing, the act of increasing comprehension, was seen as so satisfying that the student, once exposed to ideas of quality, would be motivated to continue to educate her/himself. The scholars saw children as they saw themselves.[16]

Ausubel's *Psychology of Verbal Learning*[7] portrayed the mind of a child as an information-processing system and represents fairly well the dominant psychology behind the academic orientation. His views of learning derived from the assumption that the academic disciplines are composed of hierarchically ordered concepts and that the task of education is to transmit the hierarchy into the student's mind so that the student will use it to process information. Leaving aside the question as to whether scholarly disciplines are, in fact, composed of hierarchical concepts,* the analogy of the minds of students to an information-processing system and the assumption that external processing systems can be internalized by learners gives a distinctive picture of humankind. It gives rise to a particular kind of educational objective (internalization of the structures of academic knowledge) and thus results in an advocacy of that objective.

The abstractness of the much-touted curriculum *Man, A Course of Study* illustrated rather dramatically the academic frame of reference toward the social studies and the idea of the role of the teacher that was derived from it. The curriculum was aimed towards the upper elementary grades, especially the fifth grade, and replaced a curriculum that emphasized the history of the values of the American culture and the evolution of American political and economic systems. The topic of humans as a course of study is sharply different from that of the study of the American Constitution and the expansion of the United States that was emphasized in the traditional fifth-grade curriculum. *Man, A Course of Study* began with the study of the salmon, a creature whose behaviors are almost entirely genetically derived, and then proceeded to the study of the herring gull, a creature whose behavior is largely innate but includes some social learning and a minimal communication with other members of the species. From the herring gull the study proceeded to the baboon, a creature with some social life and a much larger degree of social learning. From there the curriculum proceeded to the Bushman of the Kalahari Desert and the Netsilik Eskimo. These represent human cultures that, although primitive, derive or transmit most of their behaviors socially. The student, studying the distinction between innate and learned behavior, was presumably to arrive at the concept of culture. S/he was thus to begin to get greater insight into his/her own behavior and come to understand the social nature of human life.

The *Man, A Course of Study* curriculum emphasized an almost pure form of scientific inquiry far separated from the contemporary social issues that wracked the world in which it was produced. A greater contrast to the pro-

---

* This assumption has been inadequately explored through empirical analyses of the disciplines.

gressive mode could hardly be imagined. Small wonder that the academic reform movement bypassed the education professors, so many of whom were progressives.

There was a split between those advocates of the information-processing metaphor who, like Ausubel, favored reception learning, in which the learner *receives* concepts in verbal form, and those who believed that the student should be taught by the inductive methodologies (the "inquiry" methods) that characterized the work of scholars themselves.[29] Thus two kinds of curriculums arose, one emphasizing reception learning and the other the "practice" of inductive methodology. These were paralleled by an analogous pair of approaches to teacher education. However, both branches emphasized cognitive processes. The academic reform movement was in no small measure responsible for the resurgence of interest in cognitive psychology which began in the 1950s and continues to the present. The rediscovery of Piaget by American psychologists, given the frame of reference of the academic disciplines, made it almost inevitable that the emphasis on teaching and the structure of the disciplines would be succeeded by attempts to improve cognitive processes directly. Hence, especially in primary education, there arose many programs for children based on extrapolations from Piagetian theory. These centered on the attempt to teach cognitive processes directly and to accelerate the development of logical thinking in children.[87,95]

Most often the view of the teacher that derived from the academic stance was that of the logician and academic scholar. This view was perhaps most eloquently expressed in the handbooks which Schwab and his associates wrote for the Biological Science Study Committee Handbook for Teachers.[85] Schwab very clearly felt that it would not be possible for a teacher to teach biology unless s/he also practiced it. It would not, of course, be necessary for the teacher to be a prize-winning scholar, but s/he should have the kind of intellectual interests that would lead to exploration of the modes of inquiry of the discipline and application of them to the solution of those problems in which s/he was interested. Thus the academic reformers emphasized a mode that would train the teacher to become a practicing member of the discipline and to subsequently induct students into the practice of the discipline by expressing the discipline's concepts in an Ausubelian manner or by leading the children in the practice of the discipline in the "inquiry-oriented" manner.

The two branches of the academic reform movement, the one favoring reception learning and the other favoring inductive or process-centered learning, are reflected in the training programs which were developed for teachers. Most of these training programs exposed teachers to courses on the discipline. They were taught in a largely didactic manner and taught teachers rather directly how to use the new curriculum materials that were being developed. Often substantive and methods courses were correlated. For example, courses on the structure of mathematics appeared in the curriculum to prepare elementary teachers, and these were followed up by courses demonstrating how to use the new materials with teachers. Those who favored the deductive methodologies tended to try to produce teacher-proof materials—materials that would bypass the poorly regarded teacher and bring a more academic learning directly to the student. They favored instructing the teacher directly how to use the materials designed for children. Some of these materials actually attempted to induce the students' inductive learning by developing intricate specifications within the learning packages. The teacher, simply by following the directions, was expected to achieve a high level of inductive activity on the part of the students. Those favoring inductive activity tended to try to teach the teacher the essence of induction. Perhaps the purest example of a curriculum to prepare teachers to use inductive methods was developed at the University of Chicago during the early 1960s. Much of the teacher-candidates' work was in the academic disciplines. A coordinator of each subject area taught children in the University Laboratory School, conducted academic research in the discipline, and was expected to generate original research in his/her area of concentration. The teacher-candidate served an apprenticeship with the coordinator and also in an academic high school. Thus the teacher was being trained to be scholarly in his/her field, was being taught directly by someone who could practice the discipline, and was expected to learn to use materials designed to teach students to practice it also.

It is not surprising that very few of the students from the Chicago program (and many of the other Master of Arts in Teaching programs which were similarly designed) worked in inner-city schools, or, indeed, in any but the college preparatory curriculums in secondary schools. Both the curriculums and the teacher-training generated by the academic reform movement were almost necessarily developed for the academically talented (although there were some exceptions). The intellectual scholar, not surprisingly, was oriented toward the education of the intellectually gifted student, the prototype of which was probably his/her own child.

The academic reform movement viewed humankind as an information-processing creature. It tried to orient teachers and children toward the academic disciplines. Both its deductive and inductive branches created materials for children which assumed the teacher to be the surrogate of the disciplines. The progressives emphasized the role of the teacher as a democratic leader of a problem-solving group and cast the roles of teacher and student as *creators* of knowledge constructed in the light of social purpose. The academic reformers saw the *disciplines* as the sources of the important knowledge. Teacher and child were seen as receivers either of the concepts of the discipline (the deductive approach) or its methodologies (the inductive approach). Socialization into the academic community was central to both variations on the academic theme.

The Personalistic Reformers

Thesis: The *personalists'* focus on the uniqueness and dignity of the individual gave an idiosyncratic conception of teaching and learning. The result deemphasized any standardization of learning outcomes and teacher competencies and emphasized an empathetic, almost personal, relationship between equals.

The antecedents of person-oriented philosophical and psychological positions reach well into the past, although not until Rousseau did we have a complete articulation of the thesis that the individual human being is the basic unit of humanity, and that the purpose of education is to facilitate his/her unfolding and "natural" goodness, rather than impose upon him/her the experience of his/her more corrupt elders. Although personalistic themes were evident in Horace Mann and Henry Barnard in America and in Johann Friedrich Herbart and Friedrich Froebel in Europe, it is not until the latter part of the nineteenth century that a community of educators emerged to give personalism institutional focus in the child study movement. Since that time personalists have appeared with increasing frequency from several disciplines and with a number of shadings of concern.

From clinical psychology (Rogers [82] and Glasser,[39] for instance), individual psychology (Combs [19] and Maslow [68]), Gestalt Psychology (Perls,[75] Schutz [84]), and personalistic philosophy (Friere,[31] Buber,[18] and Greene [41]) have come strands of thought that have represented a very strong reform effort in the literature—one of the best-defined lines of writing—which has had only occasional but nonetheless dramatic implementation in schooling and in teacher education.

The stance toward the student stresses her/his uniqueness and the importance of his/her emotional makeup. Individual psychology and Gestalt theory both stress the importance of the personal perceptual field. *Peering at the world from his/her unique perspective,* the student creates an individual reality and makes that world meaningful. Relations with others are characterized by a continuous process of negotiation of frames of reference as the student seeks to express his/her perspective and to comprehend her/his neighbor's view. The unique configuration of self controls the kinds of life activities which are perceived as possible and the kinds of learning which are accessible.

From this stance one does not presume to teach. One provides an environment with much diversity and malleability—one from which the learner can choose and which *s/he can shape to conform to his/her configurations.* The curriculum is not planned in the sense that objectives are set and learning activities are organized in advance. Rather, the teacher gently helps the student to reflect on her/himself and negotiates goals with him/her.

When this view finds expression in the design of a school, the result is markedly different from the norm. Summerhill, for example, is delineated not only by what it focuses on, but by what it avoids. A. S. Neill believes that personal development should not be subverted by a structural curriculum, no matter how well intentioned. The school *avoids* imposing itself on the student and gives primacy to the student's emotional life.[73]

If the student is unique, what of the teacher? The teacher educator who emphasizes the uniqueness of the child and the importance of his/her emotionality must do the same for the teacher. Teacher education, too, has to be a process of freeing the personality and helping the prospective teacher to develop on her/his own terms. The act of teaching has to be seen as an interaction between two selves, teacher and learner, neither superior nor inferior, in which the more experienced serves as the gentlest sort of guide.

This stance is not compatible with standardized specifications of competency for the teacher. Since the actual transactions of teaching will be the product of unique personalities responding to unique circumstances and forming what has to be a special relationship, needed competence cannot be forecast—competence is idiosyncratic. The effort of the teacher educator has to focus on the development of a rich, many-sided, actualizing self rather than on training in specific skills which will be shared with other teachers.

The chief spokesperson for the personalistic education of teachers has been Arthur W. Combs.[19] The idiosyncratic nature of teaching is seen as, in Combs's skepticism, the struggles to identify common teacher competencies. He preferred to emphasize the personal character of good teaching:

> A good teacher is primarily a unique personality. If good teachers are unique individuals, we can predict from the start that the attempt to find *common uniqueness* would be unlikely to get results.
>
> A good teacher is first and foremost *a person* and this fact is the most important and determining thing about her/him. S/he has competence to be sure, but not a common set of competencies like anyone else."[19, p.6]

Combs believed that the attempt to define sets of teacher competencies leads to a mechanistic conception of the teacher, and he would replace standardization with a view of the unique self as the instrument of professional behavior. "We may define the effective teacher formally as a unique human being who has learned to use her/himself effectively and efficiently to carry out his/her own and society's purposes in the education of others."[19, p.9] This view differs sharply from the position that the teacher should be taught a repertoire of competencies which s/he applies in order to adapt what s/he does to individual and purpose. From Combs's stance, we do not teach the teacher a repertory of teaching strategies—each individual develops his/her repertory in her/his unique way. This is necessary because of the perceptual basis of behavior: "The basic concept of perceptual psychology is that all the behavior of a person is the direct result of her/his field of perceptions at the moment of his/her behaving. More specifically, her/his behavior at any instant is the result of (1) how s/he sees her/himself, (2) how s/he sees the situations in which s/he is involved, and (3) the inter-relationships of these two."[19, p.12]

To develop a change in behavior a person has to change her/his perception. Any significant change in behavior involves a change in the perceptual field. Thus, the individual self has to be the focus of education. A person's adjustment and perception, interpersonal relations, and capacity for self-education all come from her/his views of her/himself. Thus Combs concerned himself much less with the discipline-derived substance of teacher education (particularly the details of the substance) than do advocates of other approaches, but rather dealt with what is done to help the teacher develop her/his view of her/himself as a person and as a teacher. It is not that Combs believed that the teacher does not need to achieve competency and knowledge, but that he believed that these will develop only in relation to the teacher's view of himself or herself as a person and a professional, rather than as the product of an imposed curriculum.

Combs assumed that each person is striving to fulfill her/himself as best s/he can, that each person is filled with energy that expends itself on self-maintenance and self-enhancement.

> It is not the physical self that each seeks to maintain, however. It is the self of which we are aware, our *self concepts,* we seek fulfillment for. Even behaviors which at first glance seem to be self destructive turn out to be self maintaining or enhancing when they are seen from the point of view of the individual. So it is that the hero may give himself up to a certain death rather than see himself a coward or a traitor to his fellows. In our own experiences we often place our physical self in jeopardy for the sake of enhancing our concepts of self. For example, we drive too fast, eat too much, work too hard even when we know better.
>
> The need for adequacy is the fundamental motivation of every human being from conception to death.
>
> This drive has a tremendous implication for education. Its existence means it is not necessary to motivate people—a problem we have often struggled with. Everyone is *always motivated* to be and become as adequate as he [sic] can be in the situations as he [sic] sees them. Students may not be motivated as their teachers would like, but they are always motivated in terms of their own basic needs.
>
> Knowledge of this unique drive changes the whole structure of the educative process from that which our ancestors felt was essential. . . . [T]he task of the teacher is not one of prescribing, making, molding, forcing, [etc.] . . . the role required of the teacher is that of facilitator, encourager, helper, assistor, colleague and friend of the students.[19, p.16]

Thus the teacher is seen as having to develop the capacity to engage in a helping relationship, one which includes the ability to relate to people and help them in such a way as to enhance them on their own terms. A teacher needs to orient her/himself so that the focus of much of her/his own fulfillment is through helping students enhance themselves. The process of teaching is a completely idiosyncratic one, depending on the individual character of the teacher as s/he interrelates with the individual character of the student. This is why Combs said that we cannot specify the competencies of a teacher, that competencies stem from the *unique* way in which an individual develops a helping relationship with her/his *unique* students. Each helping relationship, in turn, would have to be particular to the parties. Since teaching depends on making contact between the two participants, each on his/her own terms, the primary competence is the ability to understand one's self and to learn to understand others.

To train a teacher one must help him/her develop, first, an adequate self; second, reliable ways of perceiving others and their goals; and third, the ability to learn substance when it is needed. To prepare such a teacher we must provide a helping relationship for the teacher-candidate just as s/he must provide one for his/her students. The best teacher education, then, is an environment conducive to self-actualization, for two interacting reasons: One, it is the best way to help the prospective teacher to develop an adequate self; and two, it is the best way to help her/him learn how to help others.

The Competency Orientation

Thesis: The *competency orientation* has two branches. One, the superindustrial, seeks to improve education through contemporary industrial techniques, fueled by the technitronic revolution. The other, humanistic branch, seeks to promote pluralism through technology. Both, however, perceive the teacher and his/her training by means of cybernetic analogies.

Since the turn of the century, there have been attempts to define precisely the competencies which would lead to teacher effectiveness and to develop methods which could reliably and systematically prepare teachers. During the last half dozen years these efforts have culminated in what is coming to be known as the movement for competency-based teacher education. The movement itself has a very broad base. Also, its language has been coopted by many writers on teacher education who take positions which appear to be at odds with the core ideas of the competency orientation. However, it is possible to sort out the strands that have led to it and to define the assumptions that appear to lie beneath it.

In many ways the competency orientation is a logical extension of the industrial model of the school. It is based at least in part on the desire to make schooling more efficient and to hold teacher educators and teachers accountable for the effects of their efforts. It employs many techniques originally developed in industrial or military applications of systems technology. Its emphases on computer-based management systems, the use of multimedia instructional devices, the development of data storage and retrieval systems to store program elements, and objectives-evaluation devices, all represent a look beyond the traditional age to the emerging technitronic industrial age that appears to be close upon us. In this sense, the competency orientation is futuristic.

The philosophical waters are muddied by the application of systems technologies to domains which at first appear to be inimical to them. For example, systematic programs have been developed to train human relations specialists. Personalistic modes such as Gestalt therapy have been submitted to systems analysis and the development of systematic training procedures. A new field, that of *behavioral humanism,* is emerging from this effort.[98] Some have even claimed, as does the present author, that the competency orientation is a form and a methodology rather than a philosophical orientation and is broad enough to embrace *all* the modes of education which have presently been developed.[49] This position is vigorously challenged by many. Broudy, for example, finds the competency orientation inherently atheoretical and feels it is not compatible with any important philosophical position.[14] Some proponents of the academic orientation find it to be antithetical to the academic training of the teacher.[86]

The antecedents of the movement can be most clearly discerned in the years since 1940. One apparent antecedent is the development of systems for analyzing the transactions of teaching in specific behavioral terms. Interaction analysis systems derived from the work of Anderson and Brewer just before the Second World War [4] and proceeded through the work of Withall [105] to Flanders, [30] Medley and Mitzel, [71] Bellack, [8] B. O. Smith, [91] and others. Simon and Boyer have identified about eighty instruments for classifying the acts of teacher and learner. [88] *The Handbook of Research on Teaching* appeared in 1963 after several years of preparation and anchored this literature for researchers on teaching. [33]

The behavioral analysis of teaching rested on several assumptions. One was that the acts of teaching and the responses of the learner could be reasonably analyzed into specific, even minute, behavioral components without doing violence to the essential nature of the act. The second was that the mysteries of teaching and some of the mysteries of learning would, over time, be unlocked by this type of research; that teaching is not an intuitive art but is composed of discernible patterns of behavior whose dimensions can productively be changed through training. Third, many researchers hoped to identify specific components of teacher behavior that could be related to desirable pupil growth. While normally the indices of pupil growth that were studied stemmed from the objectives of the industrial age school, many researchers were seeking clues for methods of reforming education by orienting it toward newer goals in the affective or cognitive areas. Withall and Flanders, for example, studied social climate dimensions of the classroom, trying to identify the dynamics of the acts that improved the learner's feelings of self-worth. This aspect of behavioral analysis appeared to support the personalistic orientations. Bellack, Smith, and others concentrated on describing the cognitive acts of teaching, and it is not hard to tell from their writings that they hoped to identify ways of making the classroom a more conceptual and divergent place than it ordinarily is. Spaulding and his associates are directly from the personalistic school, for they analyzed the struggles of the learner as s/he seeks to actualize her/himself in the setting of the classroom.[94]

Gradually training systems began to be developed based on the category systems. Taba,[96] Spaulding, Flanders, and others employed behavioral systems to help teachers study their teaching and set goals for the modification of their behavior. Teacher-education programs began to adopt the systems and a considerable literature grew up over attempts to modify teacher behavior in this way.[3] The categories of behavior became the goals of training, and the assumption was made that a teacher could learn to analyze specific elements of her/his behavior and could gain control over those elements, either modifying his/her patterns in a given direction or developing mastery of a greater repertoire of behaviors.

During the same period, research and development teams began to attempt to lay a basis for the creation of training systems built around specific sets of teacher competencies. Allen, MacDonald, and their associates at Stanford University developed the technique known as "microteaching." [2] They developed a set of teaching skills appropriate for the secondary classroom and employed the use of videotape recordings to train teachers to discriminate their own behaviors and to practice new ones and add those, or incorporate those, into their repertoires. McDonald's recent National Society for the Study of Education Yearbook chapter on applications of behavior modification to teacher training traces the origins of their work in behavior modification theory.[70] Popham, Baker, and their associates at UCLA[77] became the center of a movement to train teachers to select specific behavioral objectives for children, to develop appropriate instructional methodologies, and to evaluate the effect of teaching with precision.

Borg and his associates at the Far West Laboratory developed multimedia training systems built on the microteaching principle.[12] In a similar effort, Joyce, Weil, Wald, and their associates built training systems based on a systematic analysis of a variety of models of teaching.[56] These researchers and developers assumed not only that teaching is amenable to particularistic analysis but that it can be trained skill-by-skill as well—that the teacher can synthesize a repertoire of specifically taught behaviors into the totality of his/her act of teaching.

The assumption that teaching could reasonably be studied and trained in segments was operative in much of the research of the late 1960s. Gage and colleagues,[35] despairing of the global conceptions of teaching that had guided much of the research between 1900 and the mid-1950s, advocated a "micro-criterion" approach based on the very specific study of particular types of teaching acts such as lecturing, counseling, and so on, thus attempting to create a research base for specific training.

In 1968 there occurred an event that unified this movement. The United States Office of Education issued a series of requests for proposals to apply systems-analysis procedures to the development of training programs for teachers. The requests for proposals were very specific. The competencies of the teacher would be stated in terms of sets and these sets would be linked to training systems specifically designed to bring about the achievement of those competencies; the totality would be held under management systems which would be used for program evaluation and improvement.

Ten contracts were let and, less than a year later, a series of complex program models had been developed that were widely disseminated and formed much of the substantive base of the movement toward competency-based teacher education.

Common assumptions of the systems planner

The teams worked separately and completed their reports within a very short time. In addition to their use of systematic planning procedures, the ten teams operated on certain implicit but common working hypotheses about teachers and training programs, although they differed considerably in application of these assumptions to teacher-education program development. These common hypotheses were manifested throughout the program reports and represented basic, but tentative, assumptions that formed a common frame of reference about teaching and training, and that could be used to make decisions concurrently with the testing of the assumptions themselves.

1. The teacher was viewed as a clinician in much the sense that physicians are clinicians. S/he was seen as the possessor of strategies for making instructional diagnoses and as the possessor of the needed repertoire of knowledge and clinical skills for carrying out an appropriate instructional treatment.

2. The teacher was generally thought of as a member of a clinical team and frequently as a specialist on that team. Several of the models provided "career ladders" with places for many kinds of specialists in a career hierarchy.

3. It was assumed that teacher educators could define the needed competencies of the teacher in terms of specific behaviors and match those behaviors with specific learning experiences, especially short instructional modules calculated to achieve those objectives.

4. It was assumed that management and control systems could be developed to monitor teacher-training programs to provide them with flexibility, especially adaptability, to the student.

5. It was assumed that any teacher who could take major responsibility in a classroom would need a long period of training, and that a consortium of colleges and school districts were necessary to provide the conditions for academic training, preservice training, internship or practice teaching, and continuing inservice education.

6. Training programs were designed to make heavy use of simulation laboratories, where situations could be created that were somewhat less complex than the "real world of the teacher," in order to teach clinical skills.

7. The teacher was to have available knowledge from the behavioral sciences which could be used to make and carry out educational decisions.

8. Last, it was assumed that a training program should contain provisions for revision and redevelopment as a fundamental feature, not as a subsidiary element or aftergrowth. Replanning and reimplementation were assumed to be basic—as basic as training components themselves.

The assumptive world of systems planning in teacher education

The set of common aspects of the program models reflects an assumptive world that is partly made up of a commitment to the application of systematic, future-related planning procedures to education; partly of a commitment to bring educational training to bear directly on the revision of public education; and, even more, of an awareness of the possibilities of contemporary management technology. An individualized (let alone a personalized) program for a large student body, without the capacity to obtain and store vast amounts of information about students, and to maintain and deliver as wide a variety of alternative instructional experiences as deemed appropriate, cannot really be imagined. For although educators have talked about individualized curriculums for decades, they have not lived in a world in which the available technology would allow a really thorough form of individualization. Nearly all successful forms of individualized instruction have depended on a very favorable instructor-student ratio, and even then the instructors have had to be highly competent and committed to individualization and personalization.

Quality control has been similarly limited. Although curriculum theory has postulated for many years that there should be direct linkages between behaviorally stated objectives, instructional alternatives, and evaluation processes, this has not really been possible. For example, even a committed instructor teaching a course to twenty students simply cannot manufacture enough tests by her/himself to track progress adequately and adjust instruction to the varying rates of progress of his/her students.

With the advent of technologies for developing large and complex information storage and retrieval systems, there arrived also the capacity for developing management systems that could coordinate student characteristics and achievement with instructional alternatives, still maintaining reasonable levels of quality control. Very few educators have as yet become familiar with these technologies, partly because they are new and not yet disseminated throughout the education community, and partly because many educators have reacted adversely and equate "management systems" with "dehumanization."

It is safe to say that all the program model teams are comfortable with the idea of management systems and believe that when we learn how to use them, we will make education much more flexible and human. They live in an assumptive world in which one looks for ways of developing "support systems," "choice points," and "feedback systems." They develop training in "simulators" with "recycling to a more appropriate alternative" and "increasing complexity of instructional tasks." In other words, they attempt a massive task analysis of the problem of preparing a teacher, confident that the task analysis can be made and the management systems can be created to implement the results. They recognize that enormous quantities of jargon will be needed to symbolize the concepts of objectives, modular curricular alternatives, evaluation, and support systems necessary to such an effort. They believe that such a technology will eventually not only permit instruction to be tailored to individuals but also will enable many instructional goals and means to be shaped by the student her/himself.

Hence, the "model developers" live in an assumptive world consisting of management systems theory, a concern with efficiency and systematic training (cybernetic psychology), and the belief that applying these to teacher education will mean a more personal environment for the student, a more effective teacher product, and a university in which desirable innovation can be made (cycled into the system) much more easily than is possible with the present organization.

View of humankind

The conception of humankind that underlies competency-based teacher education can be inferred most clearly not only from the assumptions and common program elements of the Computer-Based Teacher Education models, but also from the steps that the systems-oriented teams followed when they created their program models. There are roughly *six large tasks* involved in the application of systems technology to the training of the teacher. Although systems procedures have by no means been standardized, the six tasks generally appear in any paradigm for systematic program construction, although they sometimes exist under different names than the ones that will be employed here. The order in which they are accomplished varies quite widely. However, there is a certain logic in the following order:

1. *The development of the performance model.* A major task is the conceptualization of the goal of the training program, and this task must be accomplished in terms of a working model of the product of the program. The working performance model should be as complete as possible and describe aspects of performance and interrelationships among the aspects. In the case of a teacher-education program, the fulfillment of this task requires the development of a working model of a functioning teacher. This model is described as an imput-output system. Furthermore, the teacher must be conceptualized in terms of the system within which s/he is operating. Classrooms and schools, as well as teams of teachers, need to be described, and it would be desirable for the conceptualization also to include the wider systems of the community within which the educational institution functions.

2. *The analysis of the performance model into sets of behavioral objectives.* The model has to be broken down into specific domains of functioning (if these are not already available within the model) and these, in turn, have to be broken down into sets of behaviors—sequentially organized wherever that is possible—so that programs can be built to achieve those objectives and to provide the trainee with the devices for integrating them into the overall performance system. This task is exceedingly complicated when one is dealing with a complex functionary like a teacher: cognitive behaviors, affective behaviors, and skills interrelate and overlap, and yet must be perceived distinctly and in relationship to each other if rational program planning is to proceed.

3. *The specification of training subsystems (the development of components and component strategies).* The next task consists of the development of program components to accomplish distinct sets of behaviors. Within each set component, distinct curricular or teaching strategies need to be constructed

and sometimes many need to be developed for a particular component. Components need not be homogeneous with respect to teaching strategies. For example, the same component may use sensitivity-training techniques to achieve certain kinds of behavior, and behavior-modification strategies within simulators for yet other sets of behaviors. However, the training subsystems need to be clarified in a modular organization. One of the interesting features of the ten developed models is the wide range of curricular strategies that are recommended within and between components. The development of components must be accompanied by the development of specifications for needed support systems (such as closed-circuit television laboratories, etc.).

4. *The development of the overall training system (the creation of interlocking relationships among components).* It is always tempting for a program planner to develop discrete components having their own distinctive strategies, their own instructional materials, and their own special procedures for staff training. However, for the sake of the student, whose life should not be fragmented unnecessarily, and in order to achieve an integrated performance at the end of the program, components need to be related to one another systematically, then modules cast in reconcilable terms. In addition, support systems need to be developed and integrated into the training components, and the performances and training of training agents must be specified.

5. *The development of management systems to monitor a large program.* To enable a large program to adjust to the individual differences among students (in terms of goals, achievement, and learning style), to build in provisions for program revision, to ensure continuous feedback and evaluation for managers, faculty, and students, and to integrate components and support systems smoothly, comprehensive management systems need to be developed.

6. *The reconciliation of the program and product with the client and the field.* A young person entering the field of education has personal needs and conceptions of teaching which s/he needs to explore and to relate to the training opportunities that are presented to her/him. S/he has to explore her/himself as a person as well as explore her/himself as a professional-in-training. Whether learning to be a teacher aide in a hierarchial team or preparing to be a specialist in a subject discipline, the prospective teacher needs to learn frames of reference that will allow the apprehension of alternative careers, ways of following them, ways of reconciling personal needs for intimate relationships with the demands of career, and ways of making a training program work for her/him, so that s/he does not become an artifact of a machine. Hence, specific procedures for humanistic guidance have to be developed for the client of the program.

Similarly, the teacher-education program must be related to the field which it serves. Teacher education has to supply institutions with competent and humanistic personnel; these institutions must share in the identification of competencies and the development of training procedures. A smooth transition needs to be provided between any training institution and the educational institution in which the teacher will work. In fact, the creation of the setting for teacher education is a joint problem for universities, training institutions, and elementary and secondary schools. The problems of reconciliation with the field become particularly acute when the training program is designed to produce a teacher who is in any way different from the typical functionary in the existing schools.

The use of systems procedures implies that we can validly use the analog of "system" to describe schools, teaching, and training. Issues over the reasonableness of this analog have fueled many of the controversies over competency-based teacher education. The issues sharpen along the question "Does the analogy partition humanity and education in an inhuman way?" Embedded in this issue is the question of whether the systems analogies represent a view of humankind which can embrace a narrow or broad ideological span. Whether systems methods can be comfortably applied to the earlier industrial orientation is not widely debated. To make an analysis of present teacher roles and develop systematic procedures for training teachers to fulfill those roles appear feasible and compatible with the economic view of humanity.

However, Broudy and Shugrue have wondered whether systems approaches can be applied to theoretical or academic views of the teacher. Combs has stated outright that the competency orientation is incompatible with the personalistic position. But many of the systems planners and behavioral humanists seriously believe that systems approaches can be applied to a broad spectrum of purposes. The position taken here is that the systems approaches *can* be compatible with all available orientations toward the teacher.

CONTEMPORARY QUESTIONS

The competition between the dominant mode of teacher education and the modes discussed above—academic, personalistic, progressive, and a branch of the competency-based movement—has underlined a series of issues that form the substance of many present arguments.

Wholists and Partists

How finely can we partition the acts of teaching?

In addition to differences in substance between the orientations, there is almost surely one of form. Personalists, progressives, and academicians tend to see the teacher as an organic whole and they resist any description of the parts unless these are well grounded in the totality.

Some of the attempts to build competency-based programs have resulted in models of the teacher made up of a great many specific competencies— often as many as 3,000. The systems-based teacher-preparation programs frequently contain as many program elements as there are competencies. It is assumed, moreover, that the competencies can be taught and assessed individually and specifically and that the teacher candidate can synthesize these specific competencies in order to engage these in teaching roles. It is hard to imagine a more mechanistic view of humankind.

By contrast, from the personalistic, progressive, and academic orientations humankind is conceptualized as an organic unity. The personalist emphasizes the uniqueness of each organism, and from this comes a pluralistic conception of teacher and learner. When the personalist considers the teacher, s/he refuses to separate skill, cognition, and emotion. In such a view all the components of teacher education flow from the need to facilitate the individual's struggle for identity. The result is an extremely unified program—one in which the teacher candidates explore themselves as human beings, investigate the nature of children, and develop styles that fit their unique personalities, but can be modified to suit the unique personalities that they will teach.

The academic orientation tends to generate relatively unified conceptions of teaching and training from the emphasis on scholarship. Academic information-processing is central and forms the core of the conception of the teacher, the major portion of training, and the modes of teaching s/he is expected to use.

Many systems planners believe that these unified conceptions of teaching can be analyzed into component behaviors and systematically taught. Joyce, Weil, Wald, and their associates [57] built a plan for teacher education in which teachers are systematically introduced to models of teaching derived from personalism, group dynamics, academic and psychological information-processing stances, and behavior modification. They believe that they have demonstrated that systems approaches are compatible with the theory and practice of many contemporary approaches to education, and that the industrial versions of educational systems planning, which have thus far appeared, have been a matter of deliberate selection based on the economic views of the teacher, rather than necessities imposed by the forms of the systems themselves. *Moreover, they believe that the development of educational pluralism in institutions and in the development of the teacher actually requires exposure to and competence in a variety of theories—that the above educational stances are not mutually exclusive.*[57]

Repertoire vs. Product Orientation in Teacher Training

Should the teacher be trained to carry out specified roles and to implement particular curriculums (a product orientation) or should s/he be prepared with a range or repertoire of competencies that s/he can integrate as needed in order to solve problems (a repertoire orientation)?

The industrial orientation has generally tried to prepare the teacher to fill the traditional classroom roles, many functions of which are relatively fixed. Production of certain kinds of learning is its forte. But both personalists and progressives have favored conceptions of teaching that emphasize the unique person of the teacher. They see personal and social life as continuous, emergent processes and favor a teacher training that facilitates the unique problem-solving capacity of the teacher. They stress a humanistic repertoire.

Some of the academic reformers, especially those emphasizing the constructionist view of knowledge, have also favored a problem-solving approach that has some common elements with the emergent conception, in that they see the teacher as inducting the young into scientific modes of thought. Others have tried to prepare the teacher to implement specific curriculums designed to impart scientific knowledge or process—a product approach.

The competency orientation has largely emphasized systematic preparation for particular roles (a product orientation), but some approaches are more pluralistic, as indicated earlier. A repertoire orientation is explicitly pluralistic. The more one sees the teacher, the learner, and thus the teaching situation as unique and emergent, the less one can subscribe to a product orientation. The more one sees a pluralistic world of shifting and constructed realities, the more one will favor the repertoire orientation.

Where the curriculum is fixed and the mode of instruction is definite, one finds a preference for a product orientation.

THE POWER IN ALTERNATIVE TRUTHS

There is a powerful message in each of the alternative stances toward the nature of humankind and its education. The *personalists* have emphasized the organic nature of the human being, both as a teacher and as a learner. Both children and teachers are real people. Their emotions and their intellect are part and parcel of the same creature, and the distinction between their domains of functioning is partly one of convenience. Any education of a teacher which does not take into account this humanness and the organic nature of human existence ignores the truth about the human condition that is underlined by the personalist stance.

The *progressives* emphasized humans as social beings. The meaning of their existence and their moral nature are derived from their membership in a society and, perhaps even more, from their membership in the species that has the apparent responsibility for carrying much of the intelligence that exists on the planet. This is the truth in the progressive stance. Teaching, which is not seen as a moral act, which does not emphasize the social responsibility inherent in the role, ignores not only the liberal philosophies of the last five centuries, but the truth that humans are social beings.

The *academic* stance teaches us that all knowledge is not equal. It is possible through scholarship to develop constructs that the untutored only rarely discover. An education that is unhinged from scholarship is an education that denies the possibility that a community of intellects can bring us beyond the state which each of us would reach alone without cumulative inquiry. Scholarship frees each person from having to discover all possible ways of thinking.

The *competence orientation* embodies the truth that we can learn skills and that each of us can improve our art with the help of science and engineering, and the *industrial orientation* grounds us in the real political and economical world of our society. It teaches us that our schooling and other social processes cannot be very separate from each other.

It should be possible for us, at this point in history, to build a synthesis that succeeds, without sinking to an absurd eclecticism; in developing views of education and the education of the teacher that can capitalize on the real truths that lie embedded in our competing philosophies. The alternatives are sufficiently clear and well developed to enable the community of teacher educators to do this if they can develop the appropriate forum for dialogue.

2

The Models of Teaching Community: Overview of a Struggle to Understand Teaching and Teacher Education

Bruce R. Joyce

In general, the work described here moves between general concepts and highly specific investigations directed at particular issues. Its purpose was and is to understand teaching more fully, both as it is carried on and as it might be. It consists about equally of descriptive studies and experimental training experiments. The general thrust of the work was relatively consistent, but there were many byways, some fruitful and some frustrating. Some lines of inquiry died because they did not prove fruitful or because we were not imaginative enough to work out technical problems. Occasionally, the results of a study pulled us in unexpected directions. The study of teachers' planning is an example. Joyce and Harootunian [79] studied teachers' preactive or planning behavior about a dozen years ago, and if that study had come out differently, we might have pursued a line of work more like that of James Popham, who devoted many years to helping teachers frame objectives more precisely. During that first study, we found that teachers simply did not frame objectives and means in the ways the curricular and instructional theorists did (that is, behaviorally) and that they rarely evaluated in the sense that evaluations and measurement specialists do. They behaved more as Phil Jackson described in *Life in Classrooms*.[71] (This may help to explain why Jackson is so popular with teachers—he thinks as they do rather than as the theorists do.) At any rate, Joyce and Harootunian became so discouraged that it was almost ten years before we again tried to study or influence teachers' planning behavior.* In that case, the results redirected our efforts by discouraging us. On the other hand, unexpected findings occasionally drew us into fresh work. For example, in the case of Tinsman's [147] study in 1966, we made a really *terrible* blunder that resulted in a whole line of fresh training research, probably the most important in the whole series. In that case, luck stepped in where skill had left.

This chapter presents the work chronologically, for the most part, partly because that is the way it happened, and partly because that organization is most revealing of our changes in thought. Still, some of the work is understood best when it is grouped by topic rather than by time, so most of the remainder of the book is organized around topics.

A FRAMEWORK FOR LOOKING AT TEACHING

Most of the early work was devoted to the search for a framework within which to look at teaching. David Hunt [60] provided a way of describing the variety of environments created by teachers, and we built a system for analyzing teaching around his concepts. This system focused on three dimensions of the classroom environment: structuring (the social organization of the classroom), feedback (the pattern of sanctions), and information processing (patterns of cognitive activity). Studies using this system [85] were first reported in 1963. They confirmed Hunt's thesis that personality and teaching are correlated. Hodges and Joyce followed these up in a series of studies designed to examine relationships among personality, natural teaching style, and susceptibility to training. (Personality *was* related to susceptibility to training; natural teaching style was *not.*) Peck,[110] Wald,[153] Seperson,[133] Weil,[155] and Brown [17] studied the natural styles of novice and in-service teachers and learned a number of things that had a considerable effect on the rest of the work. Most important was that we were not struck by the quality of the teaching that we saw in the classroom. Although we were originally disposed toward the notion that we would be able to identify a few outstanding teachers who could teach us a tremendous amount about how others could improve their teaching, we soon changed our minds—primarily because we observed so many *regularities* in teaching behavior. These regularities disturbed us because of their implications for student growth. For example, Hunt [57] postulated that personality growth is affected differently by different environments, with some environments facilitating growth and others retarding it for any given individual. In other words, growth in personality is a product of individual characteristics and the environment. The only environment that we ob-

* In contrast, Popham's (1970) first studies came out about the same time, and similar findings stimulated him to attempt to build instructional systems to change the ways teachers plan—to make them behave more as curriculum and measurement people do.

served with any frequency was one that (according to Hunt) is likely to arrest most students at the earliest stage of personality development, one which is socially unilateral and cognitively simple. The number of teachers who provided complex and integrative environments was very small indeed. The general picture was a depressing one in terms of the kind of pupil growth in which we were interested—growth of flexibility and creativity, growth that requires a range of teaching behaviors that are adjusted to the growth needs of individual students. Put more directly, "natural" teaching (by most, but not all teachers), rather than spontaneity and flexibility, appeared to be rigid and unilateral, dominated by the recitation method and focused on memorization and drill. The more flexible the personality of the teacher, the more flexible and variable the teaching. The overall picture, however, was *not* one of flexibility and adaptation. It was more like the picture of the recitation method described in Bellack's studies [11] and in the long stream of research summarized by Hoetker and Ahlbrand.[50]

What of Novice Teachers?

Brown [17] and Seperson [133] found that most student teachers changed their teaching styles in the course of student teaching until their styles approximated those of cooperating teachers. Hunt referred to this as a "funneling" of teaching style, a loss of individuality in the flow toward the mean. In our studies, novice teachers became *less* rewarding, *more* punishing, more *dominating* in conversation, and, most strikingly, did less *negotiating* with children. We concluded that the norms of practice are very powerful indeed. The novice is carried along toward a powerful river of customary practice. Seperson [133] correlated dimensions of the teaching style of novice teachers with those of their cooperating teachers and discovered that cooperating teacher influence on the styles of the novices was considerable by about the third week of student teaching and continued to be strong throughout student teaching. The influence was particularly great in the areas of structuring and feedback. Structuring became more unilateral, and there was less, and proportionally more negative, feedback. Questions designed to stimulate opinions and formation of concepts were few as student teaching began and fewer by its end.

We also found that the dimensions of teaching behavior (feedback, structuring, and information processing) were not correlated with each other. Although we confirmed Flanders' "rule of two-thirds" (that two-thirds of the time in most classrooms, someone is talking; and two-thirds of that time, the "someone" is the teacher; and two-thirds of the time that the teacher is talking, direct influence is being used),[32] we nevertheless became convinced that inductiveness and reflectiveness in the three dimensions of teaching behavior were independent of each other. When we matched what we saw against Hunt's definition of variety in learning environments, we found that very few teachers produced much variety. There *were* differences in the number and types of questions asked, and to some extent, in the amount of structuring and feedback given (and their shape). There *were* enormous *stylistic* differences (*how* questions were asked, for example). Very few of the stylistic differences, however, approximated *strategic* differences (*what* questions were asked). The teachers appeared to be using stylistic variations on a recitation strategy in which the rules for information processing and for organization were, on the whole, fairly structured, fairly simple, and fairly restrictive.

A New Lens

A second lens with which we looked at teaching was in dimensions that we referred to as *strength* and *sensitivity.* We did not see these dimensions as dichotomous, as the terms suggest. The preliminary definitions of strength and sensitivity came out of work done by Hunt, Weinstein, and Joyce in the spring of 1965. Hunt devised a communication task in which a teacher taught a role player who was programed to have a frame of reference that conflicted with the concept the teacher was instructed to present. Periodically, the role player gave cues about this frame of reference. The task was designed to determine the teacher's ability to read the frame of reference of his learner and to modulate his behavior to accommodate his client. Weinstein and Joyce were the role players in this task and had the unusual experience of observing eighty teachers give the same lesson to the same learner, played, alternatively, by themselves. As Weinstein and Joyce observed the teachers and reacted to them, Weinstein observed that the teachers were differentiated not only in terms of their ability to understand the role-player-learner *(sensitivity)* but also in terms of their ability to structure the situation (manifest *strength*). Some teachers were very persuasive, bringing the role player along with them with comfort and assurance. Others were quite reticent, and a few even required a considerable amount of prompting by the role player. Weinstein and Joyce speculated that strength was independent of sensitivity rather than opposed to it. Some of the most sensitive teachers seemed to be the strongest, whereas some very sensitive teachers were not very strong, and some strong ones showed very little sensitivity.

Two studies picked up the strength-sensitivity thread. Peck [110] used communication tasks designed to assess strength and sensitivity. She rated the teachers on eighteen dimensions of both strength and sensitivity, factor-analyzed the ratings of each dimension, and intercorrelated the factor scores. She established the partial independence of the two constructs and identified the factors that appeared to be most prominent in each. Separately, Joyce, Dirr, and Hunt [78] developed a training program designed to increase sensitivity to students. This program was largely a failure, although the teachers did modify their "approach-behavior" to the children. The conclusion was that training to influence sensitivity would have to be long-term in nature and probably should concentrate on relatively few aspects of learner behavior.

Most important, the two dimensions appeared to be reliably measurable. One, strength, measured the purpose and drive of the trainer or the teacher, the person responsible for intervening in the life of the student. The other, sensitivity, measured the empathic quality necessary to make contact with that student. Both qualities, however, defied classification by means of a simple category system, and each was very difficult to study in the hurly-burly of the classroom, where communication between teacher and learner is more diffuse than it is in a one-to-one or small-group teaching simulation.

An important side effect of these studies occurred when we correlated the behavior of teachers in the simulated teaching situations with behavior in the classroom using the three dimensions of the category system. The correlations for all dimensions were positive. That is not to say that the behavior of the teacher was identical in the classroom and the simulation or that it should be so. But it did provide evidence to support the notion that behaviors of teachers in classrooms and in simulated teaching situations are similar. Without this evidence, we could hardly support the use of the study of teaching or of training under simulated conditions. This finding (that teacher behavior is alike in simulated and "real" teaching situations) has been replicated several times, involving a variety of simulations and field settings. There are correlations between teachers' behavior in peer-teaching situations and field situations, in microteaching situations, and in large and small group teaching situations in the field. In other words, the teacher has an integrity that is somewhat independent from his/her surroundings (although it is greatly influenced by them).

THE EARLY TRAINING STUDIES: TRAINING THROUGH FEEDBACK

During the first studies of teaching, a system for observing variations in teaching styles and strategies had been developed and refined. The first training study used the categories in the observation system in two ways: first, as vehicles by which the teacher could examine his/her teaching; second, as definitions of a repertory of teaching skills. Eight of us collaborated in a year-long study in which thirty novice teachers received individual and group feedback about their teaching on a weekly basis. The training hypothesis was that first, feedback about teaching would increase the teachers' comprehension of their styles and strategies of teaching. Then, following comprehension, the teachers would strive to master new skills and expand their variety of approaches to teaching. The teachers who received feedback were compared with a group of teacher candidates who did not receive such feedback. The dependent variables were their teaching styles in the classroom and performance on a series of teaching tasks that required repeated shifts in teaching behavior. Tinsman [147] constructed these tasks to determine the extent to which members of the experimental and control groups would be able to navigate "controlled shifts" in teaching. The teaching styles of the control and experimental groups showed *no* differences throughout the year. The really interesting finding resulted accidentally from the fact that we neglected to pilot the controlled-flexibility tasks adequately before using them as part of the central study. When we piloted the tasks, we were concerned only with determining that they were viable—that the pilot teachers could navigate most of the shifts. We paid little attention to ensuring variability. In the *Tinsman* study there were very few differences between the experimental and control groups in performance on the teaching tasks for a fairly simple reason: nearly *all* members of *both* groups were able to navigate the tasks adequately. *Furthermore, both groups of teachers manifested types of teaching behavior that they had not displayed to us in the thirty weeks during which we had been tracking them in training and in the classroom!* In other words, learning to analyze teaching and receiving regular feedback had little effect on classroom behavior. However, when the teachers were asked to demonstrate some fairly unusual teaching behaviors they reached into the repertoire that they had generated from *both* conventional and experimental training techniques and were able to execute intricate patterns of teaching which they otherwise rarely manifested in the classroom. What they evidently needed to change was an explicit blueprint and an evocative situation—they were capable of flexibility beyond our most optimistic expectations.

About the same time, we had been gathering the specifications for a variety of theoretically based models of teaching which we hoped to use as the basis for a major portion of the theory component of a teacher-training program. It then occurred to us to use these as the practical components of training—as the sources of "blueprints" for patterns of teaching that could be the products of training.

We had made the same finding twice, but not until the second time did its implications become clear to us. The first time was during the search to identify "strength" and "sensitivity" in teaching. Although we could see evidence of strength and sensitivity when the teacher was in a controlled situation responding to definite stimuli, the same stimuli occurred in such random and occasional forms in the classroom that we learned that many teachers used a basic teaching strategy (the recitation pattern) so as to make sensitivity almost irrelevant, at least as we had defined it. Similarly, when we taught teachers to analyze their behavior and then followed them into the classroom to find out whether the analytic process affected their styles, we neglected the obvious. We had not defined the stimulus conditions under which behaviors other than those called for by the recitation pattern would be appropriate. Most of the behaviors in our category system were not used by teachers before or after training simply because they did not fit in with the patterns common in their classrooms. For example, a teacher doesn't ask a synthesis-level question unless it is appropriate to something that he/she is teaching. When we realized that teachers would not use skills except in meaningful conditions it occurred to us that they might have a latent repertory of behaviors that they rarely exercised simply because the behaviors did not fit with the strategies most common to classroom teaching. When teachers are "pushing" children through workbooks or drilling them over reading assignments, they have little need for most of the range of teaching skills that would be necessary to carry out inductive or cooperative teaching strategies.

THE SECOND STAGE OF TRAINING STUDIES

We now began to conceptualize the objectives of training quite a bit differently. The object of training came to be to help the teacher acquire a variety of models of teaching representing important different frames of reference toward the teaching and learning act. Skill in teaching became the mastery of the necessary repertory to manifest any of those models. The observation system was modified to become more purely a description of behavior within and across models, rather than a statement of goals for teacher training. This system was changed drastically by Weil, Gullion, and Cole,[156] in order to enable us to pick up the various elements of different models so we could determine whether teachers were able to acquire them. The chief tools of instruction became sets of instructional systems—these are described in Appendix A. These instructional systems are built around a strategy which presents the theory of a model first, then demonstrates it as a whole, then breaks it down into its parts for practice, and concludes with exercises in which the teachers synthesize the parts of the model into a more complete clinical entity and apply it in the classroom.

Over a period of four years a series of studies were planned and carried out with teachers and teacher candidates to determine whether, by means of these instructional systems, teachers could be brought to the point where they could practice models of teaching which required patterns of behavior considerably different from those normally observed in the classroom (O'Donnell,[109] Wald,[153] Weil,[155] Murphy and Brown, [106] Rude,[122] Kelly,[93] McKibbin,[102] and Gower [45]). (As indicated above, the most "normal" teaching styles we previously observed contained elements of what Hoetker and Ahlbrand have so aptly described as a recitation style.[50]) O'Donnell's study used a primitive version of the instructional system, but she nonetheless demonstrated that the teacher candidates did learn patterns of behavior that were both relatively unusual classroom behaviors and which conformed to the theoretical specifications of the models of teaching that they were to be taught. Wald's study investigated several aspects of the training problem. In the first place, she introduced teacher candidates to models requiring not only patterns of behavior different from those considered "normal" in the classroom but also very different from one another. Her study demonstrated that teacher candidates were able to produce in the classroom patterns of behavior that conformed to the theoretical specifications of each of the models. In other words, nearly all of them could learn several models of teaching. The power of the instructional systems appeared to be general with respect to models of teaching.

Wald also investigated the extent to which the normal teaching style of teachers influenced their acquisitions of the models. She correlated indices of teaching style with the clinical ratings of performance in the models and found no positive correlations in any area. In other words, normal teaching style did not influence the acquisition of the models of teaching. Teachers who normally displayed elements of particular models did not learn them any more completely than did those who rarely manifested those elements. (However, it should not be concluded that the normal style of a human being will not influence his ability to acquire a new frame of reference and act on it. As pointed out earlier, the normal teaching styles of most teachers are extremely restricted, and stylistic differences occur over only a small part of the potential teaching spectrum. Therefore, we probably do not get *real* indicators of a teaching personality in the samples of behavior we normally encounter in the classroom. The restrictions on the role of the teacher, the kind of institution he works in, the kinds of lessons he normally teaches, greatly truncate the possibilities for the play of his personality in his transactions with children.)

Wald also studied the relationship between the educational and social values of teacher candidates and their preferences for various models. Except in one case, that of the social scale of the Allport-Vernon Study of Values, she found no relationships, but the acquisition of the most socially oriented model of teaching was quite striking ($r = .60$).

Finally (à la Hunt), she looked at the relationship between personality and the acquisition of teaching styles and determined that personal flexibility was not related to the acquisition of a single model but was related to the acquisition of a repertoire of models. In other words, at least at the initial stages of training, the ready acquisition of repertory seemed to be a function of personal flexibility.

Wald advances the following principles:

Normal teaching styles contain a few elements of most models of teaching.

Teachers can learn a variety of models which they can use at will.

Teaching styles and, in most cases, personal values do not greatly interfere with training. An exception may be found in a relationship between social values and group-dynamics-oriented models.

When not practicing the models of teaching the teacher generally returns to the modes of teaching displayed prior to training. In other words, the new repertory could be displayed on call but had little effect on teaching when the recitation function was resumed.

The results of this work accord with those of McDonald, Allen, Orme,[101] and their associates at Stanford during the middle 1960s, in which they demonstrated ability to teach a repertory of teaching skills through micro-teaching. Borg, Gall, Langer, and Kelley and their associates at the Far West Laboratory [14] also demonstrated that minicourses can be used to help teachers teach themselves complex teaching skills and strategies of a sort that are not ordinarily manifested in the classroom.

This work and theirs raises several questions about what are logically the first-stage dependent variables in studies designed to influence teacher behavior. Wald and Weil's studies indicated very clearly that the teacher candidates who had been taught the repertory in models of teaching could manifest that repertory at will in the classroom and often did so on a voluntary basis as well as on call. However, when they were not practicing those models of teaching, their teaching behavior looked very much like that of any other group of teachers except that they were somewhat less punishing than the average. In other words, if the dependent variable training was the acquisition of repertory, it was successful; but if the dependent variable was the teaching style of the teacher in general, then the training was not successful. Many authors of studies of teaching skills and interaction-analysis studies have had as their object the modification of the general teaching style of the teachers with whom they were working. In other words, having taught teachers a skill, such as a questioning technique, the investigator hoped the teachers would ask better questions on a regular basis. It is our current belief that teaching style as a dependent variable is much less fruitful than is the demonstration of an acquired repertory that can be used at call. One reason for this is that it is not always appropriate to use a teaching skill or strategy. One might help a teacher acquire one and then wait weeks before it is necessary for that teacher to use it, and it might be months before it was necessary for him/her to use it and there was also an observer present. If repertory is the goal, however, one can, as in the case of the McDonald, Allen, and Orme studies, the Borg and Gall studies, and the Joyce, Wald, and Weil studies, concentrate on the teacher's ability to produce when it is needed.

Skills in Models

Weil [155] approached the analysis of skills needed to carry out specific models of teaching in several ways. First, she analyzed Wald's data and identified several types of behavior which teachers appeared to have difficulty mastering. She and Wald identified three teaching skills which they believed would have general facilitating power. They built instructional systems directed toward mastery of those skills and rated degrees of mastery in a group of teachers who were exposed to the skill training. They then exposed the teachers to a variety of models and correlated skill and model performance. They found the skills to be model-specific, and formulated the thesis that the more a model requires unusual teaching behavior, the more it requires additional skill-training in the "areas of unusualness." [153]

Further Studies on the Acquisition of Models

Rude [122] and Kelley [93] demonstrated that in-service teachers could acquire models at about the same rate as preservice teachers, and they and Gower extended the power of the clinical rating forms. Gower experimented with the use of videotape "exemplar" models of teaching as performance standards for novice teachers and worked out a system for comparing the interaction-analysis profiles of teacher candidates with those of the "exemplar" episodes in order to identify the teaching skill discrepancies between the two groups. Gower's work improved the precise description of the teaching skills relevant to each model.

Gower found a significant correlation between degree of discrepancy between the pattern of teacher candidates and the "exemplar" patterns and the high-inference clinical rating forms embedded in the instructional systems. This encouraged our use of somewhat more global analyses of teaching. Weil's intensive study of skill discrepancies between teachers rated high and low in model performance has resulted also in an elaborated description of skills which can be incorporated, with Gower's findings, into new instructional systems.

McKibbin [102] also has approached instrumentation by using Bellack's [10] and Flanders' [34] systems to study teachers across models in order to try to increase our power to analyze across-model teacher behavior. He reconstructed the observation system to make it more sensitive to stylistic and model-relevant variations.

Pupil Learning in Various Models: Models of Teaching Accessibility Characteristics

Presently our efforts are turning toward pupil learning in various models. The first work focuses on the contribution of model variables (strategy) and individual differences among teacher (style) to various types of pupil outcomes.

We have developed sets of learning materials which can be used with children with a variety of models. These consist of banks of data on communities and on historical figures, with accompanying banks of test items.

The MOTAC series (part VI) carried out at the Ontario Institute for Studies in Education by Hunt, Joyce, and associates, has explored three questions:

1. How do children who vary in conceptual complexity respond to different models of teaching?

2. How can different models of teaching be modified to adapt to children's differences in personality?

3. How do teachers' and children's personalities interact within the framework of different models of teaching?

The MOTAC series consists of carefully engineered laboratory studies in which children of varying conceptual levels are exposed to different models of teaching which are modified in deliberate ways. The biographical and community data banks are used to control content and provide the substance, and specially constructed tests are used to measure model-relevant learning outcomes.

Consistently children respond to the models of teaching in accordance with theoretical predictions or conceptual systems theory. The various models of teaching produce the predicted model-relevant effects. However, the most important finding is that children who vary quite a bit in conceptual level appear to be able to learn the processes of the different models of teaching so that they can achieve considerable levels of independence. In other words, children appear to be able to acquire a variety of strategies for teaching themselves in much the same manner that teachers can acquire a variety of methods for teaching.

The personalities of the children can reach across a variety of learning environments, but these need to be adapted to help them acquire the skills necessary to teach themselves.

The power of the learner to teach himself and to require changes in his own learning environment is vividly demonstrated in the MOTAC series. Also demonstrated is the importance of method or model of teaching. Unless a teaching strategy capable of modification is used, children who simply read the material (the "read only" control condition) frequently perform as well on tests as do those who have been taught by teachers using their natural styles (see Clark et al, part VII.)

Teaching as Information Processing

If teachers can acquire a wide range of teaching strategies and if children can learn the same range of strategies for teaching themselves, then what does this mean for the ways a teacher might think about teaching?

In a series of separate but related investigations, Clark, Marx, Peterson, Crist-Witzel, Joyce, and their colleagues (see part VII) have been studying the decision-making behavior of teachers and how that decision-making behavior can be affected as the teacher learns a wider range of teaching strategies and how to teach those to children. The completed studies depict the information-processing behavior of teachers in laboratory and field settings and their ability to respond to feedback about the characteristics and opinions of the learners. The overt behavior of teachers and learners was studied using observers, and the extent of decision making was ascertained by playing television recordings of the teaching episodes back to the teachers and interviewing them about their thoughts while teaching (the Stimulated Recall method).

Again, content was controlled using the data banks, and special measures of learning outcomes were delineated. Most of the teachers who have been observed used the familiar recitation style unless they had been exposed to training to prepare them to employ a repertoire of models of teaching. The information-processing styles of the teachers generally matched the recitation style.

The teachers made relatively few decisions of strategy but fine-tuned the recitation method for the most part. Their concerns were largely with pupil attention, coverage of content, and keeping the flow of activities going. Pupil achievement did not appear to rise with success of trials. Some teachers were, however, able to respond to feedback from their students and modify their behavior accordingly.

Morine-Dershimer, Joyce and McNair's recent studies of ten teachers in one suburban elementary school indicate considerable stability of information-processing style and that, as in the case of the laboratory studies, the parameters of decision making are within the parameters of the recitation style of teaching (see chap. 21).

At present we are beginning the first of a series of investigations to explore how teachers who acquire a variety of models of teaching think as they attempt to transfer these to their classroom situations. This set of studies should lay a basis for learning how to rethink the problems of curriculum and instruction when one considers repertoire and the differences among children.

CURRICULUM IN THE SOCIETY:
A LARGER PERSPECTIVE

In the final papers in this book we deal with the larger questions of studying teaching and rebuilding curriculum and instruction from a pluralistic stance. If teaching is seen as flexibility both in terms of the ability to radiate a wide variety of learning environments and to adapt these so that children can acquire a wider variety of strategies for teaching themselves, then how do we study teaching and what is the relationship between teaching and the general structure and environment of the school? We discuss a variety of backgrounds for thinking about these problems in an attempt to stretch ourselves and our colleagues from the narrow, almost reductionist, point of view that has in recent years pervaded schooling in the United States and the study of the teaching that goes on within it.

Teaching by itself cannot improve American education, as strange as that seems. Teaching interacts with its social context. In the school as it exists today it is very difficult for teachers to generate the kinds of learning environments that will enable their children to reach beyond themselves and become more creative and productive personally and socially. While this book is not primarily about the social context of schooling, we feel that we would be remiss not to reach beyond our specific concern here and reflect on its meaning in the larger context of social events.

This book will present some of the investigations which have been introduced in this chapter. The early field studies and the development of the concepts of teaching as the sensitive use of repertoire are presented in parts II and III. The development of the concept of Models of Teaching and the training studies are described in parts IV and V. The MOTAC studies are introduced in part VI. The studies of teachers' thinking are summarized in part VII. Finally, in part VIII a model is presented for studying teaching competence as the product of personality and skill.

PART II

Repertoire: The Search for Rationale

How do we define competence in teaching? What are the dimensions around which training can be developed?

3

Flexibility as Repertoire

Bruce R. Joyce and Richard E. Hodges

In the early 1960s, we began to struggle with the problem of the definition of teaching as we planned the program for the preparation of elementary school teachers at the University of Chicago. The program we had been asked to direct had been an interesting one for several years. The students were gifted masters' candidates and undergraduate seniors and drew on the rich resources of the University of Chicago faculty as well as the social ferment of the south side of Chicago and its social institutions. The program was operated as a group investigation into teaching by an extremely gifted faculty, including especially Kenneth Rehage, Herbert Thelan, and Philip Jackson. The students had exciting seminars and demanding and intensive experience in the Chicago schools.

The program had long been philosophically stimulating and experientially fascinating, but it lacked a concept of training. Essentially, the students had to teach themselves to teach in the Chicago schools, and most of them had an extremely difficult time doing that. It was imperative that we do something to link the powerful philosophical education the students were getting and the fascinating experiences they were having, with the kinds of instruction that would help them cope with the tasks of teaching.

We began to search for a rationale that could guide training. Clearly, it could not be narrowly based, for the environment was philosophically pluralistic, and no one of our philosophers could stand for a conception of training that omitted his preferences. Similarly, the students were diverse and interesting and wished to develop themselves in different ways. The rationale that emerged appears rather halting and wooden as we look at it today, from the perspective of fifteen years. However, its basis was rooted in the diverse philosophical and experiential demands made on our teacher candidates. They wanted to be able to use a variety of philosophies of education, through which a variety of learners could satisfy their own personal predilections.

This drove us to begin to think of teacher training as increasing the capacity for flexibility by increasing the repertoire of teaching skills and strategies that the students would have at their command. Thus, to the philosophical and experiential components of the program, we began to add one which we finally called "instructional flexibility training." It consisted of a variety of ways of boosting the skills of teaching, chiefly by means of describing those skills, modeling them for the teacher candidates, and providing the candidates with ways of obtaining feedback about their own performances. In the pages that follow, we describe the emerging rationale for teacher training that we constructed at that time, and the concept of instructional flexibility as we were able to articulate it then.

A number of calls for theoretical conceptions to guide teacher education programs and research were made in the early 1960s. The fine series of essays that resulted from the Palo Alto Conference in 1960 defined some conceptual needs of teacher education and charted a course for development that has not yet been fulfilled.[14] In 1963 an entire issue of the *School Review* [126] was devoted to teacher education with much the same result as the Palo Alto conference—a lamentation about the need for a coherent and research-able conception of teacher education. Up to that time programs of teacher education were not based on theory—they followed certification patterns for the most part, and there was little theory and less research reported in the literature. In the early sixties, a few theoreticians and researchers began limited but important work.

Some theoretical work was being produced on aspects of the education of teachers,[124,130] and some empirical work began to be carried out on training components. Examples include McDonald and Allen's work with "micro-teaching," [2] Amidon and Flanders' [3] explorations of the use of interaction analysis, the investigations by Popham [115] into teacher planning and Joyce and Harootunian's [80] explorations of teachers' decision making. However, we were in need of general, testable conceptions of teacher education as a whole. The works by Conant [24] and others, while interesting as criticisms and as mild suggestions for improvement, did not provide operational concep-tions of teacher education.

In 1954 a small teacher-education program was established at the Univer-sity of Chicago to provide a setting congenial to research in teacher education. During its early years Professors Jacob Getzels, Philip Jackson, Kenneth Rehage, and Herbert Thelen operated the program as a study in group inquiry. They organized the students into a problem-solving group that drew on other professors and resources from the Chicago metropolitan area as the need arose. Hence, there were no separate courses on the "foundations of education" or "educational methods" but, rather, a year-long seminar devoted to learning to teach.[82] Over the years, various ways of relating this seminar to field practice were tried out, and several means of structuring experiences were explored. The design presented here is an outgrowth of this history and represents a movement in the direction of a theory of teacher education.

A RATIONALE FOR TEACHER EDUCATION

The University of Chicago is primarily a graduate and research university, although it includes a highly selective undergraduate college of about two thousand students. The Department of Education is in the Graduate Division of the Social Sciences. The department exists primarily to produce research and to train doctoral students, rather than to prepare teachers. In this respect, it is unlike most education departments and colleges. Accordingly, the Elementary Teacher Education Program was created, not to produce large numbers of teachers, but to study the process of preparing teachers. Therefore, the program is kept small for easy flexibility. Further, its students are carefully selected for academic excellence. The intent is to offer preparation to individuals who can cope with and effectively use the university community.

During 1964–1965 there were fifteen students in the program. Eleven were graduate students, and four were seniors in the undergraduate college. All entered the program in September. For graduates, the program requires four quarters of full-time study, commencing in the fall. The program must be taken as a whole; no part-time students are admitted. The first three quarters were shared by undergraduates and graduates. The fourth (summer) quarter was for graduate students only. The graduate group came from several undergraduate colleges. All fifteen students were quite able academically. None had had formal instruction in education. Nevertheless, on the National Teacher Examinations special examination on Education in the Elementary School taken in the late fall the median for this group was at the 93rd percentile. Ten students ranked from the 90th to the 99th percentile.

It was possible to organize the program as an entity, rather than to build it from independent courses. Because changes could be made without interfering in the schedules of other faculty and students, it was possible to be extremely flexible in planning.

The University of Chicago maintains a well-equipped private laboratory school. In addition, the Chicago metropolitan area offers a wide spectrum of schools, and this tiny program received much cooperation from them.

The setting of the program, then, was favorable to experimentation in teacher education. The University of Chicago Elementary Teacher Education Program was conducted in a rich and varied environment; it was organized as an integrated whole by a small leadership team; it could be altered quickly; its students were extremely able academically; it was very small; and its mission was to generate ideas and research.

The Function of Teacher Education

Teaching is a complex, multidimensional art. Truly professional performance demands that the teacher effectively control the several areas of reality [81] that provide control over the dimensions of the art of teaching. Every profession functions to deal with certain problems that demand special knowledge and skill. The professional in any field is better trained to deal with certain aspects of human reality than is the average nonprofessional. The function of professional teacher education is to gain control over those aspects of reality with which the teacher has to cope in order to oversee education.

What areas of reality does the teacher have to control? *First, s/he has to control effective intellectual strategies or systems for making curricular and instructional decisions.* For example, the teacher has to be able to blend knowledge of psychology, society, learning, and subject matter into effective instructional plans. In other words, s/he has to bring to the problems s/he faces the ability to focus on productive questions and to identify and use relevant data and ideas to develop solutions to problems. This control over strategies for making decisions should be the central intellectual product of teacher education. The teacher has to know how to focus attention on the critical parts of problems and has to be able to bring appropriate information to bear on the production of solutions. However, it is not enough for the teacher to make effective curricular and instructional decisions. S/he has to be able to carry them out.

Hence, the second area s/he needs to control is teaching behavior, or the ability to organize children and carry out instructional plans. The teacher has to be able to use a wide variety of teaching behaviors and to use them when they are appropriate to his/her ends and for the children s/he teaches. It is not enough to be able to control a single teaching style effectively (to teach inductively or deductively, for example). The really professional teacher has control over several teaching styles, each serving different ends and different learners.

A third area over which the teacher must exercise control is the analysis of teaching. The professional is able to analyze her/his teaching performance and that of others. S/he is able to improve skills by deliberate acts that are a result of a rational examination of his/her teaching.

Fourth, the teacher has to be able to exercise control in interpersonal situations, coping with his/her own needs and problems, using personality effectively in interactions with pupils. The teacher has to be able to build group morale and productive group organization and to help groups analyze and improve their performance.

Fifth, the teacher has to know how knowledge is produced and revised in the field of education. S/he has to be able to participate in research and evaluative activity.

It should also be said that the effective teacher is knowledgeable in one or more scholarly disciplines. Since the Chicago program deals largely with the purely professional components of teacher preparation, education in the disciplines will be discussed only as one portion of the development of strategies for making curricular and instructional decisions. It is vital, however, that the total education of teachers include provision for acquisition of scholarly knowledge. (See Joyce and Harootunian [81] for an extensive description of what this entails.) Since the Chicago program was designed for graduate students and advanced senior undergraduates who were preparing to be generalists in elementary education, knowledge of a scholarly discipline was not made one of the functions of the program. In a four- or five-year program or a graduate preservice program for subject-matter specialists, the problem of scholarly knowledge should be defined and a component built to achieve control over it.

Components of Teacher Education and Goals of the Program

To develop a teacher-education program that would help students achieve control over these five areas of reality, we formulated clusters of activities designed to promote such control. These clusters became the components of the program. Although there was considerable interaction among the several components, we will describe them separately, together with the reasons why the components were shaped as they were.

The operational goal of the program was to develop students who achieved control over the five areas of reality listed earlier. This operational goal was developed after consideration of the purpose of the Elementary Teacher Education Program, which was to help our gifted young students function effectively in forward-looking school settings. We were concerned, then, with the development of teachers who would have great flexibility and who could modify their teaching behavior in order to experiment effectively in the classroom. The general objectives of the program were stated in terms of a hypothetical teacher of the future as follows:

> The assumption is made that the teacher of the future should not have a single fixed style of operation in teaching, but should exhibit a variety of styles which s/he can control by professional decision-making. For example, s/he should not favor either inductive or deductive teaching exclusively, but should be able to do both either singly or in combination where they appear to be most appropriate. S/he should be able to lead inquiring groups of children using knowledge of group dynamics; and s/he should be able to program a careful, logical exposition of ideas.
>
> S/he should understand the role of the social environment in education and be prepared to help develop a wide variety of learning environments as they are appropriate to the children s/he teaches. In the same vein, s/he should understand the school as a social institution and be prepared to participate in the development of institutions with deliberately designed characteristics.
>
> S/he should possess a rationale for approaching the creation of curricular and

instructional plans that defines the tasks involved and identifies stategies appropriate to the tasks. Hence, s/he should understand the nature of scholarly knowledge, the characteristics of the structures of the disciplines and the means whereby knowledge is developed and revised through scholarly inquiry. S/he should understand research into the nature of knowing and be prepared to use the findings of psychologists in planning and teaching.

S/he should desire to participate in curricular experimentation and be able to relate to and utilize the talents of behavioral scientists and scholars in the other substantive fields.

S/he should know enough about all fields of instruction 'that s/he is able to relate his/her speciality to other areas and to work with other specialists in the development of new curricular areas or focuses for instruction.

In short, it is the purpose of the University of Chicago to prepare persons who can staff experimental schools—those schools that are developing the character of the American schools to come.[82]

As indicated earlier, the approach to achieving these goals was to identify the areas of reality that an experimental teacher has to control and to develop and to organize components or clusters of activity that would be likely to develop the control desired. Hence, our rationale for teacher education consists of the five areas of reality we identified. These areas formed the bases for the components of the program we developed to help the students achieve satisfactory command over them. There was considerable interaction among the components. As each is discussed in turn, we will emphasize:

1. the reasons the area of reality was identified and selected;

2. the theoretical basis for the shape of the component and some illustrations of activities that actually took place in each;

3. the relation of each component to the other components; and

4. illustrations of devices that were created to measure the effects of each component.

The strategy component

The purpose of the strategy seminar was to develop control over systems for educational decision making. It was assumed that the teacher has to make, or share in making, many curricular and instructional decisions. Thus, the purpose of the strategy seminar was to help students develop rational strategies for approaching these educational decisions. These strategies grow out of knowledge of what questions to ask when confronted by educational problems and knowledge of what sources of data are pertinent to finding answers to the questions. For example, each teacher is faced with the task of developing continuity in his/her instructional program and of identifying, in consort with colleagues, means of developing continuity in their cumulative instructional efforts with children. Teachers need strategies for finding effective themes around which to build instructional continuity; they need to know alternative ways of achieving this condition; they need to know how to use knowledge of the child, of subject matter, and of society to select the most appropriate method.

The need for specific attention to strategies for decision making in education is well documented in research. In 1948 Sand found that the curriculum guides of few school districts reflected effective plans for achieving sequence or continuity.[123] Apparently the administrative leaders and teachers did not believe that the organization of instruction was important, or, more likely, they did not have effective strategies for developing an organizational plan. In 1960 Ammons studied the curricular plans of school districts within 250 miles of Chicago.[5] She found that only a tiny fraction had statements of educational objectives that were sufficiently operational to function as guides to making instructional decisions. Evidently teachers and administrators lacked effective strategies for locating and stating objectives.

In 1964 McClure found that the teachers of a well-known laboratory school lacked orderly strategies for approaching the curricular problems of their school.[100] Joyce and Harootunian examined the educational problem solving of beginning teachers and found that few of them considered objectives, evaluation, or organization of instruction from an operational point of view.[79] Few were able to give a rationale for their selection of procedures or to state objectives or to relate objectives and procedures to theoretical work in psychology or the substantive disciplines.

Hence, strategies for approaching decision making at the curricular and instructional levels became one of the areas of reality around which a component of the program was built. The component was named the "strategy" component.

The central element of this component was a seminar that operated largely as a cooperative group inquiry into a series of educational problems. There were five reasons for deciding on a seminar. First, it provided a model of an instructional strategy (cooperative inquiry) that the students were not likely to see in present-day schools. The students might see pupil-teacher planning, but it seemed unlikely (and the surmise proved sound) that the students would see a class operated as much by the model described by Thelen[144] as ours was.

Second, since the purpose of this component was to develop strategies for approaching educational problems, problem-solving activity in a seminar setting seemed likely to maximize transfer to actual classroom situations and to provide us with constant feedback about the quality of the strategies that were being developed. (If the seminar did not become increasingly effective as a problem-solving group, then we would know that revision of our procedures was in order.)

Third, a cooperative seminar would enable easy control of the other components of the program through cooperative decision making. It could be seen whether the students' educational practices in the classroom were functions of decisions made in the seminar.

Fourth, the sources of ideas and information useful in educational decision making could be studied in the context of the problem-solving process. For example, the structure of mathematics and methods for teaching this subject, as well as the relationships of curriculum theory and learning theory to mathematics as an elementary-school subject, were taken up as part of the group inquiry.

Fifth, the seminar could provide experience in team decision making.

Hence, the Elementary Teacher Education Program was primarily an experiment in group inquiry into the nature of the teaching and learning processes. The program was controlled by the strategy seminar, in which students identified and attempted to solve critical educational problems. Highly competent scholars and teachers were invited to participate in the education of the student. These experts did not simply structure the activities of the students. Instead, these scholars and teachers attempted to assist students in formulating possible solutions to problems identified in the strategies seminar.

It was assumed that clinical or laboratory practice should be controlled by ideas. Consequently, theoretical questions and research projects that were developed in the seminar were entwined with classroom practice.

It was also assumed that the time when one learns to teach is a time of personal stress and heightened awareness. Hence, group interaction became part of the students' studies and was designed to help the students explore together their emerging roles as teacher-scholars and as adults.

It was also assumed that today's teacher is a skilled clinician with an academic or a professional specialty, who is part of a team of specialists. Consequently, his education as a teacher should involve her/him in team activity as a curriculum planner, a maker of instructional decisions, and a classroom teacher. The group inquiry model seemed to be particularly well suited for this purpose.

As indicated, the strategy seminar was the intellectual center of the program. Much of the laboratory component and the research component was structured through the seminar also, and the bulk of the independent projects and the readings for the entire program took place in connection with seminar activities. Curriculum theory was considered in relation to all curriculum areas of the elementary school. The structures and the strategies of the various disciplines were discussed. Instructional strategies were created, and strategies for analyzing teaching were constructed and tried out in the seminar. Tape recordings and films were used in the seminar as bases of discussions and as examples of teaching styles and strategies.

The central function of this component was to teach the student strategies that s/he could bring to curricular and instructional problems. Hence, evaluation of the program was planned to investigate the strategies that students applied to problems in curriculum and instruction.

A questionnaire was devised to which the teacher candidates responded after teaching episodes. The questionnaire was designed to probe how they coped with certain problems, for example, the setting of objectives, the provision for continuity and sequence with other lessons, the analysis of content, the selection of instructional strategy, the use of knowledge about children and learning in preparing and conducting a lesson, and the selection of evaluation procedures. Each week that the students were engaged in teaching they were asked to tape-record one lesson and to fill out this questionnaire. The responses were analyzed to determine whether the student's instructional strategies were related to intended (planned) behavior and actual performance in the classroom. As the year progressed, the students' plan became more operational and more clearly rationalized. Increasingly, the students were able to carry out their plans effectively and to employ teaching styles they had selected beforehand. Increasingly, the methods and materials the students selected seemed appropriate for the objectives of the lessons.

In short, the evaluation took theory into account. Examinations were given—rather extensive ones, in fact. But the real test was the effectiveness with which the students could identify and attack problems of curriculum and instruction.

Control over teaching styles: the second component

The second area of reality that the teacher needs to control is a wide range of teaching behavior that s/he can produce at will. The third area of reality that the teacher needs to control is the analysis of teaching to diagnose and improve his/her performance.

The component *control over teaching style* was designed to achieve control over both these areas.

On the whole, recent research on teaching has indicated that there is a surprising lack of variability in teacher performance.[10] Hughes has addressed herself to this problem and has reported that a few teachers account for nearly all the variability in teacher performance.[54]

Many educational experiments in field situations have reported inconclusive results regarding variability in teacher performance. Undoubtedly, one reason is the difficulty of measuring behavior in field settings. These inconclusive findings, it is often suggested, are due to the fact that in these experiments there was not a great enough difference between experimental conditions and control conditions. The teachers involved were not, it is suggested, able to produce the desired experimental behaviors.

Each of us who has participated in attempts at educational innovation has found that it takes time and enormous effort for teachers to learn new classroom behaviors. Proponents of the "new math" have found that the new materials can be so taught that the effect is much like that of the "old math." Experimenters with team teaching have made much the same report. Considerable effort is often required to prevent team teachers (often experimentally minded teachers, too, in the special research projects) from acting as if they were still in individual classrooms.

Hough and Amidon presented evidence that teachers can become more "indirect" in teaching method if they receive feedback about their teaching behavior and learn to analyze their verbal behaviors.[51] We saw feedback on performance as crucial in learning to control performance. For this reason, feedback became central in the component that was designed to help students assess and control their behavior in accord with conscious decisions.

If an individual is to make conscious improvements in professional performance, s/he needs to be able to look at himself/herself and to analyze his/her professional functions. Only with self-knowledge can deliberate innovations in behavior be made. Hence, professional experimentation also depends on possession of well-developed means of assessing the realities of performance.

Reality-testing becomes particularly critical under stress. A young teacher testing her/his professional capacity for the first time is under considerable tension. If s/he can describe and evaluate her/his own performance, s/he can satisfy her/himself as to "how s/he is doing." If that performance cannot be described adequately, s/he has to make guesses on the basis of inadequate evidence.

We set as our goal not the production of any one set of teaching behaviors, but the development of a range of appropriate behaviors that could be produced by using rational techniques. The results obtained by Schueler and Gold [130] and associates at Hunter College with videotaped feedback sessions and the efforts of Allen at Stanford with microteaching,[2] encouraged us to build a component in which students would learn to analyze teaching behavior and receive feedback on their performance. Goals were developed that would give students direction in their attempts to enlarge upon their teaching behaviors. (See Joyce and Hodges [84] for an extensive description of this aspect of the program.)

Part of the program was based on the student teaching experience. Each cooperating teacher was asked to provide the student teacher with a small group of children, and for half an hour daily the student was to try out teaching strategies with this group. This leaf in our book was taken from Allen's work with microteaching at Stanford University.[2] The rationale is that the small group of children allows experimentation with minimal control problems. After the student has developed a new instructional strategy with a small group, s/he can transfer the strategy to larger groups.

Each week, each student was asked to make a tape recording of a lesson. Often the lesson taught was filmed, using an 8mm sound camera. Each week in the fall, groups of four students met with faculty from the program and analyzed several dimensions of their teaching—handling of content in the classroom, interpersonal relations in the classroom, teaching strategies, teacher leadership or strength.[84] By spring, each student had identified the teaching strategies that s/he employed easily and the teaching strategies that s/he had some difficulty producing.

There were three student teaching periods. In the fall, half of the students were placed in inner-city schools and half in the University of Chicago Laboratory School. After six weeks, the students switched assignments. Again, the teaching period was six weeks long.

In the spring, each student chose an environment and a grade for his teaching and prepared a teaching program, which s/he implemented for a third six-week period. For example, six students organized themselves into a team and taught an experimental unit on *Ebony* magazine to second- and fifth-graders. Cooperating teachers served as critics and observers, but the team had responsibility for the experiment.

During the last student teaching experience, each student tried to perfect his/her "natural" teaching styles and to engage in teaching behaviors that would expand that natural range.

This component of the program was evaluated in two ways. The weekly lessons were coded by an independent observer, who used taped segments of the lessons and a manual developed by Joyce.[75] The increase in variability of teaching performance was calculated. In addition, in the spring, each student was asked to teach a series of three lessons that would require very different teaching behaviors. The lessons were taped and coded to determine whether the students had learned to produce these behaviors. Increasingly, the students displayed control over wider ranges of teaching behavior. Especially, they showed greater control over cooperative planning and over inductive teaching styles. As the year progressed, they became more skilled in asking questions that caused children to raise hypotheses and to build concepts. More and more, their lessons used concept-formation models and were directed toward the higher mental processes generally.

The research component

Throughout the program, students were helped to identify research problems, to develop appropriate measuring devices, and to carry out independent studies. Each graduate student engaged in one fairly extensive investigation.

Research emphasis was balanced to provide:

1. acquaintance with techniques useful in diagnosing children's instructional needs;

2. acquaintance with the standard techniques of educational research;

3. an understanding of the means by which knowledge is produced and revised in the behavioral sciences; and

4. opportunity for students to enhance their specialization by engaging in the area of specialization.

The reason for including research as a component is probably obvious. We expected that some of the students would seek placement in experimental schools where acquaintance with research procedures and acceptance of the canons of research would be very useful. Integrating the students' research with the strategy seminar seemed good sense in terms of efficiency, for the seminar, the laboratory, and the feedback components proved so demanding that it did not seem wise to build a large separate research component.

The person-teacher component

Ultimately, all that a teacher does is conditioned by her/his capacity for self-control in stressful interpersonal situations. It may be that each teacher reflects her/his self-concept when teaching, and that personal needs are dominant in teaching strategies. Certainly, it seemed that we should develop a component addressed to this problem. But how? Who would know how to shape it?

We felt that the component should not be "taught" by the faculty members who were responsible for coordination of the remainder of the program. There seemed to be too many possible ways of detracting from both sets of roles.

A psychologist from the Department of Education volunteered to meet with the students for two sessions a week, each lasting an hour and a half. During the sessions the psychologist was to conduct a course in psychology in which the students as teachers were to provide the content of the course. Hence, for three hours each week the students studied themselves as teachers—their conceptions of teaching, of children, of teachers, of knowledge.

The psychologist who conducted the course will present his evidence on the effectiveness of this component separately,* but we can report with some confidence that all of us were better able to bear the strain of the intensive course in teacher education because there was some place besides the seminar and the professor's office where students could examine their problems. It was no small help that the analysis was scholarly and systematic rather than simply a response to students' momentary problems.

SUMMARY

We have described the rationale of teacher education that controlled the University of Chicago Elementary Teacher Education Program during 1964–1965. The program had five components, each designed to produce control over an area of reality considered essential to teacher performance. The five areas of reality around which components were built were:

1. Educational decision making.
2. Control over teaching styles.
3. Control over the analysis of teaching.
4. Control over research skills through the research component.
5. Control over self.

Teaching, then, is seen as a blend of educational decision making by a person who can implement educational decisions because s/he possesses a

* Our debt is to Benjamin Wright, University of Chicago.

wide range of teaching behaviors that can be controlled rationally. The professional teacher is a person who can cope effectively with a variety of classroom settings and can cope with personal needs as they affect her/his teaching. The professional teacher also possesses the ability to analyze his/her teaching and, through analysis, to set realistic goals for improving performance. Teacher education is seen as clusters of activity (components), each designed to produce control over the designated area of reality. Each component itself can be conceptualized on a basis of theory and research, and research can be conducted to test the theories of the components.

THE IMPLICATIONS OF THE CHICAGO PROGRAM RATIONALE

The importance of this work for us is that we began to develop a way of partitioning the acts of teaching, in order to identify the dimensions of teaching. The long-term validity of the five "areas of reality" is surely questionable, but the struggle to create a several-sided "model" of the teaching act helped us to isolate components of competence around which training components could be built. It also provided a device by which we could move from "persuasion-oriented" teacher training and toward "repertoire-oriented" conceptions. Many training programs are designed to "persuade" teachers to adopt a particular philosophy of education. The repertoire orientation acquaints teachers with a variety of approaches and seeks to help them develop the competence to use that repertoire intelligently and sensitively.

PART III

Personality and Teaching: Adaptation to the Learner

In 1963, we became acquainted with the work of David Hunt, who, with his colleagues, Harvey and Schroder, had developed an approach to the study of personality known as Conceptual Systems Theory.[47] Theirs is a stage theory of personality development which describes human development as moving along a continuum of increasing flexibility and integrative power. Up to then we had conceived of repertoire as the general capacity to radiate a wide variety of environments to children, but we had no real basis beyond intuition to give the teacher a clear idea of what environments to radiate to whom. Conceptual Systems Theory specified, or hypothesized, the environments that would be optimal for learners at different stages and provided an entirely new basis for looking at the teacher and learner. If Harvey, Hunt, and Schroder were right, teachers at different stages of conceptual flexibility would naturally radiate certain kinds of environments and would respond differently to training designed to increase repertoire. Similarly, teachers and students who were matched and mismatched in personality would be likely to generate different environments as they worked together. Finally, Conceptual Systems Theory provided the basis for the selection of environments for children. Hunt's early paper [58] described a model for the training of teachers or training agents and provided a basis for his research and thinking that resulted in the following position paper.

The interaction with Hunt opened up our minds to possibilities for research and training far beyond what we had imagined before. We began to generate small studies to determine the relationship between teacher/trainee personality and the modes of teaching style, relationships between conceptual level and teachers' ability to respond to instructional flexibility training, the nature of the interaction between teachers and learners of different personalities, and other matters. Most important, we began to see flexibility in teaching from a point of view that included the learner more fully than it had before, and, rather than try to give teachers a range of teaching skills, we began to conceive of the possibility of training them to radiate environments appropriate for various children and to discriminate children's conceptual levels.

If we conceive of teaching as the radiation of a variety of environments, then we acknowledge that different environments are appropriate to different learners, and that the teacher and learner interact so that each contributes to these environments. Thus, we begin to approximate a "grounded" theory of teaching. By the late 1960s Hunt was able to propose that: (1) education has a variety of objectives, (2) different teaching strategies are appropriate for different objectives, (3) teachers can learn to radiate varieties of environments, and (4) learners can respond differentially to a variety of educational environments and teachers. It follows that we can conceive of the task of the teacher as coordinating objectives, learner characteristics, and environments. Training becomes a matter of helping the teacher discriminate and select objectives, discriminate various learning characteristics, and select and shape appropriate environments to produce a blend that will maximize the learner's growth.

It should be emphasized that this process is construed as a fluid rather than as a mechanical process. It is not a matter of creating an industrial scheme of multiple pigeonholes through which learners are channeled so that they encounter an environment that suits their learning style and the objectives that are sought. Rather, it is a way of thinking that can make the process of teaching more rational and help the teacher as s/he feels her/his way along through the maze of materials and learners with which s/he is confronted. Hunt's formulation has been articulated separately with Edmund Sullivan in their book, *Between Psychology and Education*.[69] In the passage that follows Hunt summarizes his thinking and presents a grounded theory for teacher training.

4

Teachers' Adaptation: "Reading" and "Flexing" to Students

David E. Hunt

Teachers' adaptation to students is the heart of the teaching-learning process yet it remains poorly understood. It refers to the moment-to-moment shifts in teacher behavior in response to an individual student, a group of students, or an entire class as well as shifts over a longer period of time. Such adaptation has been called spontaneous, intuitive, implicit, or interactive. Teacher adaptation varies enormously: some teachers change their approaches to suit their students more readily than other teachers; some teachers adapt more effectively than other teachers; and some teachers adapt to students in relation to immediate circumstances, while others adapt in relation to long-term development. Whatever the label and whatever the variety or form, teacher adaptation is occurring constantly; i.e., a conservative estimate would suggest a rate of 100 occurrences per hour. Given the nearly three million teachers here in North America this would mean at least one billion occurrences each day.

Why is such a ubiquitous phenomenon so poorly understood? With a few exceptions I will mention, the phenomenon has usually received one of the following treatments: (1) not acknowledged; (2) grudgingly admitted with a narrative example (e.g., "the teacher rewards this student, stops to consider another"); (3) described as a complex "clinical" skill beyond the ken of most classroom teachers; (4) regarded as a mysterious, unanalyzable feature idiosyncratic to every teacher and every classroom; or, most frequently, buried in elaborate discussions on "individualized instruction."

The first step in demystifying teacher adaptation and in acknowledging its ubiquitous occurrence is for each of us personally to realize that we engage in the same generic activity continuously in our interaction with others. We listen, we watch, we feel the reaction of the other(s) as we attempt to communicate, and we continually adapt our verbal and nonverbal approach accordingly. This process of adaptability in interpersonal communication is so deceptively simple that we have failed to attend to its importance and give it the analytic attention it deserves. Once we sense the nature of the adaptive experience in ourselves, then we see that teacher adaptation is indeed a special case of adaptability in interpersonal communication.[6]

The simplest way to summarize the organization of this paper is to say that the traditional order in such discussions—theorist → researcher → consultant → teacher → student—will be exactly reversed. This reversed presentation is not simply a countertraditional tour de force, but is based on assumptions about the teaching-learning process and the application of theory/research to practice that will become evident in the discussion.

Therefore, I begin with (1) a consideration of "student pull," or how students influence teachers and the variation among teachers in their susceptibility to such pull. Noting such teacher variation sets the stage for (2) a description of the Communication Task, a method for assessing an individual teacher's adaptability in interpersonal communication (which includes, among other things, susceptibility to student pull). Analysis of Communication Task results indicated two basic components in the adaptive process: "reading" (sensitization) and "flexing" (modulation), which in turn serve as the basis for (3) an analysis of the specific steps in the adaptive process expressed in terms of B-P-E (Behavior-Person-Environment) features. These steps then serve as the framework for (4) a comparison of the implicit matching of teachers with the explicit matching in educational programs in matching and ATI (Aptitude-Treatment-Interaction) research, and in matching theories. Finally (5) the implications for assessing teacher effects and teacher training are considered.

"Student Pull"

Any adequate account of the interaction between teacher and student(s) must ultimately be reciprocal, acknowledging that the unit is persons-in-relation and cannot be understood in unidirectional terms. However, until very recently, almost all theory and research in teaching has been limited to the one-way effect of teachers on students, e.g., Turner's comment in 1967 [21] (p. 6): "The empirical evidence to support the hypothesis that pupils are an influence in the behavior of the teacher is wholly circumstantial."

Therefore, although the unit of analysis will ultimately be the teacher-student dyad, an intermediate step to redress the lopsided emphasis of teacher on student is to consider the effects of student pull, or the influence of students on teachers. How much a teacher's behavior varies in relation to differences in students, or is susceptible to student pull, is a general indication of a teacher's degree of adaptation to the student. Teachers may be unaware of student pull, reacting entirely on an intuitive basis. The results of a few recent studies of student-pull effects illustrate the adaptation process in its implicit, spontaneous form.

To get a feeling for what is meant by student pull, try a couple of examples. First, imagine that you are asked by a six-year-old for instructions on how to find the nearest mailbox, and then consider how your response might differ from the way you would respond to the same question asked by an adult. Second, consider how a teacher's behavior in a high school class differs from that of a teacher in a primary class.

In their recent book, *Teacher-student relationships: Causes and consequences,* Brophy and Good [2] have called attention both to the importance of considering the relation between teacher and individual student, and to the necessity of considering teacher behavior in context of desired outcomes, nature and age of students (as in the second example), time, and so forth. These authors summarize several studies on the effects of student pull (pp. 275–277).

Like the sequence of this paper, a study on student pull effects reverses the position of variables in the experimental design: student behavior becomes the independent variable, and teacher behavior becomes the dependent variable. Student behavior is systematically varied either experimentally or naturalistically with its effects being observed on a sample of teachers (who define the N) on one or more dimensions of teacher behavior.* I have described several recent student pull studies in detail elsewhere [8] so here I will simply summarize them in Table 4.1.

Perhaps a summary description of one of the studies will help to translate the telegraphic summaries in Table 4.1. The first study by Siegel & Harkins [20] did not use classroom teachers but studied adult volunteers in an institution for mentally retarded children. They investigated the effect of a listener's (student's) relative verbal ability upon the verbal behavior of an adult (teacher) who attempted to communicate without knowledge of the listener's verbal ability. The "students" were two groups of mentally retarded youngsters, one relatively high and one relatively low in verbal ability. The "teachers" were twenty-one male college students who were each assigned one low ability youngster and one high ability youngster. The teacher's task was to work with each of the youngsters separately to help him assemble a simple puzzle. Verbal interaction was recorded, transcribed, and analyzed. Results indicated that interactions with the low ability youngsters produced greater vocal out-

---

* A long chapter could be written on the methodological details of student pull studies, e.g., students as confederates, role playing adults as students, variation in student behavior induced by instructions, etc. (see Brophy & Good [2] and Hunt [6] for more information on methodology).

TABLE 4.1. Summary of "Student Pull" Effects in Five Studies

Student Characteristic Investigated	Teachers	Students	Effect on Teaching Behavior
Verbal ability (Siegel & Harkins, 1963)	21 college students	Mentally retarded youngsters varying in ability	Low ability: more words, shorter sentences, and greater repetition
Conceptual Level (Rathbone, 1970)	20 experienced teachers	Grade 6 students varying in CL	High CL: more interdependent statements
Age or grade (Joyce, Weil & Wald, 1973)	28 teacher trainees	Elementary students in K–2 vs. 3–6	Older (3–6): higher level information statements
Age or grade (Joyce, Weil & Wald, 1973)	15 experienced teachers	Elementary students in K–2 vs. 3–6	Older (3–6): higher level information statements and less negotiation
Positive or negative behavior (Klein, 1971)	24 college teachers	Manipulated variation in positive and negative behavior	Positive: more teacher clarification. Negative: more criticism and giving directions

From Hunt,[8] p. 6.

put, shorter sentences, and more repetition on the part of the adult communicators than the interactions with the high ability youngsters.

The studies in Table 4.1 are not intended to be inclusive (although there are not a great many more in education, cf. Brophy & Good [2]), but to illustrate the nature of student pull effects. Following the seminal "Direction of effects" paper by Bell,[1] research workers in developmental psychology have begun to accumulate a fairly substantial literature on the reciprocal effects of parent-child interaction that might serve as an exemplar of what the results of student pull studies might look like in ten years.

Since Table 4.1 summarizes only the general effects without reporting the variability among teachers, a final observation is required: not all teachers are equally susceptible to student pull, a point pursued in the next section. Put another way, we may ask why the effects summarized in Table 4.1 occur at all. Their intuitive reasonableness is not sufficient explanation though it does verify the general occurrence of teacher adaptation.

Assessment of Teacher Adaptation by Communication Tasks

Student pull studies are only general examples of the adaptation process because (1) they usually consist of only general variation in student characteristics, e.g., verbal ability, without precise specification of the cues provided by the student, and (2) they report general effects without considering variation among individual teachers. Therefore, behavioral tasks were devised which would vary the cues provided by the student(s) in a microteaching setting taught by one teacher.[6]

Although adaptation is constantly occurring, it is easiest to observe when the teacher encounters obstacles (Lesser,[18] p. 537); therefore, the central feature of the tasks was that the student(s) presented systematic obstacles by misperceiving, misunderstanding, or failing to comprehend the communication. Most tasks consisted of a one-to-one microteaching situation (although occasionally three or four students were involved) in which the trainee * was given a short time (twelve to fifteen minutes) to communicate a particular idea or concept to a role-playing listener or student. The trainee was given information about the concept to be taught, the specific objective, and (in some cases) information about the student (listener). During the trainee's attempt to communicate, the student (listener) interjected specific obstacles at prespecified intervals. Interest then centered on the trainee's approach and how he modulated his approach in response to the obstacles.

A prototype task to communicate the concept of the balance of power in the U.S. federal government was initially developed. The trainee was first given material describing the system of checks and balances; next, he was told that he was to meet a Venezuelan emigrant "George Lopez," who wanted to learn about the idea of balance of power in order to pass a citizenship examination; and then, before meeting George, he was given a one-page description about him. Finally, the trainee met with the role player for twelve to fifteen minutes, in which he was free to present the concept in any way he wished. The role player systematically introduced five obstacles as appropriate, e.g., "The judges are like priests . . . they tell us what's right and wrong," or "The president is in charge . . . he tells everybody what to do" (a prophetic "obstacle" in retrospect).

Variation in trainee approach was enormous. Some trainees were completely unresponsive to the role player, delivering an unremitting, inflexible minilecture in political science. Other trainees spent at least half the allotted time getting to know George and his frame of reference before proceeding with an inductively derived lesson—e.g., since George was a waiter, using the analogy of three plates to be balanced on a tray to represent the three branches of government.

---

* Although several Communication Tasks were used with teacher trainees, they were also applied to other "trainees," e.g., Peace Corps trainees, mothers, etc., as shown in table 2; thus the general term, trainee.

To capture this variation, an Adaptability Index was developed. Part of the Adaptability Index was based on the trainee's specific reaction to each of the five obstacles as follows:

Rating	Behavioral Referent
1	Completely insensitive.
3	Aware of obstacle, but does not modulate.
5	Aware of obstacle, and makes some attempt to modulate.
7	Shifts and modulates presentation in flexible fashion.
9	Modulates and explores for more information from listener's frame of reference.

Some flavor of the response variation can be conveyed by the following extreme examples of reaction to two of the obstacles.

Obstacle: "The judges are like priests . . . they tell us what's right and wrong."

Low (scored 3)
"No, they're not like priests because they're appointed to the Supreme Court by the President which must be approved by the legislature."

High (scored 7)
"In a sense, that's true, but they have no religious power; it doesn't matter what religion they are, but they do tell us what's right and wrong according to the Constitution."

Obstacle: "This sounds like it takes a long time . . . wouldn't it be better to have a revolution?"

Low (scored 2)
"No, no, why did you say revolution? I noticed that your country has been plagued by revolutions. But you see, the Constitution of the United States with these three separate branches of power is the longest standing written constitution in the world."

High (scored 9)
"It might be simpler, but I don't know that the results would be as good. What do you think? In your country do you have revolutions? Was the country better off after the revolution?"
(Hunt, 1970, pp. 330–331)

As I observed several hundred trainees in this task it seemed that successful adaptation required two general skill components: "reading" the listener's misunderstanding, and "flexing" or adjusting the communication in accordance with what was read. Factor analysis of several high-inference ratings for the total task supported the two components in that two factors emerged in two fairly equal samples of trainees which appeared to be "reading" (e.g., loading on seeking initial information) and "flexing" (e.g., loading on adaptation, language level).* Although both skill components are required for effective interpersonal communication, a trainee can "read" without "flexing," though the opposite is not possible. Several other tasks based on the balance-of-power prototype are summarized in Hunt (1970, p. 336).

Returning to a consideration of student effects, susceptibility to student pull requires the operation of both components discussed in this section: the capacity to be sensitive to the student (reading the student) and modulating the approach (flexing) in relation to the student's requirements. Teachers may not always be aware of, or able to describe, exactly how they "read" and "flex" to students, but the process must be made as explicit as possible.

Making Implicit Adaptation Explicit

The thorniest problem in teacher adaptation is trying to understand the relation between teacher's intuitive split-second shifts and explicit formulations of the adaptation process such as teaching prescriptions. The problem has often been discussed in terms of the failure of explicit matching ideas either prescribed by the psychologist or espoused by the teachers themselves to influence teachers' implicit matching in the classroom. For example, Jackson [14] distinguished teacher's "preactive" behavior (in which the teacher reflects on how he will teach while seated in an "empty classroom") from "interactive" behavior (which is the teacher's "Life in Classroom"); yet, Jackson gives little reason for the optimistic belief that the preactive experience will have a direct influence on the teacher's interactive behavior in the classroom.

Again I propose that the sequence be reversed from the question of the influence of preactive on interactive teaching to asking how teacher's adaptation in the classroom can influence the teacher's preactive (now postactive) reflection as well as exert an effect on matching programs, research, and theory. Just as student-teacher relations are reciprocal, so should the relation between practice and theory/research be viewed in reciprocal terms. The first requirement is for a means in which teachers can express how they view their teaching in their own terms because, in a sense, as I have suggested elsewhere, "Teachers are psychologists, too." [11] Like psychological researchers and theorists, teachers have ideas about their students, their teaching, their goals, and the relations among these features. More specifically, I propose therefore that teachers express their ideas in terms of the Behavior-Person-Environment, or B-P-E paradigm [9,13]: learning outcomes (B) viewed as a result of different teaching approaches (E) and different kinds of students (P). Expressed in B-P-E terms, teachers' ideas would then be in a form comparable to that of psychological theories and research investigations. For

---

* See Flavell [5] for a description of how skills similar to "reading" and "flexing" develop in children.

example, an individual teacher's conceptions of his students (P) could be related to theories and research on student individual differences. In short, implicit theories can be related and translated to explicit theories.

One way to identify a teacher's implicit psychological theory is to use a variation of the Role Construct Repertory, or REP, test [16] (pp. 219–266). For example, to find out more about a teacher's dimensions and descriptions of students (P), the teacher first writes the names of several students, each on a separate card; then sorts the cards either through triadic sorting as Kelly suggested ("Which two of these three are alike in some important way and different from the third"?) or through free sorting into groups; and, finally, describes the basis for sorting. Repeating this procedure produces a list of student characteristics which the teacher uses (or, in Kelly's terms, his repertory of role constructs). A similar approach has been used to identify teachers' concepts about teaching approaches (E) and learning outcomes (B).

One of the reasons for earlier inconsistent results in the study of teacher awareness and its influence on teacher behavior has been the failure to permit teachers to express themselves in their own terms about all aspects of the teaching-learning process (cf. Brophy & Good,[2] pp. 270–281, for a discussion of other reasons). Through the B-P-E version of the REP test, teachers' implicit concepts become explicit, and into the awareness of both the teacher and the psychologist or consultant working with the teacher. These teacher B-P-E concepts provide the idiosyncratic language within which teachers are requested to articulate their view of the adaptation process.

If teaching is viewed in B-P-E terms as E: $P \rightarrow B$ (Hunt, 1971, p. 53), then teacher adaptation is a shift from E_1 to E_2, which occurs within a specific P-B context. Therefore, the B-P-E components serve as the units in specifying the steps in the adaptation process. These steps will be first described as they apply to an individual teacher articulating his own adaptation; i.e., making the implicit adaptation explicit. In the next section the steps will be used to compare teacher's implicit adaptation with explicit prescriptions and matching research. The following five-step sequence is a telegraphic, slightly revised summary of the analysis of adaptation I discuss in more detail elsewhere (Hunt,[8] p. 11–18). In reading the steps, imagine that you are a teacher using your own language or concepts to complete each step.

Step 1: State Intention (B)

All adaptation must be viewed in relation to what a teacher is trying to do, not only because effective adaptation is goal-specific, but because teachers vary considerably in terms of their initial intentions and their organization of goal sequences, e.g., cognitive vs. affective emphasis; contemporaneous vs. developmental emphasis.

Step 2: Classify Student (P)

This step includes both collecting information about students (through questioning, observing, testing) and using such information to infer student characteristics. Of course, in microadaptation it consists only of sensing minimal cues from the student as the teacher "reads" the situation. Although teachers should initially use their own concepts to describe their students, I have recommended that students be described in terms of "accessibility characteristics" [7] (p.75) that are translatable into environmental prescriptions, e.g., visual-auditory, need for structure, rather than static person descriptions that have no relation to instructional adaptation.

Step 3: Translate Student Characteristic into Appropriate Teaching Approach (P to E)

This step is often the most difficult for teachers, and should be one of the points at which theory and research could be most helpful. It is important to reemphasize that such derivation of appropriate approaches must always take account of the objective, e.g., "spoon feeding" may work for immediate learning for a dependent student but be mismatched for developmental growth.

Step 4: Provide Appropriate Approach (E)

"Flexing," or modulation, subsumes both steps 3 and 4. If teachers' concepts of how they teach are based on their actual teaching, then the descriptions should be in terms comprehensible to them, but this does not assure that they are capable of actually teaching with a specific approach, i.e., "radiating" an environment. Therefore, this is the most critical step in the process because, if it does not occur, the whole exercise is a "non-event." [3]

Step 5: Check Effects (B)

Adaptation is an ongoing process that must be continually monitored. It requires continual openness to reading changes in the student (which does not necessarily mean simply continual change in teacher behavior). A major source of resistance to an analytic account of the adaptation process that requires an explicit classification of the student is the fear that such a classification may lead to stereotyping and inequitable treatment. [10] If adaptation is viewed as a static, one-shot classification that serves to place the student into an inflexibly prescribed environment, then of course such a procedure would be detrimental and, it might even be argued, worse than no adaptation at all.

This very telegraphic summary is similar in intent to the model for promoting proactive teaching proposed by Brophy & Good [2] (pp. 292–295). In the next section, these five steps are used to compare teachers' implicit adaptation to matching programs and research.

Comparison of Implicit and Explicit Matching

Rather than approach the difficulties in "applying" theory and research in adaptation to classroom practice by looking for defects in the teachers' "application," the sequence is again reversed. Table 4.2 summarizes the five-step analysis from three perspectives: (1) implicit teacher matching, (2) explicit matching programs, e.g., homogeneous grouping by learning style [12] and (3) experiments on matching effects (e.g., Hunt,[7] pp. 45–46 and ATI research). Note that, in addition to the distinction between implicit-explicit and interactive-preactive already mentioned, formal programs and research studies are

TABLE 4.2. Comparison of Teacher's Implicit Matching, Explicit Matching Programs, and Experiments on Matching Effects

Nature of Activity	Teacher's Implicit Matching	Explicit Matching Programs	Experiments on Matching Effects
	Intentional Action of Persons-in-Relation	Prescriptive	Descriptive
Steps in adaptation:			
1. State B	Specify objectives	Specify objectives	Determine dependent variable
2. Classify P	"Reading"	Testing students and assigning to classes	Assessing subjects and assigning to conditions
3. Translate P to E	Implicit theory	Explicit theory	Explicit theory to be verified
4. Provide E	"Flexing"	Prescribing approach	Manipulating independent variable
5. Check B	Observing or testing	Characterizing effects	Recording dependent variable

also static and nonreciprocal, while teacher adaptation is dynamic and reciprocal.

Table 4.2 permits a focus on teacher "reading" and "flexing" as the central feature to be considered in relation to matching programs or matching research. I will use a specific example from the Conceptual Level (CL) matching model [7]—its application through homogeneous classroom grouping by learning style and its relation to the teachers' implicit matching.

From a traditional view this work began with a simple theoretical idea that "low CL learners profit more from high structure and high CL learners profit more from low structure, or in some cases, are less affected by variations in structure" [7] (p. 44). Following the usual sequence in table 3, controlled experiments were conducted to verify the principle [7] (p. 45–46). Once verified, then attempts were made to "apply" the model at various levels of educational organization: within-class groupings, homogeneous grouping by CL (or learning style), and alternative schools.

In the case of homogeneous grouping by learning style [12] junior high school students were classified into one of four groups varying in learning style or need for structure (with all groups equal on achievement). Each teacher then taught four groups who varied in the teaching approach they required. We had viewed this arrangement in terms of increasing teacher efficiency through prescribing learning style-specific prescriptions of varying degrees of structure. However, we discovered that what really happened to the teachers was that the groups served as exemplars for adaptation. The teachers experienced, many for the first time, what it means to "meet a student's needs" by adapting your approach. The major effect of the program, therefore, was to *sensitize* teachers to "reading" students. In effect, the grouping confronted them with students who were easily "read," and the teachers went on to "read" and "flex" to students (both between and within classes) in ways which went far beyond the original idea of student learning style and instructional approaches varying in structure.

I cannot emphasize this point too strongly because it is the central idea of this paper and epitomizes what happens when we reverse the sequence and consider what happens from a practice → theory view. Obviously, this point has major implications for the significance of matching research or ATI studies. Rather than view such highly controlled experimental research as generating findings which will provide highly specific differential prescriptions for the explicit matching of students to forms of instruction, it may be that the effect of these results will depend on their congruence with teacher's concepts and how well the findings can serve as guiding exemplars. This is a radical change in our traditional theory-to-practice thinking, and it is bound to be initially disturbing. I know that I was enormously surprised, if not disturbed, when I came to realize that the effect we were having in our work with teachers (in applying learning style ideas) was much less influenced by the CL matching model, and much more determined by the degree that

I, or one of my colleagues, exemplified, "reading" and "flexing" in our work with teachers. Again, the reversal: I have learned to preach what I practice.[4]

Implications for Teacher Effects and Teacher Training

What are the effects on students of being taught by teachers who are effective in adaptation, i.e., high on the Adaptability Index? This question of teacher effects is very difficult to answer empirically at this time. We have data comparing four classes of Grade 9 students who were homogeneously grouped on learning style with a comparable sample who were not, which indicated that the former group showed greater increase in CL over one year. These results were encouraging, but they do not link the increase directly to the teachers' increased adaptability. The evaluation of the effect of teacher adaptability on students must proceed in designs which take account of the context: age and type of students, objectives, etc. In the meanwhile, the effectiveness of the highly adaptable teacher remains an article of faith that seems very intuitively reasonable.

The present central emphasis on teacher adaptation and the availability of methods for measuring the teacher's skill in "reading" and "flexing" provide the foundation for the development of training procedures at both the preservice and in-service level to facilitate the development of such skills. Video feedback, microteaching, modeling, systematic exposure to students varying in pull, and many other approaches have been used (e.g., Hunt [6]) or may be developed.

I conclude by repeating my own experience: it is necessary to be reflexive about adaptability in interpersonal communication. You cannot induce "reading" and "flexing" by giving a canned lecture; you must encourage the teachers with whom you work to experience adaptation through their actions and, most important, to exemplify it through your own actions.

SUMMARY

We began by considering teachers' implicit matching, or adaptation, to students, and the variation among teachers in adaptation. This matching process was explicitly analyzed in a six-step sequence using the B-P-E (Behavior-Person-Environment) system. Explicit matching was illustrated by the conceptual level matching model. The matching process was seen in terms of a shift from specifying B, to classifying P, to translating P into an appropriate E ($E_1/E_2/E_3$), and then repeating the cycle—each step requiring specific teacher skills. At its most general level, matching was viewed in terms of two components:

1. sensitivity to students (ability to "read" them); and
2. modulation to the perceived classification of students ("flexing").

Specific examples for training in these two skills were offered. The long-term aim of the application of explicit matching ideas is to facilitate teachers' implicit matching in their spontaneous adaptation to the needs of their students.

5

Strength and Sensitivity: The Battleground of Explicit Matching Behavior

Lucy Peck and Bruce R. Joyce

Hunt's extensive formulations and long and careful series of studies lay a foundation for looking at teaching as a clinical, adaptive activity. The teacher initiates, on the one hand, and adapts, on the other. Hunt invented a procedure for investigating both of these processes, and Peck and Joyce developed the study that is reported in the following pages.

SITUATIONAL ASSESSMENT OF STRENGTH AND SENSITIVITY IN TEACHING

This chapter reports an empirical study of two aspects of teaching behavior: one, *strength,* refers to behaviors by which teachers introduce structure into the interactive teaching-learning situation; the other, *sensitivity,* refers to the teacher's modulation or adaptation to the behavior of the learner. The work derives from earlier investigations by Hunt and his associates [68] into strength and sensitivity in Peace Corps candidates; Joyce, Dirr, and Hunt's [78] investigation of procedures for increasing the modulation-adaptation dimension of teaching behavior; and Weinstein's [157] constructs about the behavior needed to structure the interactive teaching situation for unruly students.

The Practical Problem

The origins of the concepts of strength and sensitivity are in the practical world of teaching. The focus on strength comes from the teacher's role as organizer and as the one responsible for order in the social system of the classroom. The job description of most teachers requires that they organize from twenty to forty youngsters. Hence, their job is not simply one of instructing and helping students engage in dialogue or learn subject matter; they need, in addition, other characteristics, including organizational ability and persuasiveness, which enable them to organize a social situation conducive to learning.

Interpersonal strength is potentially a very important component of successful teaching, and not only in inner-city teaching. Everyone who trains teachers is plagued by the fact that many young teachers who seem to like children, who are well prepared in subject matter, and who are highly motivated, appear to be unable to maintain sufficient discipline to teach in many settings. The construct of interpersonal strength as we use it refers to the ability to create structure in the interactive process of teaching—the ability to initiate sufficient structure to develop a stable social situation while interacting with the students. Strength will have different manifestations according to the instructional model one is using. It shows up differently in a highly directive or highly organized approach to teaching than it does in a nondirective or student-centered approach. Whatever the approach, strength has to be manifested in the interactive situation in order to develop a cohesive group whose members can cooperate in maintaining enough stability to enable learning to go on.

FIGURE 5.1

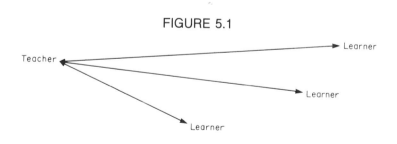

The construct of sensitivity originates also from the job description of the teacher. The teacher and learner radiate toward each other a barrage of information, potentially telling each other about themselves—their interests, values, and abilities (see figure 5.1). Sensitivity refers to the ability to reach the other person's communications and to modify one's own behavior so as to adapt to the characteristics of the other. In the case of the teacher, it means picking up clues about the character of the learner, putting them together into an integrated picture of the learner, and then adapting one's behavior so that one makes contact with the learner and can teach her/him effectively.

Empirical History

Communication tasks have been designed to investigate strength in teacher behavior. Weinstein,[157] Lesniak,[96] and Joyce[76] have engaged in separate investigations to probe strength. In the strength tasks, the same general procedures are followed as in the sensitivity tasks, with the difference that the role players are trained to resist any structure given by the teacher. For example, they may complain that they have previously engaged in the activities suggested by the teacher or that those suggested are too difficult or unpleasant. In addition, they may make personal comments about the teacher ("Are you married, teach?") and disrupt the interaction by looking away from the teacher, moving around the room, and talking to each other while the teacher is talking. The disruptions and resistant behavior are planned and scheduled to occur at regular intervals. As in the sensitivity task, raters observe and record on a strength scale the way the teachers cope with this dissident behavior. Some get quite flustered and are unable to continue their activity; others get very harsh and try to repress the dissident behavior; still others cope with the obstacles firmly yet integratively.

Weinstein[157] and Lesniak[96] used strength tasks to assess applicants for admission to the urban teacher preparation program at Syracuse University and were able to increase dramatically the rate at which interns survived teaching in the inner-city schools of Syracuse. Before the use of the strength tasks to select interns, many dropped out of the program or at least were unable to complete the internship because of disciplinary problems. After using the strength tasks to select candidates, Weinstein reported that he was able to increase survival to the point where nearly all the interns lasted the year, and many went on to inner-city teaching.

Theoretical Sources

A number of theoretical concerns stimulate a continuing interest in the concepts of strength and sensitivity and possible relationships between them. First of all, Hunt's[55] research indicates that sensitivity is probably related to conceptual complexity. Sensitivity may be a function of the general capacity of the organism to absorb information, integrate it, develop new concepts, and adapt behavior accordingly.

A series of studies by Schroder and his associates[129] attempted to measure sensitivity and strength simultaneously in the same assessment tasks. Schroder found that teachers who were unable to impose a reasonable degree of structure in the situation were also unable to manifest much sensitivity, although the tasks had been constructed so that strength and sensitivity could be measured independently of each other. In the Weinstein, Hunt, and Joyce study [158] of sensitivity many teachers seemed almost to give up and be unable to continue if they were unable to understand the cues from the learner in a sensitivity task. Hence, the following questions arise: (1) Is a certain amount of strength necessary for sensitivity or, more disturbingly, is too much sensitivity incompatible with strength? (2) Is it possible that the highly sensitive teacher (the one sought after in almost all the theoretical literature about teaching) may lack the interpersonal strength to cope with the vicissitudes of many types of classroom teaching? Thus, (3) what are the relationships between strength and sensitivity?

Purposes of the Study

The present study, conceived as a first stage in a series, was constructed to explore the relationship between strength and sensitivity in situational assessment tasks.

Design of the Study

The subjects for the study were twenty-seven students in master's level teacher education courses at Teachers College, Columbia University. Each subject taught in two communication tasks, one sensitivity and one strength. In each case, they taught students who, in reality, were role players.

In the sensitivity task, the teacher was presented with a composition by the artist Hokusai, entitled *Mount Fuji Viewed Through the Waves at Kanagawa* and instructed to teach ways in which art can communicate feelings without the use of words, with an emphasis on the concept of dynamic balance familiar in Japanese compositions. The role player tried to communicate the impression of an individual who has a fear of the sea because of a frightening experience in his past. Thus, while the teacher tried to teach him how to look at the painting, the role player was concerned with communicating his fear of the sea. If the teacher perceived this, he could deal with the role player, or student, in terms of feelings and could even make his points effectively by utilizing the role player's own experience as a springboard to the concepts.

In the strength task, two students resisted the activity of the teacher, who was instructed to organize the students to take a field trip to the United Nations. The students resisted the whole idea—they rejected the experience, questioned the kinds of things they are supposed to learn from it, and expressed lack of confidence in the teacher and a general apathy toward learning.

Hence, in the sensitivity task, the focus was on the teacher's ability to comprehend the student's problem and relate the concepts to be taught to that problem; in the strength task, the focus was on the teacher's response to a series of obstacles raised by the students. In both tasks, role players were trained to behave in a uniform way with each teacher so that the cues and obstacles would be the same. To illustrate, at one point in the strength task, a role player began to leave the room. If she was stopped or questioned by the teacher, she stated that she was getting a drink of water and then went ahead and left. Upon reclaiming her seat, she engaged in a mild quarrel over the ownership of some physical property, such as a pencil or paper with the other student. When reprimanded, both role players ceased fighting immediately. A couple of minutes later, however, they began another quarrel. In this case, they became secretive, giggled, and exchanged mild insults. This routine was repeated with each teacher.

Each student was rated on eighteen categories of strength and thirteen of sensitivity. Each set of ratings was submitted to a factor analysis, and four sensitivity and four strength factors were extrapolated.

A varimax factor rotation was made of the four sensitivity factors and four strength factors, and four further factors were extrapolated (see table 5.1): integrativeness, awareness, control, and structuring. The first of these was characterized by a combination of *learner-directedness* (from sensitivity) and *personal involvement* (from strength). *Awareness* and *modulation-supportiveness* were prominent in the factor of awareness; *persistence* (from sensitivity) and *dominativeness* (from strength) were prominent in the control factor. *Structuring* was the prominent component in the factor of that name. Thus, two of the factors are sensitivitylike, and two strengthlike.

TABLE 5.1. Varimax Factor Rotation: Interpersonal Sensitivity and Interpersonal Strength Eight Tests: Four Factors

Factors	I Integrativeness	II Awareness	III Control	IV Structuring
1	−.07	.93*	.06	.22
2	−.03	.06	−.84*	−.10
3	.09	−.59	.34	.50
4	−.79*	−.37	.06	.10
5	.30	.51	−.03	−.03
6	−.13	.02	.80*	−.32
7	.86*	−.20	−.02	.30
8	.09	−.14	.17	−.92*

* Significantly correlated.

Factors

1 Awareness
2 Persistence
3 Modulation/supportiveness
4 Learner directedness
5 Rationality
6 Dominativeness
7 Personal involvement
8 Structuring

It seems clear that strength and sensitivity, as originally defined and measured, are by no means unrelated to each other. The pattern of correlations between strength and sensitivity ratings and the factor analyses indicate that the two aspects of teaching behavior have elements in common but that there are elements, such as dominativeness and persistence, that distinguish them. The general strength factor is interesting because of its many associated dimensions and its inclusion of many of the behaviors that on the face of them might be termed sensitivity.

The implications of these findings provide a focus for our future investigations in teacher education and the study of teaching:

1. Sensitivity (modulation-adaptation to the learner) and strength (structuring the learning situation and coping with dissonant interpersonal interchanges) appear to be distinct dimensions in teaching behavior as revealed in the communication tasks. The subscores of each are so highly intercorrelated as to make it reasonable to consider strength and sensitivity in terms of relatively few component factors. The factors that emerged from the factor analysis are reasonable beginnings as focuses for training and research.

2. Strength and sensitivity, as measured, are by no means unrelated dimensions of teaching. Many of their component subscores are significantly correlated, although not so highly as are the strength or sensitivity scores among themselves. The four factors reflect the relationship, but also the distinctness, of the dimensions.

The relatedness of strength and sensitivity suggests that growth in one may depend on growth in the other. Training research can be designed to explore this question and develop findings that will reflect any causal relationship between training in one dimension and growth in the other. It may be that strength is necessary to sensitivity in teaching and that training in one will improve the other. However, they may be different enough to require different emphases in training.

6

Sensitivity Training for Teachers: An Experiment

Bruce R. Joyce, Peter Dirr, and David E. Hunt

This chapter reports the first of a set of investigations designed to develop a training program to increase the sensitivity of a teacher to the frame of reference of the learner. The first investigation examined the effects of such a program and, as an adjunct to the central study, made a comparison of the communication styles of teachers both under simulated conditions and in the normal classroom situation.

The experiment was made possible because, as indicated in chapter five, Hunt had invented a method for assessing the interpersonal sensitivity and flexibility of a teacher who is interacting with a learner. The method consists of a series of communication tasks, in each of which the teacher is presented with the problem of teaching a concept to a learner. After time has been given him to prepare a lesson dealing with the concept, he is given a fifteen-minute period in which to teach the concept. The learner is a role player trained to give to the teacher, during the course of the lesson, responses that indicate a frame of reference counter to the one implied by the concept. In other words, a situation of conflict is created, in which the concept that is the object of the lesson is mildly but firmly rejected by the learner.

As the role player provides each verbal cue to the teacher, observers rate the teacher as s/he, in turn, responds. They look for his/her recognition of the frame of reference of the learner and try to determine whether or not the teacher modifies his/her strategy in order to build a conceptual bridge between the learner's concept and the one s/he is trying to teach. Hence, sensitivity is defined as *the recognition of the learner's frame of reference and a subsequent adjustment of teaching behavior in an attempt to accommodate the learner's stance.* Some teachers grasp the problem and begin to develop a teaching strategy to build a conceptual bridge between the student and the concept. Yet other teachers went on with their presentation as if the role player had not spoken, entirely failing to recognize that the learner was not only grasping the concept but had a conflicting concept of his/her own.

The Sensitivity Training Program

Dirr, Hunt, and Joyce decided to develop a program of training designed specifically to help teacher trainees learn:

1. To discriminate cues from learners; that is, to scrutinize utterances by learners and attempt to interpret them.
2. To try to alter teaching behavior during lessons so as to accommodate the emerging frames of reference of the learners.
3. To reflect this in their classroom teaching by asking more probing questions designed to reveal the frame of reference of the learner.

The training program had the following phases:

Discrimination training

The trainees were presented with several sets of transcripts of tape-recorded episodes of other persons undergoing the communication task. Practice was given in identifying and interpreting learner cues and in analyzing the responses of the other teachers to the learners' frames of reference. Examples of sensitive and insensitive behavior were included in an effort to teach the trainees to discriminate between those two classifications of teacher response.

Practice and feedback

In this section of the training program, each trainee engaged in four communication tasks. Each of the engagements was tape-recorded or filmed, and shortly after the task, the tape-recording or film was shown to the trainee, who was helped to discriminate the learner cues and his own response or failure to respond to or interpret the cues. The role players were children of nine to fourteen trained to play the specific roles required, and the teaching tasks were of a kind familiar in school settings. One task required the teacher to correct the grammar in a written essay prepared, presumably, by the role player, who was trained to appeal to authority to defend his position. Another task required a discussion of the interdependence of foreign relations with a role player trained to reflect a concept of national autonomy and protectionism. A third task required the teaching of the use of metaphor in a poem to a role player trained to make incorrect inferences from the metaphors.

The Design of the Study

Subjects were twenty-four students in the master of arts in teaching program at a small liberal arts college for women. All were student teachers throughout the study.

The central questions explored were:

1. Did the training program result in an increase of sensitivity within the communication tasks that were part of the training program?

2. Did the training program increase the proportion of questions asked by the subjects during classroom teaching in the public schools?

3. Was the teaching behavior of the subjects under simulated conditions similar to behavior in normal public school classrooms?

In terms of direct implications for teacher education programs, the second question is the most relevant. To maximize evidence on this question, experimental and control groups were formed as follows: A communication task was administered to all twenty-four subjects and ratings of sensitivity obtained. In addition, recordings were made of three teaching episodes in normal public school classrooms and analyzed according to a system designed by Joyce to yield indices of question-asking in teaching.* Twelve matched pairs were then made up according to sensitivity scores and indices of questioning; members of each pair were randomly assigned to experimental and control groups.

The experimental group was submitted to the sensitivity training program, and ratings of sensitivity were obtained from each communication task during training. At the conclusion of the program, recordings of three more episodes of classroom teaching were obtained from all subjects and analyzed as above to yield indices of questioning behavior.

Results

Results are presented in terms of the three questions:

1. *Did the training program result in an increase of sensitivity within the communication tasks that were part of the training program?* Two scores were obtained by rating behavior within each task: an overall rating of sensitivity and a rating of rapport-building activity—probing and conciliatory behav-

---

* For a general version of this system, see Bruce R. Joyce and Berj Harootunian, *The Structure of Teaching* (Chicago: Science Research Associates, 1967).

TABLE 6.1. Sensitivity and Rapport Building During the Early and Later Communication Tasks in the Sensitivity Training Program

	Mean	SD	t	p<
Sensitivity				
In early tasks	2.71	1.46	1.06	.35
In later tasks	3.02	1.28		
Rapport Building				
In early tasks	1.75	1.12	4.35	.01
In later tasks	3.05	1.35		

ior not directly related to the teaching task. Table 6.1 presents means, standard deviations, and *t* values of the scores for the first two tasks compared with the last two tasks during the training program. It can be seen that there was no significant change in the ratings of sensitivity but that there was a large and statistically significant change in rapport building. It may be that it is easier for a teacher to learn to probe generally into the learner's background than it is to probe specifically into his frame of reference and adjust teaching tactics accordingly.

When individual differences are examined, the data suggest differential effects. Five of the subjects actually dropped in sensitivity, while seven rose markedly. Apparently the development of a sensitivity training program will require research on which a differential training model can be built.

Considering the results as a whole, it is necessary to conclude that the program did not achieve its main target with the group of subjects, but that it may have achieved a related target (rapport building) that may be a precursor of sensitivity. The apparent differential effectiveness of the program suggests that future research should include attention to the development of differential procedures.

2. *Did the training program increase the proportion of questions asked by the subjects during classroom teaching in the public schools?* For both experimental and control subjects, three teaching episodes were recorded before and after the training program and an index made of the number of questions that were asked, divided by the number of all communications judged to be rewarding to a learner (positive sanctions). Table 6.2 presents these data as a comparison of means of experimental and control groups before and after training.

With respect to sanctioning, the experimental groups changed very little whereas the control group dropped until the differences between the groups reached significance. However, when the differences were adjusted to account for initial differences, the change was not significant. In questioning, the same trend appeared, although the difference between the control and the experimental group did not reach significance. The results are similar to those obtained several times when the application of interaction analysis,

TABLE 6.2. Comparison of Means of Experimental and Control Groups Before and After the Training Program: Indices of Questioning and Sanctioning

	Pre-Training Mean	SD	Post-Training Mean	SD	Mean Differences	t	P
Sanctioning							
Experimental group	6.51	3.84	6.70	3.61	+ .19	.21	NS
Control group	5.81	2.91	5.32	3.10	− .49	.27	NS
					(Difference of differences, .68)		
Questioning							
Experimental group	11.32	5.62	11.21	5.46	− .11	.14	NS
Control group	11.71	6.01	10.34	6.12	−1.37	1.61	NS
					(Difference of differences, 1.28)		

rather than achieving a positive result, has stemmed the flow toward directness in teaching.* It must be concluded that the sensitivity-training program did not increase questioning or positive sanctioning by the subjects; both are categories of classroom behavior that might be expected to accompany increases in sensitivity.

3. *Was the teaching behavior of the subjects under simulated conditions similar to behavior in normal public school classrooms?* This question was explored because any attempts to build training programs utilizing simulation must face the problem of transfer to the normal environment of application. This necessitates laying an empirical base from which to approach the problem.

It will be recalled that three teaching episodes in public school classrooms were recorded and analyzed for each subject before and after the training program and that, in addition, four communication tasks of each subject were analyzed using the same procedure. Computation of the following indices provides a comparison of behavior in the two types of situation:

Sanctioning — The proportion of all teacher communications judged to have positive reward value compared with all other communications

Informational Communications — The proportion of all teacher communications that handled subject matter

Informational Questioning — The proportion of questions compared with other informational communication

* See, for example, Jeffrey Kirk, "Elementary School Student Teachers and Interaction Analysis," in Amidon and Hough, eds., *Interaction Analysis: Theory, Research,* and *Application* (Reading, Mass.: Addison-Wesley, 1967, pp. 299–306).

| Open Question-ing | Open-ended questions compared with all informational communications |
| Procedural Communications | The proportion of communications that organize procedures compared with all other communications |

The focus of the analysis was to determine the kinds of unexpected differences that occurred; that is, those that were a product of the environmental change but are not easily accounted for by changes in the kinds of tasks in the simulation as compared with the ordinary classroom tasks.

The indices are looked at in two ways: as a comparison of means between the two situations (did teachers reward as much under simulated conditions as they did in the classroom?), and as a matter of correlation (what was the relation between rewardingness in the two situations; did the high-rewarding teachers in one situation act the same way in the other?).

Table 6.3 presents the results for the index of sanctions.

TABLE 6.3. Index of Positive Sanctioning in Simulated and Classroom Situations

	Mean	SD	Mean Diff.	t ($p <$)	r ($p <$)
Classroom teaching	18.6	7.12			
			4.6	7.33 (.025)	.63 (.05)
Communication tasks	14.0	6.14			

We would expect teachers to reward a role player less than a classroomful of children. And they did. The amount of rewarding communication directed at the role players was, it seemed to us, remarkably high (14 percent of all communications). Apparently the communication tasks were sufficiently realistic so that the teachers did not omit reward to their simulated learners. This corroborated our informal observation that the situations held much realism for the teachers; that is, after a task developed, they seemed to lose themselves in the business of teaching. Although this was not true of all the subjects all the time, it was nevertheless a striking feature of the program. The correlation between the situations indicated that individuals reacted similarly in both situations. This suggests that teachers can be assessed for rewardingness in simulations and that it is worthwhile to try to learn to train them under simulated conditions.

Table 6.4 presents the results for informational communications.

The communication tasks were more information-oriented. This was to be expected, since the teacher was assigned a concept to teach and faced a single, cooperative learner. Again, the correlation is in the positive direction, indicating the tendency for the teachers to react to the simulated learner much as they react in the classroom.

Table 6.5 presents the results for informational questioning.

TABLE 6.4. Index of Informational Communications in Simulated and Classroom Situations

	Mean	SD	t	r
Classroom teaching	74.5	17.42		
			13.56	.54
Communication tasks	92.5	18.15	(.005)	(.10)

TABLE 6.5. Index of Questions Related to Information

	Mean	SD	t	r
Classroom teaching	39.6	17.51		
			—	.56
Communication tasks	41.6	19.12	.03	(*p* .10)
			(NS)	

The proportion of questions asked, when compared with all information-related communications, was about equal. Again, the correlation suggests a relationship between the performance of individuals in the two situations; that is, there was a tendency for those who asked a high proportion of questions in the simulations to do the same in the classroom.

"Open" questions (table 6.6) are those to which there are no fixed answers. In this sample of trainees, the proportion of open questions was very low compared with the other samples of pre-service and in-service teachers we have studied; hence, the correlation does not seem applicable. The comparison of means indicates a trend for a larger number of open questions to be asked of role players, a finding that should be explored in a further study. It may be that this indicates a real difference in the two conditions, and one wonders if this difference can be capitalized on to make simulated teaching conditions into a good setting for teaching difficult teaching maneuvers.

Table 6.7 presents the index of procedural communications.

The results indicate that the proportion of communications devoted to procedures was much lower under simulated teaching conditions. This is very likely attributable to the structure of the communication tasks in which procedures are fairly well established and only one compliant learner needs to be organized. The correlation is very low, indicating that there was little similarity in this type of behavior for individuals in the two situations.

TABLE 6.6. Index of Open Questioning under Both Conditions

	Mean	SD	t	r
Classroom teaching	3.6	2.38		
			3.23	N.A.[a]
Communication tasks	6.2	3.44	(.10)	

[a] Not applicable.

TABLE 6.7. Index of Communications Directed at Procedures

	Mean	SD	t (p)	r (p)
Classroom conditions	23.7	6.12		
Communication tasks	11.7	3.94	15.00 (.005)	.14 (NS)

The total picture encourages us to believe that the communication task provides a setting in which teachers behave in several important ways as they would in the classroom. Differences in behavior in the two settings are, in general, what would be expected. The two situations apparently measure the same characteristics to some extent.

Conclusions

1. The sensitivity training program evidently had little direct effect on sensitivity as designed but did affect a logically related behavior, rapport building, which may be the first behavior affected by such a program.

2. Although the program did not seem to affect classroom teaching in any observable way, it did arrest the flow toward directness that characterized the subjects in the control group.

3. There were consistent relations between teaching behavior in simulated conditions and in normal classrooms which indicate that the simulated settings were enough like real teaching conditions that we can hope to learn to use them as training environments.

This work resulted in a much clearer idea about the nature of the communication problem teachers face. Teachers have to read cues from a variety of learners, synthesize these into a conception of the human beings with whom they are dealing, generate environments that are tuned both to the learner and the objectives, and then continuously modify their behavior as the learner responds or fails to respond to instruction. The Joyce-Dirr-Hunt investigation, attempting to pull teachers rapidly into the ability to tune in to learners, was not very successful, but, together with a number of other failures, it led to a better conception of the ways teachers could be helped to choose environments appropriate to their students.

PART IV

Learning to Teach: The Influence of Personality, Experience, Cooperating Teachers, and Feedback

In this section of the book we explore the question, How do we learn to teach? We will consider three types of influence. One of these is the influence of the individual personality. Teaching is an extremely personal process, and the individual's makeup strongly affects the style of teaching that eventually emerges. Over the years we have done a series of investigations to determine, in particular, the influence of the individual's values and educational philosophy. More frequently, we have investigated the influence of the teacher's personality structure as defined by Hunt and his collaborators.

Again and again, relationships have emerged between the conceptual level (CL) and the teaching styles of both preservice and in-service teacher candidates. The more abstract (high CL) teachers responded differently to information about the learner, were less punitive in their teaching, developed more negotiated climates in the classrooms, and used information at a higher conceptual level. In addition, they more easily acquired a repertoire of models of teaching, thus increasing their capacity for radiating a wider variety of environments to their learners than did low CL teachers.

We have also studied social influences on learning to teach. Specifically, we have done a series of studies on the relationship between the beliefs and teaching styles of cooperating teachers and the young teachers with whom they worked. We found that, while student teachers were with cooperating teachers, they tended to take on the "teaching personality" of those cooperating teachers, but the persistence of this effect was unclear. When student teachers moved to a new cooperating teacher, they tended to take on that personality just as quickly as they did the last.

Thus, the influence of the individual cooperating teacher may be more ephemeral than we had thought previously. However, in general, unless there was a powerful training intervention, young teachers became more and more like their cooperating, experienced teachers during their student teaching experiences. Specifically, they tended to become less rewarding, more punishing, and less negotiating toward children. Also, they dominated the conversation more, and asked fewer and fewer "higher order" questions. However, training could affect this and change the natural flow toward the recitative model of teaching that has been so well documented in past research.

Our most elaborate work has been on the effects of training. We have studied the effects of providing feedback to teachers about their teaching styles, of exposure to sensitivity training and communications training and, most extensively, have studied teachers' ability to take on models of teaching that were unusual to their "natural" styles.

We found that feedback alone was enough to impede the flow toward increasing directness and punitiveness in teaching, but that it did not generally widen repertoire or variety in teaching style. Communication and sensitivity training had mixed effects. We had our greatest success with models of teaching. According to our findings, teachers can quite easily widen their repertoire of models of teaching and can learn to employ them in a variety of situations. In-service teachers appeared to acquire models of teaching somewhat more rapidly than did preservice teachers, but we are not as yet certain how to interpret that finding. Generally speaking, the "natural" teaching style of the teacher appears to have relatively little effect on his/her ability to acquire given models of teaching. Teachers who had previously displayed very little nondirectiveness, for example, appeared to be able to acquire nondirective models about as well as did teachers who seemed to lean in that direction naturally. Similarly, teachers whose natural classroom discourse rarely manifested higher-order cognitive activity appeared to be able to master quite readily models of teaching that required that kind of activity.

Presently we see the process of learning to teach as a combination of many factors: the individual's personality and beliefs, social influences on learning to teach, and training. We see the ideal effect of training as the ability to integrate a repertoire of models of teaching with the modulation of teaching behavior in response to the needs of the individual learner.

7

Teacher Trainee Personality and Initial Teaching Style

David E. Hunt and Bruce R. Joyce

This chapter describes two exploratory investigations of the relationship between the personality of teacher trainees and their initial pattern or style of teaching.* The major limitation of earlier studies investigating teacher personality is that they have been conducted in a "theoretical vacuum" [44] (p. 575). A second limitation of research in this area is reliance upon a single criterion of teacher effectiveness, i.e., "the ideal teacher" [43] (p. 575),[159] (p. 709). We have attempted to overcome the first difficulty by utilizing a theoretical network—Conceptual Systems Theory [47,55] to coordinate concepts dealing with teacher personality and teacher behavior. We have attempted to overcome the single-criterion limitation through the use of a theory-relevant, objective coding system [80] that permits classifying teacher behavior in terms of nonevaluative patterns.

If one views certain teaching patterns, for example, highly structured lesson plans, as differentially effective depending upon the characteristics of the learner and the desired educational objective,[55] then one skill important for the effective teacher is the capacity to utilize a variety of teaching patterns under appropriate circumstances. Based on a training model which analyzes the skill components for training agents in general (including teachers, therapists, case workers, as well as parents) we have called this skill "the capacity

---

*Results of this study were obtained in relation to an unpublished investigation of the modification of teaching patterns by D. E. Hunt, B. R. Joyce, and J. DelPopolo.

to radiate a wide variety of environments." [57] Stated in more educationally relevant terms, ". . . the teacher who can exhibit a wide variety of teaching styles is potentially able to accomplish more than a teacher whose repertoire is relatively limited." [84] Since it is known that the most infrequent teaching pattern is what we will call *reflective*, or one that utilizes the learner's frame of reference to encourage questioning [54,151]; further, since providing this reflective environment is also theoretically relevant,[55] we focus on the reflective teaching style. Our tentative assumption is that, if a teacher trainee can radiate a reflective environment, s/he will have expanded his/her repertoire since the reflective pattern occurs very rarely in teaching. Some of Flanders' [32] findings seem to support this assumption. Thus, the capacity to radiate a reflective educational environment also probably indicates a general tendency to radiate a wider variety of educational environments. The selection of the dependent variable—proportion of reflective teaching behaviors—thus has both an empirical and theoretical basis.

From the Conceptual Systems viewpoint, the major dimension in personality variation is degree of abstractness or conceptual level (CL). Persons at a higher CL are expected to be more flexible, more capable of using alternative solutions and more stress-tolerant. Considerable construct validity evidence supports this expectation.[127] The potential educational relevance of Conceptual Systems was indicated at an American Educational Research Association symposium in 1964 on "Conceptual Systems and Educational Research," and more recently by Joyce, Lamb, and Sieber.[88]

In one of the five theoretically derived papers at the AERA symposium, Joyce [74] reported that the occurrence of one of the teaching patterns inferred from the Anderson [6] coding system—namely, IT 14, or "helps child define, redefine, or advance a problem"—was related to the CL of the teacher trainee. Joyce selected eighteen student teachers at varying levels of conceptual development and tape-recorded a lesson taught by each student teacher. The occurrence of IT 14, which would presumably be close to what we are here calling a reflective pattern, increased in an orderly fashion as the CL of the student teacher increased from a proportion of zero in the lowest CL group to .35 in the highest CL group. Although the size of these groups was quite small, the pattern of proportions was in the expected direction.

The two studies reported here are similar in design to the earlier investigation by Joyce and Hodges [82] (see chapter 3) with the primary difference being that the present studies use a coding system more theoretically relevant to the incidence of reflective teaching patterns.

Joyce devised a "Manual for Coding Teacher Communications Relevant to Conceptual Systems Theory" [75] that can be used with adequate interrater reliability to quantify a number of categories of teacher behavior. The coding system contains four general categories—Sanctions, Procedures, Information, and Activity Initiation—each of which has subcategories. The five subcategories within the Information category are ordered roughly on a reflective-structured dimension:

I-1 Helps child evaluate information, raise hypotheses, make inferences, define or advance problem.

I-2 Helps child find information.

I-3 Asks lecture question.

I-4 Makes lecture statement.

I-5 Gives conclusion.

For present purposes, therefore, the reflective pattern was defined as the number of I-1 and I-2 behaviors divided by the total number of behaviors coded in the Information category. Other subcategories might be theoretically expected to relate to the teacher trainee's CL; e.g., child-determined standards and procedures, but the primary dependent variable in the present study was the reflective handling of information. The hypothesis was simply that, for new teacher trainees, the occurrence of reflective teaching patterns is directly related to the trainee's conceptual level—the higher the CL, the greater the occurrence of the reflective pattern. The hypothesis was studied in two separate investigations.

First Study: Master of Arts in Teacher Trainees

Subjects

Fourteen female graduate students who were candidates for master's degree in an intensive one-year graduate teacher education program were subjects.

Assessment of CL

Subjects were administered the sentence completion measure customarily used to assess CL in young adults; this measure consists of six stems (e.g. "Rules. . . ," "When I am criticized . . ." etc.) to which the subject responds in three or four sentences during the two-minute time period allowed for each stem. Each of the six responses is scored according to a manual developed originally by Schroder, Driver, and Streufert [127] and the mean of these six scores becomes the subject's CL score. Interrater reliability ranges from .85 to .95.

Assessment of initial teaching style

During the first ten weeks of training, each subject brought in at least one tape-recorded lesson related to her student teaching. For most subjects it was a recording of an initial teaching experience. Although there was the possibility of self-selection bias, the cooperating teacher also helped determine which lessons would be taped, so that possible bias was not considered to be a major factor. These tape-recorded lessons were coded according to Joyce's "Manual for Coding Teacher Communications Relevant to Conceptual Systems Theory" by a coder who was unaware of the subjects' CL. A portion of these tapes was scored by another coder, and the interrater reliability was satisfactory ($r = .87$). Although the coding method described in the manual yields other material, the present investigation was concerned only with what we will call the reflective index: the number of I–1 and I–2 behaviors divided by the total number of behaviors coded in the information category.

Results

The correlation between trainee CL and reflective index was .578 ($df = 12$, $p < .05$), which supports the hypothesis. In order to check possible biasing effects of general intelligence in this relationship, scores for these subjects on the National Teacher Examination were correlated with both CL and reflective index. In both cases the relation was exactly zero, indicating that intelligence probably does not account for the reported relation.

Second Study: Sophomore Teacher Trainees

Subjects

Sixteen female sophomore students enrolled in a methods of teaching course in a teacher-training program were subjects.

Assessment of CL

CL was assessed as in the first study, and the same scoring procedure was used. However, the CL variability in this sample was much less than in the first sample.

Assessment of initial teaching style

During the first six weeks of the semester, as a requirement in the methods course, each subject taught a lesson to a group of fourth grade children. The lessons, twenty-five to thirty minutes in duration, were tape-recorded. This was the initial teaching experience for most subjects. These lessons were coded and a reflective index computed for each subject.

Results

The correlation between trainee CL and reflective index was .476 which does not reach significance ($r = .497$ at $< .05$ level for $df = 14$). Because the constricted CL variability in this sample probably decreased the correlation, a median-split analysis was also conducted. The mean reflective index of the high CL group was .10 and the mean of the low CL group was .05, a difference which is significant ($t = .249$, $df = 14$, $p < .05$). In light of the borderline results in the correlational analysis and the significant results in the extreme group analysis, the hypothesis appeared to be replicated in this study.

Conclusions

Although both these studies were small in scale, when considered along with the similar findings reported earlier by Joyce [74] the results seem to provide fairly good evidence in support of the hypothesized relation between personality and teaching pattern. The generic nature of this relation is indicated by a finding recently reported by Cross [26] that CL of parents is significantly related to the training condition that they provide for their children, as measured by an interview. The relation between CL and the parental pattern of autonomy (which is similar to measures of reflectiveness in an educational context) was .37 for fathers and .34 for mothers, both significant $< .05$.

In reflecting on the present results it should be emphasized that we consider these relations to hold for *initial* style or pattern and that they should not be considered to imply that these teaching patterns cannot be changed through training. Indeed, the present authors are interested in providing just such training.[57] The problem of how to induce the capacity to radiate a reflective environment in low CL teacher trainees is a formidable one, but one which it is hoped can be attacked more systematically in light of the present results. We have tentatively assumed that a high reflective index indicates a capacity to radiate a wider variety of environments, but this assumption needs to be verified. As we have noted elsewhere in commenting on these results, "It is tempting to conclude from this trainee personality-preferred style relation that more abstract trainees (higher CL) have more potential but, while this *may* be so, it is nonetheless true that it may be as difficult to make structured environmental radiation available to abstract (high CL) trainees as it is to induce the availability of more reflective environmental radiation in concrete (low CL) trainees." [57]

In any case, it seems reasonable to conclude on the present and earlier evidence that the relation between teacher trainee CL and the capacity to radiate a reflective environment is established, at least in the initial phase of learning to teach. Rather than view this relation as setting limits upon potential effectiveness after teacher training, we would hope that these results would help stimulate the search for procedures that might be effective in inducing the capacity to radiate a wide variety of educational environments in trainees at varying conceptual levels.

8

The Relationship between Teaching Styles, Personality, and Setting

Clark C. Brown

The purpose of this study is to explore the relationships of the behavior and personality of student teachers, the behavior of cooperating teachers, and the effects of various training environments on the student teacher's performance.

An original study by this author investigated the relationship between five variables and the initial teaching styles of student teachers.* These variables were: (1) some teaching styles of cooperating teachers, (2) student teacher beliefs about education, (3) perceptions of student teachers regarding the educational beliefs of elementary school principals, (4) the ways in which student teachers communicated with their college supervisors in conferences, and (5) the conceptual levels of student teachers. For our purposes, only the relationships of variables (1) and (5) to initial teaching styles will be reported.

DESIGN OF THE STUDY

The subjects were twenty-nine student teachers enrolled in the Preservice Teacher Education Program, which is the Master of Arts degree program

---

* Initial teaching style refers to the teaching behaviors that beginning student teachers exhibit prior to prolonged contact with the more experienced, cooperating teachers.

in elementary education at Teachers College, Columbia University. At the beginning of their teacher education program in the fall of the year, each student was assigned to an "observation-participation" situation in the public elementary schools of the city of New York.

The twenty-nine subjects were required to turn in to their college supervisors weekly tape-recordings of lessons they had taught in their teaching situations. These tape-recordings were made available for analysis. Four usable tapes from each student teacher collected during the first four weeks of observation-participation constituted the sample of his/her initial teaching.

The student teachers taught one to five children in a tutorial situation in language arts. The lessons lasted from twenty to forty minutes. The amount of student teacher communication during lessons varied with teacher and subject matter. In the first ten complete lessons coded, the number of communications made by the student teacher varied from 90 to 560 with a mean of 400. After inspecting the data, it was determined that a sufficient sample of teaching could be obtained by coding the first 120 communications from each student teacher's lesson. All communications up to and including the first 120 were converted to percentages to accommodate for differences in length of lessons. Using Joyce's "Manual for Coding Teacher Communications Relevant to Conceptual Systems Theory," [75] six investigators coded the tapes. Interrater reliability coefficients ranged between .84 and .97.

"Teaching styles" refer to the patterns of a teacher's oral communication. Initial teaching styles were established by an analysis of four samples of each student teacher's oral communications. These communications were then described in terms of categories, subcategories, and clusters of subcategories, called "indices."

Indices of Teaching Style

Because many of the subcategories had a similar theoretical base, it was convenient to group the subcategories into indices. These indices made possible a more compact description of teaching styles and allowed for an analysis of the interrelationships among aspects of teaching styles in a more coherent way than would be possible if all the subcategories were treated separately.

Eight indices were calculated from the frequency distributions and converted to percentages. Three of these were related to the general category of Sanctions and include: (1) Sanctioning—Positive, (2) Sanctioning—Negative, and (3) Sanctioning—Convergent. Three other indices were derived from the general Information category and include: (4) Total Information Handling, (5) Information Handling—Total Questioning, and (6) Information Handling—Open Questioning. The final indices were related to the general Procedure category and include: (7) Total Procedure Handling, and (8) Procedure Handling—Reflective.

Grouping of subcategories for indices

All the positive sanctioning subcategories were grouped and compared with the total number of communications. This index of Sanctioning—Positive represented the percentage of total rewarding communications.*

The negative Sanctions were grouped and compared with the total number of all Sanctions, yielding a percentage of Sanctioning—Negative.

The Sanctioning subcategories of Attainment and Following Rules were assumed to have the function of reinforcing the attainment of a concept or skill and securing conformity to established procedures. Therefore, this index showed efforts to encourage conformity and convergence of behavior. The positive and negative valences of these subcategories were grouped and compared with the total number of all Sanctions to obtain a percentage of Sanctioning—Convergent.

In order to ascertain what percentage of the oral communications of teachers were informational, the index of Total Information Handling was determined in relation to the total number of communications.

All the question-asking subcategories of Information—namely, Child Hypothesis, Child Observation, and Lecture Questions—were grouped in the index of Information Handling—Total Questioning. The percentage of this index was calculated in terms of all communications classified as Information.

Out of the total questioning subcategories of Information, the more open questions, Child Hypothesis and Child Observation, were grouped and compared to all Information for the index of Information Handling—Open Questioning. This grouping of teacher communications was assumed to have the function of stimulating autonomous thinking on the part of the child.

In order to ascertain what percentage of the oral communications of the teacher were procedural, an index of Total Procedure Handling was determined in relation to the total number of communications.

All the cooperative communication subcategories in Procedures, Child Standards, and Child Procedures were grouped and compared with all Procedures to determine the percentage for the index of Procedure Handling—Reflective.

Samples of Cooperating Teachers

In the preservice program on which this study was based, two student teachers usually worked with one cooperating teacher. The student teachers were rotated every few weeks to different cooperating teachers and children.

---

* In this and other indices, it is important to recognize that some indices were calculated on the basis of all communications while others were calculated on the basis of a category of communications. An index of Total Sanctioning was not computed because Sanctions included both negative and positive factors.

Twenty-five student teachers had three cooperating teachers while four student teachers had two cooperating teachers during the period of this study. Twenty-eight cooperating teachers constituted the sample of teaching in this study.

In order to obtain a sample of the teaching of the cooperating teachers, a time of mutual convenience was arranged between the cooperating teacher and an observer. A minimum of twenty minutes of direct observation and no more than 120 oral communications of the cooperating teacher working with children in a variety of areas constituted a sample of teaching. Because the number of communications varied somewhat, all frequencies were converted to percentages in order to allow comparisons to be made.

Indices of Teaching Style

Since each general category in the Joyce manual is composed of different subcategories, equal means for a general category could still conceal basic differences in a subcategory. It was desirable to determine which subcategory contributed to the difference in means; thus the scores for cooperating teachers and student teachers were compared on the eight indices. Table 8.1 reveals that the differences between the groups could be accepted with confidence in six of the eight categories.

The cooperating teachers had lower mean scores than the student teachers on Sanctioning—Positive, Sanctioning—Convergent, Total Information Handling, and Procedure Handling—Reflective. On the other hand, the student

TABLE 8.1. Means, Standard Deviations, and *t* Ratios on Indices of Teaching Style of Twenty-nine Student Teachers and Their Cooperating Teachers

Index	Student Teachers		Cooperating Teachers		
	Mean	S.D.	Mean	S.D.	*t* Ratio
Sanctioning—Positive	.103	.036	.056	.018	−6.357*
Sanctioning—Negative	.203	.109	.374	.102	6.938*
Sanctioning—Convergent	.799	.098	.688	.178	−2.951*
Total Information Handling	.527	.080	.457	.078	−3.677*
Information Handling—Total Questioning	.388	.115	.430	.107	1.422
Information Handling—Open Questioning	.116	.057	.091	.069	−1.512
Total Procedure Handling	.215	.055	.361	.082	7.873*
Procedure Handling—Reflective	.206	.111	.061	.043	−6.013*

* Indicates significance at the .005 level and greater for a one-tailed test. Critical *t* with 55 $df = \pm$ 2.663.

teachers scored lower than the cooperating teachers on Sanctioning—Negative and Total Procedure Handling. These differences are significant at the .005 level of confidence.

The differences indicated in the indices of teaching style were elaborated by the comparison of the subcategories.

Subcategories

As evidenced in Table 8.2, the two groups, looked at together by subcategories, show some similarities and some differences. Neither group often rewarded or punished search behavior and interpersonal behavior in group situations. They did not often give positive sanctions for following established procedures and negative communications of general approval. All percentages in these subcategories were less than 1 percent of the total communications. The two groups showed differences, however, in that student teachers gave

TABLE 8.2. Mean Percentage of Subcategories in Lessons of Twenty-eight Cooperating Teachers Combined and Total Lessons of Twenty-nine Student Teachers Combined

	Mean %	
Subcategory	Cooperating Teachers	Student Teachers
Search—Positive	0.6	0.2
Search—Negative	0.1	0.0
Group Process—Positive	0.2	0.1
Group Process—Negative	0.6	0.4
Attainment—Positive	3.2	8.3
Attainment—Negative	1.5	1.3
Following Rules—Positive	0.6	0.0
Following Rules—Negative	3.3	0.7
Support—Positive	0.7	1.8
Support—Negative	0.3	0.0
Child Hypotheses	0.4	0.1
Child Observation	3.8	6.1
Lecture Questions	16.6	14.1
Teacher Statements	21.2	27.4
Teacher Statements—Repeat	3.7	4.5
Teacher Concludes	1.1	0.6
Child Standards	0.3	0.0
Child Procedures	1.7	4.5
Teacher Determines Procedures—Group	19.3	12.4
Teacher Determines Procedures—Individual	13.0	4.6
Teacher Determines Standards	0.9	0.1
Transition	2.0	9.1
Small Talk	4.4	3.2
Discuss Routine	0.5	0.5

over twice as many rewards for learning a concept or skill than did the cooperating teachers. Their means were 8.3 percent, and 3.2 percent, respectively. Also, there was a slight tendency for the student teachers to be more supportive than the cooperating teachers (1.8 percent and 0.7 percent, respectively). The cooperating teachers, on the other hand, were more often negative in communications concerning established rules, their mean being 3.3 percent while that of student teachers was 0.7 percent.

The only similarity in information handling between the two groups was that neither group asked an appreciable percentage of questions requiring rigor of thinking; the percentage of communications for Child Hypothesis was less than ½ percent. Differences were more frequent. Cooperating teachers asked more recall questions (mean = 16.6 percent) than did student teachers (mean = 14.1 percent); also, they gave more conclusions (mean = 1.1 percent) than did the student teachers (mean = 0.6 percent). On the other hand, the student teachers made more statements (mean = 27.4 percent) than did the other group (mean = 21.2 percent); they repeated statements children made (means = 4.5 percent and 3.7 percent); and they asked almost twice as many speculating questions (mean = 6.1 percent) than did the cooperating teachers (mean = 3.8 percent).

Additional inspection of table 8.2 shows a similarity between the groups in that rarely did they give attention to teacher or child standards. The groups were different in that cooperating teachers involved children less in determining procedures (1.7 percent) than did the student teachers (4.5 percent).

Further, table 8.2 shows a likeness in the groups in that routines were rarely discussed, about ½ percent of the communications being so classified. The groups were different in the amount of communications classified as Transitions—cooperating teachers had a mean of 2 percent while the mean for the student teachers was 9.1 percent. On the other hand, the cooperating teachers had a larger percentage, 4.4 percent, of communications classified as Small Talk than the student teachers, with 3.2 percent.

Summary and Conclusions

The findings of this study are consistent with the findings of other studies regarding cooperating teachers. Cooperating teachers in this study did not utilize a significant number of communications that were classified as "Information Handling—Open Questioning," indicating that they did not frequently ask rigorous, open questions. They acted more as dispensers of information and definers of procedures than did the student teachers.

The student teachers were similar in their styles to the cooperating teachers in that they, too, dispensed information and defined procedures with a minimum of participation by the children in the development of ideas or procedures. Rarely did they ask a question that would help the children evaluate information, make inferences, advance problems, or help determine standards of performance. The near absence of these communications limited the possibilities of: (1) autonomous and creative thinking by children; (2) child-initiated seeking and searching for information; (3) expression of the child's unique meanings and perceptions; (4) discovering the individual learning mode of the child; and (5) children interacting with each other. In general, the absence of more open and expanding communication appeared to limit the possibilities of children's active engagement in the ongoing classroom processes. The inclusion of such communications might have expanded the parameters of the classroom environment for both teacher and child.

9

The Relationship between the Teaching Styles of Student Teachers and Those of Their Cooperating Teachers

Marvin Seperson and Bruce R. Joyce

For many years it has been assumed that there are considerable relationships between the teaching behaviors of individual student teachers and their cooperating teachers, and that these relationships are cumulative due to the influence of the cooperating teacher on the student teacher.

However, there are few reported investigations of the empirical dimensions of the relationships. One of the most widely quoted is that of Shirley Flint who studied student teachers and cooperating teachers at the Hunter College Laboratory School, using Medley and Mitzel's OSCAR (an observation system for studying teacher-pupil interaction). She found some patterns of relationship in several areas of teaching behavior. Her data were obtained during a relatively short teaching experience, and no long-term patterns of influence were measured, but a brief contact provides some confirmation of the common-sense belief. Brown's study (see chap. 8) of student teachers during "participation" experiences revealed no such relationships and, in fact, illustrated considerable differences between student teachers and cooperating teachers. The students displayed much more indirect, inquiry-oriented, supportive styles than did the cooperating teachers they were exposed to as models of teaching during the "preparation" experiences.

The present investigation into the development of teaching styles by young teachers, one of a long series of investigations at Teachers College, Columbia University, attempted to explore the relationship between the teaching behavior of student teachers and cooperating teachers over a semester (about fifteen weeks) of contact.

The subjects were nineteen teacher candidates in the preservice teacher education program at Teachers College. The student teachers were in a year-long master's degree teacher-education program. All were liberal arts graduates, and each of them engaged in "observation-participation" experiences during the first semester, that is, the fall of the year, and then in full-time student teaching during the second semester of their program.

Procedures

Four samples of the teacher candidates' teaching behavior were obtained during the "observation-participation" experience when they were working in tutorial sessions with small groups of children in language arts lessons. Tape-recordings were made of each of these four lessons, and the tape-recordings were coded according to the Joyce "Manual for Analyzing the Oral Communications of Teachers." [31] Two samples of their teaching behavior were obtained early in the second semester when they were with their cooperating teachers, one sample halfway through the semester, and two more late in their experience with the cooperating teachers. In addition, three samples of their cooperating teacher's behavior were obtained during the second semester. All samples of teaching behavior were obtained through live observation during the second semester.

Two types of analyses were made of these data. Indices of teaching behavior, eight in number, were computed for each student teacher for the "initial" contact with children, that is, the teaching experiences sampled in the fall of the year with small groups prior to exposure to their cooperating teachers; the "early" student-teaching behavior was sampled early in the second semes-

TABLE 9.1. Correlation Coefficients between the Mean Indices of Teaching Style for the Initial Teaching Style of Student Teachers and the Teaching Style of Cooperating Teachers

Index	Initial Style and Cooperating Teachers
Sanctioning—Positive	−.104
Sanctioning—Negative	−.256
Sanctioning—Convergent	−.402*
Total Information Handling	−.260
Information Handling— Total Questioning	−.511*
Information Handling— Open Questioning	−.476*
Total Procedure Handling	−.319
Procedure Handling—Reflective	−.095

* Indicates significance at the .05 level for a one-tailed test. Critical *r* with 17 *df* = .389.

ter, and the "later" student-teaching experience was sampled late in the second semester when they had been with the cooperating teachers for several weeks. The same indices were calculated for each cooperating teacher. Correlations were then made between the student teachers' behavior at the preteaching level, the "early" student-teaching level, and the "later" student-teaching level, with the indices of the cooperating teachers. Part correlations then removed the effect of the early relationships to determine whether there was a cumulative relationship between the early and later student-teaching behavior.

In addition, the means of each index were calculated for the initial teaching behavior, the early student-teaching behavior, and the later student-teaching behavior, and these were compared with the means for each index for the cooperating teachers. In this way, it was possible to determine whether the individual student teachers moved toward the indices of the cooperating teachers as individuals and whether the student teachers as a group became more like the cooperating teachers with whom they worked.

Relationships between the Teaching Styles of the Cooperating Teachers and the Student Teachers

Table 9.1 presents the correlation coefficients between the indices for the initial teaching styles and the mean indices of teaching styles for the cooperating teachers.

The initial teaching style, it will be remembered, was determined from samples of the student-teaching behavior taken prior to the time when the student teachers had contact with their cooperating teachers. None of the correlations are positive. The pattern is negative, with three correlations significantly so. The negative pattern seems odd, but clearly there were no positive relationships.

Table 9.2 presents the coefficients of correlation between the indices computed for the early and later teaching styles of the student teachers and the indices of the cooperating teachers.

It can be seen that four of the eight indices of the early teaching styles are significantly correlated with the indices for the cooperating teachers, and that the others are positive, although they are not significant. Four of the eight coefficients between the later teaching style of the student teachers and the styles of the cooperating teachers are significant. These correlations represent substantial evidence that the teaching behavior of the student teachers had moved from no or negative association with the behavior of the cooperating teacher prior to student teaching to being significantly related to a number of important dimensions early in student teaching, a relationship that was maintained throughout student teaching.

Part correlations were computed to remove the effects of the associations

TABLE 9.2. Correlation between Teaching Style of Student Teachers and Teaching Style of Cooperating Teachers

Index	Early Teaching Style and Cooperating Teacher	Advanced Teaching Style and Cooperating Teacher
Sanctioning—Positive	.480	.291
Sanctioning—Negative	.334	.136
Sanctioning—Convergent	.497*	.377
Total Information Handling	.562†	.513†
Information Handling—Total Questioning	.214	.489*
Information Handling—Open Questioning	.358	.342
Total Procedure Handling	.479*	.578‡
Procedure Handling—Reflective	.163	.537†

* Indicates significance at the .05 level for a one-tailed test. Critical *r* with 17 *df* = .389.
† Indicates significance at the .01 level for a one-tailed test. Critical *r* with 17 *df* = .528.
‡ Indicates significance at the .005 level for a one-tailed test. Critical *r* with 17 *df* = .575.

between the early styles of the student teachers and their cooperating teachers. The results of those calculations are presented in table 9.3.

It can be seen that three of the part correlations are significant, indicating that even after the effects of the initial relationship were removed, a significant relationship still existed in five of the eight indices. Hence, the cooperating teachers influenced the student teachers considerably during the early weeks of student teaching. In addition, their influence continued so that an even

TABLE 9.3. Coefficients of Part-Correlation between Indices of Teaching Styles of Student Teachers and Cooperating Teachers

Index	Student Teachers With One Cooperating Teacher (*n* = 19)
Sanctioning—Positive	.016
Sanctioning—Negative	.093
Sanctioning—Convergent	.266
Total Information Handling	.365
Information Handling—Total Questioning	.461*
Information Handling—Open Questioning	.163
Total Procedure Handling	.429*
Procedure Handling—Reflective	.517*

* Indicates significance at the .05 level for a one-tailed test. Critical *r* with 16 *df* = .400.

greater relationship was observed by the end of student teaching with respect to three of the eight indices.

Difference Scores

An analysis was made of difference scores in an effort to track the patterns influence more specifically over the five lessons. In table 9.4, the difference scores are presented for each of the five lessons. Each difference score was calculated by taking the index for each student teacher for each lesson and subtracting it from the mean of the cooperating teachers' indices.

It can be seen that the difference scores did not change appreciably through the five lessons and remained, in fact, about the same throughout the lessons. Thus, although student teachers' behavior became correlated with the behavior of their cooperating teachers in several important areas, differences in behavior existed and did not diminish entirely. Also, there are fairly large ranges indicating that some student teachers behaved quite differently from their cooperating teachers.

Interpretation

The evidence seems to indicate clearly that there were no relationships between the indices of the student teachers and cooperating teachers prior to their contact but that there were relationships in several of the indices very shortly after student teaching began, and the relationships continued even when they were adjusted for the early relationships. However, inspection of the difference scores revealed no consistent pattern of influence, once the early impact of the cooperating teacher had been felt.

The evidence supports the commonsense contention that the cooperating teacher substantially influences the behavior of the student teacher, and this evidence contradicts directly a finding in the previous study conducted by Brown [7] in which no significant relationships were found between the behavior of student teachers and their cooperating teachers.

However, in Brown's study two factors were different. The period of contact was much less, and the student teachers were able to teach small groups in situations that were relatively separate from the activity of the cooperating teachers.

In addition, more recent studies by Wald, Weil, Gullion, and Joyce [57] have indicated that student teachers often behaved in a manner similar to that of their cooperating teachers *except* when planning and carrying out learning activities by employing specific teaching strategies, when their behavior was in accord with the teaching strategies and, in most cases, very different from that of the cooperating teachers. Specifically, their behavior was more student-centered and at a higher cognitive level than it was when carrying out activities planned with the cooperating teacher.

TABLE 9.4. Means and Ranges of Difference Scores Between Eight Indices of Behavior of Student Teachers and Their Cooperating Teachers

	Differences									
	Lesson #1		Lesson #2		Lesson #3		Lesson #4		Lesson #5	
Index	Mean	(Range)	Mean	(Range)	Mean	(Range)	Mean	(Range)	Mean	(Range)
Sanctioning—Positive	.05	(.18)	.06	(.29)	.05	(.22)	.05	(.19)	.05	(.25)
Sanctioning—Negative	.23	(1.33)	.23	(1.23)	.19	(.96)	.17	(.96)	.28	(1.56)
Sanctioning—Convergent	.27	(1.48)	.24	(1.36)	.23	(1.12)	.20	(1.03)	.21	(.84)
Total Information Handling	.11	(.47)	.08	(.44)	.12	(.51)	.10	(.42)	.09	(.66)
Information Handling—Total Questioning	.12	(.70)	.14	(.51)	.14	(.73)	.13	(.56)	.11	(.52)
Information Handling—Open Questioning	.11	(.50)	.11	(.40)	.15	(.81)	.13	(.54)	.12	(.58)
Total Procedure Handling	.08	(.35)	.08	(.34)	.08	(.45)	.07	(.24)	.09	(.73)
Procedure Handling—Reflective	.06	(.31)	.06	(.40)	.04	(.39)	.05	(.33)	.05	(.39)

It is worthwhile noting that the influence of the cooperating teacher was felt during the very early weeks of student teaching rather than being the result of a slow and cumulative impact. We had expected that the initial correlations might be relatively low with a gradual rise in the course of student teaching. Such was not the case. It may well be that the entire setting of student teaching influences the behavior of the student teacher almost immediately upon coming into contact with the cooperating teacher. For example, if a student teacher is put into a room where all the children are organized into small groups, and the task is to help those groups maintain their functioning and to plan with them, the student teacher is likely to have to play a facilitative role even if these new behaviors are somewhat awkward. If, on the other hand, s/he is put into a classroom where the children are lined up in neat rows, and the teacher always functions by talking to them from the front of the room, then the student teacher is likely to have to adopt a lectorial, recitative pattern of behavior, however awkward *that* may be for her/him. Hence, it may be that the cooperating teacher influences the student teacher not only by verbal behavior (which one would expect to be influential only slowly and over a long period of time), but also affects the student teacher by the entire setting that s/he creates. This setting may be influential very rapidly.

Be that as it may, the cooperating teacher apparently *is* a powerful influence for good or for ill. Since it is well known that most experienced teachers carry on deductive recitation-style teaching rather than inductive or inquiry-oriented teaching, the fact of the early influence on the student teacher should not be considered an unmixed blessing.

10

The Effects of Instructional Flexibility Training on Teaching Styles and Controlled Repertoire

Stewart Tinsman

A system of verbal behavior analysis and feedback entitled Instructional Flexibility Training [33] was used as an integral part of the training of student teachers at Teachers College, Columbia University, during the academic year of 1966–1967. It was intended to provide teachers with a systematic procedure for analyzing their classroom verbal behavior in order to recognize a variety of teaching strategies and to thereby develop flexibility of teaching style through enlarging their repertoire of learned teaching maneuvers.[21]

This integrated feedback system provides a means whereby prospective teachers can gain more control over their teaching behavior. Four steps are involved:

1. Learning to discriminate among environments by analyzing and describing classroom teaching verbal behavior. This is accomplished by using the "Manual for Analyzing the Oral Communications of Teachers (31, App. A)," developed by Joyce. This classroom observation instrument establishes behavioral categories and subcategories of classroom verbal behavior derived from the Conceptual Systems Theory. Using it, the trainee can learn to analyze teaching behavior from different frames of reference, that is, social climate, content, teaching strategies, etc.

2. Developing the prospective teacher's ability to analyze and discriminate among his/her own teaching behaviors. Using audio/video tape feedback, s/he can determine her/his initial teaching style and identify strengths and weaknesses.

3. Setting behavioral goals consistent with increasing his/her repertoire of teaching strategies.

4. Learning to radiate a wide range of training environments, through experimentation, feedback, and analysis.

Design and Procedures of the Study

This study on "controlled flexibility" was designed * to test the effectiveness of using Instructional Flexibility Training for enhancing a student teacher's ability to control the flexibility of his/her teaching behavior, and (2) to determine the relationship, if any, between that ability and teacher conceptual level.

Two hypotheses were formulated:

Hypothesis 1: Student teachers who receive Instructional Flexibility Training will manifest greater controlled flexibility [1] in their teaching styles than student teachers who do not receive Instructional Flexibility Training.

Hypothesis 2: Student teachers who function at a higher conceptual level will manifest greater controlled flexibility in their teaching styles than student teachers who function at a lower conceptual level.

To test the first hypothesis, fifty-four subjects were placed in experimental and control groups. The Paragraph Completion Test [49] was administered to all subjects to determine conceptual level. The initial teaching style variable was controlled by measuring the initial teaching style of subjects in both groups utilizing the "Manual for Analyzing the Oral Communications of Teachers." [31] (App. A) Both groups were required to teach an Initial Controlled Flexibility Lesson (Lesson 1, consisting of three different teaching models) near the beginning of a thirteen-week student-teaching assignment, and a Final Controlled Flexibility Lesson (Lesson 2, consisting of three teaching models) near the end of the assignment. The experimental group received an intensive short-term orientation to the Conceptual Systems Theory and Instructional Flexibility Training. Between Lessons 1 and 2 the experimental group received instruction in the four operational steps of Instructional Flexibility Training during weekly student-teaching seminars while the control group seminars were taught in the more conventional methodology of the standard teacher-education program.†

Therefore, in implementing the prescribed teaching models, if the trainees in the experimental group exercised significantly more controlled flexibility

---

* The term "controlled flexibility" is the investigator's. It was coined to differentiate the flexibility of teaching style brought about through direct intervention; i.e., the flexibility required of the student teachers to manifest prescriptive models of teaching used in this study, from the more general term "flexibility," which was originally used to describe a teacher's ability to shift his/her style at will; or, more lately, to adapt behavior to a learner; to meet the learner where s/he is conceptually and to produce a designated behavior.

† Preservice Program in Childhood Education, Teachers College, Columbia University, New York, 1967.

of teaching style than those of the control group, one could conclude that the application of Instructional Flexibility Training was effective in aiding prospective teachers to develop controlled flexibility of teaching style.

The dependent variable in this study was the controlled flexibility of teaching styles manifested by the student teachers in prescribed lessons, that is, the ability of the student teachers to select and employ a teaching maneuver appropriate to the attainment of a prescribed goal and to alter that maneuver appropriately when the goal was changed. Controlled flexibility was a consciously preplanned move to radiate a specific environment required by the teaching behavioral models outlined in the Initial and Final Controlled Flexibility Lessons of this study. Hunt and Joyce [23] maintain that this type of direct intervention—goal setting within lessons—is an essential step in the development of flexible modulation of teaching behavior.

Each of these lessons was divided into three phases, each phase requiring the subject to exercise a different theoretically based teaching model (see fig. 10.1). Because the purpose of Instructional Flexibility Training is to help teachers enlarge their repertoire of teaching behaviors, the phases were designed to use behaviors both manifested and not manifested in the trainees initial teaching styles.

The direct informational-authoritative procedural model is similar to the dominative teacher described by Anderson [4] or "direct influence" as defined by Flanders.[14] It combined two of the four basic teaching maneuvers that

FIGURE 10.1 Placement of Teaching Models in Controlled Flexibility Lessons.

INITIAL CONTROLLED FLEXIBILITY LESSON (Lesson 1)

Phase 1	Phase 2	Phase 3
Direct Informational-Authoritative Procedural Model (I3 I4 I5 P3 P4)*	Reflective Creative-Expressive Model (I2)	Cooperative Procedural Model (P1 P2)

FINAL CONTROLLED FLEXIBILITY LESSON (Lesson 2)

Phase 1	Phase 2	Phase 3
Cooperative Procedural Model (P1 P2)	Direct-Informational Authoritative Procedural Model (I3 I4 I5 P3 P4)	Reflective Inductive Thinking Model (I1)

* Codes (I3, etc.) refer to categories of verbal behavior designated on the coding grid of the "Manual for Analyzing the Oral Communications of Teachers."

Joyce and Harootunian [31] stress should be learned first in developing a repertoire of teaching maneuvers: (1) maneuvers to induce mastery of content and achievement of skills, and (2) maneuvers to structure activities. This model requires the teacher to radiate a dominant environment in which the teacher dispenses information, asks questions requiring the "right" answers, draws conclusions, presents the procedural directions, or sets the standards of behavior and work.

The cooperative procedural model requires the opposite type of teacher behavior. Using this model, the teacher behaves in such a way as to allow the pupils to share in the development of the standards of behavior or work to be maintained or achieved and in the formulation of procedures to be followed. This model corresponds to Joyce and Harootunian's maneuvers to induce self-direction. [31]

The reflective creative-expressive model requires the teacher to radiate an environment of freedom and support, allowing pupils to freely express themselves, encouraging them to present original and unique ideas, helping them to explore and experiment with their thoughts, rewarding invention, and being supportive about all sincerely meant creative expressions.

The reflective inductive thinking model requires the teacher to radiate a receptive atmosphere that encourages the pupils' inductive thought processes, it helps them to evaluate information, see relationships, identify organizing principles, make generalizations, form concepts, raise hypotheses, make references, or define and advance problems.

To radiate the appropriate environment prescribed by each of these models, it was necessary for each subject to change or "flex" his teaching style (controlled flexibility) twice within each lesson. In the first shift of Lesson 1 the prescription was to decrease direct informational-authoritative procedural environment and initiate reflective-creative expressive and indirect informational behaviors. In the second shift, these latter behaviors were to be decreased and a cooperative procedural environment exercised. The first shift in Lesson 2 required that cooperative procedural behavior be discontinued and flexed into a direct informational-authoritative procedural environment. In the second shift that environment was to be changed into reflective-inductive thinking and indirect informational behaviors.

The extent to which a student teacher followed a prescribed teaching model in each phase of the required lessons was measured as a percentage index showing the degree to which the student teacher manifested the behavior prescribed in the teaching model as contrasted with other behavior (see fig. 10.2). Controlled flexibility of behavior was represented by the difference between like behavioral percentage indices during shifts between phases in each of the Initial and Final Controlled Flexibility Lessons.

The second hypothesis was tested by comparing the conceptual levels of the student teachers, as measured on the Paragraph Completion Tests, to the abilities of the student teachers to control the flexibility of their teaching styles, as indicated by differences in like percentage index means during shifts

FIGURE 10.2 Percentage Index Designations and Teacher Behavior Ratios for Each Teaching Model.

Teaching Model	Percentage Index Designation	Teaching Behavior Ratios
Supportive	A	$\dfrac{S+}{\text{Total } S}$
Reflective-Inductive Thinking	B	$\dfrac{I1}{\text{Total } I}$
Reflective-Creative Expressive	C	$\dfrac{I2}{\text{Total } I}$
Indirect Informational	D	$\dfrac{I1 + I2}{\text{Total } I}$
Direct Informational	E	$\dfrac{I3 + I4 + I5}{\text{Total } I}$
Cooperative Procedural	F	$\dfrac{P1 + P2}{\text{Total } P}$
Authoritative Procedural	G	$\dfrac{P3 + P4}{\text{Total } P}$
Direct Informational-Authoritative Procedural	H	$\dfrac{I3 + I4 + I5 + P3 + P4}{\text{Total } I + \text{Total } P}$

between phases of the two lessons. According to Conceptual Systems Theory, a trainee who operates at a high level of cognitive complexity would be able to exercise a high degree of controlled flexibility of teaching behavior. Conversely, the trainee who functions at a low conceptual level would exhibit little ability to exercise flexibility of teaching style.

Results of the Study

A comparison of the initial or preferred teaching styles of the experimental and control groups demonstrated that their styles were similar and that there were no statistically significant differences for any of the twenty-four subcategories as described in the manual. Both groups manifested considerably more direct-authoritative than indirect-cooperative behavior. They exhibited a limited amount of reflective-creative expressive and cooperative procedural behavior but almost no behavior to develop inductive thinking or cooperative standards.

In performing the Initial and Final Controlled Flexibility Lessons both groups generally exhibited teaching styles similar to their initial teaching styles, that is, they manifested more direct-authoritative than indirect-cooperative behavior. They both reduced their positive sanctioning, direct informational talk, and social system maintenance behavior, while increasing their indirect informational talk and authoritative and cooperative procedural behavior. There were no statistically significant differences between the performances of the experimental and control groups in the behaviors manifested in the aforementioned twenty-four subcategories.

Figure 10.3 displays the percentage index means attained by the experimental and control groups for those teaching maneuvers required by the model in each phase of each lesson. To show the shift in required behaviors, the phase immediately preceding and/or following the phase in which the behavior was required has been included. For example, the percentage index C mean for phases 1, 2, and 3 of Lesson 1 is shown, although the reflective creative-expressive model (C) was required only in phase two. Inspection shows the predominance of direct informational-authoritative procedural behavior (H) demonstrated in both lessons by both groups. The inability of each group to reduce substantially this direct-authoritative behavior when a shift was to be made is shown. In contrast, the shifts in indirect informational (D),

FIGURE 10.3   Percentage Index Means for Teaching Models in Phases 1, 2, and 3 of Lessons 1 and 2 for Experimental and Control Groups.

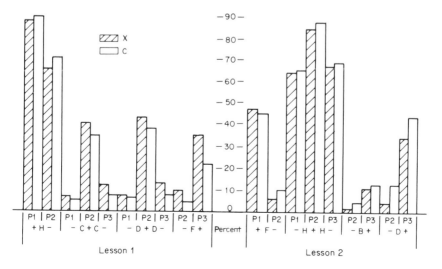

reflective-creative expressive (C), and cooperative-procedural (F) models were relatively more pronounced. Both groups encountered difficulty in radiating a reflective-inductive thinking environment (B), but the almost complete absence of this behavior in the experimental group during the phase immediately preceding the phase in which it was required, and the subsequent "flexing" to this required behavior, appear to indicate that the experimental group was beginning to make a conscious effort to manifest this seldom-used teaching behavior.

Means and range distributions for each shift of each lesson for the experimental and control groups are shown in figure 10.4. A comparison of the means of the experimental group and the control group on like indices indicates that none of the differences in performance of controlled flexibility between the two groups in both lessons were statistically significant (see table 10.1). Therefore, the null hypothesis must be accepted. However, it is important to note that (1) the experimental group did manifest more controlled flexibility on all indirect, reflective, and cooperative indices, although those differences were not statistically significant; and (2) both groups exercised considerably more positive sanctioning when demonstrating the indirect and cooperative models than when manifesting the direct and authoritative maneuvers. This latter difference was significant at the .005 level.

The evidence does indicate that both groups were able to shift their teaching behavior to manifest the prescribed teaching models in each controlled flexibility lesson. They were able to exercise the direct-informational, authoritative procedural, and cooperative procedural models. They were also able to mani-

FIGURE 10.4 Percentage Index Difference Means and Range Distributions by Shifts in Lessons 1 and 2 for Experimental and Control Groups.

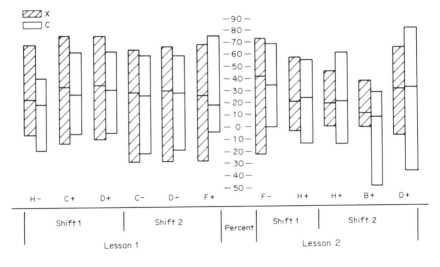

TABLE 10.1. Values of Kruskal-Wallis Statistic H for Selected Indices by Lesson and Shift

Lesson, Shift and Index	H-Values	Sample Size Exp.	Cont.
Lesson 1			
Shift 1			
Index H	1.96	27	25
C	.66	27	25
D	.16	27	25
Shift 2			
Index C	.28	28	19
D	.06	28	19
F	.02	28	19
Lesson 2			
Shift 1			
Index F	.74	25	26
H	1.36	25	26
Shift 2			
Index H	1.69	25	26
B	.11	25	26
D	.09	25	26

The value of chi square at the .05 level of significance and for observed value of $df = 1$ is 3.84.

fest the reflective-creative expressive and more general indirect informational models. The fact that both groups were able to control their behavior to initiate a reflective-inductive thinking maneuver, although this behavior was not a part of their initial teaching styles, indicates that direct intervention is fruitful in developing flexibility of teaching style.

With reference to the second hypothesis (that student teachers with a higher conceptual level will show greater controlled flexibility), the results of the Paragraph Completion Test indicated that the conceptual levels of all subjects in both groups measured on the lower end of the concreteness-abstractness continuum. On a scale of one to seven the range of fifty-four subjects' scores was 1.0 to 3.3 (experimental and control group means were 2.11 and 2.14 respectively), demonstrating that the thinking patterns of all subjects were considerably more concrete than abstract. The lack of abstract teaching did not allow for a true test of the hypothesis. This study effectively demonstrates that student teachers having low levels of conceptual development are able to follow the structured models they were required to teach within lessons, shifting between the models as required. These models included some teaching behaviors that were evident and some that were not evident in the initial teaching styles of the student teachers. Although the models that were not among those in the preferred styles of the prospective teachers were not manifested to the extent of those that were, the shifts and maneuvers exhibited were enough to demonstrate that conscious efforts were being made to "flex" and that the models were manifested. The fact that the subjects in the present study could increase their indirect informational and cooperative procedural behaviors supports the research of Joyce and Hodges [33] who determined that trainees on less abstract conceptual levels could shift toward more reflective teaching styles as well as could those on more abstract levels.

The results of this study generally corroborate the findings of the previous research—that teacher trainees can learn to expand their repertoire of teaching maneuvers. Because both the experimental and control groups were successful in this task, it would appear that such accomplishment was functional; the subjects learned to acquire performance skills, rather than to progress and raise their conceptual levels. Thus one can conclude that it is possible to train trainees with low conceptual level scores to manifest reflective teaching styles, without increasing their conceptual level.

The very extensive feedback provided by the instructional flexibility training program was unsuccessful in modifying the range of behaviors manifested by the teacher. This was in sharp contrast to the relatively short training program in which teaching strategies requiring behavior not ordinarily manifested by the students could be induced by a "modelling and practice" treatment only. The relative ineffectiveness of feedback only fits with the findings by Huff, Amidon and Flanders that feedback generally arrests the flow of the teaching style toward directness but does not induce greater indirectness or flexibility in style.

The importance of the finding of this investigation lies in displaying the relative ineffectiveness of feedback only treatments but the relatively great power of intensive direct training in alternative teaching strategies. This finding encouraged us to begin an intensive series of investigations into teachers' ability to acquire varieties of models of teaching through direct training.

PART V

Models of Teaching: Experiments in the Development of Repertoire

The most difficult thing about teaching is that it is described in such chaotic ways. Also, much of the professional and popular literature about teaching is highly emotional and connotative. Some, describing teaching as an art, do so pugnaciously as if the very idea that applied science might be useful to the teacher is heretical. Getting results from learners is sometimes described as if the learner were only clay in the teacher's hands, or an object to be moved about a chess board. Teaching is sometimes described as a unique personal interaction with a student (which it is), as if it were not also a public process of concern to groups of children and the society as a whole. Some of the orientations for teacher education were previously described in chapter 1, ''The Roots of Humanity: Views of Humankind and the Education of Teachers.''

We must live, albeit uncomfortably, with the condition of linguistic uncertainty about teaching. There is presently no agreed-upon description of the teacher. In the next pages we will try to describe portions of our struggle to define teaching as flexibility. The concepts discussed below, and throughout this book, are in a state of emergence, but the fifty or so persons who have struggled to shape them have achieved some level of common understanding about what they mean as a result of their common efforts to conduct research on teaching, prepare teachers, and reflect on their own experience in the schools. In this section, we summarize some of our empirical and conceptual trials. It is included here to provide an overview of the effort and some of the flavor of the struggle, including the role that blunders and luck have contributed to our concepts.

Our first attempts at training were relatively nondirective. We helped teachers collect samples of their behavior on film, audio-tape, and television tape. Periodically, the teacher analyzed these behavior samples with instructors who taught them to use the category system developed to study teaching styles. Teachers made their own decisions about whether or not to change their behavior and, if so, in what direction. This work was very similar to that of Amidon and Hough. It culminated in the investigation by Tinsman (chapter 10) in which this kind of training was intensively administered over a period of several months. Following the formulation of the ''models of teaching'' framework, he began to intervene more directly in helping teachers discriminate and learn to apply the various models of teaching. A critical investigation in this series is reported in a paper by Joyce, Weil, and Wald, which is presented in chapter 12.

That research bore considerable fruit and validated our thesis that teachers could easily take on a wide repertoire of models of teaching, but that direct training was necessary in order to bring this about.

We thought for a while that, by studying teachers as they attempted to carry out wide varieties of models of teaching, we could identify generic teaching skills. A study by Weil tested that hypothesis but found that teaching skills appear to be less specific in nature. In fact, the entire series of studies confirmed one of our basic beliefs: that teachers are capable and desirous of radiating a wide variety of environments, of readily responding to training, and of enjoying growth in their capacity to reach learners in increasingly diverse ways.

11

A Structure for Pluralism in Teacher Education

Bruce R. Joyce, Marsha Weil, and Rhoada Wald

In 1968 a Columbia University team was funded to develop a model for the preparation of elementary school teachers. The model required a much more systematic definition of teacher competence than any we had available to us. We were challenged to choose ways in which teachers could discriminate learners from a variety of perspectives and could gain command of the ability to generate environments appropriate to the learner and his/her objectives. The paper that follows describes the struggle to identify a model of the teacher that could serve as the basis for a precise teacher-training program.

Tinsman conducted an experiment in which he tried to modify teachers' behavior through intensive feedback (see chapter 10). For nearly a year a group of young teachers spent two to three hours a week with instructors who helped them analyze audio and television tapes of their teaching and who taught them a category system for analyzing their behavior. The purpose of the study was to see if the teachers would begin to radiate a greater variety of environments which would show up as an increasing variety of behavioral patterns in their teaching. The goal of the experiment, thus, was to help teachers gain increasing control over their behavior so that they could shift from environment to environment as it was appropriate. The criterion measure for this study was a series of teaching tasks that required quite strenuous shifts in behavior. The teacher in the course of the tasks would have to teach first one way, then a second, and then a third. At first, we were very pleased with the results of the experiment, for the experimental group of teachers who had received the feedback and learned the category system for analyzing their behavior were, indeed, able to shift from environment to environment with relative fluency. However, much to our surprise, a control group of teachers who had had a conventional experience also were able to complete the tasks successfully. The confusing aspect of the study was that both the experimental and control groups of teachers, when carrying out the teaching tasks, manifested teacher behaviors and a degree of flexible control over them that none of them had manifested during the year. In other words, the teaching tasks themselves elicited controlled flexibility and behavior to a degree that we had not seen before. It began to occur to us that it might be easier to teach teachers patterns or models of behavior rather than smaller units of behavior and to accompany these patterns with rationales for their use.

The basic concepts described in this chapter are relatively simple ones; their application and practice are more difficult. Teachers need to learn to read cues for a variety of learners while they are "in flight" carrying out the business of living and learning. Next, they have to synthesize these cues with their conception of the human being, and select and generate environments that are tuned to both the learner and the objectives, continuously modifying their behaviors as the learners respond or fail to respond to instruction. The Joyce-Dirr-Hunt study (chapter 6), in which the investigators attempted to pull teachers rapidly into the ability to "tune in" to learners, demonstrated the difficulty of doing this in laboratory or simulated settings, and it may be even more difficult for teachers to do this in the field. This work led eventually to studies of teachers' perceptions of their learners and the nature of the decisions which they make as they teach (see Part VII). It also led to the necessity to construct a way of describing educational environments in terms that teachers can comprehend and master. The development of a structure for thinking about and mastering alternative environments is the subject of chapter 13.

In this section we present the thesis that the practices and technologies of education can be described in terms of models for solving curricular and instructional problems. We contend that these models constitute the technology of education and it is from them that a content of training programs for teachers and curriculum-makers, and materials and procedures can be selected. An educator can be trained to a repertoire of few or many models and, at the highest level, be trained to develop personal models and thus add to the substance of the profession.

Although it is tempting to begin with a justification of our approach, our rhetoric will be clearer, stronger, and more vulnerable if we describe what we mean first by models for teaching. Hence, the paper is organized around the following sequence of questions:

How can we identify a model?

How can a model be analyzed and described for training purposes?

What are the advantages and disadvantages of such an approach to educational training? (We will concentrate on the advantages and hope to provoke discussion.)

HOW CAN WE IDENTIFY A MODEL FOR TEACHING?

We begin with some fairly typical teaching by three social studies teachers in three separate classrooms of a large metropolitan high school. All three teachers are working with sixteen-year-old students. Their classes are comparable, with a wide range of abilities and life experiences represented within each classroom. Their common task is to engage the students in the study of civil rights for black citizens in the United States. Emphasis is on voting rights and their exercise.

THE GROUP INVESTIGATOR

As we observe the first classroom we find that the teacher has presented his class with the Civil Rights Commission's pamphlet, *Voting Rights in Mississippi*. The pamphlet contains a report by a federal commission which details, in cases and interviews, attempts to thwart black voting rights in Mississippi. The students are angered by what they are reading, but their reactions vary, especially as they conjecture about the causes of the situation. The teacher is capitalizing on the differences in reaction and is organizing the students to explore their reactions, study how others feel, and engage in a cooperative inquiry into the whole area.

The teacher obviously enjoys teaching this way. He takes the discord among students seriously but is not bothered by it; rather, he seeks to use the involvement that is generated. "I teach through my relationship with the kids," he says. "We develop the relationship and then I confront them with puzzling situations that get them into significant study. The group interaction is the thing."

THE STUDENT OF CASES

In the second classroom we find students studying a series of "cases" involving black voting rights. The teacher has purchased some of the case materials and assembled others himself. Altogether there are twelve cases: some focusing on constitutional provisions, amendments, and statutes; some centered on litigation; and some on drives to increase black participation through combinations of litigation, registration drives, and confrontation. For each case there is a set of original source documents. Working in groups, the students investigate the cases and report their findings, which are then discussed by the entire class.

This teacher is a good organizer. He likes history himself and has done a series of short studies on local political history. He feels that the methods of history are essential if students are to learn to dig out the truth of their heritage. "The facts will leave them," he says, "but if they can get the method they can use it all their lives."

Before undertaking the study, the students read a case study of a historian who had done a similar analysis of documents related to the development of the Massachusetts state government. The students are trying to employ some rigorous methodology used by the historian in his work.

THE LECTURER

The third classroom is organized around a series of well-prepared, systematic lectures describing the subject from a social psychologist's point of view. The students are assigned readings correlated with the lectures. For example, when the teacher treats the reaction to deprivation of rights, students may read Eldridge Cleaver's *Soul on Ice,* although the lecture is not about the book as such, but includes a variety of responses. Excerpts from *Caste and Class in a Southern Town* are more directly tied in by the lectures.

"I really love to lecture," this teacher says. "Some people are against lecturing, but I believe that students need a good, strong, intellectual structure to help them comprehend complex social problems. So I lay out the structure and tie it to critical social issues. I am good at this and they usually like it."

All three classes have the same objective, and all three are studying what ostensibly is the same problem. Yet the three teachers are using very different approaches, even over common content. One is employing a group inquiry that emerges as the students identify issues and become involved in them. The teacher facilitates their study, but the students, as a group, develop their own investigation into the social issue. The second teacher is employing historical methodology; his students are analyzing documents as a historian would. Through lectures, the third teacher helps his students consider social problems within the intellectual framework of the social psychologist. (Imagine the differences that could have resulted if the content had varied more!) What other approaches might have been tried? What would be their advantages? What kind of teacher and student behavior is essential to each? What kinds of instructional materials are necessary? What views of learning and teaching give rise to the alternative approaches which might be tried? How much is the approach related to the personality of the teacher? How much should teaching be varied to reach different students?

There exists a wide variety of approaches to teaching. Moreover, there are many kinds of "good" teaching. The concept "good," when applied to teaching, is better stated "good for what?" Whether one is creating a curriculum plan, developing a course or a unit of study, developing instructional materials, or deciding what to do in response to the behavior of a student, there are many possible courses of action. A model for teaching is a coherent pattern, an abstract plan, which can be used to shape a curriculum or course, develop instructional materials, or guide the teacher's actions. As we examine models and learn their uses, we find that the task of selecting an appropriate model for any task is complex and that the forms of "good" teaching are numerous, even for any one purpose. Teaching can be described as a process by which teacher and students create a shared reality (agreements about what exists) and a shared set of values and beliefs (agreements about what is important). These in turn color reality and result in long-term motivational effects on students. The "models" of teaching that govern the teaching activities in any school have much to say about the kinds of realities that will be admitted to the classroom and the kinds of life-view that are likely to be generated as teacher and learner work together. Thus it is not surprising that people care greatly about the models they use and seek the perfect model. We find it desirable to begin by challenging the idea that there is any such thing.

The One-Right-Way Fallacy

As in the case of art, good teaching is something that many people feel they can recognize on sight, although they have difficulty expressing a reasoned basis for their judgment. Hence, implicit in many discussions about teaching is the notion that there is probably a certain kind of teaching that is really better than all other kinds. We hear of "child-centered" teaching, "inductive" teaching, "inquiry," teachers who "really work the kids," others who "really make it interesting," curriculums that are "process centered," and materials built on "behavior-modification" principles. The usual implication is that there exists a certain definable way of working with students that helps them to grow more than any other way would.

The research evidence on this question is remarkably ambiguous. There have been several hundred studies comparing one general teaching method to another, and whether curriculums are being compared, or specific methods for teaching specific subjects, or counseling sessions where different approaches are tried, the overwhelming proportion of these studies show few, if any, differences among approaches.* The results are difficult to interpret, but the evidence to date does not give encouragement to those who would hope that we have identified a single, reliable, multipurpose teaching strategy that we can use with confidence as the best approach. This conclusion annoys some people. Naturally, it bothers those who feel that they *do* know such a single broad method, and they are likely to say that the reason that one particular approach to teaching (their approach) has not yet been proven superior is because our ability to measure learning outcomes is not yet sophisticated enough to detect the true power of *their* preferred strategy.

---

* A good example of evidence and opinion which gives cause to those who feel that the issues about how to teach are largely settled in favor of inductive teaching procedures is the fine collection of essays in Lee S. Shulman and E. R. Karslar, eds., *Learning by Discovery: A Critical Analysis* (Chicago: Rand McNally, 1966).

This position may be correct. The art of measuring the outcomes of learning is still in its infancy, particularly with respect to the education of the emotions, the growth of personality, intellectual development, and creativity. It seems reasonable to suppose that, as our technology for studying teaching and learning improves, people will discover regularities in the teaching process that have not been apparent before. A few general methods *may* emerge as superior.

However, we can look at the problems of identifying and choosing teaching strategies from quite a different perspective if we hold in abeyance, pending better evidence, the search for a single right way and concentrate instead on the possibilities—the realities to be created—of the variety of models for teaching which our heritage has given us. Particularly, it behooves us to identify the approaches that made contact with individual students and to use those approaches to develop an environment in which students are facilitated in their development.

The Search for Good Teaching: "Who Focuses on What?"

If we look at the work of those interested in teaching and learning, we find that most educators concentrate on improving the creativity of the student. When they enter a classroom and begin to make contact with the student, they find themselves thinking about whether or not that student is creative, what kind of creativity may be involved, and what can be done either to awaken or to sustain the development of that creativity. Approaches to nurturing creativity are varied. Some feel that it is a spontaneous thing and that we can't do much to induce it, but that we should reward it as it appears by fanning the natural spark of creativity in the student. Others feel that it is best promoted by making the learner engage in creative activity, rather than by waiting for it to arise. Still others feel that social influences are most critical, and they attempt to put the student into an environment in which creativity is highly prized and in which s/he will see many others being creative, and thus will imitate them.

Other educators, encountering the same student, may not focus on creativity at all. Some, for instance, will be concerned primarily with mental health. When they observe the student, they will focus on self-concept, integratedness, and ego development. As in the case of creativity-oriented educators, those oriented toward mental health recommend differing approaches. Some specialize in human relations training. Others emphasize a reflective counseling relationship. Still others use awareness training. The preferred approaches are rooted in beliefs or theories about the process of growth.

In other words, educational procedures are generated from general views about human nature and about the kinds of development and environments that enhance the existence of human beings. Because of their frames of reference—their views of humanity—educators are likely to focus on specific kinds of learning outcomes and to favor certain ways of creating educational environments (which is another way of saying "teaching"). When an educator possesses an identifiable focus and a frame of reference that rationalizes it, we can then say that s/he has a model for teaching. S/he can tell us what aspects of the student are of particular interest, and what aspects of the environment are most important for growth, and we can, if we want to, model ourselves after this stance toward learning.

The workday lives of these model-builders represent a number of types of activity. Some educators who use characteristic models are practitioners, teaching in or organizing schools that describe and demonstrate their models. For example, A. S. Neill, the well-known headmaster of Summerhill School, has written and lectured extensively on his model and, of course, directs the work at Summerhill,[108] which emphasizes the role of the school in further-ing personal development and adjustment. Other model-builders engage in research as well. For fifteen years Paul Torrance has conducted studies on the fostering of creativity,[149] and the essence of his model lies in the character of his research. His frame of reference emphasizes the importance of helping students learn to originate solutions to problems—he envisions a world of cooperative, socially committed, but independently creative citizens. Some researchers conduct studies in schools and other field situations. For example, B. F. Skinner, after years of laboratory work, developed models of teaching and began to engage in field studies,[137] to work out his concern that the environmental shaping of behavior be deliberate and humane rather than accidental and, therefore, with unpredictable side effects.

Still others engage in the development of models by speculating about the implications of the nature of the subject disciplines and how to teach them. We have identified a large number of models for teaching derived from the work of persons who have developed or speculated on theories about child development or theories about the learning process. For example, although the noted Swiss psychologist Jean Piaget has conducted a massive line of research into the intellectual development of children, he has not interpreted his work extensively in terms of teaching or curriculum develop-ment. However, many others have given this area attention and have at-tempted to develop models for teaching based on Piaget's theories, stressing the importance of intellectual growth, and the role of the school in fostering that growth.

In recent years many educators have sought to translate academic disci-plines into teachable forms, and many kinds of curriculum projects have resulted, designed to teach the central ideas and research processes of the academic disciplines. Models have resulted as well from attempts to improve the society—even to reform it radically. From Plato [114] through Thoreau [145] to Dewey [29] and present-day social reformers, people have developed educa-tional models designed to socialize children to an improved social order or to prepare citizens who will develop a more perfect society. A good many humanistic educators stress the role of the school in improving social life and improving the culture.

Over the years, then, many educational models have been developed by people engaged in distinctly different kinds of educational activity. Some are based on empirical work, others on theories, some on hunches, and some on speculation about the meaning of theories and research done by others. These models have implications for curriculum (the planning of major programs of study), for the work of teachers when they are with children, and for the development of instructional materials. Educational models, in other words, can be used in three ways: for the making of curriculum plans, as guidelines for the teacher's interaction with students, and as specifications for instructional materials. All these represent a form of teaching, although only the second represents interactive teaching, which is what most people refer to when they speak of teaching.

In the last few years we have attempted to identify a large number of defensible models of teaching and examine their potential usefulness. We see these models as a reservoir of interactive teaching strategies and as a practical guide to educational literature and research. This reservoir should help the teacher identify a good number of teaching strategies, which can be used to try to achieve a considerable variety of educational purposes and to make productive contact with widely differing children. This reservoir should also have the same sort of function for curriculum makers, those who build instructional materials, and those who educate teachers. We hope to generate a dialogue about the possible models of teaching that are available to us as educators and to help curriculum makers, the creators of instructional materials, and teacher educators identify the range of educational strategies that they might employ in their work and alternative ways of developing those strategies into balanced programs for children.

THE SELECTION OF THE MODELS

So many people have developed positions on learning that can be used as models that the selection of the models to be treated was formidable. Educators, psychologists, sociologists, systems analysts, psychiatrists, and many others have produced theoretical positions about learning and teaching. Curriculum development projects, schools and school districts, and organizations representing particular curriculum areas or disciplines have also developed a large number of approaches to teaching and learning. The task of selection began with the development of a very long list of sources for models. Included on the list were the works of counselors and therapists, such as Carl Rogers,[119] Erik Erikson,[30] and Abraham Maslow.[98] Included also were learning theorists such as B. F. Skinner,[136] David Ausubel,[7] and Jerome S. Bruner.[20] The works of developmental psychologists such as Jean Piaget,[113] Larry Kohlberg,[94] David E. Hunt [59] and others were identified. Philosophers such as John Dewey,[29] William James,[72] and Harry S. Broudy [16] were included. Curriculum development projects in the academic subjects provided many examples, as did specialists in group dynamics. The patterns of teaching from the great experimental schools, such as Summerhill, made their way onto our list. Altogether, more than eighty theorists, schools, and projects were identified on the initial list.

As we examined the patterns of teaching from our first list, we discarded some names because their ideas seemed too vague to provide general models that could be communicated to a good many people. Other models were eliminated because the advocates of the models, while they were explicit enough about the specific things that teachers or curriculums should do, paid inadequate attention to rationalizations for their models, so that it was not easy to tell why they advocated those models or why they could be reasonably expected to achieve their intended aims. The remaining models fit the criteria of being communicable and rationalized.

Gradually, we began to group the models on the basis of the sources of reality on which theorists drew as they focused on the learner and his environment. Eventually, we organized the models into four families that represented different orientations toward humans and their universe. Although there was much overlapping, the four were: (1) those oriented toward *social relations* and toward the relation between the person and the culture, and which draw upon social sources; (2) those which depended on *information-processing* systems and descriptions of human capacity for processing information; (3) those that emphasized *personality development,* the processes of personal construction of reality, and the capacity to function as an integrated personality; and (4) those developed from an analysis of the processes by which human *behavior* is shaped, reinforced, and modified.

The social-interaction sources reflect a view of human nature which gives priority to social relations and the creation of a better society. They see the processes by which reality is socially negotiated as vitally important in human life. Consequently, the goals of this group were directed toward the improvement of the individual's ability to relate to others. Many of them developed from a desire to improve democratic processes and to educate students to improve the society. It must be stressed that the social relations orientation does not assume that social relations is the *only* important dimension of life. Social theorists are usually concerned with the development of the mind, the development of the self, and the learning of academic subjects; it is the rare theorist in education who is not concerned with more than one aspect of the learner's development or who does not use more than one aspect of the environment to influence the learner's development.

The second large family of models shares an orientation toward the information-processing capability of the student and systems which can be taught to improve such skills. By information processing we mean the ways people handle stimuli from the environment, organize data, sense problems, generate concepts and solutions to problems, and employ verbal and nonverbal symbols. Some of these models are concerned with the ability of the learner to solve certain kinds of problems and use studies of problem solving as a major source. Others concentrate on creativity, and yet others are concerned with general intellectual ability. Some emphasize the teaching of specific strategies for thinking, creative thinking, and thinking within academic disciplines. Again, however, it must be stressed that nearly all models from this family are also concerned with social relationships and the development of an integrated personality, although their primary sources are the student's capacity to integrate information and to process it; and systems, especially academic systems, which can help individuals to process data.

The third family shares an orientation toward the individual as the source of educational ideas. Frames of reference spotlight personal development and emphasize the processes by which the individual constructs and organizes his reality. Frequently they emphasize personal psychology and the emotional life of the individual. These models are directed toward the individual's internal organization as it affects relationships with the environment and the self. Some are concerned with the capacity to reach out into the milieu to make contact with others and to venture where one has not been before. Others are more oriented toward the feelings about the self—the self-image. Still others are concerned with helping to develop an authentic, reality-oriented view of the self and the society. Again, it is necessary to note that most of the models that are oriented around the development of the self are also concerned with the development of social relations and information-processing capacity. The distinctive feature of this category is the emphasis on personal development as a source of educational ideas. While its focus is on helping the person to view her/himself as a capable individual, it is expected that one of the products will be richer interpersonal relations and a more effective information-processing capacity. We refer to this family as the person-oriented family. None of our three teachers gave primacy to a person-oriented approach.

The fourth source of models has developed from attempts to build efficient systems for sequencing learning activities and shaping behavior by manipulating reinforcement. Students of reinforcement theory, such as B. F. Skinner, have used operant conditioning as their procedure. These behavior-modification theories rely on changing the external behavior of the student and describe him/her in terms of visible behavior. Operant conditioning has been applied to a wide variety of educational goals, ranging from military training to interpersonal behavior, and including those goals which characterize other model families.

Relationships Among the Four Families

Our families of models, therefore, are by no means antithetical to each other, and the actual prescriptions for developing learning environments that emerge from some of them are remarkably similar. Also, within the families certain of the models share many features, both with respect to goals and with respect to the kinds of means that they recommend.

Table 11.1 presents 16 models classified by family and annotated briefly. It is an illustrative list and does not include all the qualifying approaches which we have identified.

In order to describe the models as explicitly as we could (so they would be useful to a diverse clientele of educators) and to avoid doing violence to the original theories, we depicted the orientation or focus of the model, that is, the model's thesis, the kinds of goals the model builder focuses on and the reasons s/he believes that the particular means specified would be likely to achieve those goals, as well as the structure of the model.

The structure involves a description of the model in action. If a teacher were to use the model as the basis for teaching strategy, how would a lesson begin? What would happen first, second, third? What should be kept in mind in response to the activity of the learner? For example, one model begins with a presentation to the learner of a concept that is called an "advance organizer." This concept is given to the student verbally. In the second phase, the material to be learned is presented to the learner. This phase is followed by another in which the learner is helped to relate the material to the specific concept. These phases make up the structure or syntax of the model, the flow of events designed to influence the students or help them teach themselves. In a different model the first phase includes data collection by the students, then an organization of the data under concepts the students form themselves, and finally a comparison of the concepts developed with those developed by other people. These two models have a very different structure or set of phases, even though the same type of concept might emerge from both models, and they were, in fact, designed for somewhat different purposes, although both belong to the information-processing family. The first was designed for the mastery of material, and the second to teach students inductive thinking processes.

By comparing the structural phasing of models we are able to identify the operational differences between them and to make clear the roles a training agent must fulfill in order to make a model work. In table 11.2, for example, a teacher (or a mechanical agent) must trigger the concept-building activity of the second phase and shift the student's attention from the collection and identification of data to the development of concepts which group the data and otherwise make them comprehensible.

Principles of Reaction

Some models provide the teacher with principles to guide his/her reaction to student activity. In table 11.2 the teacher during Phase Two might reward concept-building activity and encourage students to compare their concepts.

TABLE 11.1. The Models of Teaching Classified by Family and Mission

Model	Major Theorist	Family or Orientation	Mission or Goals for Which Applicable
1. Inductive Model	Hilda Taba	Information Processing	Primarily for development of inductive and academic processes and academic reasoning or theory building, but these capacities are useful for personal and social goals as well.
2. Inquiry Training	Richard Suchman	Information Processing	
3. Science Inquiry Model	Joseph J. Schwab (also much of the Curriculum Reform Movement; see Jerome S. Bruner's *The Process of Education* for the rationale)	Information Processing	Designed to teach the research system of the discipline but also expected to have effects in other domains (i.e., sociological methods may be taught in order to increase social understanding and social problem solving).
4. Jurisprudential Teaching Model	Donald Oliver and James P. Shaver	Information Processing	Designed primarily to teach the jurisprudential frame of reference as a way of processing information but also as a way of thinking about and resolving social issues.
5. Concept Attainment	Jerome S. Bruner	Information Processing	Designed primarily to develop inductive reasoning.
6. Developmental Model	Jean Piaget Irving Sigel Edmund Sullivan	Information Processing	Designed to increase general intellectual development, especially logical reasoning, but can be applied to social and moral development as well (see Kohlberg).

TABLE 11.1. (*Continued*)

Model	Major Theorist	Family or Orientation	Mission or Goals for Which Applicable
7. Advance Organizer Model	David Ausubel	Information Processing	Designed to increase the efficiency of information-processing capacities to meaningfully absorb and relate bodies of knowledge.
8. Group Investigation	Herbert Thelen John Dewey	Social Interaction	Development of skills for participation in democratic social process through combined emphasis on interpersonal and social (group) skills and academic inquiry. Aspects of personal development are important outgrowths of this model.
9. Social Inquiry	Byron Massialas Benjamin Cox	Social Interaction	Social problem solving primarily through academic inquiry and logical reasoning.
10. Laboratory Method	National Training Laboratory (NTL) Bethel, Maine	Social Interaction	Development of interpersonal and group skills and, through this, personal awareness and flexibility.
11. Non-Directive Teaching	Carl Rogers	Person	Emphasis on building capacity for self-instruction and, through this, personal development in terms of self-understanding, self-discovery, and self-concept.
12. Classroom Meeting Model	William Glasser	Person	Development of self-understanding and self-responsibility. This would have latent benefits to other kinds of functioning, i.e., social.

TABLE 11.1. *(Continued)*

Model	Major Theorist	Family or Orientation	Mission or Goals for Which Applicable
13. Awareness Training	William Schutz Fritz Perls	Person	Increasing personal capacity for self-exploration and self-awareness. Much emphasis on development of interpersonal awareness and understanding.
14. Synectics	William Gordon	Person	Personal development of creativity and creative problem-solving.
15. Conceptual Systems Model	David E. Hunt	Person	Designed to increase personal complexity and flexibility. Matches environment to student.
16. Operant Conditioning	B. F. Skinner	Behavior Modification	General applicability. A domain-free approach, though probably most applicable to information-processing functioning.

TABLE 11.2. Illustration of Phasing in Models

	Phase One	**Phase Two**	**Phase Three**
Illustrative Model #1	Presentation of Concept	Presentation of Data	Relating of Data to Concepts
Illustrative Model #2	Presentation of Data	Development of Categories by Students	Identification and Naming of Concepts

In some models the teacher overtly tries to shape behavior by rewarding some student activities and maintaining a neutral stance toward others. In others the teacher tries not to manipulate rewards but maintains carefully equal status with the students.

These principles help the teacher select the reactions s/he will make as interaction with the students emerges. They provide him/her with rules of thumb by which students can be gauged and responses selected according to what the student does.

The Social System Specified by the Model

We also felt it was important to describe the model's social system. To do so we used three subconcepts: a description of student-teacher roles, a description of the hierarchical or authority relationships, and a description of the kinds of norms that are encouraged (the student behavior that is rewarded). The leadership roles of the teacher vary greatly. In some models s/he is a reflector or facilitator of group activity, in others a counselor of individuals, and still others a taskmaster. The second concept, hierarchical relationships, is explained in terms of the sharing of initiatory activity by teacher and learner, the location of authority, and the amount of control over activity that emerges from the process of interaction. Some models use the teacher as the center of activity and the source of input: as the organizer and pacer in the situation. Others provide for relatively equal distribution of activity between teacher and student, while some place the student at the center. Finally, different kinds of student behavior are rewarded in different models. In some, the student is rewarded for getting a job done and sticking to a prescribed line of inquiry. In others, the student rewards her/himself by knowing that s/he has learned something.

One way to describe a teaching model is according to the degree the learning environment is structured. That is, as roles, relationships, norms, and activities become less prescribed or externally imposed and more emergent and within the students' control, we can say that its social system is less structured.

Support System Specified by the Model

Another question we ask is what support was needed in order to create the environment specified by the model? That is, what are the additional requirements beyond the *usual* human skills and capacities and technical facilities? For example, the human relations model may require a trained leader; the nondirective model may require a particular personality; that is, an exceedingly patient, supportive one. Suppose that a model postulates that students should teach themselves with the roles of teachers limited to consultation and facilitation. What support is necessary? Certainly a classroom filled only with textbooks would be limiting and prescriptive. Rather, support in the form of books, films, self-instructional systems, travel arrangements, and the like is necessary.

The support requirements are derived from two sources—the role specifications for the teacher and the demands of the substantive nature of the experiences. Support requirements are real. Many able educational programs fail because of failure to consider or anticipate the support requirements. As a result, we feel that considering the support system is as much a part of making a model happen as learning the model itself.

General Applicability of the Model

We described the purposes of the models. Some models are designed for very specific purposes, while others have general application. Some are designed only to improve certain aspects of interpersonal relations, whereas others are intended for a wide range of academic purposes and for personal development as well. Some behavior-modification models are designed to affect *any* type of student behavior by changing responses to the environment.

Environmental effects can be direct and designed to come from the content and skills which are the bases of curricular activities, or they can be latent or implicit in the life of the environment. One fascinating aspect of models is the implicit learnings they engender. For instance, a model which emphasizes academic discipline can also (but need not) emphasize obedience to authority. Or one which encourages personal development can (but need not) beg questions about social responsibility.

Therefore, the effects of models can be categorized into the direct or *instructional* effects and indirect or *nurturant* effects. The instructional effects are those directly achieved by leading the learner in certain directions. The nurturant effects come from "living" in the environment created by the model. High competition toward a goal may spur achievement, for example, but the effects of living in a competitive atmosphere may alienate one from one's partners. Alienation would be, in this case, *nurtured* by an *instructional* method. In choosing a model, the teacher must balance instructional efficiency with nurturant effect, as shown in figure 11.1.

FIGURE 11.1

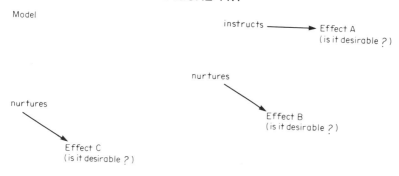

If we have two models whose instructional effects are both appropriate for our goal, we may choose between them because the nurturant effects reinforce the direct instructional effects. Suppose we favor goal "A." Three models might be considered, as shown in figure 11.2.

If we assume equal efficiency, we might choose Model 1 because its instructional and nurturant effects reinforce one another and there are no undesirable nurturant side effects.

It is possible to select a model for its nurturant effects, even if it does not have high direct efficiency. The progressive movement, for example, emphasized teaching academic subjects through democratic processes less because it would be an efficient way to teach content (although many believed it would be) than because it would be likely to nurture later democratic behavior and citizen involvement and give an opportunity to instruct citizens in democratic skills.

We can diagram the situation as in figure 11.3.

Our three civil rights teachers from the beginning of the paper might

FIGURE 11.2

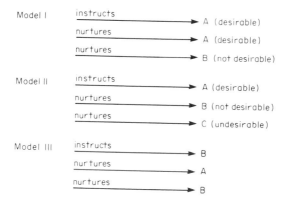

FIGURE 11.3

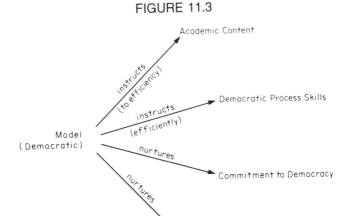

consider the instructional and nurturant values of their approaches. The lecturer, for example, is concerned with direct instructional effects. S/he might at the same time try to ascertain what that method nurtures. If s/he were to consider group investigation, s/he might question whether it was as efficient for achieving instructional goals, but s/he might value its nurturant effects and decide that the "student of cases" had a good compromise, with strong instructional values and desirable nurturant effects as well.

In the real world of education there are real decisions to be made among models that really differ from one another. By the models we choose, reality is created for our students. With so little empirical evidence to guide our choices, logic, awareness, and our own social values have to be most prominent in our selection.

THE MODELS APPROACH
TO EDUCATIONAL TRAINING

We believe that the reservoir of models constitutes the presently available technology for teachers and curriculum-workers. In fact, it contains a formidable array of ideas about how to educate people. Many ideas have already been well-developed into implementable teaching strategies. Others are relatively undeveloped. In general, the road to implementation begins with a theory (or idea which is not yet a theory), is carried into specification as an educational environment or teaching strategy, and is then ready for the development of engineering propositions necessary to bring it into existence.

| Theory or idea | $\longrightarrow$ | Educational environment or teaching strategy | $\longrightarrow$ | Engineering propositions |

Our position is that the training of curriculum personnel should be built around the development and implementation of educational models. They should learn the models and how to arrange technologies and train personnel to implement them. The curriculum specialist can then use models to develop schools and curriculums. One might build a curriculum around a single strategy or environment or around a combination of them. Single-model curriculums are fairly common, but more complex approaches are also used and probably should be used more than they are. For example, California's Contra Costa County social studies curriculum designed by Hilda Taba [141] used inductive teaching strategies as the model for most of the curriculum activities. Units of instruction were constructed around the inductive paradigm, and specific lessons within the units were built on the inductive teaching models as well. Through the collection of data and its analysis, it was assumed that many facts would be learned and that, at the same time, inductive skills would be taught. In addition, the community of students working together in induction would develop the interpersonal skills appropriate for democratic society and for vigorous scholarly analysis.

Quite a number of educational programs have been designed using behavior-modification strategies. A good example of these is the Individual Prescribed Instruction curriculums, developed at the Research and Development Center at the University of Pittsburgh; and Research for Better Schools, at the United States Office of Education Regional Laboratory in Philadelphia, which uses a variety of approaches but is characterized by liberal use of programmed instruction. [70]

Comprehensive systems planning using behavior-modification strategies has recently been applied to the development of teacher education curriculum. Michigan State University, for example, developed specifications for a program consisting of 2,700 objectives, each one of which is accompanied by an instructional module of a particular kind and all of which have been summarized and are stored in a computer retrieval system. [105]

This system is joined to a general management system which operates very much like the IPI (Individual Prescribed Instruction) system. Each student is tested and a developmental profile is created, on the basis of which that student is placed on certain developmental paths within the curriculum. As s/he proceeds through the curriculum, further evaluation is made on the basis of which the student is either recycled through segments of the program or exits into higher levels of the program. Gradually, sets of behaviors are built up, and these make up the expected competencies of the teacher as specified in the program.

Models drawn from the disciplines have been used in recent years to structure quite a number of curriculums. Such a model was used to structure the Biological Sciences Study Committee curriculum, and similar models have been used to structure curriculums in such diverse areas as social psychology for elementary-school children and anthropology for secondary-school students.[131]

Group investigation has been used to structure a good many curriculums. Theoreticians have recommended that courses in social studies especially be structured around cooperative inquiry because this may provide practice in democratic life through the simultaneous development of social skills, societal knowledge, and democratic values. John U. Michaelis, whose book, *Social Studies for Children in a Democracy,*[104] is by far the most widely used methods textbook in the social studies for the elementary school, advocates a democratic process method as the central strategy in social studies. He recommends that the teacher organize the students into a miniature democracy and that this democracy inquire into its society, attacking problems that puzzle the children and, in probing those problems, acquire knowledge about the society, problem-solving skills, democratic process skills, and commitment to democracy.

Curriculum workers need to develop clarity about the entire array of available alternatives and to codify knowledge about what is needed to bring these alternatives into existence. The ability to create multistrategy curriculums which provide different avenues for differing teachers needs to be comfortably within the engineering capacity of the curriculum worker.

The Teacher and Models of Teaching

What is the importance of a large range of teaching strategies for the practicing teacher? The answer to this question depends on one's view of teaching.

One view holds that teaching is a mysterious and exceedingly personal art. The task of each teacher is to find his/her own model. This may be created by adapting an existing model of teaching, or rationally and consciously out of personal beliefs about the kinds of conditions that will produce learning, or intuitively, through interaction with students. Of course, the teacher may not use any one model at all, but each time s/he teaches, a new kind of interaction may result out of the unique occurrence of that attempt to teach and the students' attempt to learn. For the teacher who possesses such a viewpoint, the models of teaching which others have developed provide a panorama of the beliefs concerning effective teaching and learning. This panorama should help the teacher test the adequacy of his/her own concepts and provide intellectual stimulation as well. If s/he is interested in helping students develop more adequate self-concepts, then Rogers may have something to offer. If s/he is trying to teach a skill, Skinner and Ausubel may be of interest. If s/he is trying to understand a learner, Hunt's or Piaget's or Kohlberg's ways of looking at the learner may be useful. The artistic view of the teacher would resist any notion that any of the models should be viewed as prescriptive of teaching behavior, but they should rather be sources to stimulate the imagination and get insight into the teacher's own work. The panorama of models creates a conceptual map through which the necessary artistic detachment and self-awareness can be filtered.

A different view is that teachers need to develop a solid basic style or model which they can use as the "bread and butter" of their teaching. Many teacher educators, for example, have attempted to present to teachers a good general-purpose model which they can master and then modify and eventually replace as they mature professionally. For example, the cooperative inquiry (Group Investigation) [143] model has been taught as a basic teaching strategy by teacher educators, particularly those whose historical roots are in the progressive movement. They reason that this model will give the teacher a good base for organizing the students to work with the teacher in a mutual way, solving problems and developing a mutually cooperative learning environment, so the children work at teaching themselves.

Emphasis on creative thinking could lead toward aspects of the Synectics model.[44] An emphasis on inquiry would lead toward the Science or Social Inquiry [99] model, and an emphasis on inductive thinking could lead toward the Taba or Suchman [139] approaches to inductive reasoning.

Models based on inductive thinking or inquiry have also served as staples for teachers, and there are many that hold that these are the basic models that should be taught to the future teacher and that should be used in most curriculum areas. Behavior-modification models such as Skinner's are implicit in the methods of many other teacher-education programs and are suggested as basic models for the teacher.

Our view is that the models for teaching are best viewed by the teacher as potential strategies which are applicable to a wide variety of purposes. Since no single teaching strategy can accomplish every purpose, the wise teacher will master a limited repertoire of strategies which can be brought to bear on specific kinds of learning problems. For example, the Group Investigation teaching model is a good basic element for the teacher's repertoire. It provides a means of organizing the students into a group that can work well and which will have the ability to improve its own processes. It can be used in the creative arts areas as well as in the teaching of skills and sciences. However, models derived from other sources are also valuable. The models designed from the practice of the disciplines, such as those used by the Biological Sciences Curriculum Study, are clearly relevant to the teaching of the academic disciplines. The Rogerian model is specifically applicable to helping people to become open, to freeing their inquisitiveness and their creativity, and to enabling them to develop the drive and the sensitivity to try to educate themselves. Similarly, the Laboratory Method model has great advantage for the improvement of human relations skills. Therefore, to the extent that it is possible, we urge the teacher to master a solid range of models which s/he can bring to bear on the variety of instructional problems that s/he is likely to face. This is particularly important for the teacher in a self-contained classroom, responsible for teaching a good number of children in a good number of curriculum areas. But it is also important for the subject-matter specialist, as his/her responsibilities, even if they are confined to the teaching of a single discipline to fairly mature students, imply teaching tasks for which no one single model can be completely adequate. For instance, the secondary teacher of English can draw on several models in teaching that discipline. Synectics could be used in the teaching of creative writing, Skinnerian techniques for the teaching of skills, and Rogerian methods to introduce students to a sense of their own potentialities and a willingness to capitalize on them.

Teams of teachers working together can discover the models that are most amenable to each member of the team and can orchestrate these so that they build up a strong and balanced pattern of education. Some teachers, for example, will use the counseling models effectively; others will use the behavior-modification strategies. Still others will be democratic process organizers. Together, a large team of teachers, able to draw on teacher-aides and support systems of various kinds, should be able to create a large range of opportunities for children.

To develop repertoire means to develop flexibility. Part of this flexibility is clinical and professional, and part is emotional and personal. The teacher faces a wide range of problems, and if s/he has a wide range of models of teaching to draw from, s/he should be able to offer more creative and imaginative solutions to those problems. Repertoire requires the ability to grow as a person and expand one's potential, and the capacity to teach oneself more varied and interesting ways of coping with one's need to develop. The environment for personal growth is greatly enhanced when people can define their present situations and see the alternative possibilities once this map is provided. The growing, developing person can reach out and embrace more forms of experience, explore more aspects of students, and find more ways of helping them to grow.

The satisfaction of growth and exploration should be reason enough for the teacher to reach out and set as a goal, not one or two basic models used for all purposes, but a variety which may be explored for the potential that they hold, both for the pupils *and* for the teacher.

12

Can Teachers Learn Repertoires of Models of Teaching?

Bruce R. Joyce, Rhoada Wald, and Marsha Weil

We operated on two theses—one the source of the substance of the program, and the other the source of its form. *First, if a teacher trainee masters the theory and practice of a range of models of teaching, then his/her flexibility in teaching and decision-making is increased.* From this thesis comes the conceptual core of the program—a set of models of teaching whose rationale and practice he/she explores. *Second, if the primary mode of teacher education is self-instruction, then the teacher's ability to educate her/himself—to master and generate new educational forms—is enhanced.* From this thesis comes the technical core of the program—a set of self-administering, open-ended instructional systems that the teacher trainee uses to teach her/himself alternative models of teaching.

DESIGN OF THE PROGRAM

The program extended for one year and is intended for bachelor's degree holders in the liberal arts. It begins with the fall semester and concludes at the end of the summer session. Graduates receive the Master of Arts degree in curriculum and the New York State and New York City certification.

The program design has evolved over the last five years, with components being added gradually until the present form has emerged. They are described in the order of their development, and then the current total design is presented. The major components are: Models of Teaching (four models required, others optional); Skills (three skills required, others optional); Study of Teaching (required); Clinical Laboratory: moderate experience during the fall semester, extended experience during the spring, and a trainee-operated school in the summer (required); Workshop: exploring alternative approaches to the major curriculum areas such as reading or social studies (four required).

The Models of Teaching Component

The first component was created to enable the prospective teacher to explore the theory and practice of several models of teaching. A model of teaching consists of guidelines for designing educational environments through specifying ways of teaching and learning to achieve certain kinds of goals. It includes a rationale of its likely effectiveness and may be accompanied by empirical evidence that it "works." In designing this component, we deliberately selected models representing different frames of reference toward educational goals and means so that the trainee would explore a variety of philosophical and psychological positions and be able to make them come to life in the classroom. In the beginning the trainee explores a few models representing alternative views of educating. Later s/he chooses from a larger number the ones s/he is especially interested in. Each model is presented with an instructional format consisting of five stages:

STAGE 1—explores the *theory* of the model. For example, in the instructional system that teaches the "role-playing" model, the theory of role-playing is studied in the works of Shaftel and Shaftel [51] and others who have developed approaches to role-playing for social values. The readings are combined with discussions and exercises comparing the theories with one another.

STAGE 2—*demonstrates* the model. Television tapes, transcripts, and descriptions of learning activities are combined and are analyzed to explore the dynamics of the teaching model in action.

STAGE 3—involves *peer teaching*. In this phase, trainees teach one another, using materials that have been prepared for them beforehand. This phase is designed not only to provide preliminary practice in the model but also to help each person understand what it feels like to be a student in the model situation.

STAGE 4—is *microteaching practice* with small groups of students, again using materials that have been prepared in advance. Trainees take turns observing one another, and television recordings are used to facilitate feedback for the development of precision in the teaching model.

STAGE 5—consists of *application* in a normal classroom situation, at first with materials supplied to the trainee and later with materials he/she prepares him/herself.

The Skills Component

As we observed trainees trying to master the models it appeared that mastery came most easily to those who possessed certain types of skills with students and subject matter. When several such skills were identified and measures developed for them, the correlation was confirmed. We then developed instructional systems around those skills, and these systems became the basis of the *skills component*. At present, three skills form the bulk of the component, but more will doubtless be added as our study continues. These skills are called *structuring, modulating cognitive level*, and *focusing*.

The skill of *structuring* is concerned with varying the distribution of control in the relationship between teacher and students. Goals and procedures can be *negotiated* (when teacher and student share most decisions and responsibilities) or *directed* (when they are determined primarily by the teacher) or *student-constructed* (when students make the decisions and maintain the activity). Skill in structuring is defined as the ability to bring about these conditions—to negotiate, to direct, or to facilitate student control, whichever is appropriate. The trainees must learn to bring about any of these conditions.

The skill of *modulating* is concerned with the way in which data or content is handled in the classroom. Three levels of cognitive activity—factual, conceptual, theoretical—are described as being along a continuum beginning with the identification of date and extending to the building of concepts and to the theoretical processing of data. To modulate cognitive level is to establish a certain level of intellectual activity and change it when appropriate. This modulation can be accomplished chiefly through designing activities and asking questions.

The skill of *focusing* affects the content of the learning environment. Learning activities at any cognitive level can deal with many aspects of content. The general topic of family, for example, can be studied from an economic perspective or a sociological perspective. Focusing is used by the teacher to draw, maintain, or shift the students' attention to a particular aspect of the topic or learning activity. This can be done by designating content, selecting materials, asking questions, or making statements.

Weil's [59] research has established correlations between modulating and focusing and performance with the information-processing models (about .50), and between structuring and the interaction-oriented models (about .40).

The Study of Teaching Component

To provide the trainee with a device for analyzing his/her teaching as s/he practices the models, an interaction-analysis system was devised; this employs categories that illuminate differences among the models in action, help the trainee identify difficulties s/he is having when trying a model, and facilitate research to compare the behavior of trainees as they practice the models. Figure 12.1 names the categories. These categories refer to three dimensions of teaching: structuring, information processing, and feedback. The first two correspond to the skills of structuring and modulating cognitive level, which were referred to earlier.

FIGURE 12.1 The Teacher-Innovator System

I. STRUCTURING COMMUNICATIONS

A. Planning Goals and Standards

Directive	Negotiated	Directive	Negotiated	Directive	Negotiated
1	2	3	4	5	6

B. Implementation

Instructional	Non-instructional
7	8

II. INFORMATIONAL COMMUNICATIONS

Level 1	Level 2	Level 3	Open	Opinion
9	10	11	12	13

III. FEEDBACK COMMUNICATIONS

Positive	Neutral	Negative	Corrective	Repeat	Digression
14	15	16	17	18	19

Thus the trainees employ the interaction-analysis schedule to study their teaching and that of their peers. The faculty employ it to offer advice and suggest instruction on subskills of the models. The research team employs it to study the dimension of teaching behavior as trainees practice the models. An instructional system has therefore been developed that presents the categories, offers practice in their use, and helps trainees apply them in their study of teaching.

The Clinical Laboratory

Clinical laboratory experience occurs throughout the year. It begins with moderate classroom experience during the fall semester, extends to considerable periods of contact in classrooms in New York City in the spring, and culminates in a summer school for neighborhood children, which the trainees plan and carry out, using the facilities of the Agnes Russell School at Teachers College. In creating their summer school, they are responsible for organizing a community "board" to legitimize the school, for designing the curriculum, and for training themselves to carry it out. They design the school around learning centers constructed around the various models of teaching.

Throughout the year, a trainee practices the teaching skills and models and uses the interaction-analysis system to analyze his/her own behavior and that of the teacher s/he is working with.

Teachers from the Agnes Russell School serve as supervisors, demonstrate the models of teaching, and use the television tape facilities to promote the analysis of microteaching with the models.

Workshop Components: The Curriculum Bank

Sets of workshops have been designed to help the trainees identify the alternative ways of approaching the common curriculum areas in the school and to acquaint them with contemporary projects in those areas. In the workshops they are also taught how to apply the models of teaching in the different subjects (reading, arithmetic, science, and social studies).

These workshops are backed up by "banks" of instructional materials for children representing the alternative curriculum approaches, and by television tapes in which the alternatives are demonstrated in the classroom. The workshops are conducted by the Agnes Russell staff as well as the preservice staff.

Additional Options

In addition to the teacher-innovator system, the models, the skills, the clinical experience, and the workshops, about fifty instructional systems not described above are available in a variety of areas (such as setting objectives, selecting content, selecting teaching strategies, educational philosophies, flexibility training, classroom management), and additional systems based on teaching skills and strategies have been adapted from sources such as the Far West Laboratory's Minicourse program.

The trainees are organized into small groups (inquiry groups) where they work their way through the components and help one another to learn to teach. Seminars explore theoretical issues about the models of teaching and help the trainees to organize their summer school. The components are designed around the instructional systems outlined in figure 12.2

These instructional packages consist of objectives for the component and subcomponent, instructional tasks and resource materials, and assessment tasks. The packages are designed to be self-administering in the sense that the teacher candidates can employ them to teach themselves, with faculty serving as facilitators.

RESEARCH: THE EFFECTIVENESS OF THE INSTRUCTIONAL SYSTEMS

The program is organized so that research can be conducted on the learning of the models, the effects on students, and the effectiveness of the various

FIGURE 12.2 Instructional Packages

General Domains	Specific Topics			
	Personalists	Synergists	Cyberneticists	Knowledge-Metaphors
Philosophies				
Child Study	Personal Development	Social Development	Learning Theory	Intellectual Development
Study of Teaching	Introduction to Behavioral Analysis	Social Climate	Tasks and Feedback	Informational Transactions
Teaching Skills Interactive		Structuring	Feedback	Modulating Focusing
Instructional Design	Behavioral Objectives	Designing Learning Activities	Assessing Objectives	
Models of Teaching	Personalistic Strategies	Synergistic Strategies	Cybernetic and Behavior Modification Strategies	Information-Processing Strategies
Curriculum Design	Reading	Social Studies	Science	Mathematics
Institutional Design	Team Teaching	School Organization	School Architecture	School Law

instructional systems. In this paper we concentrate on the effectiveness of the instructional systems build around the models of teaching in changing the behavior of the teacher trainees. Specifically, we ask: Is it possible to use instructional systems to teach a repertoire of teaching models to a sufficient degree that the trainee can actualize them in the classroom? And how do "normal" teaching style, personal values, conceptual flexibility, and the teaching style, personal values, and conceptual flexibility of cooperating teachers affect their actualization?

Data from one year's research are reported in terms of the following specific questions:

1. Do trainees, when attempting to actualize models of teaching, create interactive teaching patterns that are different from those manifested when they are not practicing the models, and that approximate the theoretical specifications of the learning environment contained within each of the models?

2. Is the teaching behavior of cooperating teachers related to the patterns manifested when models are practiced?

3. How does the level of the students taught (primary or intermediate) influence the interactive patterns created?

4. Are personality variables, attitudes, and values factors in the actualization of the models? (For example, can trainees whose orientation is child-centered learn models that use a good deal of external structure? Can trainees whose orientation is toward structured models learn to actualize models built around student activity?) Stated in terms of the families of teaching models, the fundamental question is whether trainees with a philosophical preference for one family or another can participate in the teaching of models drawn from the other families. Since there are very real philosophical differences among the families of models, this is a serious question of both practical and philosophical import.

General Procedures

Twenty-six trainees were exposed to the instructional systems built around three models of teaching during the fall of 1970 as a part of the program described above. The models—Synectics, Concept Attainment, and Group Investigation—were selected because they require patterns of teaching distinctly different from each other and from the patterns of teaching one generally finds in North American and European classrooms. As each trainee practiced the models in the classroom (stage 5 of the instructional system), observers coded her/his teaching behavior and the responses of his/her students using the categories shown in figure 12.1. His/her behavior was also rated in terms of the specifications when s/he was not practicing the models. Samples of teaching episodes of the cooperating teachers were collected as well. These data are the primary focus of the research, although ratings of effectiveness are used as well.

The trainees also completed the Sentence Completion Test, the Study of Values, the inventory of Teacher Conceptions of the Educative Process, and the Scale for Determining Teacher Beliefs.

The Use of the Interaction-Analysis System

Nine indices, derived from the teacher-innovator categories (fig. 12.1), were employed in the analysis of the data related to the primary questions of the study. Each index refers to an aspect of teacher or learner behavior that we believe to be important in the description of teaching style. Some refer to general aspects of teaching behavior, others are "model-relevant"; that is, they describe aspects of teaching behavior that are prominent in the descriptions of the various models.

INDEX 1—Teacher talk (proportion of all talk): relevant to Group Investigation and Synectics

INDEX 2—Negotiated structuring, teacher (proportion of all talk): relevant to Group Investigation

INDEX 3—Negotiated structuring, student (proportion of all talk): relevant to Group Investigation

INDEX 4—Higher-level information processing (proportion of all information processing): relevant to Synectics

INDEX 5—Middle-level information processing (proportion of all information processing): relevant to Concept Attainment

INDEX 6—Positive sanctioning of higher-level processes (proportion of all talk): relevant to Synectics and Concept Attainment

INDEX 7—Negative sanctioning of higher-level processes (proportion of all talk): relevant to Synectics and Concept Attainment

INDEX 8—Information processing (proportion of all talk): general indicator of style

INDEX 9—Procedural (proportion of structuring to all talk): general indicator of style.

The Effectiveness of the Instructional Systems

The first question is whether the indicators of teaching behavior calculated when the trainees were practicing the models were significantly different from their "normal" or "nonmodel" teaching styles, and especially whether the differences were in the desired directions according to the model-relevant indices. In other words, did the instructional systems pull the behavior of the trainees in the direction of the model specifications? The nine indices were calculated for each trainee.

We then asked the same question with respect to each model: Were the indices different from the normal teaching styles? Especially, were the model-relevant indices different in the predicted directions?

Synectics

Synectics is a highly structured teaching strategy that emphasizes metaphoric thinking. It culminates with the deliberate use of analogies to attack problems. The conceptualization of problems, synthesis of metaphors, and application of metaphors are critical to Synectics.

The model should result in a great deal of higher-level information processing (Index 4) and middle-level information processing (Index 5). Because it is a model of creative thinking, there should be a low evaluative atmosphere (Indices 6 and 7), and particularly low negative sanctioning. Thus, these four are the model-relevant indices for Synectics. The model, however, should also reduce teacher talk and affect procedural interaction by reducing it somewhat. Table 12.1 presents the means and standard deviations of indices computed for Synectics as compared with nonmodel practice.

The primary model-relevant index was Index 4, higher-level information processing; the Synectics model requires much activity at this level. This index rose significantly, with seven times as much communication at the higher levels as occurred in the normal teaching sessions. (More specifically, the most prominent feature of Synectics activity is synthesis. The percentages of communication reflecting synthesis as a mental activity were 6.3 for teachers and 5.6 for students, indicating that 11.9 percent of all communication was at that level while Synectics models were being practiced. This figure compares with less than 0.5 percent during normal teaching.)

Attention to procedures (Index 9) dropped as did negotiated teacher structuring (Index 2), for Synectics is a teacher-directed model, at least in the early stages. Teacher talk (Index 1) dropped significantly (about 10 percent). This probably reflects the effects of the increase in higher-order questions by teachers. (Higher-level solicitations generally result in a greater proportion of student talk in response, for the more complex questions often require discussion and debate and permit more alternative responses. In fact, the 10 percent shift here is actually smaller than one would expect had the teachers allowed an optimally rich response to their questions.) Positive sanctioning decreased slightly, both indices moving in the direction one would expect, for the model specifies that creative activity is best promoted by neutrality of feedback.

Concept Attainment

Concept Attainment is another directive strategy that emphasizes higher-level thinking, especially at the interpretation level (the intermediate cognitive level), which reflects the analysis of concepts.

When the indices computed from Concept Attainment practice are com-

TABLE 12.1. Comparison of Means and Standard Deviations of Nine Indices of Classroom Interaction for Synectics Model Teaching and Nonmodel Episodes

Index	Name	M		SD		t
		Synectics	Nonmodel	Synectics	Nonmodel	
1	Teacher talk	0.565	0.638	0.044	0.053	-5.277**
2	Negotiates structuring: teacher	0.012	0.030	0.010	0.027	-3.067**
3	Negotiates structuring: student	0.007	0.016	0.007	0.015	-2.541
4[a]	Higher-level information processing	0.273	0.045	0.163	0.046	6.857*
5[a]	Middle-level information processing	0.190	0.115	0.081	0.082	3.288*
6[a]	Positive sanctioning	0.032	0.052	0.025	0.024	-2.869*
7[a]	Negative sanctioning	0.020	0.025	0.016	0.014	-1.157
8	Information processing	0.591	0.590	0.134	0.085	0.007
9	Procedural	0.123	0.186	0.046	0.071	-3.782**

[a] Model-relevant index.
* $p < .01$ for a one-tailed test, critical t with 50 df — ± 2.40.
** $p < .01$ for a two-tailed test, critical t with 50 df — ± 2.68.

pared with nonmodel practice, the following pattern emerges. Student participation in the structuring of procedures (Index 3) dropped significantly, as did attention to procedures in general (Index 9). The critical model-relevant indices were middle-level cognitive activity and higher-level information processing (Index 4). The proportion of middle-level activity increased about 60 percent (0.115 to 0.190) while the Concept Attainment model was being practiced; in fact, about 12 percent of all discourse was at the middle level. However, student-asked questions remained very low, so that student-led exploration of concepts, which should occur in Phase Three * of the model, probably did not materialize in very many cases.

Group Investigation

Group Investigation is a democratic-process model built around cooperative problem solving. Because Group Investigation is much less directive than the other models and requires a cooperative social system, it is in some ways more complex to carry out. In addition it evolves slowly, requiring several interaction sessions at a minimum, while the others can be implemented more quickly. When we compare indices for Group Investigation practice sessions with those for normal practice sessions, a mixed picture results, with a considerable shift in structuring behavior but little change in information processing.

With respect to relevant indices, teacher talk (Index 1) dropped about 15 percent and the "negotiated procedures" indices (2 and 3) both rose significantly. Students made contributions coded as "negotiated procedures" fifteen times more during Group Investigation practice than during nonmodel practice. In general, communication related to procedures increased, while sanctioning and informational communications dropped accordingly, as expected.

Apparently the social characteristics of the model were actualized more than the intellectual characteristics, for the second and third phases should be characterized by much more higher-level information processing than was reflected by the data.

Summary: Did the Patterns Change?

In terms of the critical model-relevant indices, the bulk of the evidence points to the conclusion that the trainees did shift their patterns of verbal interaction with students in the directions specified by the models. Synectics is characterized by higher-level information processing, especially at the synthesis level, and interaction at that level rose to many times the frequency in nonmodel teaching. The negotiated structure characteristic of Group Investigation also

---

* Phases are units of activity characterized by particular types of transactions (as those at a certain cognitive level).

appeared to rise substantially while the model was being practiced, although the theoretical information processing that should also characterize the model did not appear to rise. When practicing Concept Attainment, trainees and their students interacted at the conceptual and theoretical levels much more than during nonmodel practice, though to a lesser extent at the theoretical level.

An interesting side issue is whether nonmodel behavior contributed to implementation of the model (did nonmodel style influence model behavior?). The indices for nonmodel teaching were correlated with indices for model teaching and also with ratings of effectiveness with the models. The correlations were uniformly low. Apparently, nonmodel style, as measured by the indices, did not affect behavior while practicing the models. For example, teacher trainees who exhibited middle- or higher-order information-processing behavior in nonmodel practice apparently behaved in Synectics and Concept Attainment much the same as did students, for whom such behavior was apparently characteristic.

The Cooperating Teacher as an Influence

In several past investigations (Seperson, see chap. 9) it has been established that indices of several dimensions of cooperating teacher behavior are associated with the behavior of teacher trainees, who apparently follow the patterns exhibited or modeled by their cooperating teachers. We were concerned to learn whether cooperating teacher behavior would influence practice with the models. (For instance, if cooperating teachers rarely displayed negotiating skill, would that affect the way trainees practiced Group Investigation with its dependence on negotiated structure?)

Samples of the behavior of the cooperating teachers were taken and indices computed for each of them. These were correlated with the indices for the trainees when not practicing models (the nonmodel episodes) and when practicing each model.

With respect to cooperating teacher behavior and nonmodel teaching, the indices related to structuring and feedback were significantly correlated (the two negotiated-structuring indices were correlated .50 and .60 respectively). This replicated Seperson's study and indicated an influence on nonmodel teaching.

However, only one correlation between cooperating teacher indices and trainee "model practice" indices was significantly greater than zero. Also, none of the cooperating teacher indices was positively related to the performance scores of the trainees.

Evidently the nonmodel styles of the trainees were somewhat related to the behavior of the cooperating teachers, but the model practice behavior was not related to the model of the teachers.

This finding is extremely important, since few cooperating teachers exhibit the behavior that is critical to the models (as higher-order questioning is to Synectics). Trainees must thus introduce new patterns of teaching into the classrooms if they are to implement the models they are learning.

The Age of the Students and the Practice of the Models

Students as well as cooperating teachers influence the implementation of the models. We looked at relative age as the first consideration and wondered whether younger students would respond as well to the demands for the higher-order information processing required in Synectics and Concept Attainment or the negotiation of procedures required in Group Investigation. About half the trainees practiced in the primary grades (K–3) and about half in the intermediate grades (4–6). The indices were compared for primary and intermediate grades.

At the primary level, in the case of Synectics and Concept Attainment, there was less middle- and higher-level information processing: however, in Group Investigation there was more negotiated structuring. These differences were in line with differences exhibited by cooperating teachers at the two levels. (They negotiate more with younger students, are more directive with older students, and handle information at a lower level with younger students.)

Younger students may have more difficulty at the higher levels of information processing either because of their developmental level or because higher-order communications are relatively infrequent in primary classrooms. On the other hand, there were many examples of higher-order tasks. Younger students are exposed to much negotiation and appear able to respond to Group Investigation as effectively as do older students.

The analysis indicated a need for research into the relationship of learners' maturity and responsiveness to the models.

Personality, Values, and the Behavior of Trainees

It seems certain that personality influences teaching behavior, although few previous empirical studies have confirmed this fact. Our concern here is the extent to which differences in value orientation and personality affect the learning of the models of teaching. For example, do conceptually oriented people implement conceptually oriented models (as Concept Attainment) differently from the socially oriented? Is conceptual flexibility related to mastery of a repertoire of models?

Four measures of personality and attitudinal orientation were taken of the twenty-six subjects in the study. These are:

1. The Sentence Completion Test,[24] which is a general measure of cognitive flexibility and conceptual level. It should be model-free and should rather reflect ability to explore and master a range of orientations.

2. The Study of Values,[1] which yields six scores, of which the social and theoretical orientations were especially interesting to us because they are theoretically related to the social and cognitive models.

3. The Inventory of Teacher Conceptions of the Educative Process,[58] which measures educational belief systems. Certain subscores are pertinent to specific models, such as subject-matter emphasis, personal-adjustment ideology, and student autonomy. We hypothesized that the subject-matter emphases would be related to preference for the concept-oriented model and the other subscores to preference for Group Investigation.

4. The Scale for Determining Teacher Beliefs,[43] which yields these scores: progressive (child-centered, related to Synectics), community (socially oriented, related to Group Investigation), and academic (subject-matter oriented, related to Concept Attainment).

The four measures together yielded scores representing dimensions that should affect the acquisition of specific models. The scores were correlated with the model efficiency scores, and with an overall rating performance on all the models.

Of the thirty-six coefficients only two were significant. Conceptual level was correlated with the overall score (.420); this indicates that conceptual flexibility is in fact related to mastery of all the models rather than to any specific one. The finding accords with Conceptual Systems Theory, which holds that conceptual development is value-free but would relate to ability to embrace a variety of conceptual positions.

The social scale from the Study of Values was related (.611) to performance in Group Investigation, a socially oriented model. This was the only specific value scale to be related as one would theoretically expect, but it may be an important one, for Group Investigation is a complex strategy that may require a social commitment if it is to be maximally effective.

In general, it cannot be concluded that specific educational attitudes or values affected performance to any great extent. It must be remembered that the measured performance was in limited situations in which the trainees were required to practice the models. Long-term results might be quite different, especially with respect to the extent to which trainees actually incorporate the models into their regular repertoire. However, specific educational values did not seem to affect performance in these short-term practice situations.

The relationship between conceptual level and overall practice is interesting, especially when considered in light of the evidence available in other studies [23] of the relationship between Concept Attainment and the flexibility of general teaching style. If we conceive of the "good" teacher as one with a flexible repertoire, these findings may help us understand the role of general personality structure in effective teaching.

SUMMARY: TOWARD FURTHER RESEARCH

The most important finding is the evidence of effectiveness of these first-generation instructional systems in teaching a variety of complex models.

This evidence encourages the belief that we can design an effective technology of teacher education—one offering teacher trainees the chance to master a wide range of approaches to their work.

This finding is particularly encouraging when considered along with the additional evidence that trainees were able to practice effectively in classrooms reflecting a range of cooperating teacher styles and student ages. The fact that cooperating teacher style affected performance so little suggests that the cooperating teacher need not be a roadblock to practice even of teaching models that diverge markedly from his/her own style. The finding with respect to Synectics is especially striking, for it depends on teaching moves (and pupil responses) that almost never occur in the behavior of cooperating teachers (or their students) except when models are being practiced.

Chiefly, the findings should stimulate further research, especially in the following areas:

1. *Improvement in Instructional System Design.* We need closer examination of the behavior of teachers as they practice the models. Wald [56] has provided evidence about the types of moves that were especially difficult for trainees in each model. Weil [59] has demonstrated that certain "micro-skills," if taught, facilitate behavior in each model, and that certain "cycles" of transaction differentiate the best and poorest implementers. Rude [48] has identified the behaviors that differentiate phases in each model, and Kelly [41] has delineated the relationship between the "normal" styles of experienced teachers and their behavior when learning the models. From a close study of teachers trying out various models, we may identify the critical "micro-skills" that make models come to life. On this knowledge we can build more effective instructional systems. We also need to learn the process by which teachers, having mastered the essential form of a model, incorporate it into their active repertoire and employ it regularly. The role of attitudes and personality in this process needs to be explored as well. This type of analysis, together with exploration of system-design variables (combining media in different ways, juxtaposing training in skills and models variously, etc.), should also lead to improved instructional systems.

2. *Effects on Student Learning.* Although we selected models for which there is theoretical justification and/or research evidence about effectiveness in limited situations, the effects on students when large numbers of teachers employ the models need to be ascertained. Studies are needed in which groups of teachers use several models over the same content and the students' learning is rigorously measured. These studies need to include examination of age-related and other student characteristics that might influence learning.

3. *Diagnosis of Teacher's Need for Instruction.* If we can design instructional systems that offer teachers the possibility of teaching themselves a wide range of skills and models, then we can conceive of a teacher center containing an array of these systems.

Can we also, through a combination of studies analyzing teaching styles and the effects of instruction on styles, come to an understanding of how teachers can study their behavior and select the instructional programs most likely to increase their flexibility and effectiveness?

Teacher education has usually, until now, depended on didactic instruction in theory followed by classroom practice. The connection between them has been too tenuous to permit teacher educators to accept the credit if teaching competency results. Complex multimedia instructional systems enable us to marry theory and practice in teacher education and to assess whether teacher training is actually accomplishing its purpose.

13

The Relationship of Teacher Characteristics to the Utilization of Models of Teaching

Irene S. Shigaki and Clark C. Brown

After considering Joyce, Weil, and Wald's four families of models (see chapter 11), it seemed plausible that mastery of a repertoire of models from within each of these families would lend itself to flexibility in teaching, as the teacher could then shift teaching style with confidence after assessing a particular teaching situation.

The present investigation was concerned with the utility of models to teacher education. Specifically, two stages of model utilization were explored. The first stage required the identification of the factors that would influence the choice of a model, and the second required the creation of a new model. Four variables, i.e., teaching experience, conceptual level (from concrete to abstract), creativity, and intelligence were identified as potentially influencing a teacher's utilization of a model. The relationship of the four variables to the two stages of model utilization was studied.

PROCEDURE

Subjects

The subjects for the study were twenty-eight students enrolled in a graduate level course entitled "Dynamics of Childhood Education" during the Spring term, 1970, at New York University. The students ranged in age from twenty to fifty-four with the mean age of 28.8 and standard deviation of 9.7 years.

The majority of the class members had teaching experience, with a range of from one to twenty-three years. Seven members had no previous teaching experience other than student teaching.

Independent Variables Influencing Mastery of Concept of Strategies

Teaching experience

It seemed plausible that the extent of an individual's experience in the classroom would have a positive effect on the acquisition of teaching strategies. We believed that a person who is able to draw upon years of working with children would more readily recognize the value of having at her/his command alternative modes of dealing with ideas, recognizing and providing for affect, and stimulating group processes.

Conceptual level

Harvey, Hunt, and Schroder's [18] developmental theory of personality provided the construct of conceptual level employed in the present study. The first, or most basic, level is typified by the concrete individual. Such a person would perceive and react to the environment in a unilateral fashion—something is either good or bad; people in authority are to be strictly obeyed, and so forth. Rigidity typifies this thinking and behavior.

The second level of development would be exemplified by the rebellious teenager. In psychological terms this stage might be called counterdependence. In other words, the individual no longer perceives an authority figure as being indisputably right but is not yet able to employ independent judgment. Instead, there is a tendency to do just the opposite of what a person in authority advocates. Implicit in this contrary behavior is dependence upon others for direction.

The third level of development is characterized by group orientation. At this stage an individual has come to appreciate the sense of community afforded by groups. The pleasure of group companionship may lead to the dissipation of working goals as the feeling of camaraderie in itself seems sufficient.

The fourth stage is one where the individual can recognize the complexities of interrelationships. A given situation no longer appears to have a clear cause and effect. This simplistic view is replaced by the recognition that numerous influences upon a given situation must be taken into account and this is followed by the ability to maintain autonomy in decision-making.

It was felt that a person operating on a higher level of abstraction would more readily recognize the value of a family of models, whereas one operating on a concrete level may accept one mode of operation as perfectly sufficient. The instrument designed by Harvey, Hunt, and Schroder to assess conceptual level was used in this study.

Available reliability coefficients include item-total coefficients ranging from

.57 to .75 and a split-half reliability index of .70. The concurrent validity of the instrument was demonstrated by comparing it with the Impression Formation Test by the same authors which is also a measure of conceptual level. The concurrent validity for the two measures of conceptual level ranged from .40 to .80.

Creativity

Receptivity on the part of the subject and ability to produce new models were hypothesized to be contingent upon the subject's openness to new ideas. Consequently, it appeared to be relevant to have an index of creativity which is often defined as the ability to make unusual associations. The *Torrance Tests of Creative Thinking*[55] were utilized for this purpose. They are among the few tests of creativity commercially available, although they are in a research edition. A verbal form was selected as being a sufficient index of creativity for the purposes of this study. The scoring procedures yielded three subscores: one for fluency, the total number of responses; one for flexibility, the ability to shift from category to category; and one for originality, the unusualness of the response. The manual reports test-retest reliability coefficients from .61 to .93 for the verbal form. Extensive evidence is also provided for the validity of the instrument.[55]

Intelligence

Finally, an intelligence measure was included in the battery of measurements. Research indicates that there is a low though positive correlation between intelligence and creativity on the order of from .20 to .40 in the general population.[62] Since such a low correlation leaves much of the variance still unaccounted for, one measure is not an adequate substitute for the other. Likewise, though on the surface it may appear that intelligence and conceptual level assess the same domain, empirical study has indicated that this is not the case. The entire range of conceptual levels has been found to be operating within a college sample. Consequently, an intelligence measure would contribute supplementary information about the subjects.

The *Wonderlic Personnel Test* was employed as the measure of intelligence. It has been used widely in industry and has been developed specifically for adult populations. Reliability coefficients for the instrument range from .82 to .94 which include both test-retest and split-half reliability. The test has been found to be a valid instrument in determining success for a variety of jobs. Concurrent validity computed against the *Otis Self-Administering Test of Mental Ability* resulted in correlations of from .81 to .87.[61]

Teaching Models Selected

It was felt that for an introductory exploration of models, a detailed study of four would be sufficient. The four models selected were from the family dealing with information processing and exemplify the range of possibilities within a given family. The four models have their sources in the works of Ausubel [5]; Bruner [10]; Taba [54]; and Harvey, Hunt, and Schroder.[18]

Ausubel—advanced organizer [5]

Prompted by the work of Bruner, Ausubel agreed that it was possible to teach children anything in an intellectually honest form at any age. However, he felt that in order to make this premise work, it was necessary to organize the materials by presenting the underlying concept followed by examples of that concept. One concept would be the commutative property of numbers which can be expressed by the equation $A + B = B + A$. Specific examples of this concept include $1 + 3 = 3 + 1$, $2 + 4 = 4 + 2$, etc. By presenting the organizing concept at the outset, the learner would be provided a framework for specific information, underscoring relationships rather than the accumulation of isolated facts.

Bruner—concept formation [10]

The teacher in this case may not have a concept clearly in mind. Instead, she/he helps the children formulate concepts by building their activities. Work with concepts may be initiated by asking the children to share their impressions concerning a common experience. They may then be asked to group related impressions and finally to label the groups. Grouping can be applied to varying dimensions. The children may decide upon a given dimension but are also guided to recognize that alternative modes of grouping are possible. As a result, the process of deriving a concept is emphasized, rather than that of illustrating a specific concept.

Harvey, Hunt, and Schroder—Differential Training Model [18]

Their basic contention is that individuals on different conceptual levels require different environments for optimal growth. For example, in working with an individual at Stage 1 of development, a well-structured though supportive environment is recommended. Emphasis is placed on encouraging an individual to make a distinction between a person and his beliefs. Further, the learner is provided opportunities that illustrate the varying perspectives of individuals. Finally, stress is placed on the fact that right and wrong are not definitive but situational and can be negotiated. Appropriate strategies for individuals at other stages have been defined.

Assessment of Model Utilization

Application of models

The first stage of model utilization, identification of the factors that would influence the choice of a model, was assessed through the evaluation of a written assignment in response to the question, "How do you decide on what model to use?" Criteria were established for judging the papers. Three major areas were assessed. The first dealing with *"How* do you decide?" included reference to the learner, the teacher, the support system or material available, the context and the nature of the task. The second area dealing with *"What* model?" included the dimensions of understanding the function of a model, the number of models mentioned, the use of contrasting models between and within the same family, mention of models presented in class, and inclusion of models not taught in class. The final point for evaluation dealt with the quality of illustrations employed, including the use of a variety of illustrations, the appropriateness of the model cited, clarity, and elaboration. The criteria above were judged on a three-point scale from no mention, some reference, to a major point. A score was the sum of the ratings on the dimensions listed.

Creation of models

The second stage of model utilization was the creation of a new model. The students were asked to submit in writing the parameters of a model that they had created from any source or sources they chose. Criteria were again established for assessing the papers, but, as will be explained later, the detailed criteria could not be applied to the papers. It suffices to say that the major criteria employed included the quality of conceptualization, the description of the syntax or structure of the strategy, the description of the social system, and the delineation of the principles governing the reactions or responses by the teacher or materials.

Design

The semester consisted of fifteen class sessions meeting for 100 minutes each. Three of the class sessions were utilized early in the semester for work with models. A team of three instructors, including the authors, presented the concept of models and the family structure of models. The four models selected and described above were presented to the class. Part of the presentation of the Differential Training Model included response from the subjects to the questions assessing conceptual level. A fourth class session was utilized late in the semester for administration of the creativity and intelligence instruments and for gathering background information, including the number of years of teaching experience. The subjects were required to submit their "Application of Models" paper about halfway through the term. The "Creation of Models" paper was submitted at the end of the term. The authors served as judges in assessing the two assignments.

Results

Interjudge reliability on the first or minor model paper was computed to be .67. In attempting to apply the rating sheet for the "Creation of Models"

TABLE 13.1. Means and Standard Deviations for Two Scores on Assignments and Four Teacher Characteristics

Variable	Mean	Standard Deviation	N =
Application of Models	28.9	6.3	27
Creation of Models	10.5	5.9	20
Teaching Experience	3.7	4.8	26
Conceptual Level	1.4	0.3	25
Creativity			
Fluency	56.1	8.8	22
Flexibility	68.6	12.0	22
Originality	60.4	10.5	22
Intelligence	27.0	6.3	25

assignment to the papers that were submitted, it was found that so many dimensions of the criteria were left unaccounted for in the bulk of the papers that the score was not a meaningful reflection of the quality of the paper. Instead, the papers were rank-ordered, using the original criteria as a standard. The means and standard deviations on the two assignments as well as for teaching experience, conceptual level, creativity, and intelligence are tabulated in table 13.1. Correlations were computed between the four independent variables and the scores on the two papers. The correlation coefficients appear in table 13.2.

As indicated in table 13.2, several correlations were found to be significant. Some of the significant correlations do not bear directly on the major hypotheses, but attest to the interrelationships of the measures employed. The high,

TABLE 13.2. Correlations between Two Scores on Assignments and Four Teacher Characteristics (Number of Subjects are in Parenthesis)

	2	3	4	5	6	7	8
1. Application of Models	.61** (19)	−.20 (25)	.11 (24)	.22 (21)	.23 (21)	.59** (21)	.18 (24)
2. Creation of Models	—	−.14 (19)	−.08 (18)	.29 (17)	.29 (17)	.36 (17)	.28 (18)
3 Teaching Experience	—	—	−.17 (24)	−.41 (22)	−.40 (22)	−.43* (22)	−.33 (25)
4. Conceptual Level	—	—	—	−.04 (20)	−.04 (20)	.10 (20)	.28 (23)
5 Creativity-Fluency	—	—	—	—	.89** (22)	.86** (22)	.15 (22)
6. Creativity-Flexibility	—	—	—	.—	—	.80** (22)	.26 (22)
7. Creativity-Originality	—	—	—	—	—	—	.30 (22)
8. Intelligence	—	—	—	—	—	—	—

* Significant beyond the .05 level.
** Significant beyond the .01 level.

positive intercorrelation between the subscores of the creativity measure is consistent with that reported in the literature. The correlations were .89 ($df= 22$) between fluency and flexibility, .86 ($df= 22$) between fluency and originality, and .80 ($df= 22$) between flexibility and originality, all significant beyond the .01 level. A negative correlation of $-.43$ ($df= 22$) between teaching experience and originality was significant at the .05 level. There was a correlation of .61 ($df= 19$) between performances on the two assignments. This seems reasonable as a reflection of the consistency of the subject's work. Only one significant correlation was found between one of the four independent variables and performance on either assignment. A correlation of .59 ($df= 21$), significant at the .01 level, was established between performance on the "Application of Models" paper and the originality subscore on the creativity measure.

SUMMARY AND DISCUSSION

The most interesting finding of the study was the significant correlation between the originality subscore on creativity and the score on the minor model. The finding was at first a puzzling one. Applying logic one would expect to find a stronger relationship between originality and the second assignment which required the creation of a new model, a task which would appear to require originality. In retrospect, the failure to obtain a significant correlation between these variables must be due in part to the fact that the papers for this assignment fell far short of expectation and consequently often were not in keeping with the charge to create a new model. As a result, as mentioned earlier, the scoring procedure had to be drastically revised. For the "Application of Models" paper, on the other hand, the detailed scoring procedure was quite workable and may have resulted in a more meaningful score. The assignment did not merely ask for a regurgitation of presented material, but called for synthesis and extrapolation in articulating the underlying rationale governing the use of models. It appears that originality, an aspect of creativity, does have a strong relationship to this task. In view of the recent concern for nurturing creativity in children, this finding also suggests the value of nurturing creativity in teachers, particularly in the quest for meaningful innovations. Among such attempts that deserve further study is George I. Brown's work in teaching creativity to prospective teachers.[8] In light of the significant negative correlation between the originality subscore and teaching experience, attempts to cultivate creativity early in the preparation of teachers seem warranted. The ramifications of encouraging creativity in teachers are at the very least provocative and may open new vistas.

The difficulty encountered with the "Creation of Models" assignment deserves further explanation. During the semester several obstacles became apparent. The bulk of the class failed to grasp the idea of a repertoire consisting of distinct models each appropriate for a specific task. This lack of understanding was apparent in the assignments. Many papers attempted to delineate the best model, akin to the best method of instruction. Most of these papers presented models which were eclectic in orientation. These models attempted to cover all possible contingencies. It appeared that for many students it was not sufficient to construct a thoughtful model useful for a specific, though limited, situation. Perhaps the years of training in writing general or comprehensive papers made it difficult for some subjects to see value in limiting their responses. In the same vein, during one class discussion centering around the creation of a new school building, it was striking how easily the students could criticize the status quo, but how few ideas they had concerning the construction of a new structure. Our educational practices may favor sharp criticism, as documented by Jules Henry,[19] but may do little to cultivate the creation of viable substitutes. Another factor that may have contributed to the poor quality of the second set of papers was that the time spent in instruction on models was obviously insufficient. Additional time could be spent not only with models but in an effort to counteract many entrenched and predictable responses to an assignment. Since the concept of a repertoire of models is not a prevalent one, outside reinforcement cannot be expected to occur automatically. In addition, a more gradual progression of learning activities seems necessary, providing time for the ideas to be assimilated. Perhaps spending six half-sessions rather than three complete sessions might have resulted in a better use of time.

The finding that teaching experience had a negative though nonsignificant relationship to performance on both the major and minor models and a significant negative correlation with originality would leave the relating hypothesis open to question. Perhaps with extended experience in the classroom the teacher becomes comfortable with his established practices and is insulated from fresh ideas. It may take the young, inexperienced teacher to recognize the value of, or to be willing to suspend judgment on, novel ideas.

The restricted range in conceptual levels from 0.8 to 2.0 on a seven-point scale undoubtedly contributed to the low correlation with performance on the two assignments. However, this constricted range is consistent with reported conceptual levels of other samples of teachers. Conceivably, conceptual levels are not useful in working with teacher populations as sufficient discriminations are not made.

The subscores of fluency and flexibility from the creativity test interestingly do not correlate as strongly as the originality subscores with performance on the "Application of Models" assignment despite the high intercorrelations of all three subscores. A contributing factor may have been the length of the test, which had seven sections and took forty-five minutes of actual testing time, requiring the subject to write continuously for that length of time. Many subjects complained of fatigue, with a few working haphazardly and one subject refusing to complete the test. Fatigue would certainly take its toll on fluency, which is the number of responses. It may also affect flexibility, which is measured by the number of different categories within which responses fall. Less effort is expended by responding within a narrow range of categories. There is also the possibility that taking the creativity test was a threatening situation where some subjects may have been reluctant to expose themselves, relying primarily on conventional responses.

The intelligence measure also proved to be nondiscriminating. An argument can be made for the influence of self-selection. This would certainly be present in a graduate-level course, as subjects would not be expected to represent the full range of intelligence. This attenuation of the range would contribute to a lower correlation with other variables.

A look at table 14.2 will reveal that correlations were run with unequal numbers of subjects. The unusual nature of the spring term, 1970, and the refusal of a few students to complete some tests took their toll. In May, with several class sessions remaining, the campus reaction to the invasion of Cambodia resulted in cancellation of classes, with students given an option concerning completion of course work.

To summarize, the significant correlation between originality and the "Application of Models" assignment provides data for speculation concerning the relationship of creativity to innovations in the schools by teachers. This area deserves further investigation. The negative, though generally nonsignificant, correlations of teaching experience with all other variables under study point to the importance of focusing on relatively inexperienced teachers to introduce new modes of operation. Information concerning conceptual levels of teachers corroborates earlier findings and leaves the question of their use with teacher populations a moot point. Despite the inadequacies in the presentation of creating a repertoire of models, the results were encouraging and indicated areas of future investigation.

14

Improving Inservice Training

Bruce R. Joyce and Beverly Showers

To be most effective, training should include theory, demonstration, practice, feedback, and classroom application.

We have just completed a two-year effort to examine research on the ability of teachers to acquire teaching skills and strategies.

The first message from that research is very positive: teachers are wonderful learners. Nearly all teachers can acquire new skills that "fine tune" their competence. They can also learn a considerable repertoire of teaching strategies that are new to them.

The second message is more sobering, but still optimistic: in order to improve their skills and learn new approaches to teaching, teachers need certain conditions—conditions that are not common in most inservice settings even when teachers participate in the governance of those settings.

The third message is also encouraging: the research base reveals what conditions help teachers to learn. This information can be used to design staff development activities for classroom personnel.

TWO PURPOSES OF TRAINING

Improving our teaching can be focused on "tuning" our present skills or on learning new (to us) ways of teaching. When tuning our skills, we try to become more affirmative, involve students more, manage logistics more efficiently, ask more penetrating questions, induce students to be more productive, increase the clarity and vividness of our lectures and illustrations, and understand better the subject matter we teach. In short, we work on our craft. Training oriented toward fine tuning consolidates our competence and is likely to increase our effectiveness.

Mastering new teaching strategies or models and/or learning to put alternative curriculums in place is quite a different goal. To master a new approach we need to explore and understand its rationale, develop the ability to carry out the new strategies, and master fresh content.

Generally speaking, "fine tuning" our existing approaches is easier than mastering and implementing new ones, because the magnitude of change is smaller and less complex. When we change our repertoire, we have to learn to think differently, to behave differently, and to help children adapt to and become comfortable with the new approaches, so mastery of new techniques requires more intensive training than does the fine tuning.

We organized our analysis to find out how various components of training contribute to learning. To do this we developed a typology of "levels of impact" of training and another for categorizing training components. Then we asked the question, "In the body of research on training, how much does each kind of training component appear to contribute to each level of impact?"

LEVELS OF IMPACT

Whether we teach ourselves or whether we learn from a training agent, the outcomes of training can be classified into several levels of impact: awareness, the acquisition of concepts or organized knowledge, the learning of principles and skills, and the ability to apply those principles and skills in problem-solving activities.

Awareness. At the awareness level we realize the importance of an area and begin to focus on it. With inductive teaching, for example, the road to competence begins with awareness of the nature of inductive teaching, its probable uses, and how it fits into the curriculum.

Concepts and Organized Knowledge. Concepts provide intellectual control over relevant content. Essential to inductive teaching are knowledge of inductive processes, how learners at various levels of cognitive development respond to inductive teaching and knowledge about concept formation.

Principles and Skills. Principles and skills are tools for action. At this level we learn the skills of inductive teaching: how to help students collect data, organize it, and build concepts and test them. We also acquire the skills for adapting to students who display varying levels of ability to think inductively and for teaching them the skills they lack. At this level there is potential for action—we are *aware* of the area, can *think effectively* about it, and possess the *skills* to act.

Application and Problem Solving. Finally, we transfer the concepts, principles, and skills to the classroom. We begin to use the teaching strategy we have learned, integrate it into our style, and combine the strategy with the others in our repertoire.

Only after this fourth level has been reached can we expect impact on the education of children. Awareness alone is an insufficient condition. Organized knowledge that is not backed up by the acquisition of principles and skills and the ability to use them is likely to have little effect.

COMPONENTS OF TRAINING

Most of the training literature consists of investigations in which training elements are combined in various ways, whether they are directed toward the fine tuning of styles or the mastery of new approaches. From our analysis, we were able to identify a number of training components that have been studied intensively. Alone and in combination, each of these training components contributes to the impact of a training sequence or activity. (As we shall see, when used together, each has much greater power than when they are used alone.) The major components of training in the studies we reviewed are:

1. Presentation of theory or description of skill or strategy
2. Modeling or demonstration of skills or models of teaching
3. Practice in simulated and classroom settings
4. Structured and open-ended feedback (provision of information about performance)
5. Coaching for application (hands-on, in-classroom assistance with the transfer of skills and strategies to the classroom)

THE NATURE OF THE LITERATURE

We analyzed more than 200 studies in which researchers investigated the effectiveness of various kinds of training methods. Determining levels of impact from single and combined treatments was difficult for several reasons. Most training studies were not designed to measure levels of impact on the incremental value of each training component. Rather, research questions were generally focused on differences between treatment and comparison groups.

Conclusions nearly always addressed the issue of whether skills were acquired and demonstrated. The question of transfer at the classroom level was addressed in relatively few studies. Nevertheless, we have developed working hypotheses regarding expected levels of impact from the various training strategies. The hypotheses are extrapolations derived from investigations that examined training elements for their impact on teacher behavior. Although the conclusions here are working hypotheses, we believe they adequately represent the present state of the literature and that training programs can use them reliably.

No single study used all training components and measured effects at all levels of impact. However, the training literature taken as a whole provides information on many of the possible combinations. For example, simulated practice has been studied for its impact on skills development (Cruickshank,[3] Vlcek [12]). Structured feedback has been compared to open-ended feedback and self-observation (Tuckman,[11] Saloman and McDonald [10]).

Studies combining modeling, practice, and feedback (Orme [9]); presentation, practice, and feedback (Edwards [4]); presentation, modeling, practice, and feedback (Borg [1]; Borg, Langer, and Kelley [2]) have been heavily investigated with respect to skill acquisition and transfer.

Although few studies focused on "coaching to application" as conceived here, several treatments included lengthy follow-up feedback after initial training (and these methods seemed to result in greater transfer at the classroom level). Feldens and Duncan [5] demonstrated the power of observation, feedback, and goal setting to boost the effects of training, and Borg, Langer, and Kelley [2] found permanence of fine-tuning skills in a delayed posttest after an initial training that included presentation, modeling, practice, and feedback.

Is there a clear demarcation between fine tuning and new repertoire? Sometimes it was unclear if the focus of the study was fine tuning of existing skills or redirection of teaching style. Frequently, pretraining observations of teaching were omitted from the training study, so the level of entry skills was unknown. However, we have applied several general rules of thumb to distinguish the purposes of training. First, if preservice teachers were the subjects of training, we were most likely to label the training objective "new repertoire" than if inservice teachers were the subjects. Secondly, training aimed at questioning skills, discussion skills, question wait time, attending to overlooked students, and positive reinforcement of desirable student behavior were generally classified "fine tuning." It seemed reasonable to assume that these behaviors reside in everyone's repertoire, including teachers and teacher trainees. Thus, if training involved installation of a new curriculum, instruction in inquiry strategies, or unusual models of teaching that departed radically from the usual recitation classroom process, the purpose of training was assumed to be redirection of teaching style.

Was there an awareness of the need for addressing the transfer question in the training research? Apparently, many researchers are aware of the need to assess transfer of learned skills at the classroom level. Recent carefully designed studies examining relationships between student learning and teacher training have carefully monitored teacher behavior in the classroom to assure the implementation of new strategies thought to influence student learning. Furthermore, many studies conclude with the observation that application of skills in the classroom should be the subject of future research.

What is the power of individual components? Some components were studied intensively; others were not. We discovered no studies in which presentation alone was the training strategy, but it often appeared as a "control," when it was invariably surpassed by treatments including modeling, practice, or feedback components. Likewise, no studies were reviewed in which practice alone constituted the treatment.

The evidence for modeling and feedback is the clearest. Karan, Snow, and McDonald [8] demonstrated the efficacy of modeling for redirecting teacher behavior, and Good and Brophy [7] illustrated the effectiveness of feedback in a powerful one-shot interview based on four months of classroom observation.

How conflicting were the findings? The results of training studies are remarkably consistent. Teachers learn the knowledge and concepts they are taught and can generally demonstrate new skills and strategies if provided opportunities for any combination of modeling, practice, or feedback.

Was the level of impact always discernible? The absence of fine-grained analyses that examine all levels of impact for individuals in a training program leaves many questions unanswered, for example, the percentage of trainees that achieved each level of impact following training. For the purposes of this review, we assumed that skills had been acquired if teachers were observed to exhibit the trained skills or strategies in peer teaching, microteaching, or classroom settings. If observations occurred several months after completion of training and the trained skills or strategies were in evidence, we assumed transfer had been accomplished. Now, what did we find?

EFFECTIVENESS OF COMPONENTS

1. *Presentation of Theory.* The substance of theory components is the rationale, theoretical base, and verbal description of an approach to teaching or a skill or instructional technique. Readings, lectures, films, and discussions are used to describe the approach, its conceptual base and potential uses. In many higher education courses and inservice institutes and workshops, it is not uncommon for presentation of theory to be the major and in some cases the sole component of the training experience. In research it is frequently combined with one or more of the other components.

Level of Impact. Either for tuning of style or mastery of new approaches, presentation of theory can raise awareness and increase conceptual control of an area to some extent. However, it is for relatively few teachers that it results in skill acquisition or the transfer of skills into the classroom situation (although there are some people who build and transfer skills from theory presentations alone). On the other hand, when the presentation of theory is used in combination with the other training components, it appears to boost conceptual control, skill development, and transfer. It is not powerful enough alone to achieve much impact beyond the awareness level, but when combined with the others, it is an important component.

2. *Modeling or Demonstration.* Modeling involves enactment of the teaching skill or strategy either through a live demonstration with children or adults, or through television, film, or other media. In a given training activity, a strategy or skill can be modeled any number of times. Much of the literature is flawed because only one or two demonstrations have been made of some quite complex models of teaching, thus comprising relatively weak treatments.

   Level of Impact. Modeling appears to have a considerable effect on awareness and some effect on knowledge. Demonstration also increases the mastery of theory. We understand better what is illustrated to us. A good many teachers can imitate demonstrated skills fairly readily and a number will transfer them to classroom practice. However, for most teachers modeling alone is unlikely to result in the acquisition and transfer of skills unless it is accompanied by other components. Fairly good levels of impact can be achieved through the use of modeling alone where the tuning of style is involved, but for the mastery of new approaches it, by itself, does not have great power for many teachers. All in all, research appears to indicate that modeling is very likely to be an important component of any training program aimed at acquisition of complex skills and their transfer to the classroom situation.

3. *Practice Under Simulated Conditions.* Practice involves trying out a new skill or strategy. Simulated conditions are usually achieved by carrying out the practice either with peers or with small groups of children under circumstances which do not require management of an entire class or larger group of children at the same time.

   Level of Impact. It is difficult to imagine practice without prior awareness and knowledge; that is, we have to know what it is we are to practice. However, when awareness and knowledge have been achieved, practice is a very efficient way of acquiring skills and strategies whether related to the tuning of style or the mastery of new approaches. Once a relatively high level of skill has been achieved, a sizeable percentage of teachers will begin to transfer the skill into their instructional situations, but this will not be true of all persons by any means, and it is probable that the more complex and unfamiliar the skill or strategy, the lower will be the level of transfer. All in all, research supports common sense with respect to practice under simulated conditions. That is, it is an extremely effective way to develop competence in a wide variety of classroom techniques.

4a. *Structured Feedback.* Structured feedback involves learning a system for observing teaching behavior and providing an opportunity to reflect on teaching by using the system. Feedback can be self-administered, provided by observers, or given by peers and coaches. It can be regular or occasional. It can be combined with other components; which are organized toward the acquisition of specific skills and strategies. That is, it can be directly combined with practice and a practice-feedback–practice-feedback sequence can be developed. Taken alone, feedback can result in considerable awareness of one's teaching behavior and knowledge about alternatives. With respect to the fine tuning of styles, it has reasonable power for acquisition of skills and their transfer to the classroom situation. For example, if feedback is given about patterns of rewarding and punishing, many teachers will begin to modify the ways they reward and punish children. Similarly, if feedback is provided about the kinds of questions asked in the classroom, many teachers will become more aware of their use of questions and set goals for changes. In general these changes persist as long as feedback continues to be provided and then styles gradually slide back toward their original point. In other words, feedback alone does not appear to provide permanent changes, but regular and consistent feedback is probably necessary if people are to make changes in very many areas of behavior and maintain those changes.

4b. *Open-ended Feedback.* Unstructured feedback, that is, feedback consisting of an informal discussion following observation, has uneven impact. Some persons appear to profit considerably from it while many do not. It is most likely that unstructured feedback best accomplishes an awareness of teaching style and as such can be very useful in providing "readiness" for more extensive and directed training activities. For example, teachers might begin to observe one another informally and engage in general discussions about teaching behavior and then proceed toward focused attempts at change. Modeling followed by practice and feedback can be very powerful in achieving skill development and transfer.

5. *Coaching for Application.* When the other training components are used in combination, the levels of impact are considerable for most teachers up through the skill level, whether the object is the tuning of style or the mastery of new approaches to teaching. For example, demonstration of unfamiliar models of teaching or curriculum approaches combined with discussions of theory and followed by practice with structured feedback reach the skill acquisition level of impact with nearly all (probably nine out of ten) teachers at the inservice or preservice levels. If consistent feedback is provided with classroom practice, a good many, but not all, will transfer their skills into the teaching situation. For many others, however, direct coaching on how to apply the new skills and models, appears to be necessary. Coaching can be provided by colleagues, supervisors, professors, curriculum consultants, or others thoroughly familiar with the approaches. Coaching for application involves helping teachers analyze the content to be taught and the approach to be taken, and making very specific plans to help the student adapt to the new teaching approach.

COMBINATIONS OF COMPONENTS

For maximum effectiveness of most inservice activities, it appears wisest to include several and perhaps all of the training components we have listed (see Orme [9]). Where the fine tuning of style is the focus, modeling, practice under simulated conditions, and practice in the classroom, combined with feedback, will probably result in considerable changes. Where the mastery of a new approach is the desired outcome, presentations and discussions of theory and coaching to application are probably necessary as well. If the theory of a new approach is well presented, the approach is demonstrated, practice is provided under simulated conditions with careful and consistent feedback, and that practice is followed by application in the classroom with coaching and further feedback, it is likely that the vast majority of teachers will be able to expand their repertoire to the point where they can utilize a wide variety of approaches to teaching and curriculum. If any of these components are left out, the impact of training will be weakened in the sense that fewer numbers of people will progress to the transfer level (which is the only level that has significant meaning for school improvement). The most effective training activities, then, will be those that combine theory, modeling, practice, feedback, and coaching to application. The knowledge base seems firm enough that we can predict that if those components are in fact combined in inservice programs, we can expect the outcomes to be considerable at all levels.

Future research on training should systematically address the many cells of the training components/levels of impact matrix that currently lack adequate data. An emphasis on the effects of "coaching to application" on "problem solving," with coaching administered by other teachers, principals, supervisors, and so on, should provide useful information not only on "coaching" as a training strategy but on the relative effectiveness of various training agents as well. If, in fact, coaching by peers proves to boost the magnitude of classroom implementation, an extremely practical and powerful training method can be added to the already tested strategies of theory presentation, modeling, practice, and feedback.

PART VI

Children and Models of Teaching: the MOTAC Series

If teachers can increase their repertoire of models of teaching, what then happens to their students? How flexible are *they?* Does personality affect the ability of the student to relate to alternative approaches to teaching?

David Hunt initiated what we came to call the MOTAC Series, (Models of Teaching Accessibility Characteristics) to explore the relationship between student characteristics and their ability to profit from alternative approaches to teaching. The earlier MOTAC studies investigated the relationship between student personality and preference for certain models (for example, we expected that the lower conceptual-level students would respond more positively to the more structured models of teaching, while the higher conceptual-level students would prefer relatively unstructured models). The later studies explored the susceptibility of students to training so that they could respond to models more fully. The questions were asked, "Can students learn to not only respond to alternative teaching approaches but also to share leadership in the instructional situation? Can they learn to use a method of learning independently of the teacher?" Further, can students be taught the skills essential to participation in various models of teaching?

Generally speaking, the results were parallel to those obtained in the teacher training investigations. Conceptual level does influence preference for models of varying structures and task complexities, and the preferences are in line with conceptual systems theory. Also, however, students who vary widely in conceptual level appear to be able to develop their skills to the point where they can take major leadership in the implementation of a model. That is, they can develop such skill that they become gradually free from dependence on the teacher's leadership and develop ability to generate and carry out their own learning activities, using the paradigms of the models.

In other words, a model of teaching can serve as a model of learning, as a guide for the learner as well as the teacher. The implication is quite clear: students can respond to a wide range of models and will respond more powerfully if they are explicitly taught the skills for relating to it effectively.

A conclusion is that training offered to teachers should not simply implement a model as an instructional tool but should implement it in such a way that the learners acquire the skills necessary for them to profit from it maximally. The teacher's mastery of a given model of teaching, thus, can follow a progression something like this:

1. First, the model is learned in an acceptable form. That is, the teacher learns to carry it out in a recognizable way so that it can be used for instruction.

2. The teacher learns to transform the model and combine it with other models so that it can be used in extended units of instruction.

3. The teacher learns to teach it to the students, helping them to acquire it and carry it out independently.

The repertoire of models acquired by the teacher becomes, in this sense, potential repertoire for the student.

Gradually, the students learn to respond to an increasing variety of learning environments and to profit from them.

Hopefully, this will permit students to relate more effectively to the potential learning opportunities in their learning environments. They will face some situations where instruction will be highly structured, others where independence is required, still others which require the interaction with other persons to solve problems. As the learner experiences a greater variety and acquires the skills for profiting from them, his ability to learn expands in ways parallel to that of the teacher.

15

Student Conceptual Level and Models of Teaching: Theoretical and Empirical Coordination of Two Models

David E. Hunt, Bruce R. Joyce, JoAnn Greenwood, Joyce E. Noy, Roma Reid, and Marsha Weil

Most earlier studies of the teaching-learning process have been piecemeal, either investigating teaching while disregarding students, or investigating only student characteristics. Investigations of the teaching-learning process require a theoretical framework which coordinates three components: student characteristics (person), characteristics of the teaching approach (environment), and learning outcomes (behavior). The MOTAC studies view students in terms of *conceptual level*[5] and teaching is viewed in terms of *models of teaching*.[18] They investigate the interactive effect of one or more models of teaching (environment) upon students varying in conceptual level (person) as indexed by a variety of learning outcomes (behavior). The two models—conceptual level matching model and models of teaching—have been converging theoretically for some time, but these studies are the first empirical investigations based on the theoretical coordination of the two models.

The conceptual level matching model[5] describes the differential effects of educational environments varying in structure on students of varying conceptual level (CL): low CL students are likely to profit from high structure while high CL students should profit from low structure, or learn effectively in a variety of structures. Models of teaching[18] describe a variety of teaching approaches in terms of their syntax, sequence, and structure, thus providing a systematic basis for describing educational environments of varying degrees of structure. For example, an advance-organizer approach is considered highly structured, an inductive teaching approach moderately structured, and group investigation low in structure. The design of the present studies, therefore,

TABLE 15.1

Conceptual Level (Person)	Models of Teaching (Environment)	Learning Outcomes (Behavior)
Low CL (need much structure)	Inductive Teaching	Cognitive measures at different levels
	Synectics	Model-specific measures
High CL (need little structure)	Role Playing	Attitude measures

was derived from a general B-P-E (behavior-person-environment) analysis proposed by Hunt and Sullivan [13] as shown in table 15.1.

Student CL is considered an "accessibility characteristic" [5] because it is coordinated with an environmental characteristic, degree of structure. Other accessibility characteristics such as student's need for affiliation (which is coordinated with effective learning through group discussion) have been identified, and will later be investigated as they interact with various models of teaching. Therefore, the coordinated theoretical framework is called MOTAC (Models of Teaching-Accessibility Characteristics).

The teaching-learning process does not occur in a vacuum; investigations require *content* to be taught and learned. The content vehicles in the present MOTAC investigations have been adapted from information systems or data banks, based on either cultures [17] or persons.[22] Therefore, the empirical studies combine instructional systems (models of teaching), conceptual systems (accessibility characteristics) and information systems (biographical and cultural data banks) to investigate their interactive effects.

The goal for students is to acquire a wider variety of learning styles, or to learn on their own. This developmental goal for students could be operationally stated as the capability of learning from a wide variety of models of teaching.

Relation between Models of Teaching and Matching Models

In addition to providing one operational basis for specifying the developmental goal of the CL matching model, models of teaching are compatible with matching models in several ways. First and foremost, the sixteen models of teaching have been described in terms of their degree of structure, and therefore provide the ideal companion model for the coordinated study of the teaching-learning process. For example, an advance-organizer approach (high structure) should be more effective with low CL students than a group-investigation approach (low structure). One of the models of teaching, sensitivity training, was found to have the predicted differential effects on teacher trainees: [3] high CL trainees showed greater improvement in the adaptability of their teaching under sensitivity (low structure) training while low CL trainees improved more with the Human Development Institute (high structure) approach. Since the initial classification of models according to degree of structure [18] (p. 305) was made on a logical basis, the present MOTAC studies provide an empirical basis to verify or correct the classification of models of teaching in terms of degree of structure (or may perhaps indicate the need for a more differential, multidimensional system to replace degree of structure).

Second, the system for interaction analysis to describe models of teaching has been devised with an aim to detecting CL-relevant responses. Thus, the various levels of information-processing in the objective coding system have the same theoretical basis as the different levels of conceptual development. Third, CL of the teacher trainee was found to be related to the overall capability which trainees exhibit in learning three models of teaching, though CL did not predict capability in any one single model [21, p. 50]. Thus, at a teacher-trainee level, CL seems to be an index of flexibility in teaching or "learning to learn" models of teaching.

Finally, models of teaching have been classified into four "families" [18]: information processing, social interaction, personal sources, and behavior modification, and it may turn out that certain accessibility characteristics of students are more relevant to certain families. For example:

Accessibility Characteristic	Model of Teaching Family
Cognitive orientation	Information processing
Motivational orientation	Social interaction Behavior modification
Value orientation	Personal sources

Although this diagram is speculative, it may serve to guide the selection of specific combinations of models of teaching and accessibility characteristics in future MOTAC studies.

GENERAL DESIGN AND PROCEDURE

The basic procedure in each MOTAC study consisted of (1) preselecting a group of students who were similar in a particular accessibility characteristic, for example, low in CL; who were then (2) provided with information on a topic; after which (3) the students worked on the topic through a specific model of teaching; and (4) completed various outcome measures. Thus the general procedure consisted of a three-phase sequence: information—teaching—outcome.

Formation of Teaching Groups

All students in the present series were in junior high school, Grade 7, 8, or 9. Teaching groups were small, consisting of six, eight, or twelve students, always made up half of girls and half of boys. Teaching groups in MOTAC I and MOTAC II were selected on CL; therefore, a specific teaching group consisted of all low CL students or all high CL students, but each group was equated for ability. The attempt was to make up teaching groups similar in all respects (grade, sex, ability) except CL.

Models of Teaching

To maximize the precision with which the models were taught, all models were taught by one of the two authors of *Models of Teaching*,[18] Bruce Joyce and Marsha Weil. Teaching sessions in MOTAC I were fifty to sixty minutes, and somewhat longer in MOTAC II. Teachers generally attempted to teach the model in a constant fashion to each group with a minimum of "student pull." Since all sessions were both live-recorded and videotaped, the degree to which a specific model was taught in a similar fashion from group to group could be objectively determined. Teachers were initially unaware of the CL group, but usually became aware of the nature of the CL group through students' behavior. In one study, a teaching group received only one session with one model; in one, students received one session with several models; and in another, several sessions with one model. Also, some control groups received no teaching while others received neither teaching nor information.

Outcome Measures

Learning outcome measures in as many levels of the taxonomy as possible were collected. Model-specific measures were also obtained both during and after the teaching. Attitudinal measures were collected after every teaching session.

Content Vehicles: Information Systems

The importance of subject matter or content is often underplayed in research, yet the content dealt with in the teaching-learning process is a central component. The appropriateness of a content vehicle should be considered in relation to the design, to the students, to the models of teaching, and to the learning outcomes. From the design viewpoint, the content should be in a form communicable in the forty-five to sixty minutes of the information phase. It should be both novel and interesting for the junior high school students. From the model standpoint, it should be sufficiently versatile to lend itself appropriately to a variety of models (not to deny that there may be topics more appropriate for certain models than others, but some content may have a wider area of model applicability). In terms of learning outcomes, the content should lend itself to consideration at a variety of outcome levels. The central criteria for content is that it should be complex, multidimensional, and open to a diversity of interpretations. Although the content vehicle should be potentially multidimensional and complex, it should be presented to the students initially in a form that is factual, noninterpretive, and "flat."

Content in such form was available in the biographical information systems, or data banks. They used a specifically designed category system (essentially, a taxonomy of a person's life) to organize information about a person into a random-access-and-retrieval system similar to those developed by Joyce and Joyce [17] for cultures. The first biographical data bank on Sigmund Freud consisted of 283 topics classified into 34 categories. The second bank on Ernest Hemingway was more extensive, consisting of 446 topics in 36 categories.[24]

The life and work of Hemingway was chosen for the content vehicle in the present studies. Material from the original data bank was revised to MOTAC requirements, i.e., a "minibank" was developed from the original "maxibank." Devising outcome measures was facilitated by the existing bank of 446 objective items, one for each topic in the original bank. The minibank was slightly revised for MOTAC II, and an additional set of materials describing Hemingway's work was added. In addition to decisions about design, a decision must also be made about what content vehicle to use in each MOTAC study. Therefore, we are presently developing alternate content vehicles of other persons (Freud) and cultures (Banbury, England) to serve as minibanks meeting MOTAC requirements.

MOTAC I

The first studies in the series, referred to as MOTAC I,* were primarily exploratory, and they yielded considerable information bearing on such questions as what model to use, how many teaching sessions, how many students to include in a teaching group, whether to use an intraindividual (same students/different models) or interindividual (different students/different models) design, how flexible the model should be in relation to student pull, and perhaps most important, what outcomes to observe and how to measure them.

* We appreciate the assistance of the following colleagues in conducting MOTAC I: Margo Biersdorf, Dean Flood, Robert Gower, Karen Haak, and Nancy Watson.

Two studies were conducted, a Grade 7 study in which all students experienced three different models (intraindividual), and a Grade 9 study in which each student experienced either one or no model (interindividual). Apart from this difference, the studies were almost identical. Teaching groups consisted of either low or high CL students who (1) received information about Hemingway, (2) were instructed by an inductive teaching and/or synectics model (plus a role-playing model in Grade 7), and (3) also completed a similar battery of learning and attitude-outcome measures. Both samples of students were selected from schools that are applying educational arrangements based on CL matching principles. Grade 7 students were selected from a junior high school in which students are homogeneously grouped on the basis of CL, or learning style,[9] and Grade 9 students were selected from two schools varying in their structure to serve students with different learning styles.[11]

MOTAC I—Grade 7: Method

Formation of CL groups

The Grade 7 study was conducted during a three-day period in May 1973. Two groups of twelve students each, one low in CL and one high in CL, were selected on the basis of their scores on the Paragraph Completion Method [10] from approximately 250 Grade 7 students in a suburban Ontario junior high school. Twelve high CL students, six boys and six girls, were first selected on the basis of their CL scores (1.7 or above). The low CL group was selected by pairing each high CL student with a student of the same sex and score on the Canadian Test of Basic Skills (CTBS), but with a low CL score (1.0). An alternate low CL student was selected, and because there were no absences, the low CL group consisted of thirteen students. Mean CTBS scores (administered in May 1972) in grade equivalents were identical for both groups, 6.8. Mean CL scores were 1.0 for the low CL group and 1.9 for the high CL group.

Content materials

Hemingway's life was summarized in a brief two-page chronology and a short twelve-page minibank containing information about his life—his family, interests, health, friendships, writings, and philosophy of life (see Appendix G). His writings were illustrated by (1) "The Killers," (2) "Judgment of Manitou," and (3) "El Sordo's Stand" from *For Whom the Bell Tolls.*

Models of teaching

Three models were used: inductive teaching [18] (p. 123–136) [20] (p. 3–66), synectics [18] (p. 233–252) and role playing,[20] (p. 139–178). Bruce Joyce taught each of the six teaching sessions for a period of from fifty to sixty minutes.

Interaction analysis

All sessions were live-coded by experienced coders using the system devised by Joyce, Guillion, Weil, Wald, McKibbin, and Feller.[16] All sessions were videotaped, which provided a basis for later recoding when necessary. The major coding categories of the system were structuring, information, and feedback. Structuring moves are considered either directive or negotiating; information as low, middle, or high level; open, or opinion; feedback as positive, neutral, negative, or corrective. Each statement by the teacher and by each student was coded and then expressed in terms of fifteen indices:

1. Teacher talk (proportion of all responses).
2. Structuring (proportion of all responses).
3. Information (proportion of all responses).
4. Sanctions (proportion of all responses).
5. Teacher negotiations (proportion of teacher structuring).
6. Student negotiations (proportion of student structuring).
7. Teacher middle information (proportion of teacher information).
8. Student middle information (proportion of student information).
9. Teacher higher information (proportion of teacher information).
10. Student higher information (proportion of student information).
11. Teacher opinion (proportion of teacher information).
12. Student opinion (proportion of student information).
13. Teacher positive sanctions (proportion of teacher sanctions).
14. Teacher neutral sanctions (proportion of teacher sanctions).
15. Teacher negative sanctions (proportion of teacher sanctions).

Intercoder reliability was .85.

Outcome measures

To obtain an accurate representation of effects, affective measures and cognitive measures at differing levels were obtained. Data were also collected on some model-specific measures for exploratory purposes.

1. *Attitudes:* Students were asked to answer the question, "How well did you like the method of teaching today?" by circling a number from 1 (very little) to 5 (very much) and indicating their reasons. They were also asked "How much did you feel you learned by the method of teaching used today?" and responded on a five-point scale, giving reasons.

2. *Recall:* (App. G) Students completed a twenty-item objective test on the Hemingway material (ten true-false and ten multiple choice).

3. *Essay (causal inferences):* Students were asked to write an essay with

the following instructions: "A writer's life often affects his work and his writing often affects his life. Describe as much as you can about the relation between Hemingway's life and his writing. How did his life influence his writing and how did his writing influence his life?" This task was thought to be at a higher cognitive level since it required analysis. Causal inference score was the number of causal inferences contained in the essay, and they ranged from 0 to 8. Interrater reliability for scoring was .83 ($N = 25$).

4. *Model-specific measures:* In addition to their use for communicating content in a variety of ways, most models of teaching also have process goals, i.e., attempt to facilitate model-specific skills. For example, inductive teaching aims to increase skill in forming concepts while synectics aims to increase skill in metaphorical thinking. Therefore, several model-specific items relevant to these two skills were used for exploratory purposes to note whether synectics teaching produced model-specific effects in metaphorical thinking and whether inductive teaching produced effects on items measuring concept formation.

Specific procedure

The procedure was the same for both groups with order of teaching sessions counterbalanced on the three days. Table 15.2 summarizes the procedure.

Interaction analysis indices

Results of interaction analysis are summarized by the fifteen indices described earlier that are expressed in proportions. Summarizing interaction analyses results in percentages, giving us a useful characterization which is comparable between teaching sessions; however, it does not indicate the absolute number of specific behaviors occurring in that category. Table 15.3 presents the results of the six teaching sessions by CL group. CL differences are indicated by chi-square, but it should be noted that the indices are related to one another, and the differences viewed accordingly.

Results of table 15.3 comparisons of teacher behavior can be considered in terms of "student pull." For example, the greater occurrence of teacher use of higher-level information processing for the high CL group in role playing is presumably due to the teacher's susceptibility to student characteris-

TABLE 15.2. Synopsis of Procedure: MOTAC I, Grade 7

Day	Information	Teaching	Outcome
1	Hemingway's Life	Inductive teaching	Attitude, Model-specific measures
2	No new information	Synectics	Same
3	No new information	Role playing	Attitude, Recall, Essay

TABLE 15.3. MOTAC I—Grade 7: Interaction Analysis Indices—Comparison of CL Groups

Index	Inductive Teaching		Synectics		Role Playing	
	Low CL vs. High CL		Low CL vs. High CL		Low CL vs. High CL	
1. Teacher talk	.752	.706	.731	.650 *	.540	.584
2. Total structuring	.378	.341	.254	.251	.247	.206
3. Total information	.447	.469	.519	.626 **	.703	.652
4. Total sanctions	.120	.146	.147	.075 **	.036	.095
5. Teacher negotiations	.005	.024	.009	.000	.434	.182 **
6. Student negotiations	.000	.045	.000	.000	.862	.348 **
7. Teacher middle information	.279	.374	.615	.674	.404	.226 **
8. Student middle information	.388	.575 **	.635	.808 **	.603	.158 **
9. Teacher higher information	.129	.130	.082	.014 *	.135	.432 **
10. Student higher information	.091	.090	.035	.041	.043	.392 **
11. Teacher opinion	.029	.033	.057	.159 **	.117	.178
12. Student opinion	.025	.037	.026	.096 *	.124	.240 **
13. Teacher positive sanctioning	.174	.280	.431	.235	.333	.250
14. Teacher neutral sanctioning	.739	.640	.554	.765 *	.619	.636
15. Teacher negative sanctioning	.014	.000	.000	.000	.000	.000

* = < .05   ** = < .01 (Underlining indicates higher group.)

tics. That the high CL students themselves make more such statements (.392) in this session supports this notion. Such CL differences in student behavior exemplify model-specific CL characteristics; for example, the higher incidence of student opinion for high CL students in both synectics and role playing.

Outcome results

Attitude

In expressing their attitude to synectics, the low CL (4.1) was more favorable ($< .05$) than the high CL group (3.4). It should also be noted that the synectics model was less favorably evaluated ($< .05$) by both groups combined (3.8) when compared with inductive-teaching (4.3) and role-playing (4.4) models.

Recall and causal inferences

The results of these two learning measures can best be shown in a correlational table with CL and CTBS as shown in table 15.4.

As will be noted in table 15.4, there is a clear and distinctive pattern of relationships: CL to the higher-level measure (causal inferences); ability (CTBS) to the lower-level measure (recall). The mean scores for the two CL groups were identical for recall (14.7), and the causal inference mean score was 5.8 for high CL and 3.5 for the low CL group. This significant ($< .01$) CL difference might reflect dispositional tendencies present before experiencing teaching sessions, but the results to be presented from the control group in the Grade 9 study make this interpretation unlikely.

Model-specific measures

Differences between CL groups were observed for two model-specific measures. On one inductive teaching measure which required the student to provide labels for already organized groups of statements about Hemingway, the high CL groups were significantly better ($< .01$) at providing adequate labels. On the synectics measure which reflected a student's selecting remote, or conceptually distant analogies, the high CL group scored higher ($< .05$).

TABLE 15.4. MOTAC I, Grade 7: Intercorrelation

Variable	2	3	4
CL [1]	−.03	−.07	.59 **
CTBS		.56 **	.08
Recall			.08
Causal inferences			

[1] All correlations with CL are biserial *r*'s
$N = 25$ ** $= < .01$

MOTAC I—Grade 9: Method

This study was similar to the Grade 7 study in the following: (1) formation of groups (low and high CL), (2) models (inductive teaching and synectics, but not role playing), (3) content material, (4) interaction analysis measures, and (5) outcome measures. It differed in: (1) size of teaching group (six students instead of twelve), (2) number of models experienced (one instead of three), and (3) in the inclusion of two control groups, one which received no model and one which received no model and no information. The study was conducted immediately following the Grade 7 study in May 1973.

Formation of CL groups and design

Students were selected from a pool of approximately 475 Grade 9 students in two Ontario high schools and assigned to either the low or high CL group on the same basis as the Grade 7 study. Forty-eight low CL students (scoring 1.0) and forty-eight high CL students (scoring 1.8 or above), plus a few alternates were assigned to one of four treatments—(1) inductive teaching, (2) synectics, (3) no model–control, and (4) no information–no model–control. The final actual number varied slightly from twelve in each cell. For inductive teaching, synectics, and no model–control, there were thirteen students in each CL group. In the no model–no information group there were eleven students in each CL group, or a total of 100 students in all groups.

The mean CL score for each of the four low CL groups was 1.0. The mean CL score for the high CL–inductive teaching group was 2.0, and for the other three CL groups, 1.9. In addition to varying in CL, the eight groups were designed to be equal in ability (SCAT), with an equal number of boys and girls and an equal number from each of the two schools.

Models of teaching

Although it had been initially planned to use twelve or thirteen students in each teaching group, the Grade 7 experience indicated that this number was rather large. Therefore, the four teaching groups (Low CL–inductive; high CL–inductive; low CL–synectics and high CL–synectics) were each subdivided into two smaller teacher groups of six or seven, all from the same school, similar in SCAT score and approximately equal in boys and girls. Bruce Joyce and Marsha Weil each taught one group in each of the four model combinations, but for analytic purposes, the two teaching sessions were combined.

Specific procedure

Table 15.5 summarizes the procedure.

TABLE 15.5. Synopsis of Design and Procedure: MOTAC I, Grade 9

Group	Information	Teaching	Outcome
1	Hemingway's life	Inductive	Attitude, Recall, Essay, Model-specific measures
2	Hemingway's life	Synectics	Same
3	Hemingway's life	No teaching. Film: *The Killers*	Same
4	None	None	Recall, model-specific measures

Interaction analysis indices

Table 15.6 presents the results for the two models by CL group.

Results of table 15.6 can be compared with the comparable indices in Grade 7 shown in table 15.3. The pattern of "student pull" effects is less consistent from Grade 7 to Grade 9 than is the consistency of general model indices from the two studies.

The interaction analysis results from the Grade 7 and Grade 9 studies were used in two recent dissertations, one by Gower,[2] which used these indices to define an exemplary model, and one by McKibbin,[22] who compared these indices with the same teaching sessions coded by the Flanders' system and the Bellack system of interaction analysis.

Outcome results

Attitude

No differences were found between mean attitude scores of CL or teaching groups. Surprisingly, the most favorable attitude to method was expressed by the low CL–control group who saw a "nonteaching" film (however, this score, 4.3, was not significantly higher than the others). The most interesting pattern of attitude results came from considering the correlation of attitude to method with recall and causal inference scores in the three conditions as shown in table 15.7.

Table 15.7 indicates that favorable attitude to inductive teaching is significantly related to generating inferences, which is a process goal of the inductive teaching model. No such pattern is seen in the other two conditions although attitude to synectics was positively related to recall score.

Recall

Students in the no teaching—no information control condition scored significantly lower ($< .01$) on recall (10.3) than did those in the other three conditions; however, no other significant differences were noted. Neither CL

TABLE 15.6. MOTAC I—Grade 9: Interaction Analysis Indices—Comparison of CL Groups

Index	Inductive Teaching		Synectics	
	Low CL	High CL	Low CL	High CL
1. Teacher talk	.682	.735 *	.572	.671 **
2. Total structuring	.248	.255	.267	.277
3. Total information	.608	.564	.584	.557
4. Total sanctions	.075	.108 *	.122	.078
5. Teacher negotiations	.019	.000	.038	.091 *
6. Student negotiations	.067	.000	.217	.364
7. Teacher middle information	.380	.424	.543	.589
8. Student middle information	.515	.567	.645	.662
9. Teacher higher information	.143	.164	.094	.073
10. Student higher information	.088	.085	.144	.086 *
11. Teacher opinion	.086	.026 **	.098	.113
12. Student opinion	.022	.009	.056	.065
13. Teacher positive sanctioning	.343	.174 *	.329	.397
14. Teacher neutral sanctioning	.642	.779	.608	.562
15. Teacher negative sanctioning	.000	.000	.000	.000

* = < .05   ** = < .01
(Underlining indicates higher group.)

TABLE 15.7. MOTAC I, Grade 9: Correlations Between Attitude to Method and Outcome Measures in Three Conditions

		Correlation Between Attitude to Method	
Condition	N	Recall	Causal Inferences
Inductive teaching	26	.00	.37 *
Synectics	26	.50 **	.08
Control	26	−.16	−.19

* = < .05   ** = < .01

nor SCAT correlated to a significant degree with recall in any of the three groups.

Causal inferences

Table 15.8 shows the mean causal inference scores by group.

Although the effects as indicated by analysis of variance on scores in table 16.8 were only at a borderline level of significance, the pattern of causal inference scores is worth noting. That the low CL control score is the same as the high CL control score makes it more likely that the high CL superiority on causal inference in Grade 7 was at least in part a function of the teaching. The relative decrease in low CL–synectics score compared with the high CL score is also of interest; whether this might reflect the low structure of the synectics model or the skills required in that model will require further investigation.

Model-specific measures

Although the model-specific measures were designed to index the effects of specific teaching experience, there were no differences in these measures attributable to teaching condition, i.e., inductive teaching measures were not higher after inductive teaching. However, the same pattern of CL scores described in Grade 7 was noted on several model-specific measures: high CL students (mean of all fifty in four conditions) were higher on the inductive teaching and synectics measures found earlier. In addition, the high CL group also scored higher on another inductive teaching measure (free grouping, labeling, and justifying) and a general synectics measure ("Imagine you are

TABLE 15.8. MOTAC I, Grade 9: Mean Causal Inference Scores by Model and CL

Condition	Low CL	High CL	Overall
Inductive teaching	3.7	4.4	4.1
Synectics	2.7	4.1	3.4
No teaching control	3.0	3.1	3.1
Overall	3.2	3.9	3.5

an apartment building, describe yourself"). These results suggest that within the short-term training period (one hour), the effects were not sufficient to produce measurable, model-specific results but that such measures did reflect CL effects.

Discussion of MOTAC I and Implications for MOTAC II

No specific evidence was noted in these initial studies for matching as might be indicated by differential effectiveness of a model with either a low- or high-CL group. The Grade 7 study was not designed to detect differences since learning outcomes were measured only after all three models. In the Grade 9 study the models were not selected for their differing degrees of structure, i.e., both inductive teaching and synectics were classified "moderate" in structure [18] (p. 305).

However, the MOTAC I studies raised specific questions about how the structure of a model is defined. Does structure refer to the degree of teacher-directedness, or to the model's insusceptibility to "student pull" so that a highly structured model would be identical for low and high CL students? A slightly different possibility than degree of teacher-directedness is the degree of precision with which the nature and sequence of teacher moves are specified so that a highly structured model would be more clearly identified, for example, by the pattern of interaction-analysis indices. Or does structure refer to the skill demands required of students in different phases of the model so that a highly structured model would demand less complex skills?

Each of the fourteen MOTAC I teaching sessions was the first exposure of students to that specific model. Although perhaps it should have been obvious, it seemed quite noteworthy to us that the initial session of *any* model that meets the criterion of objective specification required for a model of teaching will necessarily be fairly high in structure (defined in terms of teacher-centeredness). Thus, one would not expect CL-model differences to appear until students experienced several sessions with the model. Some hint of CL differences occurring after a longer exposure to a model is seen in the pattern of causal inference scores in MOTAC I. Following this lead we considered the effect of number of sessions by disregarding the nature of the model. Scores of Grade 7 students were considered only in terms of three sessions; scores for Grade 9 inductive teaching and synectics in table 15.8 were combined for the one-session group; and the control group scores in table 15.8 were considered no sessions. Results are summarized in table 15.9.

The results in table 15.9 are the most important outcome findings of MOTAC I insofar as they display not only orderly CL group increases, but differences *between* CL groups as a function of number of teaching sessions. In addition to number of teaching sessions, results of MOTAC I were also considered in terms of several other questions related to designing MOTAC

TABLE 15.9. MOTAC I: Mean Causal Inference Scores Reaggregated by Number of Teaching Sessions

Number of sessions	Low CL	High CL	Total	CL Difference
3	3.5	5.8	4.7	+ 2.3
1	3.2	4.2	3.7	+ 1.0
0	3.0	3.1	3.1	+ 0.1

II: (1) what model, (2) how flexible should the model be to "student pull," (3) how many students in a teaching group, and (4) what outcomes to measure and how to measure them. Inductive teaching seemed to provide the most promising results in MOTAC I (tables 16.6 and 16.7), and it also seemed most relevant to CL in terms of skill demands. If several sessions were used, the teacher could allow the model to become more susceptible to student responsibility in later sessions.

Comparing our impressions with the size of the group in the Grade 7 study (twelve to thirteen) with those of the Grade 9 (six to seven), it seemed that a number midway between, eight, should be optimal. In considering outcomes, the attitude, recall, and essay measures seemed to be worth retaining, but the results from the model-specific measures were not encouraging. As discussed, part of the difficulty may have been with the short, one-session intervention. Process measures such as skill in concept formation skills or metaphorical thinking are unlikely to be affected by a one-hour experience. Therefore, it seemed more reasonable to attempt to obtain such information from students' response *during,* rather than after, exposure to the model.

MOTAC II

MOTAC II * was similar to MOTAC I in (1) its use of low and high CL groups, (2) its use of Hemingway content materials (with slight variation), (3) its use of inductive teaching (although in elaborated form), (4) the general system of interaction analysis, and (5) some outcome measures (attitude, recall, essay). It differed from MOTAC I in (1) the number of students/ teaching group, eight, (2) its elaboration of the inductive teaching model, (3) its use of three long sessions, the final one without the teacher, (4) interaction analysis coding which identified each specific student (so that individual student measures of degree of participation and information level were available), and (5) the addition of an outcome measure, impressions. Apart from the longer period of intervention, the most important feature of MOTAC II was its explicit objective to train the students to use the model by them-

* We appreciate the assistance of several colleagues in conducting MOTAC II: Peter Adams, Dhun Berhamji, William Fehlberg, Thomas Moore, Geoff Peruniak, and Mary Rosser.

selves. The emphasis in MOTAC II, therefore, was on an articulation of the inductive teaching model so that it was not only longer (90-minute sessions) but could be repeated so that the basic intervention was 180 minutes, or three times longer than MOTAC I. The study was conducted during a three-week period in November and December, 1973.

Method

Formation of CL groups

Two groups of 8 low CL students and two groups of 8 high CL students were selected from approximately 225 students in the same school from which the MOTAC I-Grade 7 students had been selected. Formation of the groups was the same as before: the mean CL scores for each of the two low CL groups was 1.0 and for the two high CL groups, 2.0. Each of the four groups contained four boys and four girls, and each was similar in ability (CTBS). The groups were originally formed on the basis of 1972 CTBS scores, but the CTBS was administered again to the 32 students the week after completion of MOTAC II. Mean CTBS for the low CL group was 8.1 and for the high group, 8.2. There were no absences during the eight days of experimentation.

Content materials

The first portion of information was very similar to MOTAC I: chronology, minibank, and three stories. The design required a comparable portion of information on Hemingway's writing. A nineteen-page booklet of information on Hemingway's work was prepared, consisting of excerpts from his writing and portions of the *Paris Review* interview by George Plimpton with Hemingway about his writing.

Model of teaching

The inductive teaching model was elaborated by reiterating the enumeration-grouping-labeling sequence at a higher level, using the labels as stimuli. The model was also amplified in terms of required learner skill, involvement options, hypothesized model-relevant outcomes, and content outcome boosted. These various aspects are summarized in table 15.10.

The first session (A) on Hemingway's life was approximately ninety minutes and the second session (B) on Hemingway's work was also about ninety minutes. At the third session (C) the students were instructed to use the model to try to understand the relation between his life and work. Because the aim of the first two sessions was to teach the students to use the model on their own, the teacher attempted to encourage the students to become more responsible in the B phase through negotiating, talking less, etc. The involvement options listed in table 16.10 were borrowed from Greta Morine of the Far West Laboratory, especially her notion of "responsive options,"

TABLE 15.10 Scripting a Model—Concept Learning

Task	Required Learner Skill	Involvement Options	Hypothesized Model-Relevant Outcome	Content Outcome Boosted
1. Concept attainment	Discriminate attributes Infer principle Analyze strategy	Reception—Selection Sharing strategies (Move) Student leadership	Concept-attribute Concept of classification	Integration
2. Enumeration of data	Recall Select by criterion, e.g., heterogeneity triviality abstract-concreteness	Individual—Group (Number) Student leadership	Enumerate data by criterion	Recall
3. Selection of data	Develop criteria; apply criteria	Group (Number)	Apply criteria	Recall
4. Group data: Initial pass (Includes label)	Generate groups	Individual—Group—Class (Number)	Group basis of common attributes	Integration
5. Share—classify—justify—predict labels	Identify common elements of grouped data Generate multidimensional possibilities	Student—talk	Identify principles of classification Concept of classification	Integration

6. Regroup—label data of some group members	Regroup—relabel data	Student-talk	Concept of classification	Integration
7. Multidimensional grouping	Generate multidimensional possibilities	Number	Multiple classification	Integration
8. Share—classify—justify	Identify principles of multi-dimensional grouping	Student—talk	Concept of multiple classifications	Integration
9. What is a label? (Share labels)	Analyze labels	Student—talk Leadership	Nature of label	Integration
10. Alternative Labels (Generate and share)	Generate labels which refer to common attributes Compare labels against criteria of appropriateness	Student—talk	Criteria for adequacy of labels	Integration
11. Group labels	Generate concepts of concepts	Student—talk Number Leadership	Group Abstractions	Integration
12. Share groups	Analyze concepts of concepts	Student—talk Number Leadership	Criterion for grouping abstractions	Integration
13. Label grouped labels and share	Generate labels	Student—talk Number Leadership	Ability to use labels for grouped labels	Integration

and served to operationalize the increased student responsibility and decreased teacher control in Phase B.

Interaction analysis

The same basic coding manual was used with an identification of each student who made a comment. This permitted calculation of two individual scores for each student: (1) total *number of comments,* and (2) an *information index,* calculated by weighting each information comment by a score of 1 (low), 2 (middle), or 3 (high), and dividing by total information comments. Otherwise, the interaction-analysis indices were the same. Intercoder reliability was .85.

One other individual measure was obtained from the teaching session: *number of concepts* a student formed as indicated by the number of groups in the grouping phase. Each student kept his cards in retrievable form so it was relatively easy to obtain this "imbedded" measure.

Outcome measures

Attitude measures

These were the same as before and were administered after each of the three phases.

Recall

Two comparable seventeen-item objective tests on Hemingway's life were used, one after Phase A and one after Phase B.

Essay (causal inference)

The same form as for MOTAC I was used for two of the four groups so these data were available for only sixteen students (eight high and eight low).

Descriptions

Students were first asked to describe Hemingway's life as follows: "Imagine that you are describing Ernest Hemingway to someone who knows nothing about him. How would you describe Hemingway as a person? Write as many descriptions of the sort of person he was as you can—use either single words or phrases to describe what he was like."

Students' free responses to this question were coded on a five-point scale for conceptual complexity which ranged from 1 (Hemingway was either all good or all bad) to 3 (both positive and negative features acknowledged; descriptions at an inferential level) to 5 (presenting superordinate concepts to account for his positive and negative qualities). This score will be referred to as the *complexity index.*

On a second sheet students were asked to write on the following: "Now imagine you are describing Hemingway's writing to someone who knew nothing about it. What was his writing like? Write as many descriptions of his writing as you can think of. Use either single words or phrases to describe what his writing was like."

Responses to this question varied primarily in terms of whether reference was made to his writing style, e.g., simple, straightforward, or to content, e.g., adventurous, violent. Therefore, the *reference to style* measure was the frequency of such descriptions. For the first two groups, these two questions, along with the essay question on Hemingway's life and work, were administered in individual interviews after Phase A and Phase B. The repeated use of the essay question in an interview format produced very little variability in response so this data could not be used; however, the description data were quite comparable to the written form.

Specific procedure

Each of the four groups was brought from the school to the Ontario Institute for Studies in Education studio for two consecutive days. The procedure is summarized in table 15.11 (approximate number of minutes in parentheses).

Interaction analysis indices

Comparison of CL groups in Phase A

Table 15.12 summarizes indices separately for the four teaching groups and for CL groups combined.

The most striking and consistent finding is the higher incidence of both

TABLE 15.11. Synopsis of Procedure: MOTAC II

Phase	Information	Teaching	Outcomes
A	Hemingway's Life (60)	Inductive teaching on his life (90)	Attitude, Recall, Descriptions (30)
B	Hemingway's Work (45)	Inductive teaching on his work (90)	Attitude, Recall, Descriptions (30)
C	No new information	Independent inductive teaching on the relation between life and work (90)	Attitude, Essay (30)

TABLE 15.12. MOTAC II—Interaction analysis indices. Comparison of CL groups: Phase A

Index	Low CL Group 1	vs. High CL Group 2	Low CL Group 4	vs. High CL Group 3	Total Low CL vs. (1 + 4)	Total High CL (2 + 3)
1. Total teacher talk	.803	.793	.724	.747	.761	.769
2. Total structuring	.312	.316	.310	.309	.311	.312
3. Total information	.438	.381	.374	.428	.404	.405
4. Total sanctions	.131	.154	.119	.092	.125	.123
5. Teacher negotiations	.156	.128	.128	.246 **	.142	.188
6. Student negotiations	.143	.000	.000	.200	.062	.048
7. Teacher middle information	.429	.279 **	.359	.327	.402	.305
8. Student middle information	.367	.395	.353	.289	.360	.338
9. Teacher higher information	.178	.505 **	.123	.382 **	.156	.438 **
10. Student higher information	.227	.363 *	.219	.421 **	.223	.394 **
11. Teacher opinion	.127	.122	.044	.109 *	.120	.082
12. Student opinion	.049	.031	.007	.011	.028	.018
13. Teacher positive sanctions	.291	.232	.298	.164	.295	.205
14. Teacher neutral sanctions	.645	.732	.688	.800	.666	.759
15. Teacher negative sanctions	.000	.000	.000	.000	.000	.000

* = < .05   ** = .01
(Underlining indicates higher group.)

teacher higher-level information processing and student higher-level information processing in the high CL teaching groups. Whether this was due to student pull, teacher pull, or their interaction is impossible to determine though it seems most likely that the results reflect a dyadic interaction of teacher adaptation to student pull.

Comparison of CL groups in Phase B

Table 15.13 summarizes the interaction analysis indices for Phase B, which was intended to be more student responsible and less teacher controlled than Phase A.

First, the observed high CL superiority in Phase A on higher-level information processing by both teacher and student is not in evidence. The Phase B topic, Hemingway's work, was generally more difficult than that of his life in Phase A, which may account for the general decrease in higher-level processing by students.

When table 16.13 is compared with table 16.12, one notes a general increase for both CL groups in teacher negotiation, which verifies the intended shift to student responsibility. Table 16.13 also indicates that this occurrence of teacher negotiation was greater for high CL than low CL groups.

Outcome measures

Attitude

Table 15.14 shows the mean scores on attitude to method for the two groups after each phase.

Because the distributions were highly skewed, Phase C scores were compared by a median split, and the Fisher Exact Test was used.[1] The high-CL scores (15 rated C at 5) were significantly higher ($< .02$) than the low-CL group (9 rated C at 5). Therefore, the CL differences occurred, as would be expected, when students were given a chance for greater self-responsibility. This finding was further pursued by considering the reasons given by the students for their rating. Responses were scored in the three categories: internal (emphasis on freedom, opportunity to learn by oneself, etc.), external (emphasis on specific absence of teacher, difficulty with method, etc.), and neutral/indeterminate. Interrater reliability was 86 percent. When internal responses were compared with others, the high-CL group used significantly more internal responses (Fisher Exact Test $< .05$) than did the low-CL group.

Individual measures

Table 15.15 summarizes the characteristics of the major individual measures.

All the interrater reliability coefficients appeared quite adequate. Since most of the measures were administered both after Phase A and after Phase

TABLE 15.13. MOTAC II—Interaction Analysis Indices. Comparison of CL groups: Phase B

Index	Low CL Group 1 vs.	High CL Group 2	Low CL Group 4 vs.	High CL Group 3	Total Low CL (1 + 4) vs.	Total High CL (2 + 3)
1. Total teacher talk	.779	.666 **	.653	.768 **	.722	.728
2. Total structuring	.243	.338 **	.308	.276	.273	.301
3. Total information	.419	.424	.365	.404 *	.394	.412
4. Total sanctions	.141	.107	.145	.132	.143	.122
5. Teacher negotiations	.180	.319 **	.292	.314	.233	.316 *
6. Student negotiations	.333	.228	.210	.407	.245	.306
7. Teacher middle information	.365	.328	.316	.385	.351	.368
8. Student middle information	.317	.228	.309	.384	.313	.307
9. Teacher higher information	.270	.314	.166	.248	.240	.268
10. Student higher information	.309	.346	.244	.254	.275	.299
11. Teacher opinion	.140	.140	.066	.119	.116	.125
12. Student opinion	.038	.007	.019	.048	.028	.029
13. Teacher positive sanctions	.321	.239	.305	.322	.314	.294
14. Teacher neutral sanctions	.643	.674	.666	.644	.654	.654
15. Teacher negative sanctions	.000	.021	.000	.000	.000	.000

$* = <.05$ $** = <.01$
(Underlining indicates higher group.)

TABLE 15.14. MOTAC II—Mean attitude to method scores by CL group

Group	N	Phase A	Phase B	Phase C (Independent)
Low CL	16	4.38	4.44	4.44
High CL	16	4.32	4.44	4.88

B, it was possible to correlate the two measures for an estimate of stability or test-retest reliability. For the reference to style measure, the stability coefficient is a contingency coefficient; for the others, product-moment coefficients. The information index seemed quite unstable, and this is probably due to factors discussed in relation to the decrease in higher-level student information processing that occurred because of the increased difficulty of the Phase B topic (Hemingway's work). Otherwise, most measures seemed fairly stable.

Table 15.16 presents mean scores by CL group.

We have already observed that the greater difficulty of the Phase B task decreased the information index generally and therefore probably accounts in part for the lack of high CL superiority on the information index in Phase B. In keeping with the increased difficulty, number of concepts decreased for both groups although the high CL students were significantly higher. No CL differences were found in recall, but CTBS correlated significantly with both Phase A recall ($r = .46$) and Phase B ($r = .58$).

Causal inferences

The mean high CL score (6.8) was significantly higher ($< .001$) than the mean low CL score (2.4). These mean scores can be added to table 16.9

TABLE 15.15. MOTAC II—Characteristics of Individual Measures

Measure	Source of Measure	Range of Scores	Interrater Reliability	Stability (r_{AB})
Total comments	Interaction analysis	4–72	.85	.80 **
Information index	Interaction analysis	1–3	.85	.17
Number of concepts	Teaching sessions	1–12	—	.54 **
Complexity index	Descriptions	1–5	.91	.54 **
Reference to style	Descriptions	0–4	.97	.79 **
Causal inferences	Essay	1–10	.95	—
Recall	Recall	0–100	—	.34 *

* = < .05   ** = < .01

TABLE 15.16. MOTAC II—Mean scores by CL group for each phase

Measure	Phase A (Hemingway's Life)		Phase B (Hemingway's Work)	
	Low CL	High CL	Low CL	High CL
Information index	1.7	2.1 *	1.9	1.9
Number of concepts	5.44	7.00	3.69	5.82 *
Complexity index	2.50	2.75	1.75	2.82
Recall	72%	73%	65%	68%
Reference to style	0.2	1.6 **	0.3	1.3 *
N	16	16	16	16

Fisher exact test: * = < .05   ** = < .01
Underlined group is significantly greater

(since they represent the equivalent of about four sessions, or 240 minutes) in order to extend the relation between duration of teaching and causal inference score.

High CL scores, and especially high CL superiority, continued to increase while low CL scores decreased with increased teaching time. The MOTAC II relation between CL and causal inferences, expressed in terms of biserial r, was .81. Causal inference was also significantly related to total information index ($r = .51, < .05$), but as before, unrelated to CTBS ($r = .11$).

Independent phase

At the conclusion of Phase B, the teacher told the group that their task in the next teaching session (C) was to use the inductive teaching strategy to understand the relation between Hemingway's life and his work. The teacher told them that s/he would not be present for this phase, but that they would have available the enumerated information from Phase A (life) and Phase B (work) so that the enumeration phase would consist of eliminating unnecessary items. At this point the teacher asked each group how they wished to work, with a leader or without.

Our discussion of MOTAC II up to now has largely ignored the specific characteristics of each of the four groups, considering the two low CL groups together and the two high CL groups together. However, in the independent phase, and in the plans preceding it, each of the four groups displayed idiosyncratic features which will be briefly noted. From a design standpoint, the replication feature of MOTAC II was very valuable because it provided a broader basis for establishing distinctive features of low and high CL groups while also emphasizing the specifically distinctive characteristics of each of the four groups.

Leadership question

When asked if they wanted a leader in Phase C, both low CL groups were unanimous in favoring a leader, as would be expected. Both groups decided to use a formal procedure to elect the leader. Group I selected a rather quiet boy, while Group 4 selected a very dominant girl. The reaction of the two high-CL groups was equally consistent and theoretically expected: neither group wanted a leader, that is, "No, we'll do it on our own."

Group behavior in independent phase

The best way to communicate how Group 1 (low CL) reacted is to mention initially that none of the research staff thought they would be capable of carrying out the task on their own. Group 1 students had been very dependent and passive in both Phase A and Phase B so that we held serious reservations about their capability to deal with this difficult problem. We were wrong; we seriously underestimated how well these fairly dependent students could learn on their own. We share our mistaken prediction because if teachers and researchers are to take seriously the idea of student self-responsibility in learning, they must entertain the possibility that it can occur, and moreover that the teacher's presence is not essential.

Why were we wrong? First, as just indicated, we overestimated the need for a teacher's presence for any students. Second, Group 1 students coped with the task by creating the structure and support they required. They began by carefully listing each of the specific tasks (cf. table 16.10). The leader became a teacher following a lesson plan who led the group through a step-by-step application of the model. If he experienced difficulty, one of the group occasionally assisted him in his directive role. Their emphasis was almost entirely on the teaching strategy as a method to be completed with almost no attention to its problem-solving purpose, that is, how well it helped to understand the relation between Hemingway's life and work.

By contrast, Group 2 (high CL) was entirely concerned with the problem of relating Hemingway's life and work. These students discussed the functional necessity of certain steps in the model and eliminated those steps which they felt were not required. During their discussions, one girl emerged as the facilitator of the group's feelings and views though she was not a leader directing the accomplishment of tasks. While the "output" of Group 1 was their successfully accomplishing a step-by-step application of the model, the "output" of Group 2 was their shared understanding of the relation between Hemingway's life and work.

The reactions of the other two groups were similar in that they reflected CL differences. In Group 4 (low CL) the leader was much more forceful than the Group 1 leader, and she directed the group by taking the role of a highly directive teacher. Group 4 followed the sequence closely but was guided more by the strong leader than by the list of steps. Group 3 (high CL) was less concerned with the specific steps than Group 4 but was also considerably less effective than the other high CL group primarily because of two or three students who deprecated other students and disrupted the group process. Group 3 serves as a valuable reminder that high CL students are not superior in every way and that there are student characteristics other than CL. Group 3 was not always effective because some students exemplified another characteristic of some high CL students at this age: a difficulty in listening to the other person and understanding his/her view. In the process of learning self-responsibility, some high CL students may be excessively concerned with themselves and their own views, thus tuning out the ideas of others.

CONCLUSIONS

This first MOTAC series has been valuable for the questions it has raised, for the surprises it has provided, and for its reminding us of some common-sense notions easily forgotten in designing research. Students can learn to teach themselves, and the question is how to facilitate the acquisition of such self-responsible skill. Educational intervention of short duration such as one hour is unproductive both for student learning and research understanding.

The teaching-learning process is enormously complex, but the present series shows promise of gaining some understanding of this dyadic interchange and its effects. While many of our initial theoretical ideas require revision in light of these results, the general assumption underlying the MOTAC series has been strengthened: that a comprehensive understanding of the teaching-learning process can be approached through the systematic combination of models of teaching, student accessibility characteristics, and informational systems in designs permitting a maximum diversity of outcome measures.

16

Studies in Role Playing: MOTAC III

David E. Hunt, Lenora F. Butler, Joyce E. Noy, and Mary Rosser

Investigations of the teaching-learning process need to consider the interactions among students, teaching approaches, and learning outcomes. In the present study we viewed these interactions in terms of the Behavior-Person-Environment, or B-P-E, paradigm [3,5]: learning outcomes (B) are a result of the interactive effects of different kinds of students (P) experiencing different kinds of teaching approaches (E). More specifically, teaching approaches (E) are considered in terms of *Models of Teaching*,[12] and student differences (P) in terms of accessibility characteristics.[4] The studies are referred to as MOTAC (Models of Teaching-Accessibility Characteristics). The first MOTAC studies investigated primarily the effects of the Inductive Teaching model on students varying in Conceptual Level.[4]

Conceptual Level is a personal characteristic based on a developmental personality theory [2] that describes persons on a developmental hierarchy of increasing conceptual complexity, self-responsibility, and independence. The developmental goal in CL theory is to increase independence for all students, but developmental growth requires learning environments systematically varying in their structure and task complexity according to the students' initial level of self-responsibility.[4] Models of teaching [12] describe a variety of learning environments that differ in structure and task complexity (and that can be systematically modulated along each dimension). The developmental goal in models of teaching theory is to increase the students' capacity to use a wide variety of teaching models independently and to transfer these models (now models of learning) to new problems. Models of teaching, therefore, provide an operational basis for describing the goal of CL development: learning how to learn independently using a variety of models.

Earlier MOTAC studies were, therefore, designed on the assumption that certain teaching models would be more differentially appropriate to students varying in CL because the degree of structure of the model matched the students' needs [12] (p. 305). Although this notion was initially useful we came to realize after MOTAC II that, although inductive teaching may have a "moderate" degree of structure as classified in the Joyce and Weil table, and thus is more appropriate for students high in Conceptual Level (CL), the more important point was to analyze a teaching model in terms of the specific skills required to "go through the model" [10] (pp. 70–71). If students lack the skills, obviously they will be unable to learn through use of the model.

Therefore, the present study (MOTAC III) which was focused on role playing, was also designed to include a training period for some students to emphasize and train them in skills required for the Role Playing model, e.g., talking and feeling as another person. Although MOTAC studies are not intended to simulate a classroom, the inclusion of a training component is similar to what classroom teachers must do for those students requiring specific skill training in relation to a specific way of learning.

Like earlier studies in the series, MOTAC III was designed on the basis of component compatibility, precision, and control. Component compatibility means that the selection of teaching approach (E), student characteristic (P), and learning outcome (B) should be based on likelihood of producing distinctive interactive, or model-specific, effects. For example, role playing was thought to have specific effects on students' affective reaction to the topic so, in addition to most of the outcome measures (B) used earlier, a new measure intended to assess the students' empathic reaction to the topic was used. Precision means that each of the three components are measured as accurately as possible, and this precision is especially important in the model of teaching (E) since to meet this criterion requires independent, objective evidence that the students did experience the model as described. In MOTAC II, teaching sessions were coded by an interaction analysis system to establish precision and comparability of teaching to various groups. In the present study, the model was monitored by use of a detailed check-list applied to each teaching session. Otherwise, the precision for the person component (teaching groups of varying CL) and behavior component, or learning outcomes (analyzed for stability), as well as the control criterion (groups identical in terms of sex, school grade, and scores on the Canadian Test of Basic Skills) were identical to MOTAC II.

METHOD

Overview

The design consisted of three conditions: (1) role playing with training *(training)* condition in which students experienced the model and two sessions of training in model-required skills, (2) role playing with no training *(model only)* condition in which students experienced only the model, and (3) *control* condition in which the students received neither training nor experience with the Role-Playing model, only information on the topics. The training condition consisted of two low and two high CL groups while the other conditions consisted of one low and one high CL group. Students in all three conditions completed the battery of outcome measures, but the control groups did not attempt to apply the role-playing model independently. All teaching and training sessions were videotaped (approximately 25 hours). The studies were conducted in the OISE studio during January and February 1975.

Formation of CL Groups (P)

Students were selected from the total Grade 8 population of a suburban junior high school for whom Conceptual Level (CL) and Canadian Tests of Basic Skills (CTBS) scores were available.[7] Each CL group consisted of four female and four male students whose average CTBS score, expressed in grade equivalent (and collected in May 1974) was as close to 7.5 as possible. Scores on the Paragraph Completion Test [8] served to define CL groups with the low CL groups averaging as close to 1.0 and high groups to 2.0 as possible. Table 16.1 shows the CL and CTBS mean scores for the eight groups, each containing eight students.

There was very little CL variation within each of the eight groups while CTBS variation was very similar for all groups. With the exception of the slightly lower CTBS score for the Low CL-Control group, the groups were almost identical in ability (CTBS). There were no absences during the twelve days of experimentation.

Models of Teaching and Training (E)

Role-playing model. The role-playing method used is based on the description by Joyce, Weil, and Wald [10] (pp. 139–178) and is one of the many variations

TABLE 16.1. Mean CL and CTBS Scores for MOTAC III Groups

Conditions	Low CL Groups		High CL Groups	
	CL	CTBS	CL	CTBS
Training (4 groups)	1.00	7.4	1.84	7.6
	1.10	7.5	1.94	7.6
Model Only	1.16	7.6	1.83	7.4
Control	1.10	6.9	1.91	7.3
TOTAL	1.09	7.4	1.88	7.5

of the method.[11] The present version is a relatively structured version which deals with predetermined content and a specific situation to be role-played (in contrast to other versions in which the students determine the topic and situation). The steps in the model which were prominently displayed on a poster at all sessions were:

1. Read material.
2. Discuss roles and settings.
3. Select role players.
4. Instruct observers.
5. Conduct first role play.
6. Discuss.
7. Conduct second role play.
8. Discuss and conclude.

The time required to go through these eight steps with the students was approximately 90 minutes.

Training sessions. Training session I consisted of three exercises, which required a total time of about one hour: after reading a short description of a person, e.g., Huckleberry Finn, each student tried to "be" that person by saying what he might say to express his feelings with an emphasis on the student's talking as if he were that person, e.g., saying "I, (Huck Finn)" not "He would say"; (2) after reading short descriptions of a person, each student took a turn at conveying that person's feelings nonverbally through a brief pantomine; and (3) carrying out a short role-playing exercise with emphasis on completing the planning steps. In all three exercises the teacher took an active role in training by rewarding, demonstrating, correcting, and emphasizing.

Training session II required approximately ninety minutes and consisted of the teacher's conducting the group through the eight steps explicitly with emphasis on what activity was required at each step. Joyce Noy conducted the teaching and training sessions.

Monitoring precision of teaching/training sessions. MOTAC studies require an objective measure of the teaching environment to insure comparability of experience among teaching groups. Earlier studies have applied an objective coding system to the videotaped teaching sessions, to demonstrate teaching environment comparability through indices derived from interaction analysis. However, comparability of MOTAC III teaching/training sessions was measured by applying detailed checklists of questions to the videotapes for each teaching or training session. The idea for these checklists came from Marsha Weil's "Evaluation guide for role playing," [12] which had been developed as an objective evaluation for teacher trainees who were learning the model. The MOTAC III revision of this guide for the first teaching session (Phase

A) consisted of forty-six questions, e.g., "Were the students told to observe thoughts and feelings?" Applying this list of questions to a Phase A teaching session, therefore, provided both an estimate of precision (how close to forty-six) and control (similarity of six Phase A teaching sessions). Checklists were also developed for the two training sessions (forty-three questions in Phase B and fifty-nine in Phase C) and for the independent phase as will be described in the next section. Because these checklists are low-inference measures, the agreement between two raters in checking the six Phase A teaching sessions was almost perfect. Therefore, the remaining sessions were checked by one rater.

Outcome Measures (B)

Paper-and-pencil measures. These measures were very similar to those in MOTAC II (Hunt, et al., 1974) with the addition of the "diary" measures to index empathy. Specifically, the following objective measures were administered by the teacher:

1. *Attitudes:* Ratings of attitude to method, perception of amount learned, and attitude to material on a five-point scale.

2. *Descriptions:* Students were asked to describe a person or culture with as many descriptions as possible. Descriptions were coded for the number of distinct categories employed.

3. *Essay:* After the teaching session on Roussillon, students were asked to compare and contrast Roussillon and Toronto, and these essays were scored for the number of similarities and differences (relations). After the teaching session on Hemingway, students were asked the same question as in earlier MOTAC studies, "Describe how his life influenced his writing and how his writing influenced his life," and essays were scored for number of relations between life and work (causal inference).

4. *Diary:* In order to index a student's affective reaction to the topic, a diary measure was developed in a pilot study which compared role playing with inductive teaching. Students were asked to complete the entry, "Dear diary," after the person had experienced some difficulty: for Roussillon, a young boy had been forced out of a bicycle race due to injury; for Hemingway, he had just learned that he had failed to win the Nobel Prize. These diary entries were scored for (a) objective empathy by counting the number of thoughts and feelings expressed and (b) subjective empathy by rating how much the student's response established and maintained a mood. In the pilot study role playing produced higher scores on both empathy measures than inductive teaching.

5. *Recall:* A 25-item objective test consisting of true-false multiple-choice and short completion items was administered for each topic. Scores were expressed in proportion of correct responses.

Table 16.2 summarizes the characteristics of these paper-and-pencil mea-

TABLE 16.2. Characteristics of Written Outcome Measures: MOTAC III

Measure	Actual Range of Scores	Interrater Reliability	Stability
1. Number of categories	3–15	.96 **	.75 **
2. Causal inference	0–6	.96 **	—
3. Objective empathy	2–9	.96 **	44
4. Subjective empathy	0–2	.74 **	.50 *
5. Recall	48–92	—	.68 **

* = p < .05
** = p < .01

sures. The range and interrater reliability information is based on the Hemingway scores (number varied from 12 to 30) since these scores reflected training effects. The Roussillon data were almost identical. The stability coefficients describe the correlations between Roussillon scores and Hemingway scores for the control group (N = 16).

Student behavior in independent phase. The major, long-term goal of MOTAC teaching and training is to increase student competence in using the model independently; therefore, it becomes important to measure how well the students direct their own learning by using the model without the teacher's presence. In MOTAC II the interaction analysis coding system was not applicable to the independent phase because it was designed for situations in which a teacher was present. Therefore, a checklist similar to those used to establish the comparability of the teaching and training sessions was devised to apply to the independent teaching session. In this case, the

TABLE 16.3. Synopsis of Procedure: MOTAC III

Condition	Information	Teaching	Training	Outcome
Training Day 1	Roussillon	RP Model	RP I	Roussillon measures
Day 2	Hemingway		RPII	Independent Phase
				Hemingway measures
Model Only	Hemingway	RP Model	None	Independent Phase
				Hemingway measures
Control	Roussillon	None	None	Roussillon measures
	Hemingway	None	None	Hemingway measures

checklist of 32 questions provided a measure of the *dependent* variable, or learning outcome so that interest was on *difference* between conditions rather than on their similarity. This use of an objective checklist also opened the future possibility for comparing students' directing their own learning with that of a teacher trainee teaching the same model.

Content Materials

Roussillon. In addition to reading the ten-page minibank on Roussillon adapted from a longer version prepared by Elizabeth Joyce, the students saw several slides of Roussillon and a map showing Roussillon in relation to Toronto, and heard a story about a boy in Roussillon.

Hemingway. In addition to reading a two-page chronological summary of his life, a ten-page minibank, and an interview with Hemingway (all very similar to MOTAC II materials), students also saw a poster-sized version of the Karsh portrait of Hemingway, and heard his story, "The Killers."

Specific Procedure and Design

The sequence of information-teaching-outcome used earlier was the major basis for conceptualizing the three conditions: training, model only, and control. Further, the training condition was specifically defined in terms of four teaching sessions, or phases: role playing model (A), Role Playing Training I (B), Role Playing Training II (C), and Independent Phase (D). As the diagram synopsizing the procedure below indicates, the students in the model-only condition experienced only Phases A and D while students in the control condition did not experience any teaching. It should also be noted that the Hemingway outcome measures were the primary indicators of training and teaching effects; therefore, Roussillon was not used for the model-only condition. The training condition required two days, or approximately nine hours, while the other two conditions required only one day, or approximately five hours. Table 16.3 synopsizes the procedure for the three conditions.

Comparability of Teaching Environments

Table 16.4 summarizes the objective checklist scores for the four groups in the training condition and for the two groups in the model-only condition.

Reading across the three rows it seems that the teaching environments were very comparable for all groups. There is a slight tendency for the low-CL-training groups to receive slightly more precise teaching and training than the high-CL-training groups, but this would not be significant. That model-only group scores were slightly higher than training group scores at

TABLE 16.4. Check-list Scores for Six Teaching Groups: MOTAC III

Phase	Possible Score	Lo CL$_1$	Lo CL$_2$	Hi CL$_1$	Hi CL$_2$	Lo CL	Hi CL
Model	46	40	42	40	40	44	42
Training I	43	39	37	36	35	—	—
Training II	59	52	49	50	49	—	—

Phase A means only that it might be slightly more difficult to demonstrate training effects. Table 14.1 presented earlier and Table 14.4 provide evidence for the precision of the MOTAC III Person-Environment Experimental context within which the following outcomes were observed.

Analysis of Outcome Measures

Within the teaching condition × CL design, a variety of possible effects was investigated: CL, role playing (training plus model only vs. control), training (training vs. model only), and interactions. Analysis of variance was used where appropriate, and in other cases, the Fisher Exact Test was used.[1] Correlations, also, are occasionally reported. The following analysis was based on Hemingway results only.

Attitudes. A major conclusion from the pilot study was that the effectiveness of training in role playing can be evaluated partially by the degree to which it produces an increase in perceived amount of learning since this model is ordinarily perceived fairly low in terms of how much learning it produces. The scores for perceived amount of learning were compared for the training condition (mean = 4.69) with the model-only condition (mean = 4.06) by nonparametric analysis. Using a median split between 4 and 5, the trained students scored higher (22/32) on perceived amount of learning than the untrained model-only students (3/16) by the Fisher Exact Test (p = .0032). Another way to evaluate this effect is to consider the amount learned in relation to the attitude to the method where it is assumed desirable that the perceived amount learned be equal to the liking for the method. Trained students were more likely to feel that the learning potential of role playing was equal to its attractiveness as a method (24/32) than were model-only students (6/16), who saw it as "more for fun than for learning," by the Fisher Exact Test (p = .0138).

Attitude to method scores for trained students were also positively correlated with two learning outcomes: number of categories (r = .43, p < .01) and, as in MOTAC I (Hunt, et al., 1974, p. 25), with causal inference (r = .33, p < .05). No CL effects were found for attitude scores.

Number of categories. A main CL effect was found with high CL students (Mean =υ3 8.06) σχορινγ ηιγηερ ον αδθεχτιϑε χατεγοριεσ (Φ = 8.50, p < .01) than low CL students (Mean = 6.16). No treatment effects were observed.

Causal inference. No significant effects were noted although there was a nonsignificative CL-Causal inference correlation among trained students (r = .22, N = 32).

Objective empathy. No significant effects nor correlations were noted for objective empathy.

Subjective empathy. Mean scores were 1.66 for training condition, 1.50 for model-only condition, and 1.06 for the control condition. Using a median split (2 vs. 0 or 1), it was found that scores for trained students (24/32) were higher (p = .0036) than for control students (4/16). That this effect was due to role playing rather than training was indicated by the superiority of model-only students (10/16) over control students (4/16); also, by the Fisher Exact Test (p = .037). However, when only low CL students were considered, trained students scored higher on subjective empathy (13/16) than model-only low CL students (2/8) by the exact test (p = .013). Therefore, the training effects were specifically limited to low CL students, presumably since they had more room for improvement.

Recall. No significant treatment or CL effects were found. As before, a strong relation was observed between verbal achievement (CTBS) and recall: r = .45 in training condition, r = .71 in model-only condition, and r = .89 in control condition, all p < .01.

Independent phase. Checklist scores for the four trained and two model-only groups are summarized in table 16.5.

Although the average total score for the four trained groups (19) was higher than for the two untrained groups (13), there is considerable variability among the trained groups ranging from 14 to 24 so that the difference is not significant. An analysis of training effects at each stop revealed significant improvement in "Discussing roles and settings" (Trained groups 20/40 vs. untrained groups 4/20, p < .05) and in the final step, "Discussion and conclusion" (16/24 over 3/12, p = .0127).

The time spent at each step was also recorded, and since groups varied in total time in the independent phase, these times were converted into proportions of time spent in initial planning (Steps 2,3,4), role playing (Steps 5,7), and discussion and conclusion (Steps 6,8), and are summarized in table 16.6.

That training increased the time spent in planning (from 3 percent to 26 percent) is in keeping with the earlier finding of training group superiority in the initial step (table 16.5). Although the steps call for only two enactments, some groups carried out several enactments (ranging from 3 to 10). No training effects were noted for number of enactments, but the low CL groups carried out more (Mean = 7.3) than the high CL groups (Mean = 3.3). Because the number of enactments might affect the time spent in role playing and discussion, these two activities were calculated for only the first two enactments. When only time for these two activities were considered for the first enactments, the trained group spent more time in discussion (44 percent to 30 percent) while the untrained groups spent more time in role playing (70 percent to 56 percent).

TABLE 16.5. Checklist Scores for Each Group: Independent Phase MOTAC III

Activity (Steps)	Possible Score	Training					Model Only		
		Lo CL$_1$	Lo CL$_2$	Hi CL$_1$	Hi CL$_2$	Trained Average	Lo CL	Hi CL	Untrained Average
Planning (2,3,4)	14	7	4	11	7	7.2	5	1	3
Enactment (5,7)	7	6	3	7	4	5.0	3	5	4
Discussion (6,8)	11	9	7	6	5	6.8	7	5	6
Total	32	22	14	24	16	19	15	11	13

TABLE 16.6. Proportion of Time Spent in Different Activities, Independent Phase: MOTAC IV

Activity Steps	Training					Model Only		
	Lo CL$_1$	Lo CL$_2$	Hi CL$_1$	Hi CL$_2$	Average	Lo CL	Hi CL	Average
Planning (2, 3, 4)	16%	14%	50%	22%	26%	6%	0	3%
Enactment (5, 7)	52%	53%	22%	50%	44%	55%	79%	67%
Discussion (6, 8)	32%	34%	28%	28%	30%	39%	21%	30%

DISCUSSION AND CONCLUSIONS

Earlier MOTAC studies have been designed on the basis of conceptual compatibility among B-P-E components, precision, and control. The inclusion of the empathy measures thought to be compatible with (or model-specific to) the role-playing model provides environment-behavior compatibility. Precision was demonstrated for each component: Behavior (Table 16.2), Person (Table 16.1) and Environment (Table 16.4). Control was demonstrated through the design (Table 16.3) and control of student ability (Table 16.1). The design controlled for training and teaching, but the model-only and control groups also had less time in working with the model (i.e., training groups spent two days in the experiment while others spent only one). Whether one provides "nontraining" experience with the model for the untrained students is a complex issue which depends in part on the duration of training. Subsequent MOTAC training studies may include control groups with comparable time but no training. Within this qualification the following were the major results.

Training Effects

1. Training in role playing increased students' perception of the value of the model for learning.
2. Training in role playing increased low CL students' feelings of empathy for the topic.
3. Training in role playing increased students' competence to apply the model independently through increasing time spent on planning and discussion rather than excessive time in the enactments.

Role-Playing Effects

4. Role playing generally increased students' feelings of empathy for the topic.

Conceptual Level Effects

5. High-CL students provided a greater number of distinctive categories in describing the topic than low-CL students.
6. In the independent phase, low-CL students tended to be more concerned with the enactments (as indicated by their greater number of reenactments) than were high-CL students.

Training in Role Playing: MOTAC IV

The earlier MOTAC studies were designed to answer the question of how students respond to, and learn from, a model of teaching. A student must have available certain skills required in order to "go through" the model; for example, the inductive teaching model requires the student to sort data and form concepts (see Joyce [10] p. 70–71, for a list of student skills required in inductive teaching). One reason a model may appear inappropriate is that the students do not have the required skills.

MOTAC IV * was designed to include a training period to emphasize certain skills required in role playing. Such an extended application of a teaching model to include training is more like the way a classroom teacher might use a model over a longer period of time. MOTAC IV also included the two empathy measures developed in MOTAC III that were thought to reflect effects specific to the role-playing model.

MOTAC IV, like earlier studies in the series, was aimed to investigate the interactive effects of a Model of Teaching (role playing) and student Accessibility Characteristic (conceptual level) upon a wide variety of learning outcomes, but was also designed to consider the effect of training in certain skills required by the role-playing model. The B-P-E or Behavior-Person-Environment paradigm [3] is used to describe the interactive design, that is, B = learning outcomes, P = variation in conceptual level (CL), and E = role-playing model. MOTAC IV was conducted in the OISE Studio during January and February of 1975.

METHOD

Overview

The design consisted of three conditions: (1) Role playing with training *(Training)* condition in which students experienced the model and two sessions of training in model-required skills; (2) Role playing with no training *(Model only)* condition in which students experienced only the model; and (3) *Control* condition in which the students received neither training nor experience with the role-playing model, only information on the topics. The *Training* condition consisted of two low- and two high-CL groups while the other two conditions consisted of one low- and one high-CL group. Students in all three conditions completed the battery of outcome measures, but the *Control* groups did not attempt to apply the role-playing model independently. All teaching and training sessions were video-taped (approximately twenty-five hours).

---

* David E. Hunt, Lenora Butler, Joyce E. Noy, and Mary Rosser.

Formation of CL Groups (P)

Students were selected from the total Grade 8 population of a suburban junior high school for whom conceptual level (CL) and Canadian Test of Basic Skills (CTBS) scores were available.[4] Each CL group consisted of four female and four male students whose average CTBS score, expressed in grade equivalent (and collected in May 1974) was as close to 7.5 as possible. Scores on the Paragraph Completion Test [8] served to define CL groups, with the low CL groups averaging as close to 1.0 and high groups to 2.0 as possible. Table 16.7 shows the CL and CTBS mean scores for the eight groups, each containing eight students.

There was very little CL variation within each of the eight groups while CTBS variation was very similar for all groups. With the exception of the slightly lower CTBS score for the Low CL—Control group, the groups were almost identical in ability (CTBS). There were no absences during the twelve days of experimentation.

Model of Teaching and Training (E)

The role-playing model, as described by Joyce, Weil, and Wald [13] (p. 139–178) was used with slight revisions. The steps in the model (which were prominently displayed in all teaching and training sessions) were: (1) read material, (2) discuss roles and settings, (3) select role players, (4) instruct observers, (5) first role play, (6) discuss, (7) second role play and (8) discuss second role play and conclude. Completing the eight steps usually required approximately ninety minutes.

The first training session consisted of three exercises which required approximately one hour. First, after reading a short description of a person, for example, Huckleberry Finn, each student tried to "be" that person by saying what he might say to express his feelings, with an emphasis on the student's talking as if he were that person,—saying "I" (Huck Finn) "would say," not "he would say." Second, after reading short descriptions of a person, each student took a turn at conveying that person's feelings nonverbally through a brief pantomime. Third, students carried out a short role-playing

TABLE 16.7. MOTAC IV—Mean CL and CTBS Scores

	Low-CL Groups		High-CL Groups	
Conditions	CL	CTBS	CL	CTBS
Training	1.00	7.4	1.84	7.6
(four groups)	1.10	7.5	1.94	7.6
Model Only	1.16	7.6	1.83	7.4
Control	1.10	6.9	1.91	7.3
Total	1.09	7.4	1.88	7.5

exercise with emphasis on completing the planning steps. In all three exercises the teacher took an active role in training by rewarding, demonstrating, correcting, and emphasizing. The second training session, requiring approximately ninety minutes, consisted of the teacher's conducting the group through the eight steps explicitly with emphasis on what activity was required at each step. Joyce Noy conducted the teaching and training sessions.

MOTAC studies require an objective measure of the teaching environment to ensure comparability of experience among teaching groups. In experimental terms, such measures provide evidence that the independent variable was manipulated; in educational terms, they assure that students experienced the teaching (and training where appropriate) required by the design. Earlier studies have applied an objective coding system to the video-taped teaching sessions, to demonstrate teaching environment comparability through indices derived from interaction analysis.

Comparability of MOTAC IV teaching/training sessions was measured by applying detailed checklists of questions to the video-tapes for each teaching or training session. The idea for these checklists came from Marsha Weil's "Evaluation Guide for Role Playing" [15] which had been developed as an objective evaluation for teacher trainees who were learning the model. The MOTAC IV revision of this guide for the first teaching session (Phase A) consisted of forty-six questions, for example, "Were the students told to observe thoughts and feelings?" Applying this list of questions to a Phase A teaching session, therefore, provided both an estimate of precision (how close to forty-six) and control (similarity of six Phase A teaching sessions). Checklists were also developed for the two training sessions (forty-three questions in Phase B and fifty-nine in Phase C) and, as will be described in the next section, for the independent phase. Because these checklists are low-inference measures, the agreement between two raters in checking the six Phase A teaching sessions was almost perfect. Therefore, the remaining sessions were checked by one rater. Compared to interaction analysis, these checklists (1) are much easier to apply; (2) are more easily translated into a precision criterion, i.e., how close was session to the ideal model; and, because they are expressed in step-by-step procedures, they are more easily understood by teachers who want to try out the teaching or training approaches. However, interaction analysis also has certain advantages over checklists: (1) the information can more easily be compared with other research, for example, percentage of teacher talk; (2) it provides more qualitative information is supplied, for example, level of student comments; and (3) because it is a system for analyzing interactions, it is more appropriate for describing teacher-student interaction, that is, "student pull."

Outcome Measures (B)

Paper-and-pencil measures. These measures were very similar to those in MOTAC II [12] with the addition of the "Diary" measures to index empathy.

Specifically, the following objective measures were administered:

1. *Attitudes.*
2. *Descriptions.*
3. *Essay:* These were scored for the number of similarities and differences, or relationships (causal inference).
4. *Diary:* The measures developed in MOTAC III were used here. These diary entries were scored for (a) objective empathy by counting the number of thoughts and feelings expressed, and (b) subjective empathy by rating how much the student's response established and maintained a mood.
5. *Recall:* A twenty-item objective test consisting of true-false and multiple-choice items was administered for each topic. Scores were expressed in proportion of correct responses.

Table 16.8 summarizes the characteristics of these paper-and-pencil measures. The range and interrater reliability information is based on the Hemingway scores. (Number varied from twelve to thirty since these scores reflected training effects, but the Roussillon data were almost identical. The stability coefficients describe the correlations between Roussillon scores and Hemingway scores for the Control group ($N = 16$).

Student behavior in independent phase. The major, long-term goal of MOTAC teaching and training is to increase student competence in using the model independently; therefore, it becomes important to measure how well the students direct their own learning by using the model without the teacher's presence. In this case, a checklist of thirty-two questions provided a measure of the dependent variable, or learning outcome, so that interest was on *difference* between conditions rather than on their similarity. This use of an objective checklist opens the future possibility for comparing students' directing their own learning with that of a teacher trainee's applying the model.

Content Materials

Roussillon. In addition to reading the ten-page minibank on Roussillon adapted from a longer version prepared by Elizabeth Joyce, the students saw several slides of Roussillon and a map showing Roussillon in relation to Toronto and heard a story about a boy in Roussillon.

TABLE 16.8. MOTAC IV—Characteristics of Written Outcome Measures

Measure	Actual range of Scores	Interrater Reliability	Stability
1. Number of categories	3–15	.96 **	.75 **
2. Causal inference	0–6	.96 **	—
3. Objective empathy	2–9	.96 **	44
4. Subjective empathy	0–2	.74 **	.50 *
5. Recall	48–92	—	.68 **

* = $< .05$
** = $< .01$

TABLE 16.9. MOTAC IV—Synopsis of Procedure

Condition		Information	Teaching	Outcome
Training	Day 1	Roussillon	RP Model (A) RP Training (B)	Roussillon
	Day 2	Hemingway	RP Training (C)	Hemingway Independent (D)
Model Only		Hemingway	RP Model (A)	Hemingway Independent (D)
Control		Roussillon	None	Roussillon
		Hemingway	None	Hemingway

Hemingway. In addition to the MOTAC II materials students also saw a poster-sized version of the Karsh portrait of Hemingway and heard his story, "The Killers."

Specific Procedure and Design

The sequence of information-teaching-outcome used earlier was the major basis for conceptualizing the three conditions: training, model only, and control. Further, the training condition was specifically defined in terms of four teaching sessions, or phases: Role-Playing Model (A), Role-Playing Training 1 (B), Role-Playing Training 2 (C), and Independent Phase (D). As shown in Table 16.9, the students in the Model-Only condition experienced only Phases A and D while students in the Control condition did not experience any teaching. It should also be noted that the Hemingway outcome measures were the primary indicators of training and teaching effects; therefore, Roussillon was not used for the Model Only condition. The training condition required two days, or approximately nine hours, while the other two conditions required only one day, or approximately five hours.

RESULTS

Comparability of Teaching Environments

Table 16.10 summarizes the objective checklist scores for the four groups in the Training condition and for the two groups in the Model Only condition.

Reading across the three rows it seems that the teaching environments were very comparable for all groups. There is a slight tendency for the Low-CL—Training groups to receive slightly more precise teaching and training than the High-CL—Training groups, but this would not be significant. That Model-Only group scores were slightly higher than Training group scores at Phase A means that it might be slightly more difficult to demonstrate training effects.

Outcome Measures

Within the teaching condition × CL design, a variety of possible effects was investigated: CL, Role Playing (Training plus Model Only vs. Control), Training (Training vs. Model Only), and interactions. Analysis of variance was used where appropriate, and in other cases, the Fisher Exact Test [1] was used. Correlations, also, are occasionally reported. The following analysis is based on Hemingway results only.

Attitudes. The scores for perceived amount of learning were compared for the Training condition (mean = 4.69) with the Model-Only condition (mean = 4.06) by nonparametric analysis because of the distribution. Using a median split between four and five, the trained students scored higher (22/32) on perceived amount of learning than did the untrained Model-Only students (3/16) by the Fisher Exact Test ($p = .0032$). Another way to evaluate this effect was to consider the amount learned in relation to the attitude to the method where it is assumed desirable that the perceived amount learned is equal to the liking for the method. Trained students were more likely to feel that the learning potential of role playing was equal to its attractiveness as a method (24/8) than were Model-Only students (6/16), who saw it as "more for fun than for learning," by a Fisher Exact Test ($p = .0138$).

Attitude to method scores for trained students were also positively correlated with two learning outcomes: number of categories ($r = .43$, $p < .01$) and, as in MOTAC, with causal inference ($r = .33$, $p < .05$). No CL effects were found for attitude scores.

Number of categories. A main CL effect was found with high-CL students (mean = 8.06) scoring higher on adjective categories ($F = 8.50$, $p < .01$) than low-CL students (mean = 6.16). No treatment effects were observed.

Causal inference. No significant effects were noted although there was a nonsignificant CL-causal inference correlation among trained students ($r = .22$, $N = 32$).

Objective empathy. No significant effects nor correlations were noted for objective empathy.

Subjective empathy. Mean scores were 1.66 for Training condition, 1.50 for Model Only condition, and 1.06 for the Control condition.

Although the average total score for the four trained groups (19) was higher than for the two untrained groups (13), there is considerable variability among the trained groups ranging from 14 to 24 so that the difference is not significant. An analysis of training effects at each step revealed significant improvement in discussing roles and settings (trained groups 20/40 vs. untrained group 4/20, $p > .05$) and in the final step, discussion and conclusion (16/24 over 3/12, $p = .0127$).

TABLE 16.10. MOTAC IV—Checklist Scores for Six Teaching Groups

Phase	Possible Score	Training				Model Only	
		Lo CL$_1$	Lo CL$_2$	Hi CL$_1$	Hi CL$_2$	Lo CL	Hi CL
Model (A)	46	40	42	40	40	44	42
Training 1 (B)	43	39	37	36	35	—	—
Training 2 (C)	59	52	49	50	49	—	—

TABLE 16.11. MOTAC IV—Checklist Scores for Role Playing in Independent Phase

Role Playing Steps	Possible Score	Training				Model Only	
		Lo CL$_1$	Lo CL$_2$	Hi CL$_1$	Hi CL$_2$	Lo CL	Hi CL
2. Discuss roles and setting	10	6	3	8	3	4	0
3. Select role players	1	1	1	1	1	1	1
4. Instruct observers	3	0	0	2	3	0	0
5. First RP	3	3	1	3	2	0	3
6. Discuss	5	5	2	3	1	4	5
7. Second RP	4	3	2	4	2	3	2
8. Discuss and conclude	6	4	5	3	4	3	0
Total Score	32	22	14	24	16	15	11

The time spent at each step was also recorded, and since groups varied in total time in the independent phase, these times were converted into proportions of time spent in initial planning (Steps 2, 3, 4), role playing (Steps 5, 7), discussion and conclusion (Steps 6, 8), and are summarized in table 16.11.

That training increased the time spent in planning (from 3 to 26 percent) is in keeping with the earlier finding of training group superiority in the initial step (table 16.12). Although the steps call for only two enactments, some groups carried out several enactments (range from 3 to 10). No training effects were noted for number of enactments, but the low-CL groups carried out more (mean = 7.3) than the high-CL group (mean = 3.3). Because the number of enactments might affect the time spent in role playing and discussion, these two activities were calculated for only the first two enactments. When only time for these two activities was considered for the first two enactments, the trained group spent more time in discussion (44 to 30 percent) while the untrained groups spent more time in role playing (70 to 56 percent).

DISCUSSION AND CONCLUSIONS

Each MOTAC study has been designed on the basis of conceptual compatibility among B-P-E components, precision, and control. The inclusion of the empathy measures thought to be compatible with (or model-specific to) the role-playing model, provides environment-behavior compatibility. Precision was demonstrated for each component: Behavior, Person and Environment. Control was demonstrated through the design and through the control of student ability. The design controlled for training and teaching, but the Model-Only and Control groups also had less time in working with the model— training groups spent two days in the experiment while others spent only one. Whether one provides "nontraining" experience with the model for the untrained students is a complex issue that depends in part on the duration of training. Subsequent MOTAC training studies may include control groups with comparable time but no training. Within this qualification, following are the major results.

Training effects

1. Training in role playing increased students' perception of the value of the model for learning.

2. Training in role playing increased low-CL students' feelings of empathy for the topic.

3. Training in role playing increased students' competence to apply the model independently through increasing time spent on planning and discussion rather than excessive time in the enactments.

TABLE 16.12. MOTAC IV—Proportion of Time Spent in Different Activities, Independent Phase

Activity Steps	Training					Model Only		
	Lo CL₁	Lo CL₂	Hi CL₁	Hi CL₂	Average	Lo CL	Hi CL	Average
Planning (2, 3, 4)	16%	14%	50%	22%	26%	6%	0	3%
Enactment (5, 7)	52%	53%	22%	50%	44%	55%	79%	67%
Discussion (6, 8)	32%	34%	28%	28%	30%	39%	21%	30%

Role-Playing Effects

4. Role playing generally increased students' feelings of empathy for the topic.

Conceptual Level Effects

5. High-CL students provided a greater number of distinctive categories in describing the topic than low-CL students.

6. In the independent phase, low-CL students tended to be more concerned with the enactments (as indicated by their greater number of reenactments) than were high-CL students.

    These findings and other observations of MOTAC IV will be considered in designing MOTAC V on Group Investigation.

PART VII

How We Think
When We Teach

Nearly all studies of teaching have been observational studies. That is, observers are placed in a classroom, and they examine the behavior of the teacher, using a "category" system, the system developed in the ethnographic tradition. There have been almost no studies of the thought processes of teachers as they operate with their students. For that matter, there have been very few studies of the thought processes of children as they are being taught. In other words, strangely enough, although teaching is a thoughtful process and learning involves one of the most intense forms of cognitive activity, we know almost nothing about the thinking of teachers and students in the course of the instruction process.

Over the last twenty-five years there have been scarcely a half-dozen investigations of the thinking processes of teachers. We began to be concerned about what happens to teachers' thought processes as they teach and as they learn to teach, and what is the impact of personality, of the socialization of the school milieu, and additionally, the impact of training on thought. Is it possible, we wondered, for teachers who take on new models of teaching to take on the thought processes of the theoreticians who developed those models?

In the following pages we report a series of investigations designed to explore some of these relationships with teachers' planning behavior. That is, how they think when they are preparing to teach, their thinking behavior while they are teaching (what we call "interactive decision making"), the behavioral patterns that they manifest while they are teaching, and the kinds of things that children learn as a result of the actual transactions of teaching.

17

Teacher Decision Making and Teaching Effectiveness

Christopher Clark and Bruce R. Joyce

RATIONALE FOR THE STUDY

The last fifteen years have seen a number of frontal assaults on the complex problem of defining and improving teaching effectiveness. Our progress is conspicuous. Training technology now provides us with an impressive array of multimedia teacher training products [43] and with electronic devices for immediate feedback of teaching behavior to teachers in training. Organizational changes such as team teaching and open schools have broadened our conception of how teaching might be done. Behavioral objectives and competency-based teacher education have shaped both teacher-training approaches and methods of evaluating teaching effectiveness. In-service teacher training has begun to receive more emphasis, as seen by the proliferation of teacher centers.[20] The link between teacher education and teaching effectiveness is no longer the "black box" it once was.

Now that this critical mass of concepts about teaching, training techniques, and methods of assessment has come together, the importance of understanding teacher decision making is strikingly clear. Now we are asking teachers to balance learning objectives, student characteristics, teaching skills and strategies, and curriculum materials in ways which will optimize teaching effectiveness. The teacher is the human link who binds these aspects of teaching together. Decision making is the psychological process that binds these aspects of teaching together. It has suddenly become very important to learn how and why teachers make decisions and what can be done to improve the process.

Consciously and unconsciously teachers make decisions that affect their behavior and that of their students. Some decisions occur in the midst of the teaching-learning act and affect behavior for only a few minutes. Others, such as the selection of objectives, content, and methods, may guide activity for days, weeks, or months. Teachers serve on curriculum committees, helping to make plans that will guide and coordinate activities over a period of years. Occasionally a teacher even works with others to start a school or reshape one and in so doing may make decisions that affect teaching and learning for a dozen years or more. In this paper we will focus on two kinds of relatively short-term decision making: preactive decision making which takes place shortly before instruction begins and interactive decision making which occurs during the instructional process.[17]

The literature relative to both preactive and interactive decision making is relatively sparse, with the bulk of studies in the former area. Popham, Baker, and their associates [33] have found that, without specific training, very few teachers establish behavioral objectives that are tied closely to either instructional activity or evaluation devices. Popham and Baker have also developed systems for training teachers to discriminate among and select behavioral objectives, to select appropriate learning activities, and to relate their choices to evaluating devices; and they have demonstrated many times the effectiveness of these systems in affecting teachers' capability to do those things. Aside from their work and that of Marx and Peterson, there have been very few studies of preactive decision making. Joyce and Harootunian,[21] studying teachers in elementary school science, arrived at much the same conclusion as did these authors: that very few teachers use a behavioral analysis as they prepare their lessons, and that most depend heavily on instructional materials for selection of method, content, and sequence of activities.

There are virtually no reported studies of teachers' interactive decision making. That is to say, we know very little in any scientific sense about the kinds of information or cues that teachers use when making decisions "on the fly." We have not even developed major categories for classifying the acts of decision making that we know must go on regularly in the course of teaching. Louis Smith's very careful "microethnography" of an inner-city classroom [42] explored decision making as the process of establishing the social system of the classroom. His findings support the idea that much of the teacher's conscious efforts are related to the development of a coherent social system in the classroom with a defined flow of activities and a clear normative structure. Kounin's studies [24] indicate that the social dimension is as much in the teacher's thoughts as is that of activity-structure and must be given equal prominence in research on decision making, although he did not study teachers' decisions as such.

PARADIGM FOR RESEARCH

The next section of this chapter outlines a paradigm for the exploratory phase of research on teacher decision making. Here we must acknowledge an intellectual debt to Lee Shulman,[40] whose work in diagnostic decision making by medical doctors and whose advice and encouragement have been tremendously helpful. The objective of this kind of research is to develop a "map" of teacher decision making and to generate and improve instruments for studying it efficiently and comprehensively. The results should provide information or at least ideas about how to design training research which will lead to improved effectiveness in teachers' decision making.

The paradigm is a six-step cyclical process:

1. Start with experienced teachers in a simple laboratory teaching setting.

2. Collect rich but relatively unstructured data by asking the teachers to "think aloud" as they are planning and reviewing a lesson.

3. Analyze these data to determine the categories of problems or decision points teachers perceive and the types of information they use in making decisions.

4. Project the types of decisions teachers make against a background of carefully thought-out categories representing a theoretically optimal pattern for making decisions. Use these results to develop a preliminary "map" of decision making.

5. Relate the decision-making data to observed teacher behavior and student learning.

6. Repeat the process, changing the setting in one or more dimensions (for example, teacher experience, teacher role, type of students, group size, curriculum). Revise the instrumentation and revise the "map."

We suggest starting with experienced teachers in a simple setting because it seems likely that decision-making behavior in such a situation would be relatively stable. Novice teachers, novel settings, and the complexity of the teaching situation in a regular classroom would introduce unnecessary noise in this early exploratory phase.

Because so little is known about teacher decision making and because it is usually a covert if not unconscious process, the primary data from the early studies would be protocols of teachers "planning aloud" and of stimulated recall "debriefings" in which teachers viewed videotapes of their teaching and discussed the reasoning processes behind their interactive decisions.

The "map" should identify types of problems teachers solved and the styles and strategies they used to solve them. It should include the kinds of information they used, its sources, and its accuracy. It should make possible a comparison of teachers' decision-making styles. Relationships between decision making and interactive teaching styles could then be determined, and both could be explored to see if they were related to pupil learning.

As the two ways of describing decision making—the one generated by natural teacher activity and the other by a theoretical construct—are matched against each other, a basis for improving decision making through training can be generated. Part of the basis will be rooted in an empirical determination of which teacher decision-making behaviors are, or appear to be, associated with effective teaching, and part will originate in components of the theoretical structure.

DESIGN OF STUDY

As a first attempt to practice what we have been preaching here, we conducted a study of teacher preactive and interactive decision making, using the laboratories of the Stanford Center for Research and Development in Teaching during the summer of 1974.[1] Twelve experienced teachers (six males and six females) taught the same three-hour social studies unit to three classes, each consisting of eight junior-high-school students. The last group taught by each teacher returned four days later and was taught another three-hour social studies unit.

At the beginning of each teaching day, each teacher was given ninety minutes to plan the teaching session. During this planning session, the teachers were instructed to "think aloud" while their thoughts were tape-recorded.

At the end of each teaching day, five short (one to three minute) portions of the videotapes of their classroom interaction were shown to each teacher. After each part of the tape, several questions were asked of each teacher to elicit information about interactive decision making. Teacher responses to these questions were audiotaped. The design of this study is shown in table 17.1.

These procedures conform to the first two steps of the paradigm outlined above. Experienced teachers taught small, manageable groups of students in a relatively "noise-free" laboratory setting.

Having collected a rich but relatively unstructured set of teacher decision-making data, we proceeded to sketch our preliminary "map."

TABLE 17.1. Design of the Teacher Decision-Making Study

Day 1	Day 2	Day 3	Day 4
Twelve Teachers "Plan Aloud" (90 minutes)	Twelve Teachers "Plan Aloud" (90 minutes)	Twelve Teachers "Plan Aloud" (90 minutes)	Twelve Teachers "Plan Aloud" (90 minutes)
Class 1 ($n = 8$ students per class) taught social studies unit (three 50-minute periods)	Class 2 ($n = 8$ students per class) taught social studies unit (three 50-minute periods)	Class 3 ($n = 8$ students per class) taught social studies unit (three 50-minute periods)	Class 3 returns; taught new social studies unit (three 50-minute periods)
Teacher-stimulated recall, debriefing and student posttesting	Teacher-stimulated recall, debriefing and student posttesting	Teacher-stimulated recall, debriefing and student posttesting	Teacher-stimulated recall, debriefing and student posttesting

Use of Hunt's Model

The theoretical model that we used to organize and interpret these data was an application of the work of David Hunt and his associates.[15] According to this view, decision making in teaching is a matter of identifying, selecting, and coordinating educational objectives, student characteristics, and learning environments. Preactive decision making involves selecting and modifying objectives, discriminating between learners in terms of important characteristics of the learners (see table 17.2). Interactive decision-making skills are applied in generating and maintaining the selected learning environments and adapting them to the responses of the students. We will now examine the four major sections of Hunt's model of the teacher as decision maker in detail.

TABLE 17.2. A Network of Teaching Decisions

Selecting and Clarifying Objectives ←——————→ Available Options

Identifying Components of Learning Styles ←——————→ Study of Students

Selecting Appropriate Learning Environments ←——————→ Available Options

Initiating, Maintaining, and Adapting Learning Environments

Selecting objectives

Most previous studies of the teacher as a decision maker are focused on ability to select objectives. Judging from their results, teachers do *not* generally employ behavioral objectives unless they have been trained specifically to do so. Many teachers have difficulty discriminating among behavioral objectives and have difficulty using behavioral objectives as the focus of instruction. Yet the belief persists that much instruction should be goal-directed and that the selection of learning outcomes to be focused on in any given instructional sequence, whether it is explicit or implicit, is a very important part of making the process of teaching a rational and systematic one.* Even when teachers work within curriculum frameworks in which general objectives are specified, the clarification of objectives for particular instructional episodes

* The view is not without challenge; see, for example, Philip Jackson, *Life in Classrooms.*[18]

and the adaptation of objectives and materials appear to be a very important function. Prior to teaching, the teacher organizes his or her mind, whether consciously or not, to emphasize certain kinds of outcomes and to deemphasize others. During the interactive phase of teaching the teacher modifies objectives and may even change course entirely.

Using information about the learner

The importance of individual differences was well recognized long before the behavioral sciences had established regular programs of research into children's development. Since then, there has developed a vast literature reporting investigations of the interaction between student characteristics and educational treatments or environments. Hunt's model states that optimal decision making requires the teacher to obtain information about the learning styles of students, to select environments appropriate to their styles (a function belonging to preactive decision making), and to modify them during teaching to adjust to student responses (a function of interactive decision making).

For our purposes, the important questions are:

1. How do teachers perceive their students? What are the ways in which they utilize the information about students that they gain in the course of their teaching?

2. How do they relate their behavior to their perceptions both of student characteristics and of student responses to the acts of teaching?

3. What are the dimensions which teachers *might* use to perceive their students more clearly and how can they be taught to use those dimensions?

4. How can teachers use information about their students to coordinate educational environments at the preactive level and to modify them at the interactive level?

Research in this area must begin with the clarification of the dimensions that teachers presently use to perceive their students. Schroder and his associates [38] have done a preliminary investigation of the dimensionality with which teachers view students, and this work needs to be extended to clarify the types of categories they use. A study in preparation by Ronald W. Marx [26] is focused on learning how accurately teachers perceive the cognitive and affective characteristics of their students and determining which cues are used by the more-and-less accurate teachers. The next step is to conduct a series of training experiments to determine how to teach teachers to employ potentially useful dimensions of their students and to incorporate this new information into their preactive and interactive decision-making acts. (It is highly probable, for example, that teachers can only utilize two or three dimensions of information about students at any one time.)

Selecting and generating learning environments

Hunt's model suggests that the selection of learning environments should be coordinated with objectives and with learner characteristics (that is, matched to the learning styles of the students). Once an environment has been selected, the teacher uses teaching skills and strategies to bring it into existence, maintain it, and adapt it to the responses of the children.

Models of Teaching and Teacher Decision Making

Joyce and Weil [23] have provided a framework that describes and compares many of the available educational environments. They refer to these as "models of teaching," the specifications of a range of educational strategies.

The available models of teaching are useful in relation to Hunt's model of the teacher as decision maker in several ways:

1. They provide a description of available learning environments against which we can compare what teachers naturally provide for students. This permits us to make a systematic analysis of the learning environments teachers select.

2. They provide a framework for training by identifying a range of teaching strategies that teachers can learn. For example, we can investigate the effects of teacher mastery of a range of models of teaching on their preactive decision-making behavior.

3. They provide guidelines to interactive decisions when those models are being employed. Some models specify shifts in cognitive operations at certain stages (for example, from collecting data to classifying it). In so doing, they help the teacher make decisions about when to ask questions of certain kinds, when to institute particular types of activities, and so on. They help identify many of the decisions that have to be made and the bases on which to make them. Models also can sensitize the teacher to particular characteristics and responses of the learners and serve as guides in modulating activities, structure, questions, etc., to the learner.

4. Instructional models provide guidelines for the use of teaching skills in much the same way that they guide decision making. For example, they help the skillful questioner to make deliberate use of his/her questioning ability so as to maximize the impact of the skill. They help the skilled negotiator know when, what, and how to negotiate with students.

SUMMARY

We have made a case for the importance of studying teacher preactive and interactive decision making and have suggested a general design for starting the investigation. Marx and Peterson [27] report the results of our initial foray in detail. The study of teaching effectiveness is unlikely to make great progress until this line of research is pursued. We would not expect that the sheer ability to clarify educational objectives would have a powerful effect on student achievement, although Popham and Baker [33] have shown that it can have some effect. We would not expect that more accurate perception of student characteristics would function by itself to bring about a greater student learning. Nor would the possession of a repertoire of teaching skills and strategies be likely, by itself, to be associated with pupil outcomes. However, once a teacher is able to clarify objectives, select appropriate strategies, bring them into action, and coordinate them with the characteristics of students, *then* we can examine whether that complex of competencies will result in greater pupil learning of various kinds. Thus, to understand how teacher behavior is related to student learning we must first understand how teachers make decisions to control their own performance. Through several stages of research we need to learn how teachers formulate objectives and plans and guide their own activities during interactive teaching, and whether that process can be improved. As this research progresses we can expect to delineate effects on learners more precisely. If, for example, a teacher (1) decides to teach a given set of concepts, (2) perceives students' cognitive development accurately, (3) selects a strategy that is appropriate both to the teaching of concepts and to the cognitive level of those students, (4) has the skill to bring that strategy into action, and (5) adjusts the strategy as he or she receives information about pupil response, then and only then can we ask whether *those concepts* are likely to be learned as a function of teaching.

18

The Nature of Teacher Decision Making

Ronald Marx and Penelope Peterson

The first investigation probed the decision making of experienced teachers in a somewhat novel setting, that is, in the teaching labs at the Stanford Center for Research and Development in Teaching.

METHOD

Twelve experienced teachers (six males and six females) each taught three groups of eight students. The mean number of years of teaching experience for this sample was 8.3 years. Groups of junior high school students were randomly formed by stratifying on sex and verbal ability. Sex was used as a stratifying variable to control the effect it would have on interpersonal relations, and verbal ability was used because of its well-known relationship with school achievement. An attempt was made to assign siblings and friends to different groups, although in the latter case this was not always possible.

Each teacher presented three fifty-minute lessons based on an experimental social studies curriculum unit [22] to each group. The three different groups taught by each teacher met on Monday, Wednesday, and Friday. On the following Tuesday the last group returned and was taught a parallel unit but on a different topic.

On the Friday prior to the first teaching, each teacher read the social studies content materials and was familiarized with the teaching labs. Then on each morning before teaching, the teachers were given ninety minutes to plan the day's lessons. At this time the teachers were again given the content materials. After first listening to a model "think aloud" on a tape as an introduction to the procedure, the teachers were given a list of eleven cognitive and affective objectives and were asked to "think" into a tape recorder while planning their lessons.

At the end of each day's teaching, the teachers were shown videotapes of the first five minutes of their first hour of teaching and three one-to-three-minute segments of each hour of instruction. After viewing each of these four segments, the teachers responded to a structured interview concerning their decision making. These interviews were also audio-taped. The questions asked during the interview were:

1. What were you doing in this segment and why?
2. Were you thinking of any alternative actions or strategies at that time?
3. What were you noticing about the students?
4. How were the students responding?
5. Did any student reactions cause you to act differently than you had planned?
6. Did you have any particular objectives in mind in this segment? If so, what were they?
7. Do you remember any aspects of the situation that might have affected what you did in this segment?

The same procedures were followed on each day of the study.

The audiotape protocols were coded using the Teacher Decision Making Coding System (see table 18.1). Four of the categories include parallel subcategories. *Factual* refers to information that is not manipulated, interrelated or transformed in any way, but is used as given. *Conceptual* refers to information that is compared, contrasted, or interpreted, or is used for problem solving or forming concepts. *Theoretical* statements refer to generalizing or synthesizing and include statements of principles, laws, or relationships. *Affective-personal* involves the expression or formation of personal feelings, opinions, or attitudes. *Affective-social* is parallel to affective-personal but refers to the group rather than to individuals.

All the lessons were videotaped, and these tapes were coded using The Program on Teaching Effectiveness Interaction Analysis System.[32] This system allows for coding on four facets: the source and type of communication (e.g., teacher statement or student question); the focus of the communication (e.g., person or subject matter); the process of the communication (e.g., cognitive level); and the function of the communication (e.g., goals or implementations). Student achievement and attitude were measured by paper-and-pencil tests constructed for this study.

TABLE 18.1. Coding System—Teacher Decision Making

Category	Definition
Objectives Factual Conceptual Theoretical Affective-Personal Affective-Social	The end products or intended student outcomes which the teacher is working toward.
Subject Matter Factual Conceptual Theoretical Affective-Personal Affective-Social	Statements dealing with information found in the text, or concepts, principles, etc., which are clearly derived from material found in text.
Instructional Process Factual Conceptual Theoretical Affective-Personal Affective-Social	An activity or move that the teacher intends to make during instruction, including parts of large, complex strategies.
Materials Instructional materials Noninstructional materials	Considerations about or use of instructional materials or other aspects of the physical environment.
Learner Factual Conceptual Theoretical Affective-Personal Affective-Social	Accounting for one or more specific aspects of students' cognitive development, cognitive ability, ability to respond to a cognitive task, or their equivalents in the affective domain.
Miscellaneous	

Variability in Decision Making

The preactive decision-making tapes from all four days of the study were coded using The Teacher Decision-Making Coding System. The same coding system was used to code the interactive decision-making protocols from days 1 and 2. The proportion of codes for each category and subcategory were calculated for each tape. Using only the preactive protocols, it was discovered that all the subcategories except those under Subject Matter were unusable due to very low frequency of occurrence on some of the days. This kind of variable would have resolved to a dichotomy, so it was decided to drop these subcategories from analysis. The categories retained are shown in table 18.2.

Productivity refers to the total number of codes from a tape. This is the only decision-making category that is a frequency count. The other eight

TABLE 18.2. Categories from the Teacher
Decision-Making Coding
System Retained for Analysis

Decision-Making Category	Type
Productivity	Frequency
Objectives	Proportion
Subject matter	Proportion
Subject matter—lower order	Proportion
Subject matter—higher order	Proportion
Instructional process	Proportion
Materials	Proportion
Learner	Proportion
Miscellaneous	Proportion

categories are all proportions and were formed by dividing the frequency of each particular category by Productivity. This procedure adjusted for individual differences in Productivity and allowed us to explore the relationships between the various categories and other variables independent of Productivity. The scores for Objectives, Subject Matter, Instructional Process, Materials, Learner, and Miscellaneous were derived by summing across all the subcategories within the major category. Subject Matter—Lower Order and Subject Matter—Higher Order are both subsets of Subject Matter. The former is the same as the subcategory on the original coding system; the latter is the sum of two higher order categories from the original instrument. Because distributions of proportions tended to be skewed, we used an arcsin transformation of the proportions for all statistical analyses.

Preactive decision making

Table 18.3 shows the means, standard deviations, and analysis of variance results for all nine of the preactive decision-making variables for the four days of instruction. Three of the nine variables varied significantly across days. Productivity systematically decreased from the first day to the fourth. This decrease might be due to two factors. First, the teachers may have become sensitized to the think-aloud technique. Second, the basic plan was probably developed on the first day and modified thereafter so the teachers had fewer new things to say as the days progressed. Subject Matter and Subject Matter—Lower Order both decreased from the first day to the third day but increased substantially on the last day. This increase is clearly related to the introduction of new material to be taught on the fourth day. It is noteworthy that Subject Matter—Higher Order did not change systematically across days, nor did it increase on day four. The intercorrelations within days among the nine preactive decision-making categories decreased across days. The mean intercorrelations for days one through four (ignoring sign) were .40, .32, .30, and .27. This indicates that decision-making became slightly more differentiated after more experience with the procedure and materials.

TABLE 18.3. Means, Standard Deviations, and *F* Tests for the Nine Preactive Decision-Making Categories Across the Four Experimental Days

Preactive Decision-Making Category[1]		Day				F
		One	Two	Three	Four	
Productivity	$\bar{X}$	199.75	124.25	112.08	99.67	6.78**
	SD	127.78	86.76	75.17	81.29	
Objective	$\bar{X}$	.039	.039	.044	.022	0.68
	SD	.036	.047	.072	.038	
Subject Matter	$\bar{X}$	.399	.334	.210	.358	4.55**
	SD	.255	.269	.225	.229	
Lower Order	$\bar{X}$	.278	.178	.114	.271	6.32**
	SD	.209	.215	.186	.208	
Higher Order	$\bar{X}$	.095	.109	.073	.062	1.09
	SD	.097	.119	.135	.088	
Instructional Process	$\bar{X}$	.244	.316	.309	.222	2.61
	SD	.141	.208	.167	.159	
Materials	$\bar{X}$	.064	.050	.101	.062	1.34
	SD	.056	.039	.098	.073	
Learner	$\bar{X}$	.052	.071	.084	.086	0.60
	SD	.050	.046	.070	.120	
Miscellaneous	$\bar{X}$	.202	.189	.259	.165	0.97
	SD	.169	.122	.192	.204	

[1] For all categories except Productivity, means and standard deviations are arcsin transformations of the data, and *F* tests were calculated on arcsin transformations.
** $p \leq .01$

The means and standard deviations for the nine preactive decision-making variables for the teachers collapsed across days are shown in table 18.4. There was considerable variance across teachers on seven of the nine variables. The only two variables which showed low variance were Materials and Learner. There are two explanations for these findings. First, they might be due to the constraints of the study. That is, the materials available to the teachers were restricted, and the teachers did not know their students prior to the study. However, even on the fourth day when the teachers had the same students as on day three, the proportion of preactive decision making concerned with learners did not increase appreciably. The second explanation is that none of the teachers in this study were particularly oriented toward materials or learners, and these two domains may not have seemed salient enough to warrant much planning.

We have seen that teachers vary in their orientation to preactive decision making. The next question to be raised concerns the stability of decision making across time. We have seen that six of the nine preactive decision-

TABLE 18.4. Means, Standard Deviations, and F Tests for the Nine Preactive Decision-Making Categories across the Twelve Teachers*

Preactive Decision-Making Category		1	2	3	4	5	6	7	8	9	10	11	12	F
								Teacher						
Productivity	$\overline{X}$	76.75	124.75	78.25	243.00	140.25	111.50	152.75	24.25	166.75	20.50	281.00	187.50	7.07**
	SD	81.08	86.00	29.90	106.42	52.61	37.42	115.70	27.06	48.59	8.85	91.42	92.14	
Objectives	$\overline{X}$	.028	.008	.054	.014	.028	.046	.009	.000	.065	.135	.016	.031	3.48**
	SD	.056	.014	.024	.026	.028	.037	.000	.000	.047	.089	.017	.024	
Subject Matter	$\overline{X}$	.227	.287	.195	.750	.336	.206	.534	.086	.117	.094	.575	.502	11.26**
	SD	.158	.277	.086	.106	.169	.191	.123	.152	.064	.142	.124	.117	
Lower Order	$\overline{X}$	.182	.235	.090	.628	.133	.120	.465	.000	.074	.058	.220	.318	12.17**
	SD	.151	.230	.100	.077	.092	.190	.107	.000	.063	.116	.077	.169	
Higher Order	$\overline{X}$	.030	.034	.040	.062	.185	.076	.042	.047	.028	.000	.333	.140	7.27**
	SD	.037	.052	.035	.035	.120	.022	.074	.094	.032	.000	.126	.073	
Instructional Process	$\overline{X}$	.208	.256	.414	.090	.440	.359	.245	.196	.552	.204	.143	.141	8.10**
	SD	.069	.195	.123	.037	.102	.162	.106	.131	.083	.077	.078	.035	
Materials	$\overline{X}$	.049	.112	.033	.052	.057	.163	.116	.032	.065	.069	.050	.037	1.49
	SD	.057	.100	.035	.075	.069	.118	.056	.063	.264	.079	.000	.014	
Learners	$\overline{X}$	.058	.092	.131	.019	.082	.045	.013	.038	.149	.131	.082	.039	1.57
	SD	.078	.041	.086	.020	.053	.017	.017	.046	.068	.172	.057	.030	
Miscellaneous	$\overline{X}$	.430	.246	.173	.076	.057	.180	.082	.399	.054	.366	.134	.251	4.11*
	SD	.223	.201	.091	.028	.020	.046	.032	.283	.244	.092	.000	.072	

* For all the categories except Productivity means and standard deviations are arcsin transformations of the data, and F tests were calculated on arcsin transformations.
** $p \leq .01$

making variables did not show significant mean changes over the four days of instruction, but did the teachers stay the same relative to one another? Table 18.5 shows the correlations between days for the nine preactive decision-making variables. Productivity, Subject Matter, Subject Matter—Lower Order, Subject Matter—Higher Order, Instructional Process, and Miscellaneous all showed moderate to high stability for adjacent days. These variables also showed that stability when comparing nonadjacent days (i.e., days one and three, two and four, and one and four). It is noteworthy that Objectives did not show stability when comparing the first day with other days, but after day one Objectives became highly stable across teachers. Materials and Learners showed the most stability because of lack of variability across teachers.

Interactive decision making

The same categories that were used for preactive decision making were used for interactive decision making with two exceptions. There was insufficient data for Subject Matter—Higher Order and for Miscellaneous. These two categories were used very infrequently in interactive decision making; thus, they are not included in our analyses. Interactive decision-making data are reported for only the first and second days of the study.

Table 18.6 shows the means, standard deviations, and F tests for the seven interactive decision-making categories for days one and two. There was a significant increase in Instructional Process from day one to day two. It appears that on the second day the teachers were refining their original plan and were more concerned with the process of instruction than with the content, materials, or objectives.

Although the interactive decision-making variables did not show significant

TABLE 18.5. Correlations Between Days for Preactive Decision-Making Categories

Preactive Decision-Making Category	r_{12} one × two	r_{23} two × three	r_{34} three × four	r_{13} one × three	r_{24} two × four	r_{14} one × four
Productivity	.71	.69	.54	.60	.73	.58
Objectives	.06	.79	.73	−.04	.62	.06
Subject matter	.79	.92	.55	.86	.57	.65
Subject matter—lower order	.84	.91	.62	.84	.58	.65
Subject matter—higher order	.56	.77	.44	.86	.67	.36
Instructional process	.84	.63	.69	.80	.57	.43
Materials	.44	−.01	.30	.28	−.21	−.20
Learners	−.08	.16	.01	.54	.19	.19
Miscellaneous	.86	.87	.38	.60	.37	.03

TABLE 18.6. Means, Standard Deviations, and *F* Tests for the Seven Interactive Decision-Making Categories across Days One and Two

Interactive Decision-Making Category[1]		Day One	Day Two	*F*	r_{12}
Productivity	$\overline{X}$	72.50	68.00	0.89	.79
	SD	26.57	17.86		
Objectives	$\overline{X}$	.168	.111	1.84	−.08
	SD	.125	.054		
Subject Matter	$\overline{X}$	.081	.050	3.03	.45
	SD	.060	.030		
Lower Order	$\overline{X}$	.060	.038	1.38	.54
	SD	.051	.022		
Instructional Process	$\overline{X}$	.265	.354	7.10*	.45
	SD	.114	.101		
Materials	$\overline{X}$	.058	.064	0.91	.61
	SD	.054	.053		
Learner	$\overline{X}$	.425	.419	0.01	−.10
	SD	.114	.104		

[1] For all categories except Productivity means and standard deviations are arcsin transformations of the data, and *F* tests were calculated on arcsin transformations.
* $\leq .05$

mean changes from day one to day two, five of the seven categories showed moderate stability. The most highly stable category was Productivity ($r_{12} = .79$), which was also true of preactive decision making.

Table 18.7 shows the means, standard deviations, and *F* tests for the seven interactive decision-making variables across teachers. Only Productivity differed significantly across teachers; all other variables did not vary across teachers. Apparently the coding system was not as sensitive to differences in teacher interactive decision making when the protocols were obtained in a structured manner, i.e., the stimulated recall interview. This does not necessarily invalidate the procedure but points to difficulties in data reduction and analysis.

The correlations between interactive decision making and preactive decision making are not particularly noteworthy. There was not much stability in these correlations across days. On the first day the preactive vs. interactive correlations of Subject Matter and Subject Matter—Lower Order were significantly positive, but this was not replicated on day two. The one stable and interesting finding was that Productivity in preactive decision making was *negatively* correlated with Productivity in interactive decision making. Teachers who did the most preactive decision making did the least interactive decision making, and those who did the most interactive decision making did the least preactive decision making.

TABLE 18.7. Means, Standard Deviations, and F Tests for the Seven Interactive Decision-Making Categories across the Twelve Teachers

Interactive Decision-Making Category[1]		1	2	3	4	5	6	7	8	9	10	11	12	F
Productivity	$\overline{X}$	92.00	56.50	62.00	50.00	71.00	68.50	56.50	76.50	71.50	109.00	33.50	96.00	6.53*
	SD	19.80	6.36	24.04	11.31	1.41	2.12	2.12	6.36	7.78	11.31	10.61	11.31	
Objectives	$\overline{X}$	.138	.068	.166	.121	.140	.058	.080	.120	.235	.138	.268	.212	0.87
	SD	.022	.042	.014	.071	.096	.060	.040	.028	.182	.014	.275	.102	
Subject Matter	$\overline{X}$	.024	.101	.006	.119	.007	.059	.107	.078	.056	.074	.056	.080	2.58
	SD	.033	.088	.010	.100	.010	.022	.054	.010	.010	.020	.024	.049	
Lower Order	$\overline{X}$	.010	.093	.006	.084	.007	.030	.107	.046	.050	.042	.056	.032	3.23
	SD	.014	.078	.010	.052	.010	.000	.054	.010	.014	.000	.024	.000	
Instructional Process	$\overline{X}$	.319	.164	.226	.334	.422	.525	.290	.354	.273	.252	.279	.274	2.60
	SD	.037	.069	.163	.033	.090	.024	.101	.028	.128	.017	.123	.157	
Materials	$\overline{X}$	.078	.132	.019	.048	.014	.008	.124	.044	.142	.068	.000	.063	3.50
	SD	.037	.024	.026	.067	.000	.010	.017	.041	.033	.010	.000	.000	
Learners	$\overline{X}$	.428	.534	.570	.378	.418	.364	.398	.404	.294	.450	.398	.425	0.81
	SD	.000	.223	.199	.071	.177	.028	.026	.022	.010	.017	.127	.039	

[1] For all categories except Productivity means and standard deviations are arcsin transformations of the data, and F tests were calculated on arcsin transformations.
* $p \leq .05$

Finally, the average intercorrelation among the seven interactive decision-making variables increased slightly from day one to day two. For day one the average intercorrelation was .30 and for day two it was .34, indicating that the interactive decision making may have become less differentiated from the first to the second day.

Decision Making and Teacher Behavior

Preactive decision making

The nine preactive decision-making variables were correlated with eight teacher-behavior interaction variables. Table 18.8 presents correlations between the eight interaction analysis variables and the preactive decision-making variables for each day.

For day one, decision-making productivity was positively related to teacher questions, subject matter focus, and goal setting in the classroom. Teachers who generated a greater quantity of preactive decision making on the first day asked more questions, spent more time talking about the subject matter, and made more goal statements during the day's teaching sessions. They also spent less time focusing on the group (group focus) or individuals (person focus). However, the only relationship that was stable over time was the negative relationship between decision-making productivity and teacher behavior that focused on the group.

We thought that teacher decision-making behavior would be most related to interactive behavior in the organizational domain of teaching such as goal setting or summarizing during a lesson. As shown in table 18.8, there was a significant but inconsistent relationship between the amount of time that was spent on objectives during preactive decision making and the amount of time that was actually directed toward goal setting during the lesson. On the first day, there was a significant negative correlation between Goals and Objectives—a finding that was contrary to what we predicted. However, the results for the second day indicated a significant positive correlation between Objectives and Goals, and the positive trend continued on the third day. The negative relationship between Objectives and Goals on the first day might not be representative because it was the first day and teachers were unaccustomed to the "thinking aloud" planning procedure. Furthermore, perhaps teachers who did not normally set goals in their teaching felt that we wanted them to set goals or construct objectives. By the second day, the initial demand characteristics may have decreased so that the teachers who talked about objectives in their preactive decision making also tended to be those teachers who used goals interactively.

The decision-making variable for Subject Matter had a clear and consistent relationship with teaching behavior on all days. The teachers who dealt with

TABLE 18.8. Correlations Between Preactive Decision-Making Categories and Teacher Behavior Variables on Days One, Two, and Three

Preactive Decision-Making Category	Teacher Behavior Variable							
	Teacher Question	Person Focus	Group Focus	Subject Matter Focus	Lower Order Cognitive Process	Higher Order Cognitive Process	Goals	Summaries
Day One								
Productivity	.40	−.62*	−.52*	.68*	.34	.07	.42	.01
Objectives	.28	.23	.15	−.25	.24	−.24	−.54†	.03
Subject Matter	.44	−.41	−.58*	.47	.39	−.07	.58*	−.04
Lower Order	.53†	−.16	−.48	.19	.44	−.21	.48	−.11
Higher Order	.03	−.73*	−.43	.86**	.12	.28	.39	.17
Instructional Process	−.45	.12	.47	−.25	−.53*	.00	−.58*	.15
Materials	.24	.24	.22	−.36	−.21	−.34	.18	.15
Learner	−.69*	.12	.07	.07	−.28	−.22	−.02	−.38
Miscellaneous	−.27	.32	.40	−.35	−.10	.40	−.36	−.03

Day Two

Productivity	.09	−.18	−.46	.04	−.17	.10	−.17	.55*
Objectives	−.44	.30	.28	−.27	−.31	−.19	.85**	−.28
Subject Matter	.38	−.41	−.93**	.41	−.06	.15	−.36	.78**
Lower Order	.52†	−.42	−.88**	.43	.24	−.20	−.07	.81**
Higher Order	−.10	−.27	−.37	.25	−.50*	.65*	−.38	−.08
Instructional Process	−.33	.20	.84**	−.31	−.11	.08	.11	−.46
Materials	−.24	.34	.14	−.31	.24	−.56†	.82**	−.32
Learner	.37	.11	.41	.04	.66*	−.25	.00	−.37
Miscellaneous	−.16	.35	.30	−.20	.13	−.18	.02	−.48

Day Three

Productivity	.24	−.04	−.06	.17	−.07	.65*	.27	.00
Objectives	−.25	.62*	.40	−.64*	−.07	−.22	.34	−.21
Subject Matter	.52†	−.46	−.53†	.56†	−.08	.69*	.38	.36
Lower Order	.18	−.45	−.37	.44	−.19	.41	.14	.35
Higher Order	.63*	−.20	−.41	.37	.17	.57	.51†	.16
Instructional Process	−.34	.07	.48	−.20	−.25	−.20	−.21	−.04
Materials	.04	−.32	−.13	.26	.49	−.40	−.20	.41
Learner	−.55†	.21	.68*	−.34	−.56*	−.15	−.32	−.55*
Miscellaneous	−.12	.38	.02	−.31	.24	−.31	−.18	−.36

† $p \leq .10$
* $p \leq .05$
** $p \leq .01$

the subject matter in their decision making also tended to focus on subject matter in their teaching. It should be noted that because Person Focus, Group Focus, and Subject Matter Focus were all on one facet of the interaction analysis system, communications that were not coded as Subject Matter Focus would have to be coded as either Person or Group Focus. Consequently, there was a negative correlation between the proportion of subject matter communications in preactive decision making and group and individual focus in instruction. Although we cannot draw conclusions from these data, we feel that the important relationship here is between decision making concerning the subject matter and the amount of subject matter focused on in the classroom.

The "lower order" and "higher order" decision-making variables refer to the cognitive level at which the teacher planned to deal with the subject matter. The results suggested a positive relationship between the cognitive level the teacher had planned to use and the actual cognitive level of the discussion that took place during the teaching sessions. The correlations between higher level cognitive processes in decision making and teaching were .28, .65, and .57 for days one, two, and three, respectively. The results for lower order processes were somewhat mixed, and a positive relationship was not consistent for all days.

Teachers who talked about the instructional process in their preactive decision making also tended to have more communications about the group in their teaching. Teachers probably used communications about the group to initiate and maintain the instructional process. Thus, teachers who planned instructional strategies, such as role playing or group investigation, needed more communications about the group in order to keep these instructional processes going during the lesson.

The decision-making categories of Materials, Learner, and Miscellaneous will be discussed briefly. Because the variability across teachers for the first two of these categories was so low, many of the relationships with these categories might be spurious. There was a consistent negative correlation on days one and three between the teacher's focus on the learner in preactive decision making and the number of questions that were asked by the teacher during the lesson. For the second and third day, there was a positive relationship between focus on the learner in preactive decision making and focus on the group of learners interactively. Thus, teachers who were concerned about students in their planning were also concerned about students in their actual teaching.

Only one relationship was found with the Materials variable. On the second and third days, teachers who spent a lot of time talking about using materials such as slides spent less time dealing with higher order cognitive processes in their teaching.

Finally, there were no significant relationships between the Miscellaneous decision-making category and the interaction analysis categories.

Interactive decision making

Table 18.9 shows the correlations between the seven interactive decision-making variables and the eight teacher behavior variables described above. Very few of these correlations were statistically significant.

On both days teacher summarizing during instruction was negatively correlated with Productivity in interactive decision making, a finding that is difficult to interpret. A more understandable finding was the consistent negative correlation between Subject Matter Focus during instruction and an interactive decision-making focus on the learners. In sum, since there was little significant variation across teachers in the interactive decision making, it was not surprising that these variables did not show consistent correlations with the teacher behavior variables.

Decision Making and Student Achievement and Attitude

Preactive decision making

The correlations between preactive decision making and achievement and attitude are shown in table 18.10. At this point, we will discuss only the relationships that show some stability across days.

Decision-making Productivity was positively correlated with Multiple Choice achievement on the first day, but this correlation became negative on all the subsequent days. Productivity was one of the preactive variables that showed rather high stability over time. Apparently, the teachers who were prolific planners were effective on the first day and tended to spend relatively more planning time than their colleagues on subsequent days. This extra planning, however, did not help their students, but proved to be a disadvantage. Perhaps these teachers became "stale" from too much planning. A related finding was the trend for Productivity to be negatively correlated with student attitude.

The correlations between the Subject Matter decision-making categories and the student outcomes, particularly attitude, paralleled the findings for Productivity. There were nine correlations each day between the three Subject Matter decision-making variables and the three attitude variables. Thus, for the four days there were thirty-six possible correlations between preactive decision making about the Subject Matter and student attitudes. Thirty-five of these correlations were negative. Also, Subject Matter decision making was quite stable across days and highly correlated with Productivity. The picture that begins to emerge is that productive preactive decision makers in this study spent much of their decision-making time going over the subject matter. After the first day of teaching this extra time was counterproductive with regard to their students' achievement, and actually was associated with negative student attitudes toward the subject matter, teacher, materials, and selves as learners.

TABLE 18.9. Correlations Between Interactive Decision-Making Categories and Teacher Behavior on Days One and Two

Interactive Decision-Making Category	Teacher Behavior Variable							
	Teacher Question	Person Focus	Group Focus	Subject Matter Focus	Lower Order Cognitive Process	Higher Order Cognitive Process	Goal	Summaries
Day One								
Productivity	−.14	.55†	.08	−.47	.22	−.44	.06	−.60*
Objectives	−.23	−.30	−.75**	.74**	.28	.05	.49	−.19
Subject Matter	−.06	−.02	.02	−.07	.12	−.28	.42	−.27
Lower Order	.06	−.06	.09	−.04	.05	−.29	.37	−.02
Instructional Process	−.10	−.18	.75**	−.21	−.32	.32	−.48	−.28
Materials	−.05	.62*	.05	−.41	.35	−.74**	.17	−.19
Learner	.39	.36	.00	−.41	−.11	.01	−.23	.48
Day Two								
Productivity	−.30	.16	.41	−.06	−.12	−.07	.47	−.45
Objectives	−.24	.00	.25	.19	−.29	.47	−.14	−.32
Subject Matter	−.43	.32	−.15	−.49	−.26	−.40	.46	.08
Lower Order	−.38	.23	−.32	−.40	−.21	−.40	.27	.20
Instructional Process	.08	−.60	−.19	.47	−.63*	.60*	.03	.18
Materials	.21	−.16	.03	.14	.32	−.39	.23	.32
Learner	.04	.62*	.06	−.54†	.66**	−.57†	−.19	−.13

† $p \leq .10$
* $p \leq .05$
** $p \leq .01$

Stable relationships appeared for the preactive decision-making categories of Objectives, Materials, and Learners. There was a tendency for decision making about the instructional process to be negatively correlated with some of the essay scores, but this relationship was not stable across all days.

The positive, and often highly significant correlations between Miscellaneous preactive decision making and student attitude were somewhat puzzling. Perhaps the answer lies in the nature of the communications coded Miscellaneous. They were often musings and mutterings that dealt more with adjusting to the "think-aloud" procedure than with planning the lessons. Perhaps more relaxed teachers responded in this manner, and the correlations between Miscellaneous and attitude were the result of stylistic differences in the teachers. Thus, the significant correlations for Miscellaneous suggest that we are measuring an important construct in teacher preactive decision making that is not "miscellaneous." This construct deserves further consideration as an additional category in the coding system.

Interactive decision making

The correlations between interactive decision making and student achievement and attitude are reported in table 18.11. We noted two important relationships. First, the correlations between interactive decision-making Productivity and the student attitude measures were uniformly positive. Thus, teachers who were more productive in the stimulated recall sessions had students who had more positive attitudes. Recall that the correlation between preactive and interactive decision-making Productivity was strong and negative, suggesting different styles of decision making. Teachers who were highly productive preactive decision makers tended to have students with more negative attitudes; teachers who tended to be less productive preactive decision makers were *more* productive interactive decision makers and had students with more positive attitudes.

The second important finding was the negative correlations between the two subject matter decision-making variables and the students' abstract scores on the essay test. Since Subject Matter was highly correlated with Subject Matter—Lower Order in interactive decision making (.90 and .93 for days one and two), it follows that teachers who focused on subject matter in the stimulated recall interviews were really focusing on lower order subject matter, namely, facts and figures, and their students tended to do more poorly on essay tests requiring more abstract reasoning.

SUMMARY AND CONCLUSIONS

This study was a first attempt to examine teacher preactive and interactive decision making. We had two goals in our investigation. One was to develop a methodology for investigating teacher decision making. Our second goal

TABLE 18.10. Correlations Between Preactive Decision-Making Categories and Student Attitude and Achievement Across Four Days

Preactive Decision-Making Category	Achievement					Attitude	
	Multiple Choice	Essay: Concrete	Essay: Abstract	Essay: Total	Teacher, Method, Subject	Self as Learner	Total
Day One							
Productivity	.62*	.10	.04	.11	−.37	−.14	−.34
Objectives	−.34	−.12	.34	−.00	.61*	.24	.56†
Subject Matter	.59*	.26	−.10	.21	−.35	−.02	−.30
Lower Order	.38	.37	−.17	.28	−.30	.00	−.25
Higher Order	.64*	−.25	.09	−.20	−.32	−.12	−.30
Instructional Process	−.48	−.21	.10	−.16	.35	−.07	.29
Materials	.11	.07	.44	.22	.15	−.24	.08
Learner	−.35	−.45	.09	−.39	.31	.20	.30
Miscellaneous	−.40	−.12	−.21	−.17	−.11	.04	−.08
Day Two							
Productivity	−.50†	−.27	−.39	−.39	−.68*	−.51†	−.70*
Objectives	−.48	−.14	.01	−.13	−.13	.19	−.07
Subject Matter	.03	.30	−.53†	.12	−.46	−.49	−.50†
Lower Order	−.06	.49	−.59*	.28	−.27	−.41	−.33
Higher Order	.13	.04	.07	.07	−.35	−.16	−.33
Instructional Process	−.35	−.55†	.44	−.39	.06	−.02	.05
Materials	−.19	.26	−.04	.24	.18	.57†	.28
Learner	.27	.39	.52†	.55	.36	.34	.38
Miscellaneous	.64*	.02	.12	.05	.71**	.70*	.77**

Day Three

Productivity	-.46	-.78**	-.11	-.69*	-.39	-.52†	-.42
Objectives	-.18	.20	-.18	.11	.01	.08	.02
Subject Matter	-.35	-.51†	.04	-.41	-.40	-.71**	-.46
Lower Order	-.19	-.05	.10	.00	-.29	-.58*	-.34
Higher Order	-.37	-.79**	-.11	-.71**	-.28	-.44	-.31
Instructional Process	-.25	.00	.28	.08	-.26	.03	-.22
Materials	.00	.12	-.23	.04	-.05	.01	-.04
Learner	.08	-.21	-.04	-.21	-.24	.09	-.19
Miscellaneous	.61*	.47	-.15	.36	.69*	.68*	.70*

Day Four

Productivity	-.58*	-.29	-.31	-.32	-.50†	-.07	-.44
Objectives	.02	.24	-.09	.07	.40	.27	.39
Subject Matter	.02	-.33	-.24	-.31	-.35	-.33	-.36
Lower Order	.20	-.40	.00	-.30	-.37	-.37	-.38
Higher Order	-.33	.06	-.54	-.09	.06	.11	-.07
Instructional Process	.08	-.62*	-.77**	-.73**	-.52†	-.32	-.50†
Materials	-.02	-.39	.16	-.30	-.39	-.17	-.37
Learner	-.14	.16	-.27	-.02	.20	.19	.20
Miscellaneous	.18	.49	.17	.52†	.24	.02	.20

† $p \leq .10$
* $p \leq .05$
** $p \leq .01$

TABLE 18.11. Correlations Between Interactive Decision-Making Categories and Student Outcomes on Days One and Two

Interactive Decision-Making Category	Achievement				Attitude		
	Multiple Choice	Essay: Concrete	Essay: Abstract	Essay: Total	Teacher, Method, Subject	Self as Learner	Total
Day One							
Productivity	-.32	.11	.02	.11	.51†	.50†	.52†
Objectives	.47	-.15	-.03	-.16	-.08	.23	-.03
Subject Matter	-.11	.09	-.44	-.06	-.35	.00	-.30
Lower Order	-.11	-.05	-.41	-.18	-.53†	-.27	-.50
Instructional Process	-.54†	-.46	.23	-.34	.14	.15	.15
Materials	-.36	.00	-.32	-.11	-.05	-.12	-.07
Learner	.23	.53†	.20	.56†	.16	-.28	.08
Day Two							
Productivity	.14	.05	.56†	.23	.40	.35	.42
Objectives	.39	.03	.59*	.23	.15	.10	.15
Subject Matter	-.40	-.28	-.60*	-.47	-.17	.11	-.13
Lower Order	-.40	-.28	-.63*	-.48	-.27	.03	-.23
Instructional Process	-.32	.01	.03	.04	-.37	-.75**	-.48
Materials	-.20	-.14	-.20	-.21	.24	-.07	.19
Learner	.31	.10	-.05	.06	.19	.66**	.31

$† p \leq .10$
$* p \leq .05$
$** p \leq .01$

was to explore the nature of teacher decision making and its relationship to teacher behavior and student achievement and attitude.

Our first attempt at developing instruments to assess teacher decision making has been successful. The "think-aloud" procedure for preactive decision making has generated some interesting findings. Our next step is to explore the factors affecting the quantity and quality of these data. Changes in the constraints of a study will probably affect the nature of the data. For example, we restricted the materials that the teachers could use, and we had the teachers instruct children they did not know. Perhaps decision making in a classroom situation where teachers are free to choose their materials and are teaching children they know would result in more variance in the Materials and Learner decision-making categories.

Now that a first generation of instruments has been developed, we can turn to experimental studies from which causal inferences can be drawn between environmental constraints and teacher decision making. The result of such studies might suggest more about the cognitive processes involved in teacher decision making.

The interactive decision-making data were not as fruitful as the preactive data. One obvious problem was in the coding system. A different data reduction system may have to be used for the "stimulated recall" protocols. We feel that the stimulated recall procedure, however, has merit, and that modifications in the interview format and procedures for videotape playback will produce more rewarding data than reported here.

We are not yet ready to make generalizations concerning decision-making styles in teachers, or the relationships among these styles and teacher behavior and student outcome. We have some interesting leads. For example, there is the negative relationship between preactive and interactive decision making Productivity, and the relationship between Productivity and student attitudes. Similarly, the relationship between preactive decision making about subject matter and teacher focus on subject matter during instruction is intriguing, as is the negative relationship between subject matter decision making and student attitude. With replications of these findings with new samples, our confidence in these relationships may grow. Intensive work with larger numbers of teachers and students may enable us to generate structural models of teacher decision making, teacher behavior, and student achievement and attitude.

19

Stimulated Recall

Christopher Clark and Penelope Peterson

The model in figure 19.1 represents the way we thought about teaching as we designed this study and analyzed the data. Following the approach to research on teaching suggested by Lee Shulman,[40] we conceived of teaching

FIGURE 19.1   An Information-Processing Model of Teaching.

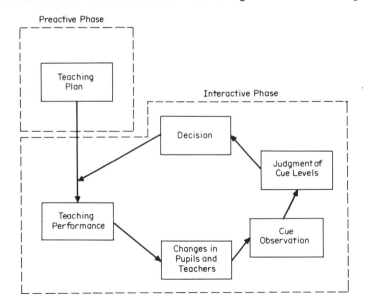

as clinical information processing. According to Shulman, "The phrase [clinical information processing] is meant to communicate two perspectives—a view of the *task* of teaching as fundamentally *clinical* in nature and a view of the human being who performs those tasks as an information processor." We have employed Jackson's [17] preactive-interactive distinction to describe the two major phases of teacher decision making.

DESIGN OF MODEL

In this model, the teacher begins with a teaching plan. The teaching plan is composed during the preactive phase of teaching. The teacher begins the interactive phase of teaching with some teaching performance or opening gambit that is part of the teaching plan. This initial move by the teacher produces some changes in both teacher and pupils. Some of these changes are observable by the teacher, and some are not. A given teacher probably places more weight on some changes than on others. We call the most important observable changes "cues." The teacher observes these cues and makes judgments about whether these cues fall within the range of acceptable values for this teaching plan. If the cues do fall within the acceptable range, the teacher decides to continue the teaching plan, and so the cycle is repeated as before. If some of the cues fall outside acceptable limits, the teacher may decide to continue with the teaching plan (hoping things will get better) or to modify the plan in a way that should restore the cues to acceptable limits.

As described above, teacher interactive decision making was explored using a stimulated recall procedure. This procedure consisted of showing each teacher videotaped segments of the day's teaching in order to "stimulate recall" of what he or she was thinking about while teaching. After viewing a videotaped segment, the teacher responded to a structured interview. The questions in the interview correspond to the boxes in our model of interactive decision making:

1. With regard to *teaching performance,* the first box in the model, the teacher was asked:
   What were you doing in this segment and why?

2. *Changes in pupils and teachers,* the second box in the model, were reflected in the videotaped segment viewed by the teacher. To get at possible internal changes taking place in the teacher, we asked the following question:
   Were you thinking of any alternative actions or strategies at that time?

3. To find out what changes in pupils were important to the teacher, we inquired:
   Did you have any particular objectives in mind in this segment?
   If so, what were they?
   Cue observation was then explored with the query:
   What were you noticing about the students?

4. *Judgment of cue levels* was elicited by the follow-up question:
   How were the students responding?

5. Finally, to ascertain whether the teacher made a conscious interactive *decision,* we asked:
Did any student reactions cause you to act differently than you had planned?

RESULTS

Now let us describe how teachers responded to these questions.

Teaching Performance

The first question in the stimulated recall interview was "What were you doing in this segment and why?" Teachers were able to describe in general terms what they were doing in each segment and to put it into context but seemed to be less able to articulate why. In most cases, the implicit reason for their behavior was either that they had planned to behave in this way, or that they were simply going with the flow of events—doing what came naturally.

Changes in Pupils and Teachers

The second question, "Were you thinking of any alternative actions or strategies at that time?", was asked a total of forty-three times to the twelve teachers in our sample. The teachers responded affirmatively only eight times to this question. Three of the twelve teachers gave a single affirmative response, one teacher gave two affirmative responses, and a fifth teacher gave three affirmative responses. These data indicate that it is relatively rare for teachers to be thinking about alternative actions or strategies while they are teaching.

This question was asked of each teacher with reference to the beginning, middle, and end of their lessons. No teachers indicated that they were considering alternative actions or strategies at the beginning of their lesson. That is, all the teachers in this sample seemed to have planned a single opening strategy and implemented it without considering alternatives. Similarly, only one affirmative response was received concerning the final part of the teachers' lessons. In the later stages of a lesson teachers did not seem to be considering alternatives because they felt that there would be insufficient time to make a meaningful change, even if they felt that a change was in order. Thus, seven of the eight occasions on which teachers reported having alternative actions or strategies in mind occurred during the middle period of the lessons.

When teachers did consider alternatives, it seemed to be because things were going poorly. For example, one teacher reported that at one point in the lesson he felt that he ought to be doing something different because the students were unenthusiastic, uninterested in the material, and not giving many verbal responses. Later in the session the same teacher reported that he was *not* thinking of alternative actions or strategies because "I was pleased with what was happening here. Not like before when I was sort of struggling with what was going on." What this finding seems to indicate is that *the interactive decision making of the teachers in this sample was not aimed at optimizing instruction.* That is, they were not particularly concerned with improving an adequate situation. Rather, their decision making came into play only when they felt the need to salvage an unacceptable situation.

Cue Observation

Parts of the responses given to the question on alternatives pertain to Cue Observation, the third box in the model. The main cue that our teachers used to judge whether alternative actions or strategies would be considered was student participation and involvement. The experimental situation was essentially a small-group discussion setting. The teachers seemed to feel that if the majority of the students were participating in a discussion, regardless of the quality of that discussion, things were going well. Conversely, if the students were behaving unresponsively, things were going poorly and an alternative strategy might be attempted.

The cues observed by a teacher should be related to what changes in pupils are considered important by the teachers. Thus, the relative weight given to different pupil changes should be reflected by the teacher's response to question 3, "Did you have any particular objectives in mind during this segment, and, if so, what were they?"

The objectives mentioned can be grouped into three categories: organizational, affective, and cognitive.

Organizational objectives are objectives that have to do with establishing roles, setting ground rules for behavior, informing students of the teacher's intended plan, and carrying out the plan. The most frequently mentioned organizational objective was to carry out the teaching plan. This objective was cited fourteen of the nineteen times that organizational objectives were recalled. In a sense, this response barely qualifies as an objective since it does not refer to desired changes in students' behavior. The teachers seemed to be saying "My objective was to do what I was doing." This response should perhaps be treated as indicating that the teacher, in fact, had no particular objective in mind at that time. (Incidentally, no teacher ever said directly that he or she had no objective in mind during any of the teaching segments viewed.)

Among the affective objectives, teachers most frequently recalled their intention to create a group feeling such as rapport, relaxation, familiarity, or unity. This objective was mentioned eleven times of the total of eighteen mentions of affective objectives. It was frequently mentioned in response to viewing the opening segment of the first teaching session.

The largest number of cues noticed about students were in the global student states category. These cues were relatively high-inference observations of the mood or state of the class as a group. The terms used to describe the students in this category were tense, relaxed, quiet, shy, cooperative, interested, tired, attentive, and positive. Cues in this category were often used as explanations of why the teacher-student interaction was proceeding as it was. For example, in discussing a teaching segment late in the day, one teacher said, "I guess I was noticing the tiredness of the group and their wanting to have side conversations instead of going on at that point."

In the category of student behavior in relation to teaching process, the cue that was mentioned by eleven of the twelve teachers was student participation and involvement. This cue was mentioned three times as often as the next most frequent cue in any category.

The next category of cues noticed by teachers had to do with the intellectual characteristics and performance of the students. Surprisingly to us, only four of the twelve teachers mentioned cues in this category. An example of this was a statement by one teacher that her students had "excellent factual recall." Another teacher noticed that his students did not have "any skill in asking analytical questions." It seemed that much more attention and energy was focused on the mood of the group and the smoothness of the group process than on the learning being done.

The final category of cues noticed by teachers were specific overt student behaviors. The cues included smiles, posture, and silly behavior. Smiles and posture were mentioned by one teacher, and silly behavior was mentioned by only one other teacher. Thus, it was rare for teachers to mention low-inference student behavior.

In describing what they were noticing, six of the twelve teachers spoke predominantly about students as a group; that is, they seemed to be using the class as their unit of analysis. Three of the teachers spoke primarily of individuals within the group when recalling what they had noticed about the students. The remaining three teachers gave approximately equal treatment to group characteristics and individual cues.

Judgment of Cue Levels

After cue observation, the next box in our model is judgment of cue levels. The question, "How were the students responding?" was expected to elicit some judgment on the part of the teacher as to whether the observed cues fell in the range of acceptable values defined by the teacher's teaching plan. The vast majority of teacher responses to this question indicated that the students were responding well, or as favorably as could be expected under the circumstances. In those instances in which the teachers were dissatisfied with how the students were responding, it was largely because of insufficient student participation or involvement. The *quantity* of student participation seemed to be the dimension on which judgment was passed. *Quality* of student participation was mentioned by only one teacher, who reported that his students were not able to ask analytic questions.

Decision

Finally, we come to the last box in the model, which represents the decision made by the teacher in response to his or her judgment of cue levels.

In response to the final question about whether the teachers had changed their behavior based on student reactions, twenty-two of the thirty-one responses were negative. Teachers did not tend to change their plans or behavior in response to student reactions. In five of the nine cases in which the teachers did report changing their behavior, it was unclear what the nature of the change was. That is, the teachers gave the impression that they had been influenced in some way by student reactions, but they were unable to articulate the specific results of that influence. In the four remaining instances, the nature of teacher behavior change seemed to be either to continue with and elaborate upon an activity in progress (in response to favorable student reactions) or to digress or shift to a new activity (in response to generally unfavorable student reactions).

CONCLUSIONS AND IMPLICATIONS

In conclusion, our information-processing model of teaching appears to be a useful way of conceptualizing what teachers think while they are teaching. When we applied our model to teachers' stimulated recall of interactive decisions, we found the following three generalizations which might have implications for teacher training:

1. Teachers considered alternative strategies only when the instructional process was "going poorly." That is, the teachers were not trying to optimize instruction.
2. Pupil participation and involvement were the primary cues used by teachers to judge how well the instructional process was going.
3. Teachers rarely changed their strategy from what they had planned even if instruction was going poorly.

20

Teachers' Utilization of Feedback from Students

Janet Crist-Witzel

Some promising research on changing teacher behavior within the past twenty years has investigated a method of providing teachers with student feedback that is more systematic than the spontaneous and filtered feedback a teacher receives during classroom interaction. This method is the feedback of students' observations of teacher behavior obtained through ratings of the teacher by students.[11] A number of studies have shown that such feedback can influence teacher behavior as measured by subsequent student ratings following feedback.[1,2,12,13,30,44]

This study was designed to determine the effects on teachers' behavior of receiving focused impact feedback in the form of summarized student ratings about amount and direction of desired change for teaching performance. Relationships between teacher characteristics, such as attitude toward feedback, verbal ability, and conceptual level, and types of reactions to feedback are examined. Comparisons of effects on teacher behavior are made between teachers who were classified as positive or negative toward student feedback. Finally, student outcomes are compared for three groups of students: those whose teachers received feedback from them and were positive toward the feedback; those whose teachers received feedback but were negative toward it; and those whose teachers received no feedback.

METHOD

As reported in chapters 17 and 18, twelve experienced teachers (six women, six men), as part of a larger experiment, each taught one social studies unit about a European town and its inhabitants to three different randomly assigned groups of eight junior high school students (stratified on sex and verbal ability). The three groups were taught over three days (Monday, Wednesday, and Friday) of one week. For each class the social studies unit was taught in three fifty-minute sessions in one day. Students were tested for achievement (multiple-choice recall and essay) and attitude at the end of the day. For the present study, which was part of the larger experiment, the teachers and their third day's (Friday's) class returned four days later (the following Tuesday) when a parallel social studies unit (on a different European town) was taught. Eight randomly selected experimental teachers received feedback about desired change in their behavior in the Friday session from their students before Tuesday and following each session on Tuesday.

Instrumentation

Prior to the study, teachers were administered four aptitude tests, measuring verbal ability (Extended Range Vocabulary Test, Parts I and II), reasoning ability (Necessary Arithmatic Operations, Parts I and II), analytic ability (Hidden Figures Test, Parts I and II), and conceptual level (Paragraph Completion Test).[16]

A Student Opinion Form (SOF), developed for this study, contained thirteen items of observable low-inference organizational, cognitive, and affective teacher behavior. Students rated on a five-point Likert-type scale how much and in what direction they would like to see the teacher change on each item, based on the session just ended. In addition, students rated approximately how often they thought each type of behavior actually occurred in the session (not at all, 1–2 times, 3–4 times, 5–10 times, 11–20 times, or over 20 times). A teacher self-rating form on desired teacher behavior changes, similar to the student form, was also used in the study.

An evaluation questionnaire, completed by teachers at the conclusion of the study, asked teachers to indicate on a five-point Likert-type scale (from "Strongly Agree" to "Strongly Disagree") their feelings about student feedback in general, reliability of their students' ratings, general usefulness of the ratings, their use of the ratings to evaluate their teaching, and their satisfaction with their feedback.

Design and Procedure

For the present study, the students in Friday's group returned on the following Tuesday and were taught a second social studies unit (on a different European town) by the same teacher. There were again three fifty-minute sessions. Thus, except for attrition and some replacements by extra students, teachers taught the same group on two separate days. Eight teachers were randomly assigned to an experimental group (E) who received student feedback on their teaching, and four teachers were randomly assigned to a control condition (C) and received no feedback.

Following each session on Friday, the students filled out a Student Opinion Form (SOF) to rate desired behavior change of their teacher on thirteen items of teaching behavior. They also indicated their estimate of how many times each behavior occurred in the session just ended. At the end of the day on Friday, each teacher also rated his or her own desired behavior change on the basis of the day's teaching on a Teacher Opinion Form (TOF).

Teachers returned on Monday to acquaint themselves with the content of the new unit and to make their teaching plans for the following day. Before receiving the new unit, E teachers received summarized feedback of their students' ratings from all three Friday sessions. For each session, on a copy of the Student Opinion Form, the mean student rating for each item was marked with a small round green sticker (dot), and the distribution of responses was indicated by the number of students who marked each category. E teachers continued to receive summarized feedback after each teaching session on Tuesday. C teachers did not receive any feedback.

Each time the E teachers received their feedback they were given instructions for interpreting it, were asked not to discuss the feedback with students or with other teachers, and were asked to "think aloud" and tape-record their reactions to the feedback they received. They were asked to talk about what the information meant to them, how they felt about it, and whether it was useful to them. They were asked to give their general reactions, as well as their reactions to each of the items in any order they wished. At the end of the instructions and guidelines for reacting, they were encouraged to use the feedback information in their lession planning if they found it useful.

Using teachers' responses from the evaluation questionnaire, average scores over nineteen items were derived for each teacher, and teachers were ranked according to the positiveness of their attitude toward feedback. On this basis, five teachers were clustered toward the positive end of the continuum and three toward the negative end: thus, the first five teachers formed the "positive" experimental group (E+), while the latter three formed the "negative" experimental group (E−).

The transcripts of the eight experimental teachers' tape-recorded reactions to their feedback were coded, with identifiable statements or thought units categorized according to the *type* of verbal statement and the *focus* of the statement. In addition, the total number of coded statements for each teacher was used as a productivity measure.

RESULTS AND DISCUSSION

Teacher Characteristics and Reactions to Feedback

Table 20.1 shows general profiles of the experimental teachers on the various teacher characteristics or aptitudes. Teachers are categorized as positive (E+) or negative (E−) toward student feedback and classified as either high or low on Verbal Ability, Reasoning Ability, Analytic Ability, Conceptual Level, and General Satisfaction with teaching (as measured by responses on the final evaluation). Attitude Toward Feedback was significantly correlated with Satisfaction With Teaching ($r = .71$, $p < .05$) and had a high moderate correlation (.57) with Verbal Ability. These were the two highest correlations among aptitudes. Since Feedback Attitude and Satisfaction with teaching were measured with the same instrument and, since the two variables may be related to a feeling of success and general attitude toward the teaching situation in the study, their high correlation was not surprising. Except for near-zero correlations between Attitude Toward Feedback and Reasoning Ability and between Verbal Ability and Conceptual Level, and low positive r's between Conceptual Level and the two variables of Attitude Toward Feedback and Verbal Ability, all correlations were low moderate to high moderate and positive.

Frequencies of coded categories from the Feedback Reaction Coding System were converted to proportions because of variability in total number of statements, or productivity. Productivity remained scaled as a frequency count. Some categories were dropped for analysis due to low frequencies.

Coding categories retained for analysis are shown in table 20.2. Table 20.3 shows overall means and standard deviations for these categories, as well as the usage of each category by each teacher in reacting to his or her feedback. For all teachers, a majority of time was spent making statements of repetition and focusing on ratings and items, although there was considerable variation among teachers. Some teachers (note teachers 9, 11, and 3) spent very little and others (note teachers 7 and 4) spent a very large proportion of their time in these categories. The distributions and variability of the eight teachers' usage of all categories were good, with the exception of justifying statements and statements focusing on Other Teaching or Teaching Beliefs; in each of these cases it was primarily a couple of teachers (in both cases E− teachers) who used them, with low usage by some and no usage by several others. Since Other Teaching or Teaching Beliefs were used primarily by one teacher, and thus had a more skewed distribution, they are not included in other tables.

Attitudes toward Feedback and Reactions to Feedback

Correlations of teacher characteristics with categories of reaction to feedback are given in table 20.4. Scattergrams of selected categories plotted against

TABLE 20.1. Categorization of Teachers as High (Above Median) or Low (Below Median) on Teacher Characteristics and Intercorrelations Among Characteristics

Group and Teacher	Verbal Ability	Reasoning Ability	Analytic Ability	Conceptual Level	General Satisfaction with Teaching
E+					
2	Low	Low	High	Low	Low
7	Low	Low	Low	Low	High
9	High	High	High	High	High
10	High	High	High	High	High
11	High	High	Low	High	High
E−					
3	Low	High	High	High	Low
4	High	Low	Low	Low	Low
8	Low	Low	Low	Low	Low

	Verbal Ability	Reasoning Ability	Analytic Ability	Conceptual Level	General Satisfaction with Teaching
Attitude Toward Feedback	.57	−.01	.50	.21	.71 *
Verbal Ability		.53	−.04	.31	.47
Reasoning Ability			.47	.56	.40
Analytic Ability				.52	.54
Conceptual Level					.41

* $p < .05$

TABLE 20.2. Coding Categories
Used in Analysis

Category	Abbreviation
Productivity [a]	Prod
Type of Statement [b]	
Intent to Change	Int+
Repetition	Rep
Reflective	Ref
Analytic	Ana
Contrast	Cont
Interpretive	Interp
Justifying	Just
Conflict	Confl
Accord	Accord
Focus [b]	
Ratings	Rat
Items	Items
Teaching Moves	Tch
Students	Stu
Class Activities	Cl Act

[a] Productivity is the total number of coded statements and is measured in frequencies.
[b] Categories of type and focus are measured as proportions of total number of coded statements.

teacher Attitude Toward Feedback are presented in figure 20.1 to show some of the relationships more graphically and to determine whether they are linear. In these scattergrams, teachers who tended to be outlying cases are marked with boxes. In addition, intercorrelations among feedback reaction categories are given in tables 20.5 through 20.7.

As table 20.4 and figure 20.1a show, there is a strong positive linear relationship between measured Attitudes Toward Feedback and the proportion of statements of Intent To Change teaching behavior on the basis of student ratings ($r = .88$). This relationship was expected, and even with such a small number of cases was significant at the .01 level. Attitude Toward Feedback was also strongly related to the proportion of statements that focused on what students did during a teaching session. This relationship was also fairly linear, as figure 20.1b shows.

The relationship between Feedback Attitude and Intent To Change and Focus On Students would be even stronger and more linear with the effect of Teacher 7 (an outlier in both cases) removed. Teacher 7 was the only teacher in the E+ group who scored low (below the median) on all the ability measures. These low aptitudes may have somehow minimized his ability to internalize and process relevant information beyond the items and ratings.

There were moderate positive correlations between Attitude Toward Feedback and proportion of Analytic, Contrasting, and Interpretive statements,

TABLE 20.3. Category Means and Standard Deviations Over All Teachers and Usage of Each Category by Individual Teachers

Group and Teacher	Prod	Type									Focus					
		Int+	Rep	Ref	Ana	Cont	Interp	Just	Confl	Accord	Rat	Items	Tch	Stu	Cl. Act	OT,TB
E+																
2	78	.10	.22	.04	.17	.18	.12	.01	.03	.04	.29	.18	.14	.18	.05	.01
7	183	.03	.71	.01	.00	.02	.01	.00	.00	.06	.39	.33	.03	.01	.00	.00
9	233	.07	.09	.14	.28	.17	.09	.03	.01	.02	.27	.08	.20	.16	.15	.004
10	108	.06	.20	.11	.07	.11	.16	.00	.01	.12	.32	.18	.14	.08	.03	.00
11	131	.10	.14	.11	.16	.07	.18	.02	.04	.10	.36	.05	.15	.30	.05	.00
E−																
3	250	.01	.16	.14	.11	.04	.02	.17	.08	.16	.40	.10	.19	.10	.02	.10
4	140	.02	.51	.04	.01	.06	.07	.05	.06	.09	.51	.30	.10	.01	.00	.01
8	21	.00	.24	.00	.00	.05	.10	.00	.05	.00	.14	.24	.00	.00	.10	.00
$\bar{x}$	143	.05	.28	.07	.10	.09	.09	.04	.04	.07	.34	.18	.12	.11	.05	.02
S.D.	77.1	.04	.21	.06	.10	.06	.06	.06	.03	.05	.11	.10	.07	.10	.05	.03

TABLE 20.4. Correlations Between Teacher Aptitudes and Categories of Reaction to Feedback

	Prod	Int+	Rep	Ref	Ana	Cont	Interp	Just	Confl	Accord	Rat	Items	Tch	Stu	Cl. Act
							Type							Focus	
Attitude toward Feedback	.01	.88 **	.03	.11	.44	.44	.45	−.53	−.70 †	−.08	.09	−.20	.23	.63 †	−.01
Verbal Ability	.13	.61	−.36	.51	.51	.27	.66 †	−.32	−.37	.03	.05	−.54	.40	.64 †	.33
Reasoning Ability	.36	−.06	−.19	.62 †	.02	.31	.22	.20	−.05	.64 †	.26	.33	.31	.11	−.15
Analytic Ability	.38	.53	−.25	.67 †	.44	.43	.25	.14	−.33	.58	.36	−.38	.72 *	.39	−.21
Conceptual Level	.51	.26	−.53	.75 *	.51	.08	.09	.33	−.15	.40	−.17	−.72 *	.56	.49	.22
Satisfaction with Teaching	.49	.18	.34	.23	.17	−.03	−.01	−.24	−.72 *	.19	.35	.00	.37	.21	−.21

* $p < .05$, two-tailed
** $p < .01$
† $p < .10$

FIGURE 20.1 Scattergrams of Selected Categories of Teachers' Reactions to Feedback Plotted Against Their Attitude Toward Feedback (Shown on *x*-axis).

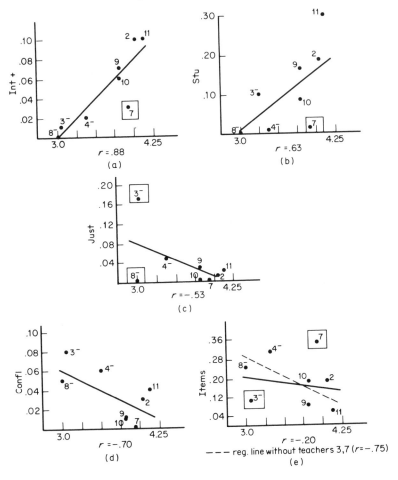

indicating that those teachers verbalizing intent or the decision to change tended to go beyond the mere repetition of the information given. All three of these relationships would be stronger and more linear (figures not shown) if the effect of Teacher 7, again, were removed. There was a small but positive relationship between Feedback Attitude and Focus On Teaching. Teachers 3 and, again, 7 were outliers: Teacher 3 was negative toward feedback but high on most abilities and was high on use of both Reflective and Justifying statements, both of which often focused on teaching. Teacher 7, positive but low on Ability measures, has been discussed.

There was a negative relationship between Attitude Toward Feedback

TABLE 20.5. Selected Correlations[a] Between Types (and Productivity) of Verbal Statements Made and Focus of Statements

	Prod	Int+	Rep	Ref	Ana	Cont	Interp	Just	Confl	Accord
Rating	.51		.47			-.32	-.32	.41		
Items	-.32	-.54	.89**	-.84**	-.81	-.41	-.46	-.34		.66†
Teacher	.61	.50	-.65†	.91**	.84**	.54		.51		
Students		.85**	-.63†	.57	.77*	.47	.61			.47
Cl. Act			-.63†		.63†	.56				-.65†

* p < .05
** p < .01
† p < .10
[a] Only correlations ≥ .30 are shown.

TABLE 20.6. Selected Intercorrelations[a] Among Types of Verbal Statements

	Int+	Rep	Ref	Ana	Cont	Interp	Just	Confl	Accord
Prod				.40		-.53	.64†		.45
Int+		-.39	.32	.69†	.70†	.67†	-.37	-.44	
Rep			-.68†	-.70†	-.54	-.57			
Ref				.70†	.31				.54
Ana					.77*	.32	.52		
Cont						.46			
Interp							-.49	-.36	-.35
Just								.74*	.65†
Confl									.40

* p < .05
** p < .01
† p < .10
[a] Only correlations ≥ .30 are shown.

TABLE 20.7. Selected Intercorrelations [a] Among
Foci of Verbal Statements

	Item	Tch	Stu	Cl. Act
Rating	.31			−.74 *
Items		−.79 *	−.83 **	−.49
Teacher			.65 †	
Students				

* $p < .05$
** $p < .01$
† $p < .10$
[a] Only correlations $\geq .30$ are shown.

and proportion of statements justifying teaching in a session (−.53, see fig. 20.1), largely due to the effect of Teacher 3. This relationship was expected to be opposite to that for statements of intent to change, as justifying or rationalizing what one did should tend to inhibit decisions to change; this expectation was confirmed for this small sample. Teacher 3 tended to digress to general feelings and philosophy about teaching methods or usual teaching—both aspects outside the relevant experimental situation—and tended to justify teaching moves on these bases. Teacher 3 was also the only teacher to express intent not to change, which occurred in five statements. Teacher 3, thus, appeared to exhibit the most overt resistance to feedback and change.

A high negative correlation (−.70) was found between Attitude Toward Feedback and statements evidencing Conflict with teachers' own beliefs about their teaching (see fig. 20.1). General Satisfaction with teaching in the experimental situation, highly related to Attitude Toward Feedback, also had a high negative correlation with statements indicating feedback information conflicted with a teacher's own beliefs. It may be that when teachers were more satisfied with their teaching, this indicated that the teaching was generally more successful, that students and teacher both evidenced higher satisfaction, and that students' views of the session didn't conflict with their own.

A small but negative relationship occurred between Attitude Toward Feedback and statements focusing on the Items. However, as figure 20.1e shows, this low relationship was highly influenced by outlying teachers 3 and 7. Teacher 3, though negative, was more reflective and focused on student ratings and things that happened more than on the items themselves. Teacher 7, as mentioned above, was a positive teacher with lower aptitudes than most E+ teachers and spent almost his entire time repeating items and ratings. Without these two teachers, the negative relationship is much stronger and more linear. There were no relationships observed between Attitude Toward Feedback and Productivity, statements of Repetition, statements focused on Ratings, or Class Activities. However, without the influence of one teacher, Teacher 8, the correlation between Feedback Attitude and focus on Ratings would be −.57 with a relatively linear relationship. Teacher 8, a negative teacher, had a very low Productivity score due to a great deal of confusion about the ratings and consequently did not focus much on them.

Other Teacher Aptitudes and Reactions to Feedback

Some interesting relationships between conceptual level (CL) and Reactions to Feedback might be expected and were, in fact, confirmed for this sample. There was a significant positive relationship ($r = .75$, $p < .02$) between CL and Reflective statements as shown in table 20.3 and figure 20.2a. Those with higher Conceptual Level tended to reflect back on a teaching session more often and recall and talk about what happened. CL was also positively related to Productivity ($.51$) and statements Focusing On Teaching moves, as figures 20.2c and 20.2d show: Productivity may be measuring much the same ability that CL does; and Teaching moves were very often the focus of Reflective statements. Thus, these relationships are not surprising. Without the effect of Teacher 4 in all these cases (see fig. 20.2a,c,d) the relationships would be even stronger. Teacher 4 had the lowest CL score and was low on all other abilities except Verbal Ability, which may have been related to her higher verbalization (compared with other low Aptitude teachers, particularly 7 and 8) of elements of the teaching situation rather than focusing practically all her statements only on the information itself in the feedback (i.e., items, ratings). As shown in table 20.4 and figure 20.2b, there was a significant and linear negative correlation between CL and Focus on Items

FIGURE 20.2 Scattergrams of Selected Categories of Teachers' Reactions to Feedback Plotted Against Their Conceptual Level (CL) Scores (Shown on x-axis).

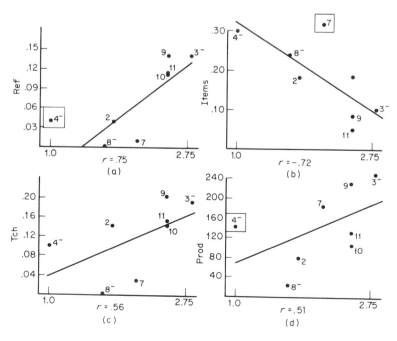

as would be expected. There was a similar but more moderate correlation between CL and Repetition.

Verbal ability had strong positive relationships with Intent to Change, Interpretive statements, and Focus On Students; moderate positive relationship with Reflective and Analytic statements; moderate negative relationships with Focus On Items and Other Teaching or Teaching Beliefs; and low moderate negative correlations with statements of Repetition, Justification, and Conflict with one's own beliefs about teaching in the sessions.

Correlations of the other Aptitudes (namely, reasoning ability and analytic ability) with Feedback Reactions are shown in table 20.4 but will not be discussed here.

Intent to change teaching behavior and interrelationships
of feedback reaction categories

Table 20.6 shows that Intent To Change teaching behavior as a result of feedback was significantly and positively correlated (at $p < .01$) with Focus on Students; teachers who made decisions to respond to feedback by planning to change their teaching tended to be those who also focused on what their students did, as well as their own teaching ($r = .50$); Intent To Change was negatively related to Focus On Items. Table 20.7 shows that stating decisions of Intent to Change was strongly correlated with statements of Analysis, Contrast, and Interpretation ($p < .10$ for all). Teachers who did plan to change tended to go beyond the information given them as feedback by talking about why the students rated them as they did, comparing different ratings, and what the information meant. Table 20.8 indicates that teachers tended to focus either on ratings or items from the feedback itself or on aspects of the teaching situation (students, teaching, and, to a lesser extent, class activities—$r = .27$ with students, $r = .20$ with teaching). These two types of focus were inversely related to each other.

Thus it appears that, at least in this small sample, teachers who verbalized decisions to alter their behavior after receiving feedback were also able to internalize and make use of the information they received, relating it to their own teaching and to their students or to other aspects of the teaching situation. This may require a certain level of verbal ability, conceptual complexity, or other abilities in order to facilitate this analysis and application of the information received as feedback. On the other hand, there was evidence that teachers who did not verbalize plans or intent to change were either teachers who were lower in measured abilities and who did not or could not go beyond stating the information given on the feedback form, and thus did not relate it to the teaching situation, or those who tended to rationalize or justify how they taught in a session.

Student Outcomes

Student cognitive and affective outcomes were compared by teacher and group (E+, E−, C) to examine changes from prefeedback to postfeedback. On the cognitive measures, Recall and Essay Total, patterns were quite variable among teachers within groups (no tables or figures shown here). On the recall test, group means remained quite equal and stable from pretest to posttest. On Essay Total, the E— group was higher than the others on both pretest and posttest; both experimental group means declined for pretest to posttest, and the control group mean increased. There was less variability among E— teachers than in the other groups, as no E— teacher had an increase in class mean as posttest (one E+ and two C teachers did).

On Attitude Total, there was also variability within groups, but some slight differences in trends among groups emerged. As figure 20.3 shows, more teachers in the *E*+ group had increases in class mean attitude (three out of five) than in the other two groups (one each). The E+ group had a slight increase in mean at posttest, whereas the E— and C groups had decreases. Roughly the same patterns occurred for Attitude toward Situation and Attitude toward Self, the subscales. However, due to the variability in

FIGURE 20.3   Pretest (Friday) and Posttest (Tuesday) Mean Scores on Attitude Total by Teacher (Identified by Numbers) and by Group (Indicated by Heavy Lines).

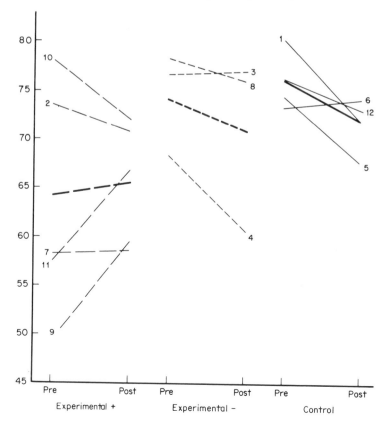

class means within the E+ group and low pretest means in the three E+ class that had increases, the differences among groups in pretest to posttest attitude changes may be explained by regression toward the mean. On the other hand, it might be that student attitude may have been influenced by teachers attempting to adapt their teaching styles to their students; teachers who were positively disposed toward student feedback and who experienced more negative student attitudes may have changed their teaching the most and found that the students reacted positively. No conclusions can be made based on this study, but further investigation may be fruitful.

SUMMARY AND CONCLUSIONS

This study has made an initial attempt to examine processes involved in teachers' reactions to feedback from their students. A coding system was developed to categorize statements made by teachers when they "thought aloud" about their reactions. These categories were used to characterize the ways different teachers responded to feedback, and we have seen that teachers did respond differently. The ways teachers responded were related to various teacher aptitudes. We have seen that teachers who were more positive toward feedback were the ones who made decisions to alter their teaching in an attempt to conform to students' wishes and who tended to be satisfied with their teaching. The teachers who indicated plans to change tended to relate the information received in the feedback to themselves and the students rather than to deal with only the items or the ratings given. To some teachers, examination of the feedback seemed to serve as a stimulus to reflect back on the teaching situation: in a sense, then, it facilitated stimulated recall, but only for some teachers.

Certain aptitudes, such as Verbal Ability or Conceptual Level, were related to teachers' reactions to feedback, especially their application of information to the specific teaching situation. Results of the exploration of relationships in this study suggest support for the hypothesis that to benefit from feedback, a teacher needs to have positive attitudes about self in the situation, and positive attitudes toward the task, as well as aptitudes that facilitate a capacity to change.[10]

There was a trend of evidence in this study that teachers who received feedback and were positive toward it tended to evidence changed behavior as perceived by their students, although changes were small. The relationship between feedback and student outcomes was unclear, although students' attitudes may well be more affected by their teachers' receipt and use versus nonuse of feedback than is the case of cognitive outcomes.

It must be emphasized that no conclusions can be drawn from this study: it was designed to be exploratory only, and used a small-group laboratory setting, which is different from the typical teaching situation. Therefore, even the tentative results of the study cannot be generalized to other situations.

However, some interesting relationships have been observed that might be studied in other contexts as well, to advance knowledge and methods for utilization of feedback.

Questions not dealt with in this study are: What role does teacher self-evaluation of desired change play? Does the teacher's actual observed behavior change after feedback? Do teachers' responses to feedback carry over into their actual plans for the lesson? How does such feedback affect their interactive decision making? These and other questions warrant further investigation in an attempt to facilitate use of feedback as a means of teacher self-improvement.

Thinking While Teaching

The findings of this series of investigations were surprising in a variety of ways. First of all, Clark and Joyce indicated that, for most teachers, preactive decision making did not promote advancement toward behavioral objectives during the actual classroom interaction. Following their suggestions for further research in this area, Marx and Peterson found that teachers tended to be consistent in their focus (be it on subject matter or instructional process) during preactive and interactive decision making; further, that extensive preplanning of materials by teachers tended to create negative attitudes among the students toward the teacher, the subject matter, and themselves.

Clark and Peterson's work indicated that, although cognitive objectives (as opposed to affective or organizational) were stated as priorities by their sample of teachers, the interactive decision making was directed primarily by pupil participation and involvement cues. Crist-Witzel's paper showed that teachers were responsive to student feedback and able to alter their behavior in ways that students could perceive.

It appears that teachers have various "rationalizations" for what they do, how they do it, and why they didn't do it differently. Are these variations in thinking consistent with the goals of "flexibility in teaching,"—that teachers have available to them a wide array of teaching skills and frameworks? Is this the other side of the coin from the kind of teacher described in several chapters of this book as of low conceptual development, rigid in thinking, preoccupied with subject matter, and alienating to students? Will the methodologies suggested by Clark and Joyce, if developed, be sufficient to help us measure, predict, and alter thinking behavior in teachers, and, if so, what criteria for change shall we use?

All this leads us to ask, "Are the traditional educational goals of teaching subject matter and maintaining control over the classroom incompatible with positive attitudes and learning in students?"

21

Toward a Theory of Information Processing in Teaching: The South Bay Study

Bruce R. Joyce

Studies of teaching have for the most part concentrated on the visible events of classrooms and other places where teaching takes place. Over one hundred systems have been developed that permit us to record and categorize teacher and student behavior in a variety of ways.* The use of these systems has resulted in a growing field of knowledge about the visible behavior of teachers and students as they interact with one another.

TEACHING AS BEHAVING: THE VISIBLE ACTS

The results of the inquiries into teaching can be interpreted from several points of view. One interpretation suggests that extremely strong normative pressures operate to shape teaching behavior. These pressures have great force in the early years of teaching (including the training period). The resulting pressure moves teachers toward what Hoetker and Albrand have termed "a recitation style" of teaching.[12] This interpretation emphasizes the finding that so many teachers appear to use similar approaches (usually variations on the recitation style). Some researchers have reported that variety in teaching is associated with pupil learning [8] suggesting that those who are not

---

* See Anita Simon and Gil Boyer, eds. *Mirrors for Behavior* (Philadelphia: Research for Better Schools), for a compendium of instruments.

completely coopted into the recitation style are more effective teachers because their wider repertoire enables them to reach more learners and pursue more goals than those who use one style regularly. Dunkin and Biddle [7] have organized the research somewhat differently, providing a picture of the relationships between variations in teaching style and skill and measures of effectiveness (usually measures of student learning). Dunkin and Biddle are generally pessimistic because correlations between measures of teacher behavior and student learning are frequently quite low. Rosenshine [25] on the other hand, has taken an optimistic view, emphasizing that a number of studies of certain teaching "skills" report positive correlations with measures of student learning. Gage presents the picture as one of a growing base of understanding. He believes that teaching is a complex art which science informs gradually. To expect a few dimensions of teaching to correlate directly and highly with any few measures of pupil learning belies both its many-sidedness and the state of development of inquiry into teaching. Gage's view that teaching is complex, and that concepts describing it will have to reflect that complexity is supported by the findings of several recent studies. For example, McDonald [17] and Berliner [2] in separate phases of the same large, long-term investigation, reported evidence that clusters or patterns of teacher behaviors may be associated with complexes of variables of student achievement. They suggest that single aspects of teacher behavior are unlikely to be powerful determinants of student learning.

There are still questions about how stable teaching styles are, that is, how consistently teachers behave over time. Medley [18] has reported that a number of dimensions of teaching style are relatively stable (that measures of teaching behaviors at one point in time are correlated with those measures at another point in time). Shavelson [26] emphasizes that the correlations between aspects of teacher behavior across time are moderate—too low to permit characterization of teachers in terms of style regularities. In our opinion, it can be reasonably argued that certain aspects of teacher behavior *are* reasonably stable across time (Medley's position) and that there are probably clusters of teacher behavior which are related to certain aspects of student achievement (McDonald and Berliner's opinion). However, there is a long way to go before causal relationships can be established between important dimensions of teacher behavior and student achievement, although knowledge accumulates gradually and much more is known today about teaching than was known twenty years ago.

TEACHING AS THINKING: THE INNER ACTS

In sharp contrast to the large amount of research on the observable aspects of teaching behavior is the tiny quality that has been devoted to the study of how teachers process information. What do teachers think about the individuals they interact with? What kinds of decisions do they make? What kinds of information do they receive from the confusing world of the classroom and how do they deal with that information? How do teachers plan lessons and units? What constraints do they perceive? How many alternatives do they consider? How do they categorize their students and why?

Most of the tiny group of studies of teacher thinking have not been designed from a naturalistic point of view. Zahorik [28] has pointed out that planning has typically been studied from a prescriptive stance, focusing on ideal models and recommendations rather than how teachers in practice typically prepare for lessons. For example, much research on preactive decision making has assumed that teachers diagnose student learning, develop behavioral objectives, and otherwise follow classic "instructional-systems" models. Naturalistic investigations have indicated that very few teachers actually use such a behavioral analysis in preparation for their lessons. [22] Fifteen years ago Joyce and Harootunian, [14] studying the major decision-making processes of preservice teacher candidates, discovered that the major decisions were made in relation to instructional materials for children. The teachers' major sources of information about science came from children's literature rather than from adult-oriented books or manuals that accompany the instructional systems that are prepared by textbook publishers. Scientific knowledge about the kinds of information that teachers use for making "inflight" decisions (that is, the decisions that they make as they interact with children) is almost nonexistent.

Except for the investigations by Clark, [4] Petersen, Marx, Crist-Witzel, [6] Joyce, [13] Morine-Dershimer and Vallance, [20] there have been almost no studies of information processing during teaching prior to this study. Thus, although *overt* teacher behavior has been subjected to analysis by numerous category systems, there are few ways of classifying the kinds of teacher thinking that goes on regularly during the course of teaching. Yet, until we explore the thoughts and feelings which occur during teaching, we may not understand the visible behaviors we observe. When a teacher asks a question we can record the visible behavior clearly enough without understanding the mind that formulates the question. However, what we have is only a record. Unless we know what thought is behind the utterance, we know little about what caused it. Especially if we care to use information about teaching as a basis for improving it, we need to understand *why* teachers behave as they do.

THE SOUTH BAY STUDY

The present investigation builds on this limited body of research to explore and try to explain relationships between the teaching styles of a small group of teachers in one school and the types of information that those teachers seek and use as they teach.

RELATIONSHIP TO PRIOR STUDIES

The South Bay study builds directly on the studies discussed in chapters 17–20 and a study conducted by Morine-Dershimer at the Far West Laboratory.[19,20] The Stanford study examined teacher decision making in a laboratory setting. Teacher planning,[21] interactive decision-making,[5] and teacher judgments of pupils [28] were all examined in this study. The Beginning Teacher Evaluation Study (BTES) conducted by the Far West Laboratory examined teacher decision making in a semicontrolled setting. Forty elementary school teachers identified as "more effective" or "less effective" [1] taught two lessons based on curriculum content new to them to a randomly stratified sample of pupils from their own classrooms and later engaged in some simulated planning tasks. Teacher planning (both short-term and long-term), interactive decision making, teacher judgments of pupils, teacher judgments of other teachers, and pupil perceptions of teachers were all examined in the BTES investigation.

These two previous studies, using somewhat different techniques to collect data on teacher decision making, arrived at complementary findings. The South Bay study incorporated some data collection procedures from these earlier studies, as well as instituted some new procedures. The similarities and differences are described here to illustrate the continuity of these three studies.

The Investigation of Short-Term Planning

In the study directed by Joyce at Stanford teachers were given new curriculum materials and provided with a period of time to plan a day's unit of instruction. These teachers were asked to "think aloud" as they planned, and their oral planning was tape-recorded and later coded, using categories such as objectives, materials, subject matter, and process. This study found that teachers spent most of their planning time dealing with content to be taught. Their second area of concentration was on instructional processes (teaching strategies and lesson activities), and the smallest proportion of their planning time was spent on identifying lesson objectives.

In the BTES study, Morine-Dershimer collected teachers' written plans for two lessons in mathematics and reading, dealing with content provided by researchers and new to teachers. These plans were analyzed to determine degree of specificity, type of format, and amount of attention to goals, pupil readiness, evaluation procedures, and alternative procedures. Teachers in this study tended to be fairly specific in their written plans and use of an outline format, but they included very few statements regarding behavioral goals, diagnosis of student needs, evaluation of learning, or possible alternative activities. The more effective teachers made more specific statements in their written plans, and more often mentioned instructional processes to be used.

In the South Bay study, teachers planned and taught lessons in reading to ongoing groups of pupils in their own classrooms, following the curriculum that they normally used. These teachers were interviewed about their plans in the morning before their reading lessons began. They described their general plan, and then probing questions were asked to gather further information on teacher thinking about diagnosis of pupil needs, use of instructional materials, specific lesson objectives, teaching strategy, and seating arrangements. While diagnosis of pupil needs, lesson objectives, and seating arrangements were seldom mentioned in the initial plan statements, teacher responses to probing questions clearly demonstrated that these aspects of the lessons were not being ignored but were part of their "mental image" or set of expectations for the lesson.

The Investigation of Interactive Decision Making

In the Stanford study interactive decision making was investigated by use of a "stimulated recall" technique. An interviewer showed each teacher four brief (2–3 minutes) videotaped segments of classroom interaction, randomly selected from a 50-minute lesson. After viewing each segment, the teacher answered a series of questions, as follows:

1. What were you doing here?
2. What were you noticing about pupils?
3. Did you have any instructional objectives in mind at this point?
4. Were you considering any alternative actions here?
5. Was there anything in this situation that caused you to behave differently than you had planned?

The principle findings of this study were that teachers considered alternative strategies only when the lesson was going poorly, that the primary cue used to judge how well the lesson was going was student participation and involvement, and that teachers rarely changed from their planned strategy, even when instruction was going poorly.

The BTES study also used a stimulated recall technique to explore interactive decision making, but in this case the entire twenty-minute lesson was videotaped and played back to the teacher, who was instructed to stop the tape at any point where he/she was aware of having made a decision. In addition, the interviewer stopped the tape at a point where a pupil gave an incorrect answer and at a point where there was a transition from one activity to another. At each decision point the teacher was asked:

1. What were you thinking about here?
2. What were you noticing that made you stop and think?

3. What did you decide to do?

4. Did you consider any alternatives?

The decision points identified by teachers in this study were related mainly to interchanges (decisions stemming from immediate verbal interaction) or planned activities (interactive decisions stemming from preactive decisions). Teachers focused on instructional process in discussing the substance of their decisions but shifted to a focus on pupil characteristics when discussing the basis for these decisions. Few alternatives were considered. The less effective teachers tended to mention a larger number of items that they were taking into account on almost all aspects of decisions discussed. That is, they appeared to be attempting to process more information at a given decision point than the more effective teachers.

The South Bay study incorporated some techniques from both previous studies in conducting stimulated recall interviews, as well as adding some new investigative procedures. A teacher was videotaped during two reading lessons on the same day, one with a high-ability group, and one with a low-ability group. At the end of the day both lessons were played back to the teacher, first using two random stops for each lesson (as in the Stanford study), then playing the lesson back in toto, stopping the tape at teacher-identified decision points (as in the BTES study). Interviews were conducted at four different points in the school year, to investigate changes over time. Interactive behavior during lessons was observed and coded to compare teacher decision making with classroom behavior.

The Investigation of Teacher Judgments About Pupils

In the Stanford study teachers were asked after each of these lessons to predict the rank-order of their students in that lesson (unknown to them before the lesson) on a cognitive achievement test and an attitude inventory, which were administered after the third teaching episode. Each lesson was taught to be a different group of pupils. In addition, teachers were asked to describe the student cues that they used in making these predictions. The most frequently mentioned cue was "student participation." Regression equations using the behavioral cues identified by teachers were not good predictors of actual student achievement or attitude inventory results. Findings suggested that teacher judgments about student attitudes were more accurate than their judgments about cognitive achievement.

In the BTES study a "pupil sort task" was used to explore teacher judgments about pupils. After each of two lessons teachers were asked to sort their pupils into groups, using as a basis something that they had observed about pupils during the lesson. The procedure was repeated until the teacher could think of no new basis for regrouping pupils. The most frequently used basis was pupil participation. The more effective teachers generated more groupings using cognitive characteristics as bases for categorizing and also formed more groups where a pupil was "singled out" as being too different on a given characteristic to be grouped with other pupils.

The South Bay teachers were interviewed using the pupil sort task at five different points in the school year, in order to explore changes over time in pupil characteristics being observed. At three points (September, November, and June) teachers were asked to predict pupil success in reading. These predictions were compared to pupil performance on standard Achievement tests to determine teacher "accuracy" in making judgments. The predictions were compared to teacher rankings of pupils on other teacher-identified pupil characteristics to identify the cues used by teachers in making predictions.

The Continuity of Investigation

These three studies can be viewed as a series of investigations that explore a basic set of questions, using somewhat different research settings and data collection techniques. The findings of the first two studies complement and support each other in important ways. The findings of the South Bay study to be reported in some detail in the body of this report, extend, refine, and throw new light on the findings of the earlier exploratory studies. In addition, the results of the South Bay study suggest new questions for future research.

THE PURPOSE OF THE SOUTH BAY STUDY

The major objective was to develop one or more paradigms for viewing the ways that teachers process information, and to generate and adapt methodologies by which information processing can be studied efficiently and comprehensively. The South Bay Study is essentially a case study approach at a single elementary school in a large metropolitan area. It focuses on the variety and stability of information processing behavior of ten of the teachers in this school.

The South Bay School is staffed by twenty teachers, a principal, an assistant principal, two secretaries, and three specialists who are shared with other schools. South Bay School qualifies for additional ESEA Title I (federal) and SB 90 EDT (state) funds by virtue of the economic conditions of the neighborhood.

The ten teachers who participated in the study work in grades one to five. One of the teachers is male. Nine are Caucasian and one is Black. All teachers have taught at least three years. The school utilizes a graded structure. Three of the ten teachers are assigned to grade one, two to grade three, one to grade four, two to grade five, and two are special education teachers.

In recent years state and national funds have resulted in teachers' participation in the selection and purchase of extensive instructional materials, especially in the areas of reading and mathematics. These include self-instructional stations for reading and arithmetic, "concrete aids," "supplementary readers," and a variety of audiovisual materials and "skill-builders."

Design

The South Bay study examined three aspects of teacher behavior and thinking:

1. Interactive teaching styles, as revealed by observation of verbal interaction, including an examination of variations between teachers and also stability of styles over time.

   "How do the teachers teach?" "How are they similar?"

   "How do they differ?" "How consistently do they teach?"

2. Thought processes while teaching, as revealed through "stimulated recall" techniques.

   "What do they think about as they teach?" "How similarly (differently?) do they think?" "How consistent are their thoughts over time?"

3. Teacher conceptions of pupils, as revealed by categories used to describe students and predict their behavior.

   "How do they describe the children?" "How similarly (differently) do they perceive the children?" "How (and how well) do they predict performance?"

The Investigation of Teaching Styles

Each of the ten teachers was observed twelve times in the course of the 1976–77 academic year for a total of 120 observations.

Observers were trained to use a complex category system which has been developed over the years which is sensitive to variations in teaching style and strategy. These data were analyzed to describe between teacher and across time similarities and differences, to determine stylistic differences between curriculum areas, and to determine whether the transactions between teachers and students varied with the ability of the students. The purpose of this aspect of the investigation was to develop a picture of the kind of teaching going on in the school and its stability and variety.

The Study of Information Processing

Altogether sixty lessons were videotaped as the teachers worked. Each of these tapes was played back to the teacher concerned and (s)he was interviewed to recapture the thoughts that were in his/her mind as events occurred during that teaching episode. The protocols derived from these "stimulated recall" interviews formed the basis for the descriptions of interactive information-processing. The analysis of these protocols was focused on the content of the recalled thoughts and was structured to determine similarities and differences among the teachers and across time, between subject areas, and between ability groups of students. In addition, the analysis attempted to determine relationships between teaching styles and decision-making styles.

Each teacher was also interviewed to ask their perceptions of their teaching styles and information processing behavior. Characterizations were developed of the teaching and information processing styles of each teacher, and these were reported to the teacher for confirmation or disconfirmation.

Conceptions of Pupils

On five occasions throughout the year the teachers were asked to categorize their students and to describe the bases they used to observe the children as they worked with them (what cues they used, how they put together those cues to describe the children, and the naming of these descriptions for decisions that they made in their teaching). These data were analyzed to determine normative tendencies, differences between teachers, and the stability of characterizations of the students across time. The data were also analyzed to try to learn how the teachers arrived at their characterizations of their students, whether or not changes resulted from continued exposure to the children and the influence of a variety of sources of information about pupils (direct observation, conferences with parents, test scores, etc.).

The substantive report can be found in the special Summer 1979 issue of *Education Research Quarterly*, which is devoted to the South Bay study.

The following material interprets the South Bay Study, linking its findings to the Stanford and the BTES investigations.

THE SOUTH BAY STUDY: AN INTERPRETATION

As in any other cumulative line of inquiry our first task is to try to learn the facts, and in this case we are interested in what is going on in a teacher's mind. As data accumulates, we can construct concepts that explain and clarify events and guide our next steps.

In the study of information processing in teaching we are currently at the fact-finding stage. Finding the facts would be easier if we knew precisely *where* and *how* to look. However, at present this work is truly exploratory— we have some primitive tools and a limited vision. Even so, as we reflect on the findings from this and the handful of other recent investigations we are beginning to develop some "sense" of the area and are starting to develop concepts that can guide our future investigations.

In this section we present those concepts and propose a framework for looking at thinking in teaching. To some extent we have drawn on information-processing research in fields other than teaching, but the major concepts have emerged as we have developed a better "feel" of our specific area of concentration.

Relevant Research on Information Processing

Research which is relevant to the present effort comes from both basic studies and applied research on information processing. An example of the former is highly controlled experiments in which stimuli are systematically varied so that types of potential cues can be investigated as variables. Examples of the latter occur in the development of instructional systems to train personnel, such as airline pilots, who in the course of their duties are required to process varieties of information. Instructional systems developers investigate ways of displaying information and study what kinds and amounts are processed in performing various tasks.

Garner's [10] summary of the experimental studies has emphasized both the roles of stimulus variation and the functions of cognitive structure in determining what kinds of information will be selected and how it will be integrated. He argues that most stimuli are simply not perceived at all because human beings simply do not scan fields of stimulus tasks as an impersonal, multidimensional information-processing system might. Human beings, rather, perceive what they have been taught or choose to attend to. Thus, most of the information potentially available in any given setting is probably not attended to at all. In any field we are thus faced with the problem of determining what kinds of stimuli are available and what kinds of cognitive structures exist that influence selection of what will be perceived.

Shiffrin's [27] review emphasizes that capacity to process information is multi-faceted. There are varying degrees of "masking" involved in perception—with respect to visual perceptions; for example, the human perceiver simply "covers over" stimuli which do not appear to be relevant, and the perception of those stimuli is forgotten almost immediately. *Selective attention* refers to this process of differentiation of stimuli on the basis of whether they are potentially relevant. The selection of stimuli to be focused on in a complex, unstructured situation involves the development of a problem-frame. Consciously or unconsciously the perceiver imposes a structure. When instructional systems are constructed, considerable attention is paid to the "display" of information—to the provision of a structure that will guide attention to relevant stimuli.

If we postulate that teaching is done in an extremely unstructured situation, where a framework of attention has to be imposed, it is probable that the kinds of "attention-focusing" structures that are developed by teachers will have quite an effect on the kinds of stimuli which they believe are relevant. We would expect considerable individual differences in the structure and in ability to divide attention among the multiple potential inputs in a teaching situation.

Personality as a factor

Hunt and his associates have contributed a theory that describes individual differences in information-processing capacity. The theory focuses on the ability of individuals to differentiate stimuli and to integrate information as it is received. Differentiation and integration capabilities are seen as unitary in the sense that persons who are better able to differentiate are also better able to integrate. The most capable "differentiators and integrators" are characterized by more complex and flexible conceptual structures. The least flexible individuals attempt to maintain their existing cognitive structure. They ignore or distort information which does not fit into that structure. Persons with more flexible and complex structures are able to receive information that does not fit into their present categories and modify their conceptual structure in order to integrate that information.

In several studies of teaching it has been established that variety in teaching styles is a function of complexity of conceptual level and, in addition, teachers displaying more complex conceptual structure have a greater ability to acquire new approaches to teaching and integrate them into their ongoing styles. It would not be surprising if information processing were also a function of personality.

Marx's [16] study of teachers' perception of students using Brunswick's "lens model" indicated that the types of cues utilized by teachers as they make judgments about pupils vary considerably and also that teachers differ quite a bit in their accuracy—including their ability to judge pupil achievement in learning situations. The ability to structure the problem frame to differentiate relevant cues and integrate them accurately probably varies widely.

Elements of Information Processing in Teaching

From this general perspective we begin to see "inflight" information processing as a series of overlapping dimensions: the flow of cues, perception of cues, interpretation, processing, and responding.

The flow of cues

Information processing begins with the flow of cues (potential stimuli) from students—this is the raw material. These cues are incredibly numerous and consist of verbal and nonverbal behavior. The cues are not independent of the tasks presented to the students by the teacher. The students are not free simply to behave—they respond to tasks, other children, and a variety of other influences from within and without the school.

Perceiving the cues

Perception is the first stage of information processing. Theoretically, the proportion of potential stimuli actually perceived can range from zero to 100 percent. That is, if one were oblivious, then the cues would pass by— they would not be turned into stimuli. Similarly, it is theoretically possible to perceive *all* the cues which are presented. The first question, then, is how much and what kind of cues are perceived.

Interpretation: accuracy and distortion

Perception is not simply a mechanical process. Impressions of stimuli are not simply "xeroxed" by the mind as they appear in the objective world. There is always a certain amount of distortion and interpretation. For example, if a student lifts his/her hand, the teacher may perceive (assuming that s/he is aware of it) a smaller or a larger movement than actually takes place. In addition, symbolic value is immediately attached to a stimulus. A raised hand may be seen as a call for attention, or a gesture of annoyance.

Processing

Once perceived, the stimuli are *processed* in some way, first for relevance to the teacher's field of concern. If the lifting of the hand, for example, is interpreted as an attempt to relieve a cramp caused by writing, it may be processed as irrelevant. If it is classed as relevant, then it may be processed for comprehension (to understand it better) and possibly for action. *Next to an understanding of the stimulus field, the interpretation of stimuli is probably the most important of the mysteries to be unraveled at the outset of investigations into information processing.*

Responding

The action resulting from processing information is *behavior* by the teacher. The behavior may be overt or covert, the activity may be immediate or delayed.

Thus, in order to understand the nature of the information processing by teachers we have to understand the nature of the flow of potential stimuli, perception, interpretation, and the responses (behaviors which occur as a result). Occasionally, these stages can be seen clearly—as when there is a distinctive stimulus from a child; the teacher manifests verbally an awareness of the stimulus and how it is interpreted, clearly decides whether it is relevant, and acts in response. One of our problems is that such a clear and full connection is rarely displayed. Evidence about one or another stage is frequently missing. At certain times we get information about the stimulus awareness (perception), at other times about processes, and still at other times, about behavior. However, we have obtained enough instances in which these dimensions are revealed, at least partially, to tell us that we can begin to put the pieces together in a preliminary framework. Also, the teachers have proved to be generous informants about what they see and how they interpret it—they help to fill in the gaps. Reflecting on the South Bay Study, we have begun to sense how these stages occur in the world of the classroom.

The Teacher as an Agent in Determining the Stimulus Flow

It is worthwhile to conjecture what the stimulus field might be like if the teacher were not present. In that case the flow would be from the natural behavior of the children as they interact and pursue their own activities. Were we simply to gather twenty or thirty children together in a room, the primary source of stimuli would be the children themselves, albeit somewhat affected by the nature of the environment. Teacher behavior changes the stimulus field in several ways:

1. First the teacher *establishes tasks.* The process of establishing activities itself produces stimuli, but, most important, the teacher shapes the students into a flow of activities which characterize that particular classroom. These activities constitute the curricular and instructional system. For example, if a teacher organizes the students to select books from the library and read them silently, coming to the teacher only when there is a question of comprehension, then some of the *natural* behavior of the students is replaced by the activities of selecting and obtaining the books, reading them, attempting to give the students direction, and so on. Those activities generate patterns of behavior, become part of the stimulus flow.

2. The teacher builds a *social system* or a community within the classroom. The social system is manifest; for example, expressions of affection are legitimate within some communities, whereas a relatively task-oriented, businesslike behavior is required in others. Some social systems are relatively spontaneous and induce free expression, whereas others are more constrained with a much narrower range of legitimate behaviors.

3. The teacher *regulates the stimulus flow* through instructional moves with respect to both pace and diversity. In oral reading cues about word attack skills will be plentiful. Unless there is discussion, there will be relatively few cues about comprehension of what is read. Some teachers tolerate stimuli from many students simultaneously, others from relatively few. Some teachers control stimulus emissions so as to reduce types of stimuli which cannot be conveniently responded to by automatic routines.

Thus, the teacher is a powerful agent in determining the kinds of information which can be processed by reducing the amount of natural behavior by the children, instituting instructional patterns, building a social system, and regulating the instructional process. We can see the stimuli as partly natural behavior by the children and partly behavior induced by the activity flow. The patterns of interaction—structuring, information handling, and feedback—which the teacher institutes further affect the flow of cues. Our thesis is that to understand the information-processing behavior of teachers, it will be necessary to understand the types of activity flow that are created by each teacher, the teacher's structuring, information handling, and feedback patterns, and the nature of the social system that is generated in the classroom. It will also be necessary to understand the types of stimuli which are generated by this combination of teacher-induced and student-generated behavior. Without a map of the potential stimulus field, studies of thought processes will be severely limited.

Perception

Individuals differ widely in the extent to which they are aware of the behavior of others. The stimulus field of the classroom is a particularly complex one. Repeatedly, during stimulated recall interviews, the teachers reported that on the playing of the videotape they became aware of behavior that they did not notice at the time of interaction. With so much happening all the time, there simply has to be some kind of selectivity.

The effect of the activity flow can be seen in the process of selectivity. As the teacher establishes the activities, (s)he *expects* to see certain kinds of behaviors. (S)he thus becomes especially sensitive to whether or not those behaviors are occurring. In other words, it is plausible that the teacher's very act of setting up activities prepares him/her for awareness. If the teacher wants students to work quietly at their seats, s/he will look around occasionally, simply to determine whether quiet seat-work is going on and so be more sensitive to indications of task-orientedness than to stimuli relevant to some other dimension of student behavior. In such a situation, Teacher 104 scanned sixteen times in one five-minute span, Teacher 101 twelve times in *one* minute; apparently just to check on whether the children were at their seats.

Processing for relevance

Awareness of a cue is not sufficient to ensure that much energy will be expended processing it. Perceptions are screened for relevance according to a variety of criteria which differ from teacher to teacher. The determination of relevance is a sorting process by which it is determined whether the stimulus has sufficient meaning to warrant further thought. Those cues determined to be irrelevant do not stay long in the forefront of consciousness. For example, a teacher may notice that a student is scratching his foot but dismiss the information immediately as not relevant. Again, we believe the basic activity flow sets up implicit or explicit criteria by which relevance is determined.

Once the stimulus is determined to be relevant it can be subject to processing by one of several available routines. We have come to believe that there

294 / How We Think When We Teach

are at least three types of routines—*immediate action* routines, *delayed action* routines, and *comprehension* routines.

An *immediate action* routine includes the rapid determination of relevance, the institution of a quick interpretation within a clear category system, and an immediate, almost reactive, behavior by the teacher. For example, when one of the teachers in the sample scans the students for attention at their seat-work while she is working with a group of readers, her routines are held "at the ready." If a student leaves his seat and is observed, the cue is interpreted to be relevant and to match one of the "inattention" criteria. The teacher either gives the child a "dirty look" (an emphasis employed when the child has visual contact with the teacher, snaps his/her fingers to obtain visual contact and follows that with a meaningful look, or snaps the fingers and also beckons to the child. These behaviors occur with considerable rapidity following the cue (if it is observed).

The second kind of routine processes the information, but for *delayed action*. One of the other teachers in the group, noticing the same kind of behavior as the first, and determining it to be relevant also as an indicator of inattention, waits until she can make eye-contact with the aide and then nods toward the child. It is then the aide's responsibility to observe the child and to determine whether the inattention persists and take some sort of mild action. The important difference is that the information is noticed in the same way, determined to be relevant by the same criterion, and stored for later delayed action.

Third, the information is stored for later *comprehension*. For example, another teacher noticed that one of the children was having difficulty persisting in tasks involving the use of a sound system for teaching word attack skills. The information was stored in order to follow it up later to determine whether the activity was an appropriate one for the child. After accumulating enough evidence, a diagnosis would be made.

There is a fourth situation—one where no routine is available. It is in these cases that teachers must make a conscious decision about what to do. They may scan the elements of the activity flow which has been instituted and try to determine what the alternatives are. One sees this when an activity breaks down. The teachers introduce an activity and then notice the children are not behaving in terms of the criteria for successful task performance. Teacher 107, at one point, listened to five consecutive errors by children in an oral drill. If "unacceptable" stimuli continue to build up, the teacher may interrupt the activity and turn to another one. In this example, 107 considered changing the activity. However, if the decision is made to persist with the activity, then a number of decisions have to be made about how to structure and handle information in order to shape the students into appropriate responses. Teacher 107 chose to stop the activity and carefully reexplained the directions. As indicated above, behavior may be overt or covert, it may be immediate or delayed. It may involve a very simple adjustment or the institution of new activities.

Thought and Action in the South Bay School

All the teachers worked within the "recitation style" of teaching, and their concerns about pupils and their interactive decision-making styles reflect the tasks of the recitation pattern. Nearly all decision making was of the "fine-tuning" variety rather than a reflection on alternatives which would considerably affect the pace and flow of activities in the classroom. These teachers had established a materials-based, tutorial flow of activity in which the teacher works with an individual or small group of children while the others occupy themselves with self-instructional materials or attend to the teaching aide.

The flow of activities that is generated in the recitation pattern enormously affects the stimulus field in two ways: first, by greatly influencing the behavior of the children (the field of potential stimuli); and second, by providing the teacher with criteria about which types of stimuli to scan for and which stimuli will be relevant. For example, the students who are at their seats are expected to be working relatively quietly at the tasks which have been assigned to them. The teacher scans for evidence of on-task and off-task behavior. A framework for detecting off-task behavior develops so that attention is focused on certain acts, while most other behaviors by students (scratching, sharpening pencils, etc.) are usually not noticed. If a child leaves his/her seat to sharpen a pencil the teacher generally will note this, and will glance up shortly afterwards to see that the student has returned to the assigned task. As to the group or individual being worked with directly, the teacher usually controls the flow by calling on one child or another and asking a question or requesting some performance. The teacher scans the performance for error and generally does not respond to specific correct responses, except to reinforce errorless behavior. Behavior judged to be in error is processed according to routines developed by each individual teacher. The result of the routine can be seen in overt behavior—Teacher 107 responds by reiterating the directions of the activity, while 106 responds with immediate instruction. Teacher 102 responds by storing the information and waiting until a similar task appears in the materials and judges whether the student is, in fact, having difficulty with the task or whether the original error was random, while 101 responds by asking the student to repeat the task performance, and 103 accumulates information until enough students have been identified, making the same type of error so that this teacher can give instructions to several persons simultaneously.

Within this style, the teacher concentrates on the children with whom s/he is directly interacting, simultaneously scanning the rest of the class for presence or absence of task-oriented behavior. The teacher has developed a number of relatively clear and simple routines for dealing with information from the students being interacted with directly. These routines also result in visible behavior—if a student responds correctly, s/he is reinforced. If s/he does not, the student is corrected or the information is stored for future use. If one of the children not directly occupied with the teacher manifests off-task behavior, the teacher reminds the child of the desired behavior, notifies the aide, or reprimands the student, depending on the severity and type of infraction. Several teachers stand out as somewhat different than the others. Teacher 108 has great difficulty keeping the activity flow going and is more preoccupied with student behavior and giving directions clearly. Teacher 101 works almost impassively with one student at a time, listening to the student read aloud but offering little corrective feedback—she is unusual in that she engages in almost no instructional behavior at all.

Teacher 103 works with a great many "homemade" materials, many adapted or borrowed from a system created by a local curriculum developer. This teacher engages in cooperative planning more often than the others and is much concerned that the students learn to engage themselves in activity and maintain their own flow rather than needing the teacher continuously for reinforcement or direction.

Teacher 102 uses a skill-oriented oral recitation system and stores and utilizes information about learner responses more fully and at a more rapid rate than any other teacher. When a student makes an error 102 does not respond immediately but stores the information and returns to the student later. 102 can store information for as many as seven children at a time. This teacher adapts the materials continuously to the learners and modifies their assignments, depending on their responses, thus operating a highly efficient recitation system.

Testing the Concept: What Do the Teachers Think about Our Thoughts about Their Thinking?

A series of précis were generated describing the information-processing routines, which each of the teachers in the study appeared to be following. These précis were developed by analyzing the data describing their teaching styles and by analyzing the stimulated recall protocols. Then, interviews were conducted with each teacher. At the beginning of the interview the teacher was asked to describe his/her system of teaching, following which our description of his/her system of information processing was revealed to the teacher for confirmation or disconfirmation. In all cases the teachers confirmed the chief elements of the précis.

Because all the teachers were working within the recitation style of teaching and because they showed such small variability in decision-making styles, it is relatively difficult to make a general test of the concept of information processing which is presented in this chapter. However, teachers' confirmation of the descriptions of the information-processing paradigms that they use is encouraging. Several interesting variations appeared, confirmed by the interviews.

The social system within the recitation pattern is a task-oriented one.

Teachers, however, differ quite a bit in terms of the details of that social system. Teacher 103 is distinguished by a cooperative social climate. Although s/he works with first-grade children, s/he is very careful to plan the activities with them. When a student appears to be engaged in off-task behavior, 103 responds by asking whether the student is clear about what s/he is doing, and will interrupt the activities to replan with the student. Teacher 102 permits students to interrupt while working with an instructional group and encourages them to come for help at any time. Teacher 104 does not want to be interrupted unless there are serious difficulties and will ask a student who is confused simply to wait out the period and come for help at a point of transition to the next activity. Teacher 105 uses the aide to help students with problems when 105 is working with one instructional group. Teacher 109 interestingly changed in the course of study. 109 worked without an aide for some time and had considerable difficulty with discipline. S/he responded to off-task behavior within the instructional group or the seat-work group by annoyed, nagging behavior. When an aide was placed in 109's classroom in the middle of the year, s/he used the aide to circulate among the students who were working at their seats, providing them with instructional help and bringing them back on task. The aide did this quite successfully, and 109's nagging behavior was reduced markedly. S/he then turned more attention to instruction with the small group of children s/he was working with at any given period. During this period 109 gradually became more sensitive to cues about responses to instruction and apparently ignored many cues related to on-task/off-task dimensions.

Impressions from the South Bay Study: Concepts to Guide Our Next Studies

In the course of conducting the investigation and analyzing the data, we have arrived at a series of impressions about the factors that influence teacher's information processing. These impressions have directed us toward the development of the sets of concepts which we believe will be useful in our further investigations.

The influence of long-term decisions

We have formed the impression that most of the important preactive decisions by teachers are long-term in their influence (as opposed to the influence of lesson-by-lesson planning).

Relatively early in the year, most teachers set up a series of conditions that will be powerfully influential on the possibilities of decision making thereafter. Lesson planning, to the extent that it goes on consciously, involves the selection and handling of materials and activities within the framework that has been set up by the long-term decisions. We believe this is why investigations of teacher's lesson planning [4,6,14,22] have found that teachers plan lessons in terms of activities and arrangements for those activities rather than using the objectives-activities-evaluation paradigm favored by most theoreticians of instructional design. Specific lessons occur within the general flow—their objectives are implicit, and decisions are concentrated around the materials at hand and the adjustment of procedures for the episode.

The flow of activities and the selection of materials

Most of these important, long-term, preactive decisions involve the selection of instructional materials and the development of a flow of activities that will enable children to approach the tasks embedded in the material. In conformity to expectations by other teachers, school administrators, community members (chiefly parents), and (occasionally) the trends in curriculum and instructional theory, a set of instructional materials is selected and assembled. In the case of reading and arithmetic a basal text or equivalent materials are usually selected.

An activity flow is built around those materials, and that flow of activities becomes the most powerful influence in subsequent information processing. *In effect the selection of materials and the subsequent activity flow establishes the "problem frame"—the boundaries within which decision making will be carried on.*

Within this activity flow most teacher information-processing behavior represents the fine-tuning of the system of activities that has been established. The establishment of the activity flow greatly influences the potential stimuli to which the teacher can respond and establishes routines through which (s)he will respond. It also establishes the parameters within which off-task and on-task behavior will be defined, as well as appropriateness or correctness of response. Nearly all teacher information-processing responses are to signals of off-task behavior or "inappropriate" responses by the children. Most of the routines which are established are to bring about increased on-task behavior and appropriate (substantively correct) response to instructional tasks.

By constraining pupil behavior the development of the instructional flow influences the availability of stimuli, creates routines to be used to deal with task-related responses by the students, and establishes the parameters within which the fine-tuning of the system will take place.

Once the activity flow has been established teachers very rarely make decisions which change the direction of instruction or mobilize resources outside of that activity flow frame. Differences in friendliness toward learners, conceptual complexity, personal philosophy, and momentary disposition influence information-processing behavior *within* the broad flow of activities and its network of routines.

Teacher concerns divide themselves into those oriented toward pupil achievement (appropriate response to the content of tasks) and involvement (the maintenance of the on-task behavior). Thus, the selection of an instructional model, either through the adoption of materials or a philosophy of instruction, establishes the problem-frame and more powerfully influences information processing than does stylistic variation (individual differences) among teachers.

We have been greatly influenced by this impression that relatively few major decisions are made once the basic "activity flow" is established; and the corollary impression that most information processing is nonetheless complex. Within the flow of activities teachers are constantly receiving information, processing it, and responding to the information received. They rarely make decisions which radically change the direction of instruction.

When we commenced our work we anticipated that we would find a fair amount of directional decision making, that is, that teachers would be receiving information which resulted in their deciding to use a different method, different materials, or major regroupings of the students. Such was not the case. The picture that emerges is that the teachers work within the general framework and fine-tune that system. In other words, teachers do not think as instructional designers do, continuously selecting new methods and materials and ways of reaching children, but work within a general design that has emerged in the classroom. Thus, future investigations should concentrate on ways that teachers process information within the context of long-term decisions. We would hypothesize that unless the activity flow completely breaks down few teachers will, in the ordinary course of events, redirect it. In fact, the activity flow so controls the kinds of information that teachers receive that they are very unlikely to process information in such a way as to move into a major decision-making frame.

Our next steps will be to probe the nature of the potential stimulus field and the nature of the criteria used to select from it as scanning goes on. It is important also to learn how much the findings from this study are a result of the instructional approach used here. Would the teachers behave the same were they teaching inductively or nondirectively? Would the use of a different approach to teaching change the available cues, the nature of the criteria for selecting the cues to attend to, and the routines for processing information and responding? Thus we will study teachers as they use a variety of models of teaching and compare the findings to those obtained here within the prevalent style at the South Bay School.

PART VIII

Effectiveness in Training: Improving Designs for Research

22

Vehicles for Controlling Content in the Study of Teaching

Bruce R. Joyce

There are two reasons the control of content and learning materials is important in research on teaching. One is that both content and learning materials influence the behavior of teachers and students. It is conceivable that some teaching skills are content- and/or learning-material-specific. The other is that many kinds of learning cannot be measured except in terms of specific content. Recall of information and learning of concepts are examples of outcomes that are content-specific. Attitudes, on the other hand (toward teacher, self, and process) are not necessarily content-specific, although they *may* be. Process outcomes, whether social or cognitive, are not usually specific to content, but, again, they *may* be. Many of the measurement tasks involved in the search for teacher effectiveness require situations in which content and material are dealt with by teacher and learner, and measurement can be made of the mastery of information and concepts in relation to that content.

Any series of investigations designed to identify variations in teaching styles or strategies and to relate these to different amounts of pupil learning has to consider the content vehicle dimension. The importance is underlined by the increasing evidence that consistency of relative teaching effectiveness has been found in a number of investigations where content and materials of learning have been controlled but only occasionally where these have been left uncontrolled.

CRITERIA FOR CONTENT MATERIALS

Thus far individual investigators have usually generated their own criteria for the construction of content and content "vehicles" (instructional material embodying the content). It appears time to begin to examine the pros and cons of various types of content and vehicles for controlling it.

Thus, we will now examine the issues relative to the selection of content vehicles, that is, those materials that can be put into the hands of teachers and learners for experiments ranging from teaching interventions of one or two hours up to forty or fifty hours. We will deal with five criteria relative to the *substance* of the material, that is, the topics that best serve the purpose, and seven criteria relative to the *form* of the material, i.e., the media through which the substance is presented and the organization imposed upon it. Finally, we will discuss the problem of constructing material relative to teaching roles. These criteria are suggested for content vehicles used in investigations of the effects of style and strategy in teaching, e.g., where one is trying to determine either the effects of "natural variability" in teacher behavior or the effects of teacher training on teacher behavior and student learning. The focus, in other words, is on the production of knowledge about teaching as a *generic* form of activity. Studies of special, subject-specific methods might require other criteria.

Criteria for Substance

We propose five criteria for selecting the substance of content vehicles— the nature of the topics which should be embodied in them.

First, they should be *unusual,* that is, not normally taught in the schools of today and not likely to have been learned incidentally through TV, newspapers, etc. This increases the likelihood that the students who are the subjects of experiments will have little, if any knowledge of the content. Therefore, what they learn will be more a product of their own efforts and the teachers' than the result of prior curriculums or instruction.

Second, the topic should *not be esoteric.* The material, in other words, should be within the normal world. It should not require leaps of fantasy or inference beyond those which we normally make in the course of our daily existences. Extremely unusual material, while "new," requires adjustments by teachers and students that may introduce abnormal variables into the situation.

Third, the material should *not be technical* unless it is desired to investigate learning in a particular technical area. That is, it should be substantively ordinary in the sense that it should not require special knowledge to comprehend it. If material is excessively technical, then prior learning probably would enormously influence both achievement and acceptability. Materials should be well within the comfortable range with which we are accustomed to dealing. An example of the difficulty which can be produced by technical material occurred in some of Ausubel's studies where content on endocrinology was employed. Prior knowledge of biology greatly influenced the effect which Ausubel's "advance organizers" had on learning, thereby muting the contributions of those studies to their main purposes.

Fourth, content should be *multifaceted.* It should be open to entry from a number of points of view rather than having simply one kind of entrance. An example of limited-facet material is calculus, which can be approached in several ways but virtually *requires* certain sequences. Trigonometry is even more unifaceted. Since logarithms are expressions of numbers in terms of ten to the zero power, the meaning of that type of expression has to be comprehended before the material can be entered. Once it is entered from that vantage, many subsequent learning steps are very nearly programmed. Multifaceted materials, in contrast, permit greater latitude and hence are amenable to greater variety in teaching styles and strategies.

Fifth, the substance of the material should be *organic.* That is, its parts should be related so that relational concepts can be developed by the students and also so that entry into any part of the substance may result in a full exploration of its totality or at least of many other facets of it. The material, in other words, should hang together in some systematic way. The organic quality should be inherent in the substance of the material.

Criteria for Form

Amenability to variation in approaches

Teachers should be able to approach the content in many different ways and learners should be able to expand their learning styles and utilize their frames of reference in reconstructing the material. Therefore, the material should have random accessibility. It should be presented to student and teacher in a way that is amenable to many approaches. The student or the teacher should be able to determine order and hierarchy in presentation and/or information. Otherwise variations in style and strategy are muted. Also, the material should be expandable or contractable—it should respond to a variety of terms of teaching and learning. This is partly a criterion of convenience for it is often useful to conduct experiments for varying terms where control of content is helpful. However, it is not theoretically unimportant, for there are many serious questions about the length of time necessary to arrive at outcomes of different sorts; material which can be handled in varying lengths of time is indispensable to investigations of duration.

Low-inferential quality

The material should be written or otherwise presented in such a way as to contain as few inferences as possible. In other words, it should present information rather than conclusions to students and teachers so as to leave maximum room for conceptualization by the teacher and students. Both teacher and learner should have to put together the facts in order to arrive at complex concepts relative to the substance under discussion. Otherwise, learning outcomes will be confined to paired-associate learning.

Multimedia nature

The material should be moderately *multimedia* in composition. It should utilize print, charts, graphs, pictures, and other forms of presentation so the combinations of these can be explored in relation to one another. Thus a random-access information storage and retrieval system produced in such a way as to minimize the number of generalizations that are presented and the use of many media is an optimal form for a content vehicle.

Age-appropriateness

Explorations of teaching and learning need to cross age levels of children in order for comparisons to be made about learners of various cognitive levels and other important developmental variables. The content vehicles, therefore, should be amenable to at least a reasonable spectrum of ages. It is too much to expect the material can be amenable to *all* ages equally, but if the material meets the above criteria (unusual, not esoteric, not technical, multifaceted, and organic; not programmed but amenable to many approaches, written at a low inference level) it might well be accessible to at least four or five years of age differences, enough to cross developmental stages and permit replication at several stages. For example, if the material can be used by children in grades 4 to about 8 it would include persons in the stage of concrete operations, some in transition to formal operations and others who have achieved that stage. Without cross-age capability developmental variables are likely to dominate the findings.

Roles

Since teachers operate in a variety of teaching roles, it is desirable to have materials which can be appropriately used by teachers and studied by learners within a variety of role contexts. Otherwise, findings cannot be generalized across roles.

The following illustrate some of the roles which need investigation.

The laboratory facilities of the Stanford Center for Research and Development in Teaching were constructed to magnify three types of roles that teachers play in the lives of children: (1) as a *facilitator* to a student working in a computer-assisted instructional system, (2) as a *leader* of small groups (whether with a cognitive or a group dynamics orientation), and (3) as a lecturer or a *presenter* to a large group. The teaching laboratories vary in ways appropriate for each of the three roles.

Facilitator to the individual

The CAI teaching laboratory at SCRDT is equipped with the Ampex Random Access Information Retrieval System (Pyramid) which can store multimedia instructional programs and information sources. In this laboratory, teachers can be studied as they help students both to orient themselves to instructional systems and to utilize stored information. For example, teachers can diagnose learning difficulties and relate types of students to types of instructional programs. Or they may help students to formulate the plans for inquiry, using materials that are stored in the Pyramid System.

Although the media and the storage and retrieval features of the Pyramid System are somewhat more advanced than those in common use in most American public schools at this time, the role of the teacher as the facilitator to individual students is a very common one. Also, there are many curriculum materials which, although not automated, are similar to the ones that can be placed in the Pyramid System.

It can be expected that empirical studies of teacher decision making in this role will reveal patterns and training needs quite different from those in other roles.

Small-group teaching

Groups of five or six or as many as fifteen children are in the size range most frequently recommended for instruction in today's schools, and it can be expected that the bulk of instruction will increasingly be done in groups of this size. The SCRDT small-group laboratories are equipped with television, audio-recording facilities, and one-way viewing mirrors connected to observation booths. These permit the intensive study of teacher and learner behavior. At the outset the role of the teacher as a group leader will be thought of in terms of two subroles: one in which the teacher is functioning primarily in relation to cognitive tasks that are presented to the students, and the other in which s/he is working from a group dynamics orientation. These two subroles overlap considerably, but they represent the two major orientations from which teachers work when they are with groups of this size.

Large-group instruction

The third SCRDT laboratory is a setting for large-group instruction. It consists of a 200-seat auditorium equipped with contemporary audiovisual equipment that can be controlled from the lectern. At each seat is a keyboard that the student can use to respond to test items and attitude inventories. Student responses can be fed to the presenter through television displays. Television and audio-recording equipment can be placed in many locations throughout the auditorium.

Although large-group instruction in the form of stand-up presentations by lecturers will probably not dominate American education much longer, it will continue to be commonplace, and mass instruction through media probably will become an important feature of American secondary schools and universities. The presentational role, as typified by the lecture and standard audiovisual presentations, needs to be studied as much as the others. It can be expected that the skills of lecturing and the skills of decision making involved in lecturing will be somewhat different than those involved in the other two roles. For example, it seems reasonable to suppose that lecturers will utilize information about students much differently than would teachers who are individualizing instruction or who are working with small groups of students.

The three roles, *facilitator, leader,* and *presenter,* need to be studied in their own right and to be compared. What kinds of learning outcomes are most fostered by each role? What differences in decision making and in cognitive and social behavior emerge as teachers adapt to the roles? What skills in each domain are important in each role? How different are the results of training?

Materials with cross-role capability enable the control of content and material while exploring teacher behavior in the different roles.

An Example: Data Banks

An example of materials which approach the criteria are sets of curriculum materials (called data banks) that provide both children and teachers with access to information about selected aspects of a number of communities representing different cultures. These banks are adapted from fairly large and complex ones developed by Joyce and Joyce at Columbia University during the late 1960s.[15] In these banks a combination of print, pictorial, and iconic material is provided within categories that represent various aspects of life in the various communities. The print material has been rewritten from original sources, and material for the pictorial representations and icons were created on site. Each bank contains between 50 and 100 pages of print material and from 20 to 50 pictures.

The categories of material can be approached by students or teachers in any order. Hence the material does not program instruction. The written material has been constructed at the lowest possible inference level so that the students and teachers have to do much of the work of conceptualization. It is impossible, however, to present only factual data and, therefore, some conceptual material is interspersed throughout the text. The banks provide information about an English town (Banbury, England), a French town (Roussillon, near Avignon), a medieval English town (largely developed around Ludlow Castle in Wales), and a New Mexico pueblo (thirty five miles southwest of Santa Fe). In both form and substance the data banks meet the criteria outlined above. They are not esoteric, yet students have relatively little prior and specific information about them. The material does not require a highly technical vocabulary or unusual prior conceptual knowledge; yet the interpretation of charts, graphs, and maps and the construction of communities are organically related so that students can enter the subject from many points of view and find their way to the core of the material. The combination of icons, pictures, and print material provide reasonable multimedia capability. The random accessibility provides much room for many types of learning styles and teaching strategies. Also, the material can stretch over a variety of time periods.

These materials have previously been used in experiments lasting from as little as one hour to as much as thirty hours. Control of content can be maintained by feeding specific amounts of information into the situation at designated intervals. Test items have been constructed over the material in each of the categories at both the "recall" and "higher order" levels. In addition, the set of data banks permits the construction of tasks to determine the extent to which students are able to transfer cognitive and social processes which they have learned. For example, if teachers try to help students acquire inductive strategies over one substantive vehicle, the students can be presented with another vehicle to determine whether or not they are able to use the inductive processes that they have been taught.

The banks are most appropriate for instruction in the curriculum areas of social studies and language arts. Comparable vehicles have been developed at the Ontario Institute for Studies in Education on the lives of Ernest Hemingway and Sigmund Freud. Comparable material does not yet exist in other areas but can, we believe, be constructed (for testing purposes) when it comes time for the Program on Teaching Effectiveness to investigate the generality of teaching skills in various substantive areas. While the material was *not* constructed to be controversial, directly relevant to the daily lives of children, or crowd-pleasing in texture, inquiry into the banks has always been popular, and independent students have sustained inquiry, even working as individuals, for thirty to forty hours distributed over several weeks.

Applications

Content vehicles which meet criteria such as these should enable us to approach a number of problems where we have been vexed by lack of experimental control in field situations. For example, the staff of the Program for Teaching Effectiveness at Stanford Center for Research and Development of Teaching used the banks described above in an investigation into the stability of teacher effects on pupil learning. The problem of determining stability of effects in more than the shortest-term investigation has been a serious one. Rosenshine's review [24] indicated that the bulk of long-term studies resulted in very low stability coefficients. Brophy's investigations [3] have employed several design improvements resulting in somewhat higher stability coefficients, but even the pattern of his findings is mixed.

Against this background we are attempting to determine whether any aspects of decision-making style or interactive style of teaching are consistently related to increased amounts of pupil learning.[10] I am convinced that we need to develop a language for describing criteria for content vehicles and employ these as part of our description of the experiments we conduct in order that the influence of the nature of the learning materials be included as one of the important factors influencing the outcome of experiments.

23

The Relative Effects of Content Vehicles in Educational Research

Thomas Kluwin, Ronald Marx, and Elizabeth Joyce

RATIONALE

There are two reasons why it is important to consider methods of controlling content in the study of teaching. First, a number of descriptive studies of the process of teaching [1, 92] have indicated that teaching patterns are content-specific, that is, the substance of what is taught affects *how* it is taught. Consequently, if the content that teachers present during a research study is unknown or uncontrolled, it is difficult to evaluate the differences that occur in teaching behavior. Put simply, if we want to learn about differences among teachers, we may have to control for content either by standardizing it or by varying it systematically. Second, content acquisition, the goal of many teaching methodologies, cannot be adequately measured without reference to specific content. Partly, this is a problem of measurement. The phenomenon of regression towards the mean renders standardized general achievement measures poor evaluators of student learning. Partly it is a problem of exposure of students to similar content. If teachers TEACH different material, how can we compare effectiveness by a common standard?

A number of investigators have explored ways of maintaining the consistency or comparability of content in studies of relative teaching effectiveness. Popham and Baker [77] controlled objectives in a study of effectiveness among teachers. Both Gall and Crown [38] as well as Gage and his associates [34] have used units on ecology to control for content in their research. These consist of "resource" units for teacher and pupils and test of achievement. Recently,

Berliner and his associates [10] developed two-week units on grade school level reading and arithmetic in order to compare the relative effectiveness of teachers.

Primarily, researchers have generated their own criteria for the construction of instructional material for their particular research. Criteria have not been discussed systematically, and the properties of "experimental teaching units" or "content vehicles" have varied widely. The differences may explain differences in findings among studies and problems such as the lack of consistency in effectiveness of teachers even within the same study. Further, no one has investigated content vehicles to understand how their properties affect teaching and learning in studies of teaching (despite the fact that researchers such as Dale and Rothkoff have developed systems for examining the properties of materials and property-related effects). Ideally, researchers of teaching styles, strategies, and effectiveness should have available to them sets of instructional materials of known properties, accompanied by batteries of tests, so that these materials can be provided to students and teachers when control over content is desired and precision of measurement of learning outcomes is essential to an investigation.

In this chapter we will discuss criteria for the development of such units, describe several sets of materials developed, and report a study designed to investigate some of their properties. Our goal is to refine these materials, construct others, and develop a general knowledge base in the area. Eventually, the hoped-for product would enable researchers to manipulate content and instructional materials in studies of teaching and its effects, or possibly to understand better how to take into account variations in content vehicles in studies of teaching.

BACKGROUND

Teaching can be thought of as the interaction of:

1. Style (learner *and* teacher)
2. Strategy (a deliberate design for the teaching-learning process)
3. Instructional material (vehicles for content)

The third of these is the focus of this paper.

To provide for greater comparability between studies or greater flexibility of content within studies, it would be useful if the content vehicles were interchangeable. Consequently, the present study was conducted to test the comparability of the Joyce and Joyce content vehicles. In order to determine if content vehicles could be created that were comparable under research conditions, three questions were considered. First, do students do equally well on content acquisition when there is no effect for teacher or method, that is, could the students simply read the material and learn from it or were certain vehicles more effective than others? Second, is the order of presentation a variable in content acquisition? Third, are the vehicles comparable across categories of content? Before these materials can be used interchangeably in research on teaching behavior, methods, or effectiveness, it must be first established that relatively though not radically different content vehicles are comparable. One would hardly expect identical teaching practices in the teaching of particle physics and literary criticism, but the question of to what degree apparently compatible material is similar in its effects must be answered. This study sought to establish that within a logical range of compatible materials there were specific content vehicles that were comparable.

DESIGN OF THE STUDY

Sixty students were selected from sixth-grade classes of two San Francisco Bay Area schools and randomly assigned by school to each of six sequence pattern groups—four from school A, six from school B. To produce the six sequence patterns listed below each content vehicle was read by a group of children and a second vehicle was read by the same group on the second day.

Having read one of the content vehicles, the students were immediately tested on what they had read. Test forms were crossed with banks and grouped to produce the counter-balanced design described in table 23.1. Teachers and methods were controlled by having the children simply read the materials and take the tests. The reading ability of the students was not measured, but it was felt that it was adequately controlled by the random assignment of students and the fact that the content vehicles had similar Flesch readability indices. The students were allowed a maximum of fifteen minutes to read the material before testing, but all finished before the time limit.

A potential complication in discussing the results of this study is the fact that one school consistently did better on all measures as shown in table 23.2.

TABLE 23.1. Design of the Study

Group	Day 1	Day 2	Test Form on 1	Test Form on 2
1	Medieval	Roussillon	A	B
2	Medieval	Banbury	B	A
3	Banbury	Medieval	A	B
4	Banbury	Roussillon	B	A
5	Roussillon	Medieval	A	B
6	Roussillon	Banbury	B	A

TABLE 23.2. Reading Time and Test Results by School

Measure	School 1 Mean	SD	School 2 Mean	SD	t-Test Value
Reading time (in minutes)	37.460	11.03	41.42	8.73	7.444 *
Essay 1 (# themes)	5.100	4.273	4.186	3.117	7.016 *
Essay 3 (# themes)	0.560	0.837	0.400	0.623	6.189 *
Essay 3 (# themes)	2.480	1.233	2.157	0.942	8.411 *
Test Form A (score)	12.920	3.392	12.086	3.810	6.818 *
Test Form B (score)	12.520	3.436	12.171	4.068	0.275
Both Forms (score)	25.440	6.082	24.257	7.140	5.279 *

* $p \leq .05$

It is not unusual to find that children who can read faster are able to do better on tests of content. While there is a clear difference on these measures between schools, the difference was not expected to affect the results of this study due to the use of a stratified and counterbalanced design. The random assignment of students by schools to each of the groups was designed to introduce into each group the same amount of variance attributable to the schools.

Instruments

The instruments used in the study consisted of an open-ended essay test and a content achievement measure. The essay was prefaced by the proposition: "Suppose one of your friends, who has never heard of Roussillon (or Banbury or Ludlow Castle) suddenly found that he/she was to move there." The students were then instructed to write a letter to the hypothetical friend and describe what life would be like when the friend moved there. There was no time limit on the test, and students were asked to complete at least one full page, preferably two. The essays were subsequently read to evaluate them on the total number of themes generated, the number of concrete themes generated, and the number of abstract themes generated. Themes were defined as the use of categorical information from the data banks. Concrete versus abstract themes were distinguished on the basis of the use of factual data as opposed to conceptual information. The content achievement instruments were two parallel form twenty-three-item multiple-choice tests for each of the three content vehicles that contained both "recall" and "higher order" questions. For the six tests, the Cronbach alpha coefficient [25] ranged from .557 to .702 based on a sample size of forty for each test (table 23.3). Allowing for a small sample size, the reliability of the tests was adequate although it could be improved in subsequent studies by combining items from the two forms.

Each test consisted of nine items that were unique to the particular content vehicle and fourteen items that were common throughout all three. In the original design of the content vehicles, sixty-one content areas were described, but during the development of the content vehicles, all categories could not be filled for all content vehicles. Consequently the tests were written to reflect

TABLE 23.3. Cronbach α's

Content Vehicle	Form A	Form B
Medieval	.557	.685
Banbury	.640	.702
Roussillon	.548	.628
$N = 40$		

the relative amounts of common and unique material found in each bank. An examination of figure 23.1 shows the mean total score for each category of item broken down by content vehicle and test form. The mean total score is the number of correct responses for test items within a category averaged over persons taking the test. It is apparent that students consistently did less well on the Medieval items. In spite of a rise for Medieval Common items, Form B, the average of A and B would still fit the overall pattern of Medieval being lower than the other two. Differences between Roussillon and Banbury tend to cancel each other out making them nearly identical. The lower mean total scores for the Medieval items are not reflected in unusually low generalizability coefficients, implying that, across the board, students did less well on the Medieval test items than on the other and that the difference was not due to special items.

Test intercorrelations for all content vehicles over all students (table 23.4) support the general impression provided by the generalizability coefficients,

FIGURE 23.1 Mean Total Score by Content Vehicle and Item Category.

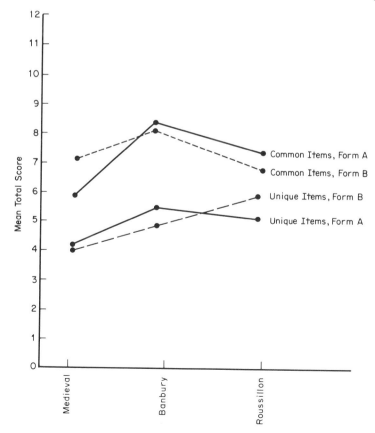

TABLE 23.4. Test Intercorrelations for All Content Vehicles $n = 120$

	Essay	2	3	Form A	Form B	Both
Essay 1	—					
Essay 2	−.002	—				
Essay 3	.756 *	.169 *	—			
First Form A	.1862 *	.207 *	.134 †	—		
First Form B	.2145 *	.200 *	.239 *	.623 *	—	
Both Forms	.221 *	.226 *	.208 *	.897 *	.905 *	—

* $p \leq .05$
† $p = .07$

that is, that the tests are moderately reliable as measures of content acquisition. Essay 1 is the total number of themes generated in the essay test, a rough measure of verbal fluency. Across all students, it correlates moderately well with the content acquisition tests since a child who is verbally fluent is more likely to be brighter than a child who is less verbally fluent. The correlations between Essay 1 and Essay 2 can be disregarded since they are so small; this suggests that no relationship exists between total number of themes and number of concrete themes. Since one would anticipate brighter students to produce more abstract themes, the correlation between the number of abstract themes (Essay 3) and the content acquisition measures is hardly surprising. The moderate correlation between the two forms of the content acquisitions tests suggests that the tests are moderately reliable measures of the same content, a fact borne out by the generalizability coefficients.

The lower correlation coefficients for tests within content vehicles (tables 23.5, 23.6, and 23.7) is partially due to the smaller sample size for each content vehicle.

The Medieval content acquisition measure intercorrelations, as well as the generalizability coefficients, reflect a moderately reliable set of measures, but the fact that the more divergent thinking measures (the essay tests) do not consistently relate to the content acquisition measures, suggests a deadening of either motivation or divergent thinking. Coupled with the apparent gross variation in reading time for the Medieval content vehicle (see table

TABLE 23.5. Test Intercorrelations for Medieval Vehicle $n = 40$

	1	2	3	Form A	Form B	Both
Essay 1	—					
Essay 2	−.111	—				
Essay 3	.703 *	.197	—			
Form A	.095	.659 *	.044	—		
Form B	−.044	.271 *	.024	.720 *	—	
Both	−.019	.190	−.007	.910 *	.943 *	—

* $p \leq .05$

TABLE 23.6. Test Intercorrelations for Banbury Content Vehicle

	Essay 1	2	*n* = 40 3	Form A	Form B	Both
Essay 1	—					
Essay 2	−.083	—				
Essay 3	.766 *	.063	—			
First Form A	.068	.440 *	.177	—		
First Form B	.203	.331 *	.285 *	.588 *	--	
Both	.156	.429 *	.262 *	.878 *	.904 *	—

* *p* ≤ .05

TABLE 23.7. Test Intercorrelation for Roussillon Content Vehicle *n* = 40

	1	2	3	Form A	Form B	Both
Essay 1	—					
Essay 2	.143	—				
Essay 3	.841 *	.218	—			
Form A	.280 *	.210	.364 *	—		
Form B	.424 *	.032	.468 *	.553 *	—	
Both	.403 *	.132	.474 *	.869 *	.893 *	—

* *p* ≤ .05

23.8), a pattern of negative attitudes toward the Medieval content vehicle emerges.

While the Banbury material yielded high correlations between the number of concrete or abstract themes produced and content acquisition, suggesting a more normal result, the Roussillon material produced a greater correlation between abstract or divergent thinking and content acquisition. Simply put, Banbury was more dependable while Roussillon was more inspiring. The

TABLE 23.8. Average Reading Time (in minutes)

	Day 1 *n* 20	Day 2 *n* 20	Average of Both *n* 40
Medieval			
mean	44.90	30.30	37.60
SD	6.00	6.75	9.72
Banbury			
mean	42.55	38.00	40.28
SD	10.92	8.69	7.74
Roussillon			
mean	40.85	42.10	41.48
SD	8.09	11.22	9.68
Mean	42.80	36.80	39.78

Medieval material produced no pattern of intercorrelations, suggesting that there was no consistency of effect.

Except for the Roussillon content vehicle, total number of themes was not a good predictor of success on any of the other measures. These results suggest that there is some characteristic of the Roussillon content vehicle which made it more "inspiring" than the other two; that is, the Roussillon material not only produced higher content acquisition but produced more conceptualization about the content.

RESULTS

It is apparent from an initial consideration of the data that there was a clear effect for materials, that is, different content vehicles produced different effects. The question of why this was so can be answered partially by comparing average reading time for each content vehicle.

T-tests calculated for the means of the total reading times for each content vehicle revealed that overall the Medieval material was read in less time than the Banbury or Roussillon material while Banbury and Roussillon were not significantly different. The source of the difference between the Medieval material and the other two is obviously due to the second day. This suggests a clear motivational effect. When students were introduced to the three content vehicles on the first day, the Medieval material required slightly more time to read—probably because of its unfamiliar terminology. On the second day, students who had the other two content vehicles found the content of the Medieval material more difficult or less interesting than the first day and "gave up" on the activity, taking tests with less preparation. The results of the *t*-tests that substantiate this hypothesis are listed in table 23.9.

The lack of preparation in the Medieval content vehicle would explain the lack of correlation between the essay measures and the content acquisition measures since lack of exposure to the material or an aversive reaction to it would tend to produce less conceptualization. Having less exposure to material would also tend to pull down the content acquisition scores for a single vehicle.

A one-way analysis of variance was calculated for the essay measures and the content acquisition measures separately. Tukey's Honestly Significant

TABLE 23.9. *t*-Tests on Average Reading Time

	t value
Medieval—Banbury	3.996 *
Medieval—Roussillon	5.572 *
Roussillon—Banbury	1.818

* $p \le .05$

Difference (HSD) statistic was then calculated for all combinations of cell means where the *F* value in the ANOVA had reached a *p* value of .05.[62] Tukey's HSD test is a multiple comparison test among cell means allowing for all pairwise comparisons. While other statistical procedures might be more appropriate for rejecting the null hypothesis, it was felt that a less conservative test would better serve the purposes of this study. Table 23.10 lists the *F* values and sample sizes for both the ANOVA calculated to compare content vehicles and the ANOVA calculated for the effects of sequence on content acquisition.

Materials

There were no significant effects produced for themes generated during the essay tests; however, there was a consistent effect for the content achievement measures. In seven out of the nine measures the cell mean for the Medieval group was significantly low. This is the same trend observed when the mean total scores were compared for each of the item categories. There was no consistent pattern of differences between the Banbury and the Roussillon

TABLE 23.10. ANOVA—*F* Values (Sample Size: Materials—60; Sequences—40)

Measure	Materials	Sequence 1	Sequence 2	Sequence 3
Essay 1	0.288	7.354 *	3.204 *	1.584
Essay 2	0.308	1.221	1.684	0.556
Essay 3	1.750	2.490	4.735 *	1.224
Test Items				
Unique A	3.528 *	1.043	1.947	0.539
Common A	8.764 *	1.113	0.175	2.233
Unique B	8.253 *	0.284	0.705	0.456
Common B	3.544 *	0.992	0.662	1.392
Total A	8.325 *	2.224	0.171	1.470
Total B	1.945 *	0.516	0.528	1.114
Unique Item	7.839 *	1.005	1.507	0.574
Common Item	6.456 *	1.092	0.325	2.568
Grand	5.590 *	1.276	0.337	1.637

* $p \le .05$

Sequence 1: Medieval/Roussillon, Medieval/Banbury, Banbury/Medieval, Roussillon/Medieval.

Sequence 2: Roussillon/Medieval, Roussillon/Banbury, Medieval/Roussillon, Banbury/Roussillon.

Sequence 3: Banbury/Medieval, Banbury/Roussillon, Medieval/Banbury, Roussillon/Banbury.

materials either in the cell means in the ANOVA done on total scores or the mean total scores generated out of the item analysis. There was a difference between the Roussillon tests and the Medieval (table 23.10) only in the categories Unique Items B and Total Unique. Since the Total Unique category sums across Unique A and Unique B, the effect in the Total may be the effect in Unique B, making it a problem of specific items on a specific form and not a feature of the content vehicle. In Unique B, Roussillon was different from Medieval but not from Banbury whereas in Total Unique, both Roussillon and Banbury were different from Medieval but not from each other. This last statement best describes the overall pattern. Medieval is the source of the variance while Banbury and Roussillon are comparable across all measures. Although the Banbury cell means from the ANOVA and the mean total scores from the item analysis were consistently higher there is no pattern of significance to the differences.

Sequence Effect

The only significant difference for the first sequence of comparisons was for the total number of themes generated. When the Medieval material was presented first, more themes were generated than when the other materials were presented first. Another way to consider the result is that when the Medieval material was presented after the other material, it had a dampening effect on the number of themes generated. Since it was the only effect found for that sequence, it is also difficult to evaluate. Only replication of the study would establish whether it is a true effect or not. However, the general pattern set so far supports the hypothesis that the Medieval material had a dampening effect.

In the second sequence, the Roussillon material presented before the other materials was contrasted with the Roussillon material presented after the other materials. The Roussillon material presented before the other materials was the source of the variance in the measures that were significant. The Roussillon material presented first was significant for "emotive" or "creative" measures but not for content. The best generalization to be drawn from the data is that a teacher who wants to have students respond more positively to subsequent content should begin with the Roussillon material rather than the other two.

In the third sequence, the Banbury materials were presented before the other materials and then after them. There were no significant results for this sequence.

Except for the essay results when the Roussillon materials were presented first, there was no appreciable, or, more accurately, regular effect for sequence.

The Roussillon material presented first sequence did produce an effect for "emotive" or "creative" measures. There was no effect on content achievement due to the sequence of presentation although there may have been an effect on the students' feelings toward subsequent material due to the order of presentation.

The content vehicles investigated in this study were designed to have equivalent effects on students. Indeed, we use the words "content vehicles" to denote that the materials are to be used as a means of investigating other variables in educational research and, thus, the effects of different vehicles should be comparable. When a study is designed to investigate teaching effects, any mathemagenic properties of the curriculum used in teaching will confound results. The extent to which these content vehicles produce variations in learning limits their use in research, particularly when more than one is used in a study.

The results of this study indicate that the Medieval content vehicle is somewhat more difficult than either Banbury or Roussillon. There is also some evidence, although weak, to suggest that Banbury is slightly easier than Roussillon. These differences appear when the content vehicles are compared with one another, and when sequence effects are explored. In the latter analysis, performance deteriorated slightly on the essay test for Roussillon when Roussillon was read following another content vehicle. More importantly, the Medieval content vehicle elicited significantly lower reading time from students when it was read following another content vehicle. This effect was substantial, representing average reduction in reading time of about 33 percent.

The overall conclusion from this study is that the three content vehicles differed somewhat. The differences were not substantial but were largely related to the Medieval content vehicle, particularly when it followed other content vehicles. These differences might be a function of some of the vocabulary, which in Medieval is relatively unique and technical. The students may have found the second day of participation in the study less engaging than the first, and when confronted with a more technical set of materials, motivation may have suffered. This is corroborated by the attenuated Essay Concrete scores, which reflect the sheer amount of material produced. Less motivated students probably would have written less on this test, hence lower scores.

One caveat is required. The findings of this study may have been the result of variations in the difficulty of the multiple-choice tests. It was impossible in this study to separate variance due to test from variance due to content vehicle. There were differences in the two forms of each test as reflected in the moderate correlations between forms for each content vehicle. However, since the few differences among content vehicles that did emerge tended not to be on the multiple-choice tests, we conclude that the differences due to multiple-choice test incomparability were negligible.

The results of this investigation point out the great difficulty of establishing control over content vehicles as a variable in educational research. Even though these materials were engineered to be comparable in structure, readability, style, and type of content, some differences emerged—the three were not completely homogeneous in effect. We speculate that differences in learning materials may have contributed wide variance to learning outcomes in educational research, and that the results of many investigations might have been interpreted quite differently had the effects of content vehicles been known.

Progress has been made, however, and the existing data banks offer us greater flexibility and control than we have had before. We shall, nonetheless, treat any differences in content vehicles as variables in any experiment we conduct and urge that others do so as well.

24

The Short-Term Effects of Self-Administered Teacher-Training Products

Thomas Kluwin, Michael McKibbin, and Elizabeth Joyce

RATIONALE

Recently, a large number of self-administered teacher-training products have been developed from the concepts first put forth by Dwight Allen and his associates at Stanford University.[2] Several assumptions underlie all these materials. The most obvious assumption is that they can make teachers better and teaching more effective. A somewhat less obvious assumption, but clearly a dominant one, is that teaching skills are hierarchical and, consequently, there must be a sequence for teaching them. Teaching is deemed to consist not of a collection of related and unstructured actions, but rather as a progression of steadily more complex or more subtle types of behavior. Coupled with this is the assumption that knowledge of the rationale for a new behavior or the theory that supports the new behavior is a factor in the teacher's acquisition of the particular skill. To put it simply, the more the teacher knows about the behavior to be acquired, the better he or she will acquire it. Finally, the same assumption that underlies all empirical research on teaching underlies the training of teachers; that is, teaching itself is a behavior that lends itself to a variety of descriptive systems. In short, all the training products assume that teaching behavior is analyzable, hierarchical, and capable of being taught.

Some examples of self-administered teacher-training products are the minicourses devised by Far West Laboratory and the products created by Horace Albertine of Texas, which are adaptations of Allen's original microteaching format. Joyce, Weil, Wald, and others at Teachers College, Columbia University, and later at Stanford, have developed a series of products around models of teaching and related teaching skills. Also, the Northwest Laboratory has developed products to train classroom teachers in human relations skills. The number of products is now so great that catalogues of them are beginning to appear. The earliest catalogue listed nearly 200 items while the most recent, a catalogue developed by Gage and his associates at Stanford,[36] contains more than 650 titles. Production of teacher-training materials promises to become an occupation in itself, as suggested by the Houston catalogue with its 850 titles carried in several supplements.

Many developers have studied the effects of their products on the short- and long-term behavior of teachers. Borg,[13] Gall, and their associates at Far West Laboratory [38] have reported that their products changed teachers' behavior in the desired direction and that the changes persisted over a period of time. Joyce and his associates [54] have demonstrated that teachers can acquire a wide variety of models of teaching (even ones quite unusual to their normal styles of teaching) and that the repertoire thus acquired persists. An important and relatively unstudied problem relates to the effectiveness of different types of products in the acquisition of different kinds of teaching skills and strategy. Some of the products are extremely complex, requiring teachers to spend 40–80 hours working through them, while others are relatively simple. The simple products utilize less television modeling of teacher behavior, generally contain fewer practice exercises, and provide fewer feedback devices for the teacher.

It is clear that, if nothing else, time is a factor in all these teacher-training packages. Since teacher time is either expensive or nonexistent when it comes to activities outside normal classroom teaching, districts or educational institutions must be concerned with the relative time required by different types of teacher-training materials. Further, there are obvious cost factors involved when one is comparing a booklet with a training system that includes film or videotape components. Time and cost effectiveness cannot be ignored on practical grounds since they are both quite finite quantities. Theoretically, there are also implications in comparing amounts of time in training procedures or complexity of products. If one initially assumes that teaching behavior is hierarchical, a conclusion that might be drawn is that the training material should also be hierarchical. Less complex or less subtle skills should be acquired through simpler training modes, or one may have to redefine the behavior hierarchy. Whether it is a practical issue of time and money or a theoretical issue of taxonomy definition, there is a need for research based on some measure of training package complexity.

Cozine [21] reported that the training mode of products was important to the potential trainee and that the more complex the mode the more acceptable it was to the trainee. While Cozine found that product acceptability can be evaluated by a simple questionnaire, the issue of whether or not the trainee's view of the product is the essential criterion in determining its usefulness is still open. Although product acceptability is a concern to teacher trainers, product effectiveness must also be evaluated, if only as a practical matter of cost in dollars and time.

Although there is a considerable body of research regarding teacher-training packages that shows that a variety of teacher behaviors can be acquired, they have been studied using relatively simple training modules. Examples are Lamb's work [65] with beginning teachers or Kircher's study [61] with experienced teachers. On the other hand, Weil, Flood, and Reed [104] found that teachers with differing learning styles developed different levels of competence depending on the complexity of the behavior to be learned; that is, the crucial variable was not the characteristics of the teachers but the characteristics of the material to be learned. Although Klingsted [63] was unable to find differences in the behavior of teachers as the result of differing levels of feedback during training, his lack of results seems more due to an inability to get interrater reliability than to differences in the teacher-training packages he used. The issue of the effects of training material complexity still remains to be evaluated.

DESIGN OF STUDY

The present study is the first in a series supported by the National Teacher Corps Program and the Competency Based Teacher Education Center, Teachers College, Columbia University. The design of the investigations is relatively simple. A large number of teacher-training products, which deal specifically with clinical teaching behaviors and which have as their target direct classroom teaching skills, have been selected and classified by Cozine [21] along a continuum of product complexity. In the course of making his classifications, Cozine found that, while nearly all the products follow the same general sequence, the sequences have different levels of complexity. Nearly all of them have a description or theory stage in which they describe and justify the teaching behavior to be acquired, followed by a demonstration stage that may be very brief or omitted in the simple products, followed by the practice of simplified skills and components of the strategy with or without television feedback, and concluded by a device so teachers may analyze their behavior as they try to carry out the skill or the strategy. Smith [93] found that with this type of training procedure the practice and feedback components were the most essential for concept acquisition. The training packages used in this study followed this basic pattern with the distinction between simple and complex being made on the basis of the essential categories of practice and feedback. Complex training packages allowed for videotaped practice and extensive feedback while the simple modules frequently contained only a pencil-and-paper type of practice and feedback component.

Method

Six experienced teachers matched for age, teaching experience, and level of education were observed under three separate sets of conditions. First, they were observed teaching prior to any training. Second, they were observed following either simple or complex training in the establishment of set induction skills. Third, they were observed following simple or complex training in questioning skills to produce the following matrix:

Teacher	Session 1	Session 2	Session 3
1,2,3	No training	Complex training in set induction	Simple training in questioning skills
4,5,6	No training	Simple training in set induction	Complex training in questioning skills

The typical pattern for each training session was that a teacher would arrive on the morning of the experiment and go through the particular type of training. Following the completion of the training, the teacher would evaluate the usefulness of the training package, prepare a lesson based on a content vehicle,[104] and then teach a sixty minute lesson to a microclass of five to eight students. During this time, the teacher was videotaped. The videotapes were later analyzed using the Teachers College Skills and Strategies Interaction Analysis System. The students completed a twenty-one item attitude inventory and a twenty-six item opinion inventory following each session. The attitude inventory included items covering the students' attitudes toward the teacher, the content of the lesson, and themselves.

The study was designed to sample different training contents as well as the complexity of the training. Consequently, an Analysis of Variance for a fully crossed design was used. The main effects were the sequence of training, which contained two levels, the first group of teachers and the second group of teachers, and the day of training, which contained three levels: no training, set-induction training, and questioning skills training. Certain a priori assumptions were tested for the main effects and the interaction. For the sequence of training, the distinction between simple types of training and complex training materials was tested. For the day of training, the two orthogonal contrasts were first the contrast between training and no training and second, the contrast between the first training—set induction—and the second training—questioning skills. Although there is a natural confounding between the day of training and the type of training in this experiment, it was decided that differences due to day of training would be evaluated individually rather than ignored.

The fully crossed model was used since it had been decided to simply dichotomize the complexity variable rather than treat it as a continuous variable. Either approach offers pitfalls. Treating it as a continuous variable would have precluded the use of the more powerful parametric statistics since the variable could only be defined on an ordinal scale. Dichotomizing the complexity variable allowed for the most efficient use of a small sample size.

The ANOVA was calculated over four categories of classroom behavior and three types of student attitude, that is, seven ANOVAs, were done and are presented in five tables. Teacher's questions and statements, as well as students' questions and statements, were coded on transcripts of the videotapes of the class sessions using the Teacher's College Skills and Strategies Interaction Analysis System (see table 24.1). The results of the ANOVA for each of these categories of classroom behavior are presented in tables 24.2 through 24.5. Table 24.6 presents the results of three ANOVAs done on the student attitude measures. It was possible to combine the results for the attitude measures because the Interaction Analysis System has nineteen categories combined under three main headings of Structuring, Information Transmission, and Feedback. These three main headings were used in tables 24.2 through 24.5.

Interaction analysis system

The system was developed by Marsha Weil, Chris Guillon, and Diane Cole to replace an earlier interaction analysis system devised by Bruce Joyce. Table 24.1 explains the categories under each heading.

TABLE 24.1. Teacher's College Skills and Strategies
Interaction Analysis System

I. STRUCTURING COMMUNICATIONS

A. Planning Goals and Standards

Directive	Negotiated	Directive	Negotiated	Directive	Negotiated
1	2	3	4	5	6

B. Implementation

Instructional	Non-instructional
7	8

II. INFORMATIONAL COMMUNICATIONS

Factual Level 1	Conceptual Level 2	Theoretical Level 3	Open	Opinion
9	10	11	12	13

III. FEEDBACK COMMUNICATIONS

Positive	Neutral	Negative	Corrective	Repeat	Digression
14	15	16	17	18	19

INTERACTION CATEGORIES

Structuring	Those communications that organize classroom activity
PLANNING	Moves that establish an activity prior to its occurrence
Goals	Decisions involving the expected outcomes of a classroom activity
Content	Moves that set the context of the lesson in a larger framework
Procedures	Set the details of who will do what and how it shall be done
IMPLEMENTATION	Direction of student behaviors while an activity is in progress
Instructional	Control the use of instructional materials or the behavior of students for instructional purposes
Noninstructional	Maintain the social and physical environment of the classroom
Information Processing	Generate and manipulate data through interactive teaching including verbal and nonverbal cues
COGNITIVE LEVELS	
Factual	Recall, identification, enumeration, description, translation
Conceptual	Interrelations, causation, interpretation, application
Theoretical	Generalization, synthesis, hypothesizing, evaluation composition
OTHERS	
Open	Indeterminate questions or statements
Opinion	Expressions of personal opinion or prejudice
Feedback	Reactions to instructional and noninstructional behaviors
Positive	Moves indicating acceptable behavior
Neutral	Short, relatively noncommital reactions
Negative	Opposite of positive feedback
Corrective	Qualified response to another's behavior to get other to alter behavior
Repeat	One's repetition of another's communication
Digression	Interactions that stray from the substantive focus of the lesson.

Results of the Study

To avoid inflating the degrees of freedom in the Analysis of Variance done on the teaching behaviors, each one of the four possible classroom interchange components was considered separately and is presented in table 24.2.

There was no effect on teacher questioning considering any of the three main categories. Neither the sequence of training nor the specific type of training package had any effect on teacher questioning behavior. This does not mean that teacher questioning behavior is unaffected by the type of training. The result must be regarded in the light of two cautions. First, the power of this study is quite low due to the small number of teachers used. Second, teacher questioning behavior is quite persistent [37] and attempts to evaluate altered patterns may require large changes. The required effect size coupled with the small sample size would preclude any final judgments on the complexity of training modules for altering questioning behavior. It can be said neither that there is a difference nor that there is no difference due to training.

Table 24.3 indicates that teacher statements were more affected by training than were teacher questions. Complex training reduced the use of teacher feedback behavior. Training increased the teacher's use of structuring statements of all kinds while teacher structuring statements were not affected by the complexity of the training. The overall category of information transmission was not affected by the sequence of training or type of training, but the individual category of conceptual level statements (not shown in table 24.3) was increased by the use of simple or complex training in questioning skills; that is, the content rather than the complexity of the training increased the use of conceptual level statements by the teachers (t value of contrast $= 2.273$, $p = .042$).

Considering the three main headings of classroom interaction, student questioning behavior was not affected by the training of the teacher; but

TABLE 24.2. Teacher Questioning Behavior

Source	df	Structuring F value (t value)	Information F value (t value)	Feedback F value (t value)
Sequence of Training	1	.950	1.249	0.391
(simple vs. complex)	(1)	(1.154)	(−0.542)	(−1.022)
Day of Training	2	.938	0.620	0.696
(none vs. training)	(1)	(−0.847)	(−0.504)	(0.590)
(first vs. second training)	(1)	(1.076)	(0.993)	(−1.022)
Sequence by Day	2	1.065	0.620	0.522
Residual	12			
Total	17			

TABLE 24.3. Teacher Statements

Source	df	Structuring F value (t value)	Information F value (t value)	Feedback F value (t value)
Sequence of Training	1	0.144	0.174	0.512
(simple vs. complex)	(1)	(0.486)	(−0.181)	(−2.324) **
Day of Training	2	3.253	0.264	1.228
(none vs. training)	(1)	(−2.525) *	(0.682)	(−0.236)
(first vs. second				
training)	(1)	(0−359)	(−0.253)	(1.550)
Sequence by Day	2	0.656	0.112	2.703
Residual	12			
Total	17			

** $p = .038$
* $p < .05$

students asked significantly more factual level questions for both groups of teachers following the teacher's training in set induction skills. Cell means were similar following the baseline and questioning skills sessions, but they were higher following the training of the teacher in set induction. This would suggest that the type of training is effective in altering student behavior but that complexity of training is not important. As the teacher tries to establish a concept within the framework of the classroom interchange, it would be more necessary for the students to ask questions regarding specific details of the concept.

Student feedback statements were affected by the type of teacher-training content. Also, of all the classroom language behavior, this category was the most affected in terms of the individual categories that make up the interaction analysis system. The training in questioning skills ($p < .016$) had the greatest effect on student feedback statements. Training in questioning skills increased the amount of student feedback regardless of the complexity of the training the teacher underwent. Further, teacher training decreased the student's use of noninstructional implementation moves; that is, as the teachers were trained

TABLE 24.4. Student Questioning Behavior

Source	df	Structuring	Information	Feedback
Sequence of Training	1	0.101	0.694	3.048
(simple vs. complex)	(1)	(0.000)	(−0.645)	(−1.336)
Day of Training	2	0.648	2.804	0.905
(none vs. training)	(1)	(−1.122)	(−1.238)	(0.154)
(first vs. second				
training)	(1)	(0.194)	(−2.019) *	(−1.336)
Sequence by Day	2	0.308	0.307	0.905
Residual	12			
Total	17			

* $p = .066$

TABLE 24.5. Student Statements

Source	df	Structuring	Information	Feedback
Sequence of Training	1	0.072	1.047	0.391
(simple vs. complex)	(1)	(0.027)	(−0.031)	(−0.766)
Day of Training	2	0.494	0.198	5.196 **
(none vs. training)	(1)	(−0.993)	(0.280)	(−2.011)
(first vs. second				
training)	(1)	(−0.027)	(0.564)	(−2.791) *
Sequence by Day	2	0.010	0.091	0.481
Residual	12			
Total	17			

** $p = .016$
* $p < .05$

it was less necessary for the students to engage in behavior to establish the social climate of the classroom. The teacher's training in questioning skills increased the student's use of theoretical information questions (t value of contrast $= 2.213$, $p = .047$). Although the training in questioning skills increased the students' production of theoretical information responses, the complexly trained group of teachers produced four times as many theoretical information statements in their students than did the simply trained teachers. Although the result is not significant statistically, it suggests that complex training in a specific skill may be very effective. Further, the students offered fewer qualified responses to the teachers following questioning skills training of both types (t value of contrast $= 3.154$, $p < .008$), but the teachers who received complex training received fewer qualified responses (t value $= \upsilon 3$ 2.580, $p < .024$) to their questions than did the teachers with the simple training. It may be belaboring the obvious to mention that there was an interaction between the training unit content and the sequence of training (f value $= 4.000$, $p < .046$) for student's qualified responses to teacher questions. The complexly trained teachers following the questioning skills module produced the fewest qualified questions from their students. Teacher training in questioning skills also reduced the number of student digressions (t value of contrast $= -3.377$ $p < .006$), suggesting that teacher training in questioning skills reduces extraneous activities in the classroom.

TABLE 24.6. ANOVA for Student Attitude

Main Effects	d	Toward Content	Toward Teacher	Toward Self
Sequence	1	0.281	8.730 **	0.146
Day	2	0.134	0.320	0.657
Sequence by Day	2	0.083	3.625 *	1.001
Residual	12			
Total	17			

** $p < .01$
* $p < .05$

Teacher-student interaction in the classroom is based on the assumption of teacher dominance of the language pattern,[89] consequently the changes in the student behavior must be accounted for in terms of the changes in teacher behavior. Due to the low power of this experiment, it is not possible simply to dismiss teacher questioning behavior changes as a possible cause for the changes in student statements; however, since there were no statistically significant changes in teacher questioning behavior, those data cannot be used to account for the changes in student behavior. The size of the change in teacher feedback statements suggests that the increases in student theoretical information statements and the decreases in student qualified responses are an interactive result of complex changes in teacher behavior brought about by complex teacher-training packages. The paradigm would be that complex training reduced teacher feedback behavior that in turn opened up more opportunities for students to expand in their responses and at the same time reduced their inhibitions about talking. The significant increase of teacher use of all types of structuring statements with training is followed by the decrease of student's noninstructional implementation statements; that is, as teachers increased their use of all types of structuring behavior through training, the students were required to engage in less behavior of their own to establish the social climate of the classroom.

Findings for student attitude

Student attitude toward the content did not change significantly throughout the course of the experiment, and thus it is not reported here. Student attitude toward the teacher did not change during the experiment, but it was apparently not a function of simple or complex teacher training. The students preferred the second group of teachers over the first. The Sequence by Day interaction for student attitude toward teacher was due largely to the students' preference for the second group of teachers over the first. Student attitude toward themselves did not change during the course of the experiment.

The preference for the second group of teachers is further supported by the results of an opinion poll that was administered to the students after each class session. In response to questions asking the students if the teacher let them interact more, gave them more positive reinforcement and was more interested in the students themselves, the results were consistent and statistically significant in favor of the second group of teachers. The students perceived the second group of teachers as being more interested in the students themselves. The distinction of simple versus complex training was not important, but the preference for the second group of teachers was clear.

Conclusions

Although teachers prefer complex training packages, the complex training modules had a greater effect on teacher behavior than did the simple training packages. The only clear trend from this study was that teacher feedback statements were changed by complex training and that, consequently, students produced more higher-order statements and fewer qualified responses. Content of the training package was found to be a more major factor than all others. However, the study of short-term effects of teacher-training packages may require different or more sensitive types of measurements than were used in this study. It will take studies with larger groups of teachers and more complex research designs to clearly establish if the complexity of teacher training modules is a factor in teaching effectiveness training. For the present, it hardly seems worthwhile to discard the simpler training modules, for we have found nothing to suggest that they are not generally at least as effective as the complex packages and they are definitely less costly both in terms of dollars and time.

One question that this study did settle is whether or not small simple studies will be able to determine the short-term effectiveness of teacher training modules using the complexity of training modules as a variable. Larger and more complicated studies will be needed to isolate the effects of complexity of training. In the meantime, practical considerations of time, expense, and trainee attitude as suggested by Cozine can be used to determine the nature of teacher-training packages.

Epilogue

In a real sense we began with a summary in chapters 1 and 2. Chapter 1 discussed the context of the entire field of teacher education and its development and the currents of reform that have guided it during the century. Chapter 2 introduced the community of individuals who have worked together to try to understand teaching as a fluid process which combines the ability to generate learning environments with the ability to adapt them to the student. Most of the investigations described in this book have been relatively simple in design and one problem has been attacked at a time. We have dealt with the following questions:

1. What is the normal range of teaching styles?

2. How do they develop over time? How much is a product of one's personality? How much is the result of the influence of other teachers as models? How much is the result of traditional training practices?

3. How do "strength" and "sensitivity" interact in teaching? Is the ability to structure and manage different from or incompatible with the ability to "read" the student and modulate and adapt to his/her characteristics?

4. Does the long excursion into sensitivity training depress teachers' sensitivity to the learners' behavior?

5. Can teachers increase their repertoire of teaching strategies?

6. How effective is feedback in assisting teachers in modifying their behavior, in planning, and in becoming more flexible?

7. What kinds of information do they collect about their students?

8. How do they deal with the realities of curriculum objectives, students, needs, and the nature of the school and classroom environment?

9. What is the pattern of the flow of activities in the classroom situation, and how does it affect the teaching-learning process?

10. Finally, how much can teachers learn from "self-training" devices?

At least for those of us who have worked together, this series of investigations has helped to clarify the nature of teaching and the conditions under which teachers can increase their competence. Clearly, teaching is pressed toward a normative mode which is largely bureaucratic in nature, yet, within the familiar patterns of teaching there are rich and interesting personalities trying to relate to one another to create productive environments. Teachers can indeed increase their repertoires. There is a rich array of models of teaching and almost all of the teachers who have participated in these investigations were able to acquire them in some form. If the research into strength and sensitivity is any indication the ability to instruct, to relate to the learner adaptively, and to manage the classroom situation are all interrelated. Finally, it appears that teachers have great self-training capability. Even the relatively limited products which were investigated here confirm the findings of the more extensive and powerful training into models of teaching to reveal that the teacher controlled in many ways by the massive demands of the situation in which s/he works can reach out and learn new skills and strategies with relative ease, *provided* that the conditions are brought about which enable that to happen. Exposure to theory, a variety of demonstrations, the opportunity to practice with structured feedback, and the opportunity to receive coaching in the classroom suggests that nearly all teachers have great capability to expand their flexibility and acquire the models of teaching necessary to enable them to reach more learners and more objectives. As we continue this work we will hopefully clarify more fully the nature of skill in teaching, come to a greater understanding of the influences which shape our teaching styles and most important develop ways that enable us to think and feel more humanely as we interact with learners at whatever level we teach. The nature of good teaching appears to be pluralistic and to reside in flexibility rather than the ability to use a single approach with force and precision. Eventually we hope that teachers will see themselves very much as the best actors do—as human beings reaching out and connecting with their students to explore the rich and many-sided ways that they can relate together. The great frontier in teaching is really the learner.

How can teachers help learners relate to their environment so that they can profit from the rich variety of learning opportunities that this society presently provides? We dedicate this book to that hope and offer this work as our contribution as we seek together to understand how we can grow together.

References

For Chapters 1, 23, and 24

1. Adams, R. S., and Biddle, B. J. *Realities of Teaching: Explorations with Video Tape.* New York: Holt, Rinehart, and Winston, 1970.
2. Allen, D., and Ryan, K. *Microteaching.* Reading, Mass.: Addison-Wesley, 1969. Also, McDonald, F. T., and Allen, D. *Training Effects of Feedback and Modeling Procedures on Teaching Performance.* Report (OE–6–10–078) to the United States Office of Education, Stanford University, 1967.
3. Amidon, T., and Hough, J. *Interaction Analysis.* Reading, Mass.: Addison-Wesley, 1967.
4. Anderson, H. H., and Brewer, J. E. *Studies of Teacher Classroom Personality II.* Stanford, Cal.: Stanford University Press, 1946.
5. Ausubel, D. *The Psychology of Meaningful Verbal Learning.* New York: Grune & Stratton, 1963.
6. See, for example, the conceptions of the teacher and the recommendations for facilitating his growth that appear in the yearbooks of the Association for Supervision and Curriculum Development. These mingle the heritage of the progressives with a generous portion of personalism.
7. Ausubel, D. *The Psychology of Meaningful Verbal Learning.* New York: Grune & Stratton, 1963.
8. Bellack, A. *The Language of the Classroom.* New York: Teachers College Press, 1966.
9. Bereiter, C., and Engelmann, S. *Teaching Disadvantaged Children in the Preschool.* Englewood Cliffs, N.J.: Prentice-Hall, 1966.
10. Berliner, D. *Beginning Teacher Evaluation Study.* Proposal for Phase III: BTES submitted by Teacher Education Division, Far West Laboratories for Educa-

tional Research and Development to State of California Committee for Teacher Preparation (revised July 1974).

11. See the textbooks which were generated during the nineteen-forties and fifties. For example: Blough, G., and Hupgett, A. J. *Methods and Activities in Elementary School Science.* New York: Dryden Press, 1951. Jacobsen, W., and Tannenbaum, H. E. *Modern Elementary School Science.* New York Bureau of Publications, Teachers College, Columbia, 1961.

12. Borg, W. *The Mini Course*, Beverley Hills, Calif.: MacMillan Educational Services, 1970.

13. Borg, W. R. *Research and Development as a Vehicle for Improving Teacher Competence.* Paper presented at AERA, New Orleans, February, 1973. ED076 584.

14. Broudy, H. S. *A Critique of PBJE.* Washington, D.C.: American Association for Colleges of Teacher Education, 1973.

15. Broudy, H. S., and Palmer, J. R. *Exemplars of Teaching Method.* Chicago: Rand McNally, 1965.

16. The spirit of the movement was captured in a conference of scholars from many disciplines at Woods Hall, Mass., in 1958, and reported by Jerome Bruner in *The Process of Education* (Cambridge, Mass.: Harvard University Press, 1959).

17. Bruner, J. S. *Toward a Theory of Instruction.* New York: Norton, 1966.

18. Buber, M. *I and Thou.* New York: Scribners, 1958.

19. Combs, A. W. *The Professional Education of Teachers: A Perceptual View of Teacher Education.* Boston: Allyn and Bacon, 1965.

20. Combs, A., and Snygg, D. *Individual Behavior.* New York: Harper, 1949.

21. Cozine, D. *Teacher Perceptions of the Acceptability of Teacher Training Products.* Stanford Center for Research and Development in Teaching, Stanford University. R & D Monograph #141.

22. Cremin, L. *The Genius of American Education.* Pittsburgh: University of Pittsburgh Press, 1965.

23. Cremin, L. *The Transformation of the School.* New York: Knopf, 1961.

24. Crist, J.; Marx, R. W.; and Peterson, P. *Program on Teaching Effectiveness.* "Teacher Behavior in the Organizational Domain." School of Education, SCRDT, Stanford University, 1974.

25. Cronbach, L. T.; Glaser, G. C.; Nonda, H.; and Rajarafnam, N. *The Dependability of Behavioral Measurements.* New York: Wiley 1972.

26. Dewey, J. *Democracy and Education.* New York: Macmillan, 1916.

27. Edwards, J. *A Treatise Concerning Religious Affections.* Edited by John E. Smith. New Haven: Yale University Press, 1959.

28. Erikson, E. *Childhood and Society.* New York: Norton, 1950.

29. See, for example, Edwin Fenton, *The New Social Studies.* New York: Holt, Rinehart and Winston, 1967.

30. Flanders, N. *Analyzing Teacher Behavior.* Reading, Mass.: Addison-Wesley, 1970.

31. Freire, P. *Pedagogy of the Oppressed.* New York: Herder and Herder, 1970.

32. Gage, N. L. "An Analytic Approach to Research on Instructional Methods." *Phi Delta Kappan* (1968), **49**:601–6.

33. Gage, N. L., ed. *Handbook of Research on Teaching.* Chicago: Rand McNally, 1963.

34. Gage, N. L. *Program on Teacher Effectiveness,* "A Brief Summary as of February, 1975." School of Education, Stanford University, SCRDT, 1975.

35. Gage, N. L. *Teacher Effectiveness and Teacher Education.* Palo Alto: Pacific Books, 1970.

36. Gage, N., et. al. *Program on Teaching Effectiveness* (1974), "Teacher Training Products: The State of the Field." Research and Development Memorandum

No. 116, Stanford Center for Research and Development in Teaching, Stanford University.

37. Gall, M. D. "The Use of Questions in Teaching." *Review of Educational Research* (1970), **40**:707–721.

38. Gall, M., and Crown, K. A. *Research Design—Questioning Study (Minicourses H9).* San Francisco: Far West Laboratory for Educational Research and Development, 1973.

39. Glasser, R. *Schools Without Failure.* New York: Harper & Row, 1968.

40. The earlier years of the academic movement were chronicled by John Goodlad (curriculum reform movement) in a report for the Ford Foundation. (New York: Ford Foundation, 1968).

41. Greene, M. *Teacher as Stranger.* New York Bureau of Publications, Teachers College, Columbia University, 1973.

42. Guba, E. G., and Snyder, C. A. "Instructional Television and the Classroom Teacher." *AV Communication Review* (1965), **13**:5–26.

43. Hofstadter, R. *Anti-Intellectualism in America.* New York: Knopf, 1963.

44. Hunt, D. E. "Matching Models in Education." In C. Beck et. al. (eds.), *Moral Education.* Toronto: University of Toronto Press, 1970.

45. Hunt, D.; Joyce, B. R.; Greenwood, J.; Noy, J. E.; Reid, R.; and Weil, M. "Student Conceptual Level and Models of Teaching: Theoretical and Empirical Coordination of Two Models." *Interchange,* (1974), **5**:19–30.

46. Ivins, W. *Print and Visual Communication.* Cambridge, Mass.: Harvard University Press, 1953; McLuhan, M. *Understanding Media.* New York: Signet Books, 1964.

47. James, W. *Talks to Teachers on Psychology and to Students on Some of Life's Ideals.* New York: H. Holt & Co., 1889.

48. James, W. *Talks to Teachers on Psychology.* New York: H. Holt & Co., 1939.

49. Joyce, B. "Variations on a Systems Theme." In Bruce Joyce and Marsha Weil, eds., *Perspectives on Reform in Teacher Education.* Englewood Cliffs, N.J.: Prentice-Hall, 1972.

50. Joyce, B. "Vehicles for Controlling Content in the Study of Teaching." Chapter 22 of this book.

51. Joyce, B, and Joyce, E. "The Creation of Information Systems for Children." *Interchange* (1970), 7, no. 2.

52. Joyce, B., et. al. *The Teacher-Innovator.* A Report to the U.S. Office of Education. New York: Teachers College Press, 1969.

53. Joyce, B., et. al. "Teacher Innovator System for Analyzing Skills and Strategies." Unpublished paper, Teachers College, Columbia University, 1972.

54. Joyce, B.; Morine, G.; Weil, M.; and Wald, R. (eds.) *Materials for Modules: A Classification of Competency-Oriented Tools for Teacher Education.* U.S. Office of Education, 1971.

55. Joyce, B., and Weil, M. *Models of Teaching.* Englewood Cliffs, N.J.: Prentice-Hall, 1972.

56. Joyce, B., and Weil, M. *Perspectives for Reform in Teacher Education.* Englewood Cliffs, N.J.: Prentice-Hall, 1972.

57. Joyce, B.; Weil, M.; and Wald, R. "Content for the Training of Educators: A Structure for Pluralism." *Teachers College Record* (Winter, 1972).

58. Joyce, B.; Weil, M.; and Wald, R. "Models of Teaching in Teacher Education: An Evaluation of Instructional Systems." *Interchange,* Winter, 1974.

59. Kersh, B. Y. *Classroom Simulation.* Monmouth, Oreg.: Teacher Research of the Oregon State System of Higher Education, 1963.

60. Kilpatrick, W. H. *Philosophy of Education.* New York: Macmillan, 1951.

61. Kircher, S. E. "The Effectiveness of a Training Package on ESL Teachers

in A B E Programs." MA thesis, Colorado State University, February, 1975, ED 110 739.

62. Kirk, R. E. *Experimental Design: Procedures for the Behavioral Sciences,* Belmont, California: Brooks/Cole Publishing Co., 1968.

63. Klingsted, J. L. "Effectiveness of Three Feedback Products in Developing Set & Establishing Skills." Texas University, El Paso, Texas, November, 1974. ED 113 302.

64. Kohlberg, L. "Moral Education in the Schools." *School Review* (1966), 74:1–30.

65. Lamb, G. "An Effective Protocol Model for Training Science Teachers to Ask a Wide Cognitive Variety of Questions." ED 116 948, 1975.

66. Lindsey, M., and Stratemeyer, F. *Working With Student Teachers.* New York Bureau of Publications, Teachers College, Columbia, 1958.

67. Mailer, N. *Of a Fire on the Moon.* Boston: Little, Brown, 1971.

68. Maslow, A. *Motivation and Personality.* New York: Harper, 1954.

69. Maslow, A. *Toward a Psychology of Being.* Princeton, N.J.: Van Nostrand, 1962.

70. McDonald, F. "Behavior Modification in Teacher Education." In *Behavior Modification in Education,* the 72nd Yearbook of NSSE, edited by Herman Richey. University of Chicago Press, 1973.

71. Medley, D. N., and Mitzel, H. E. "A Technique for Measuring Classroom Behavior." *Journal of Educational Psychology* (1958), **49**:86–92.

72. Montessori, M. *The Advanced Montessori Method.* Cambridge, Mass.: R. Bentley, 1964.

73. Neill, A. S. *Summerhill.* New York: Hart Publishing, 1960.

74. Parker, J. F. Jr., and Downs, J. E. *Selection of Training Media.* Washington, D.C.: Office of Technical Services, U.S. Department of Commerce, 1961.

75. Perls, F., et. al. *Gestalt Therapy.* New York: Julian Press, 1962.

76. Piaget, J. *The.Origins of Intelligence in Children.* New York: International Universities Press, 1952.

77. Popham, J., and Baker, E. *Establishing Instructional Goals.* Englewood Cliffs, N.J.: Prentice-Hall, 1970.

78. Pyatte, J. A. "Protocol Materials: A New Answer to An Old Problem?" (1974) ED 111 818.

79. Research for Better Schools. *Teaching in IPI Mathematics: A Program of Teacher Preparation.* Philadelphia, 1969.

80. Roback, A. A. *A History of American Psychology.* New York: Collier, 1952.

81. Rogers, C. *Client-Centered Therapy.* Boston: Houghton Mifflin, 1951.

82. Rogers, C. *Freedom to Learn.* Columbus, Ohio: C. E. Merrill, 1969.

83. Rosenshine, B. "The Stability of Teacher Effects Upon Student Achievement." *Review of Educational Research* (1970), **40**, No. 5.

84. Schutz, W. *Joy.* New York: Grove Press, 1967.

85. Schwab, J., ed. *The Biology Teacher's Handbook.* 1st ed. New York: Wiley 1963.

86. Shugrue, M. *Performance-Based Teacher Education and the Subject Matter Fields.* Washington, D.C.: American Association for Colleges of Teacher Education, 1973.

87. For an advocacy position, and empirical investigations, see: Sigel, I., and Hooper, F., eds. *Logical Thinking in Children.* New York: Holt, Rinehart and Winston, 1968.

88. Simon, A., and Boyer, G. *Mirrors for Behavior.* Philadelphia: Research for Better Schools, 1967.

89. Sinclair, T. M., and Coulthard, R. M. *Towards an Analysis of Discourse.* Oxford University Press, London, 1975.

90. Skinner, B. F. *Verbal Behavior*. New York: Appleton-Century-Crofts, 1957.

91. Smith, B. O. *Teachers for the Real World* (Task Force reprint). Washington, D.C.: American Association of Colleges for Teacher Education, 1969.

92. Smith, B. O., and Meux, N. O. *A Study of the Logic of Teaching*. Urbana, Illinois: University of Illinois Press, 1962.

93. Smith, E. "The Influence of Four Instructional Components on Concept Acquisition." Paper presented at AERA, Washington, D.C., 1975. ED 103 355.

94. Spaulding, R. *Educational Intervention in Early Childhood*. Final Report for the Ford Foundation: Durham, N.C., 1970.

95. For an analysis of the extrapolation of cognitive psychology to curriculum, see Sullivan, E. V. *Piaget and the School*. Toronto: Ontario Institute for Studies in Education, Bulletin #2, 1967.

96. Taba, H.; Levine, S.; and Ellzey, F. *Thinking in Elementary School*. Cooperative Research Project No. 1574. San Francisco: San Francisco State College, 1964.

97. Thelen, H. A. *Dynamics of Groups at Work*. Chicago: University of Chicago Press, 1954, and *Education and the Human Quest*. New York: Harper, 1960. Descriptions of the elementary teacher education program at the University of Chicago during the early 1950s.

98. Thoresen, C. (ed.) *Behavior Modification in Education*. Chicago: NSSE Yearbook, University of Chicago Press, 1973.

99. Toffler, A. *Future Shock*. New York: Random House, 1970.

100. Turner, R. L. "Levels of Criteria." In B. Rosner et. al. (eds.), *The Power of Competency-Based Teacher Education*. Princeton, N.J.: Educational Testing Service, 1971.

101. Wald, R. "The Effects of Models of Teaching as a Program for the Training of Teachers." Ph.D. diss., Columbia University, Teachers College, 1973.

102. Weil, M. Unpublished paper, 1972.

103. Weil, M. "Deriving Teaching Skills from Teaching Strategies: A Paradigm for Competency-Based Education." Ph.D. diss., Columbia University, Teachers College, 1973.

104. Weil, M.; Flood, D.; and Reed, P. "A Study of Teacher Trainee Learning Styles and the Development of Competence." AERA Paper, April, 1975, Washington, D.C. ED 113 325

105. Withall, J., and Lewis, W. W. "Social Interaction in the Classroom." In Gage, N. L. (ed.), *Handbook of Research on Training*. Chicago: Rand McNally, 1963.

For Chapters 2–3, 5–8, and 11

1. Allen, Dwight W. "A New Design for Teacher Education: The Teacher Intern Program at Stanford University." *The Journal of Teacher Education* (1966), 17:296–300.

2. Allen, Dwight W., and Fortune, Jimmie. "An Analysis of Micro-Teaching: A New Procedure in Teacher Education." Paper presented to the American Educational Research Association, Chicago, Illinois, February, 1965.

3. Amidon, Edmund, and Flanders, Ned. *The Role of the Teacher in the Classroom*. Philadelphia: Research for Better Teaching, 1967.

4. Amidon, Edmund and Hunter, Elizabeth. *Improving Teaching: The Analysis of Classroom Verbal Interaction*. New York: Holt, Rinehart and Winston, 1966.

5. Ammons, Margaret Perry. "Educational Objectives: The Relation Between the Process Used in Their Development and Their Quality." Ph.D. diss. University of Chicago, 1961.

6. Anderson, Harold H. "Dominant and Social Integration in the Behavior of Kindergarten Children and Teachers." *Genetic Psychology Monographs* (1939), **21**:288–385.

7. Ausubel, David. *Psychology of Meaningful Verbal Learning.* New York: Grune & Stratton, 1963.

8. Bandura, A. "Behavioral Modification through Modeling Procedures." In *Research in Behavior Modification,* edited by L. P. Ullman. New York: Holt, Rinehart and Winston, 1965.

9. Bell, R. Q. "A Reinterpretation of the Direction of Effects in Studies of Socialization." *Psychological Review.* **73** (1968): 81–95.

10. Bellack, Arno (Ed.). *Theory and Research in Teaching.* New York: Bureau of Publications, Teachers College, Columbia University, 1963.

11. Bellack, Arno; Khiebard, Herbert; Hyman, Ronald; and Smith, Frank. *The Language of the Classroom.* New York: Teachers College Press, 1965.

12. Bloom, B. S. (Ed.). *Taxonomy of Educational Objectives.* New York: Longman, Green, 1954.

13. Brim, O. J. *Education for Child Rearing.* New York: Russell Sage, 1959.

14. Borg, Walter; Kelley, Marjorie; Langer, Philip; and Gall, Meredith. *The Minicourse.* Beverley Hills, Calif.: Collier-Macmillan, 1970.

15. Bradford, L. P.; Gibb, J. R.; and Benne, K. D. *T-group Theory and Laboratory Method.* New York: Wiley, 1964.

16. Broudy, Harry S., and Palmer, J. R. *Exemplars of Teaching Method.* Chicago: Rand McNally, 1965.

17. Brown, Clark. "A Multivariate Study of the Teaching Styles of Student Teachers." Doctoral diss. New York: Teachers College, Columbia University, 1967. (Unpublished)

18. Brown, George I. "An Experiment in the Teaching of Creativity." *School Review.* 72 (Winter 1964):437–50.

19. Brown, Clark, and Joyce, Bruce. "The Initial Teaching Style of Student Teachers." *Educational Leadership.* 32 (May 1974): 473–479.

20. Bruner, Jerome S. *Toward a Theory of Instruction.* New York: Norton, 1966.

21. Campbell, D. T. "Conformity in Psychology's Theories of Acquired Behavioral Dispositions." In I. A. Berg & B. M. Bass (Eds.), *Conformity and deviation.* New York: Harper, 1961, 101–142.

22. Chan, R. "Learning by Discussion as a Function of Need for Affiliation." Doctoral diss. in progress, University of Toronto.

23. Combs, Arthur. *The Professional Education of Teachers: A Perceptual View of Teacher Preparation.* Boston, Mass.: Allyn and Bacon, 1965.

24. Conant, James B. *The Education of American Teachers.* New York: McGraw-Hill, 1963.

25. Cronbach, L. J. "How Can Instruction Be Adapted to Individual Differences?" In R. M. Gagne (Ed.), *Learning and Individual Differences.* New York: 1967.

26. Cross, Herbert J. "The Relation of Parental Training Conditions to Conceptual Level in Adolescent Boys." Doctoral diss. New York: Syracuse University, 1965. 238 pp.

27. Cruickshank, Donald R. and Broadbent, Frank. Ongoing work at (for example) the State University of New York at Brockport.

28. Davitz, J. *The Communication of Emotional Meaning.* New York: McGraw-Hill, 1964.

29. Dewey, John. *Democracy and Education.* New York: Macmillan, 1916.

30. Erikson, Erik. *Childhood and Society.* New York: W. W. Norton and Company, 1950.

31. Fantini, M. D. *Public Schools of Choice.* New York: Simon & Schuster, 1973.

32. Flanders, Ned A. *Teacher Influence, Pupil Attitudes and Achievement.* Final report, U.S. Department of Health, Education and Welfare, Office of Education, Cooperative Research Project No. 397. Minneapolis: University of Minnesota Press, 1960. 126 pp.

33. Flanders, N. A. *Teacher Influence, Pupil Attitudes and Achievement.* Final report, U.S. Office of Education, CRP #397, University of Michigan, 1962.

34. Flanders, Ned. *Analyzing Teaching Behavior.* Reading, Mass.: Addison-Wesley, 1970.

35. Flavell, J. H. "Developmental Studies of Verbal Communication Skills." Paper read at Soc. Res. Child Develpm., Berkeley, California, 1963.

36. Flavell, J. H. "The Development of Inferences about Others." In T. Mischel (Ed.) *Understanding Other Persons.* Oxford, England: Blackwell, Basil, & Mott, 1974, 66–116.

37. Flavell, J. H.; Botkin, P. T.; Fry, C. L.; Wright, J. W.; and Jarvis, P. E. *The Development of Role-Taking and Communications Skills in Children.* New York: Wiley, 1968.

38. Foltz, Karl and Foltz, Margaret. *Cybernetic Principles of Learning and Educational Design.* New York: Holt, Rinehart and Winston, 1966.

39. Formanek, Ruth. *Course Outline and Workbook for Elementary Education 105.* New York: Hofstra University, 1966.

40. French, E. G. "Effects of the Interaction of Motivation and Feedback on Task Performance." In J. W. Atkinson (Ed.) *Motives in Fantasy, Action, and Society.* Princeton, N.J.: Van Nostrand, 1958, 400–408.

41. Gage, N. L.; Runkel, P. J.; and Chatterjee, B. B. "Changing Teacher Behavior Through Feedback from Pupils: An Application of Equilibrium Theory." In W. W. Charters, Jr. and N. L. Gage, *Readings in the social psychology of education.* Boston: Allyn Bacon, 1963, 173–181.

42. Gallagher, J. and Aschner, M. J. "A System for Classifying Thought Processes in the Context of Classroom Verbal Interaction." In Simon, A. and Boyer, E. G. (Eds.) *Mirrors for Behavior.* Philadelphia: Research for Better Schools, 1967. Vol. II.

43. Getzels, Jacob W. and Jackson, Philip W. "The Teacher's Personality and Characteristics." *Handbook of Research on Teaching.* (Edited by Nathaniel L. Gage.) Chicago: Rand McNally, 1963. Chapter 11, 506–582.

44. Gordon, William J. *Synectics.* New York: Harper and Row, 1961.

45. Gower, Robert. "The Use of an Exemplary Teaching Profile to Assess Teaching Performance in an Induction Model." Unpublished doctoral diss., Columbia University, 1974.

46. Haller, E. J. "Pupil Influence in Teacher Socialization: a Sociolinguistic Study." *Sociology of Education,* 1967, *60,* 316–333.

47. Harvey, O. J.; Hunt, D. E.; and Schroder, H. M. *Conceptual Systems and Personality Organization.* New York: Wiley, 1961.

48. Heath, Robert W., editor. *The New Curricula.* New York: Harper, 1964.

49. Heck, E. J. "A Training and Research Model for Investigating the Effects of Sensitivity Training for Teachers." *Journal of Teacher Education,* 1971, *22,* 501–507.

50. Hoetker, James and Ahlbrand, William. "The Persistence of the Recitation." *American Educational Research Journal 6* (March 1969), 145–167.

51. Hough, John B. and Amidon, Edmund. *Behavioral Change in Pre-Service Teacher Preparation: An Experimental Study.* Philadelphia: Temple University, 1964.

52. Howard, Elizabeth Z. "Needed: A Conceptual Scheme for Teacher Education," *School Review, LXXI* (Spring 1963), 12–26. a

53. Howard, Elizabeth Zimmerman. "Elementary Teacher Training Program, University of Chicago." Unpublished manuscript, University of Chicago, 1963b.
54. Hughes, Marie M. "Utah Study of the Assessment of Teaching." *Theory and Research on Teaching.* (Edited by A. A. Bellack.) New York: Teachers College, 1963. 25–36.
55. Hunt, D. E. "A Conceptual Systems Change Model and Its Application to Education." Paper presented at Office of Naval Research conference, "Flexibility, Adaptability, and Creativity: Nature and Developmental Determinants," Boulder, Colorado, March 19–21, 1964.
56. Hunt, David E. "The Communication Task." Syracuse, New York: Syracuse University, 1965. (Unpublished)
57. Hunt, David E. "A Model for Analyzing the Training of Training Agents." *Merrill Palmer Quarterly. 12*: 137–155; April 1966.
58. Hunt, David E. "Matching Models and Moral Training," in C. Beck, B. Crittenden, and E. V. Sullivan, eds. *Moral Education.* Toronto: University of Toronto Press, 1970a.
59. Hunt, D. E. "Adaptability in Interpersonal Communication Among Training Agents." *Merrill Palmer Quarterly, 16,* 325–344, 1970b.
60. Hunt, D. E. *Matching Models in Education.* Toronto: OISE, 1971.
61. Hunt, D. E. "Person-environment interaction: A Challenge Found Wanting Before It was Tried." Invited address to the Division of Educational Psychology, American Psychological Association meeting, Montreal, Quebec, 1973.
62. Hunt, D. E.; Greenwood, J.; Brill, R.; and Deineka, M. "From Psychological Theory to Educational Practice: Implementation of a Matching Model." Symposium presented at American Educational Research Association meeting, Chicago, 1972.
63. Hunt, D. E.; Greenwood, J.; Noy, J.; and Watson, N. "Assessment of Conceptual Level. Paragraph Completion Method." Toronto: OISE, 1973.
64. Hunt, D. E. and Joyce, B. R. "Teacher Trainee Personality and Initial Teaching Style." *American Educational Research Journal,* 1967, *4,* 153–259.
65. Hunt, D. E.; Joyce, B. R.; and Del Popolo, J. "An Exploratory Study in the Modification of Students' Teaching Patterns." Unpublished manuscript, Syracuse University, 1964.
66. Hunt, D. E.; Joyce, B. R.; Greenwood, J.; Noy, J. E.; and Weil, M. "Student Conceptual Level and Models of Teaching: Theoretical and Empirical Coordination of Two Models." Paper presented at the meeting of the American Educational Research Association meeting, Chicago, April, 1974.
67. Hunt et. al. *Student Conceptual Level,* ibid.
68. Hunt, D. E.; Joyce, B. R.; and Weinstein, G. "Application of Communication Task: An Assessment of Peace Corps Trainees." Report submitted to Peace Corps, Syracuse University, 1965.
69. Hunt, D. E. and Sullivan, E. W. *Between Psychology and Education,* Hinsdale, Illinois: Dryden, 1974.
70. *Individually Prescribed Instruction.* Philadelphia, Pennsylvania: Research for Better Schools, 1966.
71. Jackson, Philip. *Life in Classrooms.* New York: Holt, Rinehart and Winston, 1966.
72. James, William. *Talks to Teachers on Psychology and to Students on Some of Life's Ideals.* New York: H. Holt & Co., 1889.
73. Jones, E. E. and Thibaut, J. W. "Interaction Goals and Bases of Inference in Interpersonal Perception." In R. Taquiri and L. Petrullo (Eds.) *Person Perception and Interpersonal Behavior.* Stanford: Stanford University Press, 1958, 151–178.
74. Joyce, Bruce R. "Summary of Exploratory Research in Education Utilizing the Theory of Conceptual Systems." Paper presented at symposium on "Conceptual

Systems Theory and Educational Research." American Educational Research Association, Chicago, Illinois, February 1964a. (Mimeo.) 39 pp.

75. Joyce, B. R. "A Manual for Coding Teacher Communications Relevant to Conceptual Systems Theory." Unpublished manuscript, University of Chicago, 1964b.

76. Joyce, Bruce R. "Exploration of the Utilization of Supervisory Personnel When Taping, Filming, and the Behavioral Analysis of Teaching are Introduced into the Student Training Program." Report to the Office of Education, U.S. Department of Health, Education and Welfare (OEG 1–6–051079–0808). New York: Teachers College, Columbia University, 1967.

77. Joyce, Bruce R. and Dirr, Peter. "Sensitivity Training for Teachers: An Experiment." Paper presented to the annual meeting of the American Educational Research Association, New York, 1967.

78. Joyce, Bruce; Dirr, Peter; and Hunt, David E. "Sensitivity Training for Teachers: An Experiment." *The Journal of Teacher Education 20:* 75–83; Spring 1969.

79. Joyce, Bruce R. and Harootunian, Berj. "Teaching as Problem Solving," *Journal of Teacher Education, XV* (December 1964), 420–27.

80. Joyce, Bruce R. and Harootunian, Berj. *The Structure of Teaching.* Chicago: Science Research Associates, 1967.

81. Joyce, B., et al. *The Teacher-Innovator.* New York: Teachers College Press, 1969.

82. Joyce, Bruce R. and Hodges, Richard E. "The Elementary Teacher Education Program at the University of Chicago," September 1964 (mimeographed for introprogram use).

83. Joyce, Bruce R. and Hodges, Richard. "A Rationale for Teacher Education." *Elementary School Journal 66:* 154–66; February 1966a.

84. Joyce, Bruce R. and Hodges, Richard E. "Instructional Flexibility Training." *Journal of Teacher Education. 17:* 409–416; Winter 1966b.

85. Joyce, B. R. and Hodges, R. E. "The Use of Developmental Studies of Teaching Styles for Research on Teacher Education." Paper delivered to the American Educational Research Association, Chicago, February 1966c.

86. Joyce, Bruce and Hunt, David. "Personality and Teaching Styles." *Journal of Teacher Education,* Summer 1967.

87. Joyce, Bruce R. and Hunt, David E. "Personality and Teaching Style." To be published.

88. Joyce, Bruce R.; Lamb, Howard and Sieber, Joan. "Conceptual Systems and Information Processing: A Study of Teachers." *Journal of Educational Research. 59:* 219–22; January 1966.

89. Joyce, B. R. and Weil, M. *Models of Teaching.* Englewood Cliffs, N.J.: Prentice Hall, 1972.

90. Joyce, B. R.; Weil, M.; and Wald, R. "The Teacher Innovator: Models of Teaching as the Core of Teacher Education." *Interchange,* 1973, *4,* 2/3, 47–60.

91. Kahn, R. L. and Cannell, C. F. *The Dynamics of Interviewing.* New York: Wiley, 1957.

92. Kelly, G. A. *The Psychology of Personal Constructs.* New York: Norton, 1955.

93. Kelley, Joseph. "An Analysis of the Moves Made by Elementary School Teachers in Operationalizing Two Theoretically Based Teacher Models." Unpublished doctoral diss., Columbia University, 1973.

94. Kohlberg, Larry. "Moral Education in the Schools." *School Review,* Vol. *74,* 1966, 1–30.

95. LaGrone, Herbert F. and Wedberg, Desmond P. "An Introductory Report on a Project to Improve the Professional Sequence in Pre-Service Teacher Education

through the Selective and Planned Use of New Media." Washington, D.C.: American Association of Colleges for Teacher Education, December 1963.

96. Lesniak, R. "Predicting Classroom Behavior of Urban Teacher Candidates Through Use of a Classroom Behavior Task." Doctoral diss., Syracuse, New York: Syracuse University, 1969. (Unpublished)

97. Lippitt, R.; Watson, Jeanne; and Westley, B. *The Dynamics of Planned Change.* New York: Harcourt Brace, 1958.

98. Maslow, Abraham. *Toward a Psychology of Being.* Princeton: D. Van Nostrand and Company, 1962.

99. Massialas, Byron and Cox, Benjamin. *Inquiry in Social Studies.* New York: McGraw-Hill, 1966.

100. McClure, Robert. "Procedures, Processes, and Products in Curriculum Development." Unpublished doctoral diss. Los Angeles: University of California at Los Angeles, 1965.

101. McDonald, Fred. "Behavior Modification in Teacher Education." In Richey, Herman (Ed.) *Behavior Modification in Education,* The 72nd Yearbook of the National Society for the Study of Education, Chicago: University of Chicago Press, 1973.

102. McKibbin, Michael. "The Application of Three Instruction Analysis Systems to Investigate Models of Teaching." Unpublished doctoral diss., Columbia University, 1974.

103. McLachlan, J. F. C. and Hunt, D. E. "Differential Effects of Discovery Learning as a Function of Student Conceptual Level." *Canadian Journal of Behavioural Science,* **5**, 1973, 152–160.

104. Michaelis, John U. *Social Studies for Children in a Democracy.* Englewood Cliffs, N. J.: Prentice-Hall, 1963.

105. Michigan State University, *Behavioral Science Elementary Teacher Education Program* (OE 58024, 2 vols.) Washington, D.C.: USOE, 1968.

106. Murphy, Patricia D. and Brown, Marjorie M. "Conceptual Systems and Teaching Styles." *American Educational Research Journal* 7:519–40; November 1970.

107. National Education Association: Teacher Education and Media Project. See #95.

108. Neill, A. S. *Summerhill.* New York: Hart Publishing Company, 1960.

109. O'Donnell, Katherine. "Natural Teaching Styles and Modes of Teaching: The Production of Classroom-Unusual Teaching Behavior." Unpublished doctoral diss., Columbia University, 1974.

110. Peck, Lucy and Joyce, Bruce. "Situational Assessment of Strength and Sensitivity in Teaching." *Journal of Teacher Education.* 23 (Spring 1972), 67–69.

111. Peterson, C. L.; Danner, F. W.; and Flavell, J. H. "Developmental Changes in Children's Response to Three Indications of Communication Failure." *Child Development,* 1972, **43**, 1463–1468.

112. Phenix, Philip. *Realms of Meaning: A Philosophy of the Curriculum for General Education.* New York: McGraw-Hill, 1964.

113. Piaget, Jean. *The Origins of Intelligence in Children.* New York: International Universities Press, 1952.

114. Plato. *The Republic.* Frances MacDonald Cornford, trans. New York: Oxford University Press, 1945.

115. Popham, James W. "Professional Knowledge and Student Teaching Behavior." A paper presented to the American Educational Research Association, Chicago, Illinois, February, 1965.

116. Popham, James and Baker, Eva. *Establishing Instructional Goals.* Englewood Cliffs, N.J.: Prentice-Hall, 1970.

117. Popham, W. J. and McNeill, J. D. "The Influence of Taped Instructional Programs on Certain Cognitive and Affective Behaviors of Teachers." Paper presented

to the annual meeting of the American Educational Research Association. Chicago, February 1965.

118. Rathbone, C. "Teachers' Information Handling Behavior When Grouped with Students by Conceptual Level." Unpublished doctoral diss., Syracuse University, 1970.

119. Rogers, Carl. *Client-Centered Therapy.* Boston: Houghton Mifflin, 1951.

120. Rosenshine, B. and Furst, N. "Research on Teacher Performance Criteria." In B. O. Smith (Ed.) *Research in Teacher Education.* Englewood Cliffs, N.J.: Prentice-Hall, 1971, 37–72.

121. Rosenthal, R. and Jacobson, L. *Pygmalion in the Classroom.* New York: Holt, Rinehart and Winston, 1968.

122. Rude, Eugene. "The Analysis of the Intersection Patterns Characteristic of Phases of Models of Teaching." Unpublished doctoral diss., Columbia University, 1973.

123. Sand, Ole. "Continuity and Sequence in Social Studies Curriculums." Unpublished doctoral diss. Chicago: University of Chicago, 1948.

124. Sarason, Seymour B.; Davidson, Kenneth S.; and Blatt, Burton. *The Preparation of Teachers: An Unstudied Problem in Education.* New York: Wiley, 1962.

125. Schaefer, Robert J. *The School as a Center of Inquiry.* New York: Harper, 1967.

126. *School Review, LXXI* (Spring, 1963).

127. Schroder, Harold M.; Driver, Marvin; and Streufert, Sigmund. *Information Processing in Individuals and Groups.* New York: Holt, Rinehart and Winston, 1967.

128. Schroder, H. M.; Karlins, M.; and Phares, J. *Education for Freedom.* New York: Wiley, 1973.

129. Schroder, H. M. and Talbot, T. "The Effectiveness of Video Feedback in Sensitivity Training." Report submitted to Peace Corps, Princeton, N.J.: 1966.

130. Schueler, Herbert and Gold, Milton J. "Video Recordings of Student Teachers," *Journal of Teacher Education, XV* (December, 1964), 358–64.

131. Schwab, Joseph, ed. *The Biology Teachers Handbook.* New York: John Wiley and Sons, 1963.

132. Scott, W. A. "Flexibility, Rigidity and Adaptability: toward Clarification of Concepts." In O. J. Harvey (Ed.) *Experience, Structure and Adaptability.* New York: Springer, 1966, 369–400.

133. Seperson, Marvin. "The Relationship Between Teaching Style of Elementary School Student Teachers and the Teaching Style of Their Cooperating Teachers." Unpublished doctoral diss., Columbia University, 1970.

134. Siegel, G. M. "Verbal Behavior of Retarded Children with Pre-Instructed Adults." *Journal of Speech and Hearing Disorders,* Monograph supplement, 1963, **10**, 47–53.

135. Siegel, G. M. and Harkins, J. P. "Verbal Behavior of Adults in Two Conditions with Institutionalized Retarded Children." *Journal of Speech and Hearing Disorders,* Monograph supplement, 1963, **10**, 39–47.

136. Skinner, B. F. *Verbal Behavior.* New York: Appleton-Century Crofts, 1958, 1–57.

137. Skinner, B. F. *The Technology of Teaching.* New York: Appleton-Century Crofts, 1968.

138. Smith, Elmer R. (editor). *Teacher Education: A Reappraisal.* New York: Harper, 1962.

139. Suchman, Richard. *The Elementary School Training Program in Scientific Inquiry.* Report of the U.S. Office of Education Project Title VIII, Project 216. Urbana, Illinois: University of Illinois, 1962.

140. Sullivan, Edmund. "Piaget and the School Curriculum: A Criteria Appraisal," *Bulletin #2 of the Ontario Institute for Studies in Education.* Ontario, Canada, 1967.

141. Taba, Hilda. *Teachers Handbook for Elementary Social Studies.* Palo Alto, California: Addison-Wesley Publishing Company, 1967.

142. Thelen, Herbert A. *Education and the Human Quest.* New York: Harper and Row, 1960.

143. Thelen, Herbert. *Education and the Human Quest.* New York: Harper and Row, 1961.

144. Thelen, H. A. *Classroom Grouping for Teachability.* New York: Wiley, 1967.

145. Thoreau, Henry David. *Walden.* New York: Heritage Press, 1939.

146. Tiberius, R. G. "Investigations into a Dialogical Pedagogy." Doctoral diss. proposal. University of Toronto, 1974.

147. Tinsman, Stewart. "The Effect of Instructional Flexibility of Student Teachers' Teaching Style." Unpublished doctoral diss., Columbia University, 1971.

148. Tomlinson, P. D. and Hunt, D. E. "Differential Effects of Rule-Example Order as a Function of Learner Conceptual Level." *Canadian Journal of Behavioral Science* 1971, **3**, 237–245.

149. Torrance, Paul. *Guiding Creative Talent.* Englewood Cliffs, N.J.: Prentice-Hall, 1962.

150. Torrance, E. P. "Different Ways of Learning for Different Kinds of Students." In E. P. Torrance and R. D. Strom (Eds.) *Mental Health and Achievement: Increasing Potential in Reducing School Dropout.* New York: Wiley, 1965, 253–262.

151. Travers, Robert M. W., and others. *Measured Needs of Teachers and Their Behavior in the Classroom.* Final Report, U.S. Department of Health, Education and Welfare, Office of Education No. 444. University of Utah, 1961, 184 pp.

152. Turner, R. "Pupil Influence on Teacher Behavior." *Classroom Interaction Newsletter,* 1967, **3**, 5–8.

153. Wald, Rhoada. "The Effects of Models of Teaching as a Program for the Training of Teachers." Unpublished doctoral diss., Columbia University, 1972.

154. Warren, Marguerite Q.; Palmer, T.; and Turner, J. K. "Community Treatment Project: an Evaluation of Community Treatment for Delinquents." CTP Research Report No. 5. Sacramento, California, 1964.

155. Weil, Marsha. "Deriving Teaching Skills from Models of Teaching." Paper presented to the Annual Meeting of the American Educational Research Association, 1973.

156. Weil, Marsha; Gullion, Christine; and Cole, Diane. "The Teacher's Innovator Skills and Strategies Interaction Analysis System." Unpublished manual, 1971.

157. Weinstein, G. "A Method for Assessing Ability to Control and Regulate Classroom Behavior." Unpublished Manuscript: Syracuse University, 1965.

158. Weinstein, G.; Hunt, D. E.; and Joyce, B. R. "Situational Assessment of Urban Teacher Candidates." Syracuse, New York: Syracuse University, 1965. (Unpublished)

159. Withall, John and Lewis, W. W. "Social Interaction in the Classroom." *Handbook of Research on Teaching.* (Edited by Nathaniel L. Gage.) Chicago: Rand McNally, 1963. 683–714.

160. Witkin, H. *The Role of Cognitive Style in Academic Performance and in Teacher-Student Relations.* Princeton, N.J.: Educational Testing Service, 1973.

161. Wright, Benjamin. "The Influence of a Teacher Model on Self-Conception During Teacher Training and Experience." *Proceedings of the 73rd Annual Convention of the American Psychological Association.* Washington, D.C.: American Psychology Association, 1965. 297–98.

For Chapter 4

1. Bell, R. Q. "A Reinterpretation of the Direction of Effects in Studies of Socialization," *Psychological Review,* 1968, **73**, 81–95.

2. Brophy, J. E., and Good, T. L. *Teacher-Student Relationships: Causes and Consequences.* New York: Holt, Rinehart & Winston, 1974.

3. Charters, W. W., and Jones, J. E. "On the Risk of Appraising Non-Events in Program Evaluation." *Educational Researcher,* 1973, **2,** (November) 5–7.

4. deCharms, R., and Hunt, D. E. "There is Nothing So Theoretical as Good Practice." Unpublished ms., Toronto: Ontario Institute for Studies in Education, 1976.

5. Flavell, J. H., Botkin, P. T., Fry, C. L., Wright, J. W., and Jarvis, P. E. *The Development of Role-Taking and Communications Skills in Children.* New York: Wiley, 1968.

6. Hunt, D. E. "Adaptability in Interpersonal Communication among Training Agents." *Merrill Palmer Quarterly,* 1970, **16,** 325–344.

7. Hunt, D. E. *Matching Models in Education.* Toronto: Ontario Institute for Studies in Education, 1971.

8. Hunt, D. E. "Teachers' Adaptation to Students: Implicit and Explicit Matching." Stanford, Calif.: Research and Development Memorandum No. 139, SCRDT, 1975a.

9. Hunt, D. E. "The B-P-E Paradigm in Theory, Research, and Practice." *Canadian Psychological Review,* 1975, **16,** 185–197b.

10. Hunt, D. E. "Person-Environment Interaction: A Challenge Found Wanting before It Was Tried." *Review of Educational Research,* 1975, **45,** 209–230c.

11. Hunt, D. E. "Teachers Are Psychologists, Too: On the Application of Psychology to Education." *Canadian Psychological Review,* 1976.

12. Hunt, D. E., Greenwood, J., Brill, R., and Deineka, M. "From Psychological Theory to Educational Practice: Implementation of a Matching Model." Symposium presented at the Annual Meeting of the American Educational Research Association, Chicago, 1972.

13. Hunt, D. E., and Sullivan, E. V. *Between Psychology and Education.* Hinsdale, Ill.: Dryden, 1974.

14. Jackson, P. W. *Life in the Classroom.* New York: Holt, Rinehart & Winston, 1968.

15. Joyce, B. R., Weil, M., and Wald, R. "The Teacher Innovator: Models of Teaching as the Core of Teacher Education." *Interchange,* 1973, **4,** (2/3), 47–60.

16. Kelly, G. A. "The Psychology of Personal Constructs." New York: Norton, 1955.

17. Klein, S. S. "Student Influence on Teacher Behavior." *American Educational Research Journal,* 1971, **8,** 403–421.

18. Lesser, G. "Postscript: Matching Instruction to Student Characteristics." In G. Lesser (Ed.), *Psychology and Educational Practice.* New York: Scott Foresman, 1971, pp. 530–550.

19. Rathbone, C. "Teachers' Information Handling Behavior When Grouped with Students by Conceptual Level." Unpublished doctoral dissertation, Syracuse University, 1970.

20. Siegel, G. M., and Harkins, J. P. "Verbal Behavior of Adults in Two Conditions with Institutionalized Retarded Children." *Journal of Speech and Hearing Disorders,* Monograph supplement, 1963, **10,** 34–47.

21. Turner, R. "Pupil Influence on Teacher Behavior." *Classroom Interaction Newsletter,* 1967, **3,** 5–8.

For Chapters 9–10, 12–13

1. Allport, G. W.; Vernon, P. E.; and Lindzey, G. *A Study of Values: A Scale for Measuring the Dominant Interests in Personality.* (3d ed.) Boston.

2. Amidon, E., and Flanders, N. *The Role of the Teacher in the Classroom.* Philadelphia: Research for Better Teaching, Inc., 1967.

3. Amidon, T., and Hough, J. B., eds. *Interaction Analysis: Theory, Research and Application.* Palo Alto, Calif: Addison-Wesley, 1967.

4. Anderson, H. H., and Brewer, H. M. "Studies of Teachers' Classroom Personalities. I. Dominative and Socially Integrative Behavior of Kindergarten Teachers." *Applied Psychological Monograph of the American Psychological Association* (1945), **6.**

5. Ausubel, D. P. *The Psychology of Meaningful Verbal Learning.* New York: Grune & Stratton, 1963.

6. Borg, W.; Kelley, M. L.; Langer, P.; and Gall, M. *The Mini-course: A Micro-teaching Approach to Teacher Education.* Beverly Hills, Calif.: Macmillan Educational Services, 1972.

7. Brown, C. "The Relationship of Initial Teaching Styles and Selected Variables in Student Teaching." See chapter 8.

8. Brown, G. I. "An Experiment in the Teaching of Creativity." *School Review* (1964), **122:**437–50.

9. Broudy, H. S., and Palmer, J. R. *Exemplars of Teaching Method.* Chicago: Rand McNally, 1965.

10. Bruner, J. S. *The Process of Education.* Cambridge, Mass.: Harvard University Press, 1961.

11. Bruner, J. S. *Toward a Theory of Instruction.* New York: Norton, 1966.

12. Dewey, J. *Democracy and Education.* New York: Macmillan, 1916.

13. Erikson, E. *Childhood and Society.* New York: Norton, 1950.

14. Flanders, N. A. "Teacher Influence, Pupil Attitudes and Achievement: Studies in Interaction Analysis." United States Department of Health, Education, and Welfare: Office of Education, Cooperative Research Project No. 397. Minneapolis: University of Minnesota, 1960.

15. Flint, S. H. "The Relationship between the Classroom Verbal Behavior of Student Teachers and the Classroom Verbal Behavior of their Cooperating Teachers." Ph.D. diss., Teachers College, Columbia University, New York, 1965.

16. Glaser, R. *Training Research and Education.* Pittsburgh: University of Pittsburgh Press, 1962.

17. Harvey, O. J. "Conceptual Systems and Attitude Change." In *Attitude, Ego-Involvement and Change,* edited by C. W. Sherif and M. Sherif. New York, 1967.

18. Harvey, O. J., Hunt, D. E., and Schroder, H. M. *Conceptual Systems and Personality Organization.* New York: Wiley, 1961.

19. Henry, J. *Culture Against Man.* New York: Vintage Books, 1963.

20. Hunt, D. E. "A Conceptual Systems Change Model and Its Application to Education." Paper presented at Office of Naval Research Conference, *Flexibility, Adaptability, and Creativity: Nature and Developmental Determinants,* Boulder, Colorado, March 19–21, 1964.

21. Hunt, D. E. "A Model for Analyzing the Training of Training Agents." *Merrill-Palmer Quarterly of Behavior and Development* (1966), **12:**137–56.

22. Hunt, D. E. *Matching Models in Education.* Toronto: Ontario Institute for Studies in Education, 1971.

23. Hunt, D. E., & Joyce, B. R. "Teacher Trainee Personality and Initial Teaching Style." *American Educational Research Journal* (1967), **4:**253–259.

24. Hunt, E. D.; Lapin, S.; Liberman, B.; McManus, J.; Post, R.; Sabalio, S.; Sweet, S.; and Victor, J. B. "Manual for Coding Paragraph Completion Responses for Adolescents." Unpublished paper, Syracuse University Youth Development Center, 1968.

25. James, W. *Talks to Teachers on Psychology and to Students on Some of Life's Ideals.* New York: Holt, 1899.

26. Joyce, B. R. "Flexibility in Teacher Behavior." *Classroom Interaction News-letter* (1967), **2**:5–11.

27. Joyce, B. R. "Method and Methods in Teacher Education: 'Geist,' Substance and Form." *The Journal of Teacher Education,* (1969), **20**:509–20.

28. Joyce, B. R. ed. *The Teacher-Innovator: A Program to Prepare Teachers.* Washington, D.C.: Office of Education, Dept. of Health, Education and Welfare, 1969.

29. Joyce, B. R. "The Curriculum Worker of the Future." In *The Curriculum: Retrospect and Prospect.* The 70th Yearbook of the National Society for the Study of Education. Chicago: University of Chicago Press, 1971.

30. Joyce, B. R.; Guillion, C.; Weil, M.; Wald, R.; McKibbin, M.; and Feller, M. "Teacher Innovator System for Analyzing Skills and Strategies." Unpublished paper, Teachers College, Columbia University, 1972.

31. Joyce, B. R., and Harootunian, B. *The Structure of Teaching.* Chicago: Science Research Associates, 1967.

32. Joyce, B. R., and Hodges, R. "A Rationale for Teacher Education." See Chapter 3.

33. Joyce, B. R., and Hodges, R. E. "Instructional Flexibility Training." *The Journal of Teacher Education* (1966), **17**:409–16.

34. Joyce, B. R., and Hodges, R. E. "The Use, for Research in Teacher Education, of Developmental Studies of the Teaching Styles of Elementary Teacher Education Students." Paper presented at American Educational Research Association Annual Conference, Chicago, February, 1966.

35. Joyce, B. R.; Morine, G.; Weil, M.; and Wald, R. *Materials for Modules.* New York: Teachers College, Columbia University, 1971.

36. Joyce, B. R.; O'Donnell, K.; Brown, C.; Apple, M.; Wald, R.; O'Neal, J.; and Lehane, S. "The Student Teacher as Institution-Builder." *Journal of Teacher Education* (1972), **23**:348–51.

37. Joyce, B. R., and Weil, M. *Models of Teaching.* Englewood Cliffs, N.J.: Prentice-Hall, 1972.

38. Joyce, B. R., and Weil, M., eds. *Perspectives for Reform in Teacher Education.* Englewood Cliffs, N.J.: Prentice-Hall, 1972.

39. Joyce, B. R.; Weil, M.; and Wald, R. *Basic Teaching Skills.* Palo Alto, Calif.: Science Research Associates, 1972.

40. Joyce, B. R.; Weil, M.; and Wald, R. *Three Teaching Strategies.* Palo Alto, Calif.: Science Research Associates, 1972.

41. Kelly, J. "An Analysis of the Moves made by Elementary School Teachers in Operationalizing Two Theoretically Based Teaching Models." Ed.D. dissertation, Teachers College, Columbia University, 1972.

42. Kohlberg, L. "Moral Education in the Schools." *School Review* (1966), **74**:1–30.

43. Kraitlow, B. W., and Dreier, W. "Appendix B: A Scale for Determining Teacher Beliefs." *Elementary School Journal* (1966), **36**:326–27.

44. Maslow, A. *Toward a Psychology of Being.* Princeton, N.J.: Van Nostrand, 1962.

45. Murphy, P. D., and Brown, M. M. "Conceptual Systems and Teaching Styles." *American Educational Research Journal* (1970), **7**:529–40.

46. Piaget, J. *The Origins of Intelligence in Children.* New York: International Universities Press, 1952.

47. Rogers, C. *Client-Centered Therapy.* Boston: Houghton Mifflin, 1951.

48. Rude, E. "The Analysis of the Interaction Patterns Characteristic of Phases of Models of Teaching as Practiced by Teacher Candidates." Ed.D. diss., Teachers College, Columbia University, 1972.

49. Schroder, H. M.; Driver, M. J.; and Streufert, S. *Human Information Processing.* New York: Holt, Rinehart and Winston, 1967.

50. Seperson, M. A., and Joyce, B. R. "The Teaching Styles of Student Teachers as Related to the Teaching Styles of Their Cooperating Teachers." See Chapter 9.

51. Shaftel, F. R., and Shaftel, G. *Role Playing for Social Values: Decision Making in the Social Studies.* Englewood Cliffs, N.J.: Prentice-Hall, 1967.

52. Skinner, B. F. *Verbal Behavior.* New York: Appleton-Century-Crofts, 1957.

53. Skinner, B. F. *The Technology of Teaching.* New York: Appleton-Century-Crofts, 1968.

54. Taba, H. *Teachers' Handbook for Elementary Social Studies.* Reading, Mass.: Addison-Wesley, 1967.

55. Torrance, E. P. *Torrance Tests of Creative Thinking.* Norms-Technical Manual, Research Edition. Princeton, New Jersey: Personnel Press, 1966.

56. Wald, R. "The Effects of Models of Teaching as a Program for the Training of Teachers." Ed.D. diss., Teachers College, Columbia University, 1972.

57. Wald, R.; Weil, M.; Gullion, C.; and Joyce, B. "The Behavior of Student Teachers When Experimenting with a Variety of Models of Teaching." Unpublished manuscript, Teachers College, Columbia University, 1971. (Available from the author.)

58. Wehling, L. S., and Charters, W. W., Jr. "Dimensions of Teacher Beliefs about the Teaching Process." *American Educational Research Journal* (1969), **6:**7–30.

59. Weil, M. "Models of Teaching as a Research Paradigm for a Competency-Based Teacher Education Program." Ed.D. diss., Teachers College, Columbia University, 1972.

60. Winer, B. J. *Statistical Principles in Experimental Design.* New York: McGraw-Hill, 1962.

61. Wonderlic, E. F. *Wonderlic Personnel Test Manual.* Northfield, Illinois: E. R. Wonderlic & Assoc., 1968.

62. Yamamoto, K. "Threshold of Intelligence in Academic Achievement of Highly Creative Students." *Journal of Experimental Education* (1964), **32:**401–5.

63. Zaken, J. "An Assessment of the Effects of Practice on Execution of the Taba Model." Ph.D. diss., Teachers College, Columbia University, 1972.

For Chapter 14

1. Borg, W. R. "Protocol Materials as Related to Teacher Performance and Pupil Achievement." *Journal of Educational Research* 69 (1975): 23–30.

2. Borg, W. R.; Langer, P.; and Kelley, M. L. "The Minicourse: A New Tool for the Education of Teachers." *Education* (1971): 232–38.

3. Cruickshank, D. R. "Simulation." *Theory Into Practice* 7 (1968): 190–93.

4. Edwards, C. H. "Changing Teacher Behavior Through Self Instruction and Supervised Microteaching in a Competency Based Program." *Journal of Educational Research* 69 (1975): 219–22.

5. Feldens, M. G. F., and Duncan, J. K. "A Field Experiment: Teacher-Directed Changes in Instructional Behavior." *Journal of Teacher Education* 29 (1978): 47–51.

6. Friebel, A. C., and Kallenbach, W. W. "Effects of Videotape Feedback and Microteaching as Developed in the Field Test of Minicourse I with Student Teachers." Paper presented at the California Educational Research Association, Los Angeles, March 1969.

7. Good, T. L., and Brophy, J. E. "Changing Teacher and Student Behavior: An Empirical Investigation." *Journal of Educational Psychology* 66 (1974): 390–405.

8. Karan, M. L.; Snow, R. E.; and McDonald, F. J. "Teacher Aptitude and Observational Learning of a Teaching Skill." *Journal of Educational Psychology* 62 (1971): 219–28.

9. Orme, M. E. "The Effects of Modelling and Feedback Variables on the Acquisition of a Complex Teaching Strategy." Ph.D. dissertation, Stanford University, 1966.

10. Salomon, G., and McDonald, F. J. "Pretest and Posttest Reactions to Self-Viewing One's Teaching Performance on Videotape." *Journal of Educational Psychology* 11 (1966): 86–90.

11. Tuckman, B. W.; McCall, K. M.; and Hyman, R. T. "The Modification of Teacher Behavior: Effects of Dissonance and Coded Feedback." *American Educational Research Journal* 6 (1969): 607–19.

12. Vlcek, C. "Classroom Simulation in Teacher Education." *Audiovisual Instruction* 11 (1966): 86–90.

For Chapter 15

1. Finney, D. J.; Latscha, R.; Bennett, B. M.; and Hsu, P. *Tables for Testing Significance in a 2 x 2 Contingency Table.* Cambridge University Press, 1963.

2. Gower, R. "The Use of an Exemplary Teaching Profile to Assess Teaching Performance in an Inductive Model." Ph.D. diss., Teachers College, Columbia University, 1974.

3. Harvey, O. J.; Hunt, D. E.; and Schroder, H. M. *Conceptual Systems and Personality Organization.* New York: Wiley, 1961.

4. Heck, E. J. "A Training and Research Model for Investigating the Effects of Sensitivity Training for Teachers." *Journal of Teacher Education* (1971), **22:** 501–7.

5. Hunt, D. E. *Matching Models in Education.* Toronto: OISE, 1971.

6. Hunt, D. E. "Person-Environment Interaction: A Challenge Found Wanting Before It Was Tried." Invited address to Division of Educational Psychology. American Psychological Association meeting, Montreal, 1973.

7. Hunt, D. E. "The B-P-E Paradigm in Theory, Research, and Practice." *Canadian Psychological Review* (1975), **16:**185–97.

8. Hunt, D. E.; Butler, L.; Noy, J. E.; and Rosser, M. *An Exploratory Study in Role Playing.* Unpublished manuscript. Toronto Ontario Institute for the Study of Education, 1975.

9. Hunt, D. E.; Greenwood, J.; Brill, R.; and Deineka, M. "From Psychological Theory to Educational Practice: Implementation of a Matching Model." Paper presented at the meeting of the American Educational Research Association, Chicago, April 1972.

10. Hunt, D. E.; Greenwood, J.; Noy, J. E.; and Watson, N. "Assessment of Conceptual Level: Paragraph Completion Method." Unpublished paper, Ontario Institute for Studies in Education, 1973.

11. Hunt, D. E.; Greenwood, J.; and Watson, N. "Alternative Approaches in Two York County Secondary Schools." Interim Report. Ontario Ministry of Education, 1973.

12. Hunt, D. E.; Joyce, B. R.; Greenwood, J.; Noy, J. E.; Reid, R.; and Weil, M. "Student Conceptual Level and Model of Teaching: Theoretical and Empirical Coordination of Two Models." *Interchange* (1974), **5:**19–30.

13. Hunt, D. E., and Sullivan, E. V. *Between Psychology and Education.* Hinsdale, Illinois: Dryden, 1974.

14. Joyce, B. R. "Listening to Different Drummers: The Effect of Teaching on Learners." In *Assessment in Competency-Based Teacher Education,* edited by R. Houston. San Francisco: McCutcheon, 1974.

15. Joyce, B. R. "Listening to Different Drummers: Evaluating Alternative In-

structional Models." In *Competency Assessment, Research, and Evaluation.* Syracuse, N.Y.: National Dissemination Center for Performance Based Education, 1974.

16. Joyce, B. R.; Guillion, C.; Weil, M.; Wald, R.; McKibbin, M.; and Feller, M. "Teacher Innovator System for Analyzing Skills and Strategies." Unpublished paper, Teachers College, Columbia University, 1972.

17. Joyce, B. R., and Joyce, E. H. "The Creation of Information Systems for Children." *Interchange* (1970), **1**:1–12.

18. Joyce, B. R., and Weil, M. *Models of Teaching.* Englewood Cliffs, N.J.: Prentice-Hall, 1972.

19. Joyce, B. R.; Weil, M.; McKibbin, M.; and Gower, R. "Scripting a Model—Concept Learning." Unpublished paper, Teachers College, Columbia University, 1973.

20. Joyce, B. R.; Weil, M.; and Wald, R. *Three Teaching Strategies for the Social Studies.* Chicago, SRA, 1972.

21. Joyce, B. R.; Weil, M.; and Wald, R. "The Teacher Innovator: Models of Teaching as the Core of Teacher Education." *Interchange* (1973), **4**:27–60.

22. McKibbin, M. "The Application of Three Instructional Analysis Systems to Investigating Models of Teaching." Ph.D. diss., Teachers College, Columbia University, 1974.

23. Noy, J. E., and Hunt, D. E. "Student-Directed Learning from Biographical Information Systems." *Canadian Journal of Behavioural Science* (1972), **4**:54–63.

24. Noy, J. E., and Hunt, D. E. "Training in Information Processing through Biographical Information Systems: Systematic Search and Hypothesis Formation." Unpublished paper, OISE, 1974.

25. Weil, M. "Deriving Teaching Skills from Models of Teaching." Paper presented at AERA meeting, New Orleans, 1973.

26. Weil, M. "Evaluation Guide for Role Playing." Unpublished manuscript, Teachers College, Columbia University, 1975.

For Chapter 16

1. Finney, D. J., Latscha, R., Bennett, B. M., and Hsu, P. *Tables for Testing Significance in a 2 x 2 Contingency Table.* Cambridge, Eng.: Cambridge University Press, 1963.

2. Harvey, O. J.; Hunt, D. E., and Schroder, H. M. *Conceptual Systems and Personality Organization.* New York: Wiley, 1961.

3. Hunt, D. E. "The B-P-E Paradigm in Theory, Research, and Practice." *Canadian Psychological Review,* 1975, *16,* 185–97.

4. Hunt, D. E. *Matching Models in Education.* Toronto: OISE, 1971.

5. Hunt, D. E., and Sullivan, E. V. *Between Psychology and Education.* Hinsdale, Ill.: Dryden, 1974.

6. Hunt, D. E., Butler, L., Noy, J. E., and Rosser, M. *An Exploratory Study in Role Playing,* unpublished ms., OISE, September 1975.

7. Hunt, D. E., Greenwood, J., Brill, R., and Deineka, M. "From Psychological Theory to Educational Practice: Implementation of a Matching Model." Paper presented at the meeting of the American Educational Research Association, Chicago, April 1972.

8. Hunt, D. E., Greenwood, J., Noy, J. E., and Watson, N. "Assessment of Conceptual Level: Paragraph Completion Method." Unpublished paper, Ontario Institute for Studies in Education, 1973.

9. Hunt, D. E., Joyce, B. R., Greenwood, J., Noy, J. E., Reid, R., and Weil, M. "Student Conceptual Level and Model of Teaching: Theoretical and Empirical Coordination of Two Models." *Interchange,* 1974, 5(3), 19–30.

10. Joyce, B. R. "Listening to Different Drummers: The Effect of Teaching on Learners." In R. Houston (Ed.), *Assessment in Competency-Based Teacher Education.* San Francisco: McCutcheon, 1974a.

11. Joyce, B. R. "Listening to Different Drummers: Evaluating Alternative Instructional Models." In *Competency assessment, research, and evaluation.* Syracuse, N.Y.: National dissemination centre for performance based education, 1974b, pp. 61–81.

12. Joyce, B. R., and Weil, M. *Models of teaching.* Englewood Cliffs, N.J.: Prentice-Hall, 1972.

13. Joyce, B. R., Weil, M., and Wald, R. *Three Strategies for the Social Studies.* Chicago: Science Research Associates, 1972.

14. Shaftel, F., and Shaftel, G. *Role Playing for Social Values: Decision-Making in the Social Studies.* Englewood Cliffs, N.J.: Prentice-Hall, 1967.

15. Weil, M. "Evaluation Guide for Role Playing." Unpublished ms., Teachers College, Columbia University, 1975.

For Chapters 17–20

1. Aubertine, H. E. "An Experiment in the Set Induction Process and its Application in Teaching." Ph.D. diss., Stanford University, 1964.

2. Bryan, R. C. "Reactions to Teachers by Students, Parents, and Administrators." Kalamazoo, Mich.: Western Michigan University, U.S. Office of Education, Cooperative Research Project No. 668, 1963.

3. Centra, J. A. *The Utility of Student Ratings for Instructional Improvement.* Princeton, N.J.: Educational Testing Service, 1972.

4. Centra, J. A. "Effectiveness of Student Feedback in Modifying College Instruction." *Journal of Educational Psychology* (1973), 65:395–401.

5. Conference on studies in teaching: "Teaching as Clinical Information Processing." Washington, D.C.: National Institute of Education, 1975.

6. Daw, R. W. "Changing the Behavior of Elementary School Principals through the Use of Feedback." Ph.D. diss., Stanford University, 1964.

7. Daw, R. W., and Gage, N. L. "Effect of Feedback from Teachers to Principals." *Journal of Educational Psychology* (1967), 58:181–88.

8. Edwards, R. L. "Changing Teacher Behavior through Feedback from Students: An Intensive Study of Four Physical Education Teachers." Ph.D. diss., Stanford University, 1973.

9. Flanders, N. A. *Analyzing Teaching Behavior.* Reading, Mass.: Addison-Wesley, 1970.

10. Fuller, F. F., and Manning, B. A. "Self-Confrontation Reviewed: A Conceptualization for Video Playback in Teacher Education." *Review of Educational Research* (1973), 43:469–528.

11. Gage, N. L. *Teacher Effectiveness and Teacher Education.* Palo Alto, Calif.: Pacific Books, 1972.

12. Gage, N. L.; Runkel, P. J.; and Chatterjee, B. B. "Changing Teacher Behavior through Feedback from Pupils: An Application of Equilibrium Theory." In *Readings in the social psychology of education,* edited by W. W. Charters, Jr. and N. L. Gage. Boston: Allyn and Bacon, 1963.

13. Hayes, R. B.; Keim, F. N.; and Neiman, A. M. *The Effect of Student Reactions to Teaching Methods.* Harrisburg, Pa.: Bureau of Research, Administration and Coordination, Department of Public Instruction, 1967.

14. Hovenier, P. J. "Changing the Behavior of Social Studies Department Heads through the Use of Feedback." Ph.D. diss., Stanford University, 1966.

15. Hunt, D. E. "Adaptability in Interpersonal Communication Among Training Agents." *Merrill Palmer Quarterly* (1970), **16**:325–44.

16. Hunt, D. E. "Matching Models in Education: The Coordination of Teaching Methods with Student Characteristics." Monograph Series No. 10, Ontario Institute for Studies in Education, 1971.

17. Jackson, P. *The Way Teaching Is.* Washington: National Educational Association, 1965.

18. Jackson, P. *Life in Classrooms.* New York: Holt, Rinehart, and Winston, 1968.

19. Jones, M. B. "The Effects of Feedback and Commitment to Change on the Behavior of Elementary School Principals." Ph.D. diss., Stanford University, 1969.

20. *Journal of Teacher Education,* 25 (1), 1974.

21. Joyce, B., and Harootunian, B. "Teaching as Problem-Solving." *Journal of Teacher Education* (1964), **15**:420–27.

22. Joyce, B. R., and Joyce, E. A. "The Creation of Information Systems for Children." *Interchange* (1970), **1**:1–12.

23. Joyce, B. R., and Weil, M. *Models of Teaching.* Englewood Cliffs, New Jersey: Prentice-Hall, 1972.

24. Kounin, J. *Discipline and Group Management in the Classroom.* New York: Holt, Rinehart, and Winston, 1970.

25. Laroesch, W. P.; Pereira, P. D.; and Ryan, K. A. "The Use of Student Feedback in Teacher Training." Final Report, Project No. 8-E-115. Chicago: University of Chicago, 1969.

26. Marx, R. W. "Cues Used by Teachers to Make Judgments of Cognitive and Affective States of Their Students." Stanford University Ph.D. dissertation in preparation.

27. Marx, R. W., and Peterson, P. L. "The Nature of Teacher Decision Making." Paper presented to the American Educational Research Association, 1975. See Chapter 18.

28. Masucci, D. A. "The Effects of Student Feedback on Changes in a Teacher's Classroom Behavior." Master's thesis, San Jose State College, 1973.

29. Miller, M. T. "Instructor Attitudes Toward, and Their Use of, Student Ratings of Teachers." *Journal of Educational Psychology* (1971), **62**:235–39.

30. Nelson, M. A. P. "Attitudes of Intermediate School Children toward Substitute Teachers who Receive Feedback on Pupil-Desired Behavior." Ph.D. diss., University of Oregon, 1972.

31. Pambookian, H. S. "Initial Level of Student Evaluation of Instruction as a Source of Influence on Instructor Change after Feedback." *Journal of Educational Psychology,* (1966), 66:52–56.

32. Peterson, P. L., and Anton, J. L. "An Interaction Analysis System to Assess Dimensions of Teacher Behavior: An Application of Generalizability Theory." Paper presented to the American Educational Research Association, Washington, D.C., April, 1975.

33. Popham, J. W., and Baker, E. *Establishing Instructional Goals.* Englewood Cliffs: Prentice-Hall, 1970.

34. Ryan, K. A. "The Use of Students' Written Feedback in Changing the Behavior of Beginning Secondary School Teachers." Ph.D. diss., Stanford University, 1965.

35. Ryan, K. A. "The Use of Feedback from Students in the Preservice Training of Teachers." Paper presented at the annual meeting of the American Educational Research Association, Chicago, 1974.

36. Salomon, G., and McDonald, F. J. "Pre- and Posttest Reactions to Self-viewing One's Teaching Performance on Videotape." Stanford University, Stanford

Center for Research and Development in Teaching (Research and Development Memorandum No. 44), 1969.

37. Savage, M. "Changes in Student Teachers through the Use of Pupil Ratings." Ph.D. diss., University of Illinois, 1957.

38. Schroder, H. M.; Karlins, M.; and Phares, J. *Education for Freedom.* New York: Wiley, 1973.

39. Shack, D. M., and Owen, S. V. "The Evaluation of Teacher Performance by Elementary School Students." Paper presented at the annual meeting of the American Educational Research Association, Chicago, 1974.

40. Shulman, L. S., and Elstein, A. S. "Studies of Problem Solving, Judgment and Decision Making." In *Review of Research in Education:* III, edited by F. N. Kerlinger. Chicago: F. E. Peacock, in press.

41. Siegel, S. *Nonparametric Statistics for the Behavioral Sciences.* N.Y.: McGraw-Hill, 1956.

42. Smith, L., and Geoffrey, W. *The Complexities of the Urban Classroom.* New York: Holt, Rinehart, and Winston, 1968.

43. Stanford Program on Teaching Effectiveness. *Teacher Training Products: The State of the Field.* (Stanford, Calif.: Stanford Center for Research and Development in Teaching, R & D Memorandum No. 116, 1974).

44. Tuckman, B. W., and Oliver, W. S. "Effectiveness of Feedback to Teachers as a Function of Source." *Journal of Educational Psychology* (1968), 59:297–301.

45. Tustin, A. "Feedback." In *Communication and Culture,* edited by A. G. Smith. New York: Holt, Rinehart & Winston, 1966.

For Chapters 21–22

1. Berliner, D. *Developing a Sample of Teachers for Intensive Analysis of Classroom Teaching.* Beginning Teacher Evaluation Study Technical Report. Far West Laboratory, 1975.

2. Berliner, D. "Impediments to the Study of Teacher Effectiveness." *Journal of Teacher Education,* 1976, 27 (1), 5–13.

3. Jere E. Brophy. *Stability in Teacher Effectiveness.* R & D Report, Series 77. The Research and Development Center for Teacher Education. University of Texas at Austin, July 1972.

4. Clark, Christopher and Joyce, Bruce R. "Teacher Decision Making and Teacher Effectiveness." In *Flexibility in Teaching,* edited by Bruce R. Joyce et al. New York: Longman Inc., 1980.

5. Clark, C. M., and Peterson, P. L. "Teacher Stimulated Recall of Interactive Decisions." Paper presented at American Educational Research Association meetings, San Francisco, 1976.

6. Crist, Janet, Marx, Ronald W., and Peterson, Penelope L. "Teacher Behavior in the Organizational Domain." Paper submitted to N.I.E., August 20, 1974.

7. Dunkin, M. S. and Biddle, B. J. *The Study of Teaching.* New York: Holt, Rinehart and Winston, Inc., 1974.

8. Flanders, N. A. *Teacher Influence, Pupil Attitudes and Achievement.* Final Report. Cooperative Research Program Project No. 397, Minneapolis, Minn.: University of Minnesota, 1960.

9. Gage, N. L. *The Scientific Basis of the Art of Teaching.* New York: Teachers College Press, 1978.

10. Garner, W. R. *The Processing of Information and Structure.* Hillsdale, N.J.: Lawrence Erlbaum Associates, 1974.

11. Harvey, O. J.; Hunt, David E.; and Schroder, Marry. *Conceptual Systems and Information Processing.* New York: Wiley, 1963.

12. Hoetker, James and Albrand, William. "The Persistence of the Recitation." *American Educational Research Journal,* VI (March 1969) pp. 145–167.
13. Joyce, Bruce R. "The Teacher Innovator System: Molar and Molecular Codes for Analyzing Teaching Styles and Models." Stanford, 1977.
14. Joyce, Bruce R. and Harootunian, Berj. *The Structure of Teaching.* Chicago: Science Research Associates, 1966.
15. Joyce, Bruce R., and Joyce, Elizabeth. *Data Banks for Children.* New York: Teachers College, 1969.
16. Marx, R. W. "Teacher Judgments of Students' Cognitive and Affective Outcomes." Unpublished doctoral dissertation. Stanford University, 1978.
17. McDonald F., and Elias, P. "The Effects of Teacher Performance on Pupil Learning." Beginning Teacher Evaluation Study: Phase II, Final Report: Vol. 1. Princeton, N.J.: Educational Testing Service, 1976.
18. Medley, D. M. *Teacher Competence and Teacher Effectiveness: A Review of Process-Product Research.* Washington, D.C.: American Association of Colleges for Teacher Education, 1977.
19. Morine, Greta and Vallance, Elizabeth. "A Study of Teacher and Pupil Perceptions of Classroom Interaction." BTES Special Report B. Far West Laboratory, 1975.
20. Morine-Dershimer, Greta and Vallance, Elizabeth. "Teacher Planning." BTES Special Report C. Far West Laboratory, 1976.
21. Peterson, P. L., Marx, R. W., and Clark, C. M. "Teacher Planning, Teacher Behavior, and Student Achievement." Unpublished manuscript, 1977.
22. Popham, James W., and Baker, Eva. *Establishing Instructional Goals.* Englewood Cliffs: Prentice-Hall, 1970.
23. Program on Teacher Effectiveness: "A Brief Summary as of February 1975." School of Education, Stanford University, Stanford Center for Research and Development in Teaching, February 1975.
24. Rosenshine, B. "The Stability of Teacher Effects Upon Student Achievement." *Review of Educational Research.* Vol. 40, No. 5, December 1970.
25. Rosenshine, Barak. *Teaching Behaviors and Student Achievement.* London: National Foundation for Education Research, 1971.
26. Shavelson, R. J. "Teachers' Decision Making." In *Psychology of Teaching Methods,* edited by N. L. Gage. 75th Yearbook of the National Society for the Study of Education (Part 1). Chicago: University of Chicago Press, 1976.
27. Shiffrin, R. M. "Capacity Limitations in Information Processing, Attention, and Memory." In *Handbook of Learning and Cognitive Processes,* edited by W. K. Estes. Vol. 4. Hillsdale, N.J.: Lawrence Erlbaum Associates, 1976.
28. Zahorik, J. A. "Teacher's Planning Models." Paper presented to the American Educational Research Association, Washington D.C., 1975.

Index